American Voices:

A Historical Reader
Volume I

American Voices:
A Historical Reader
Volume I

Robert Marcus and David Burner
State University of New York at Stony Brook

Scott, Foresman and Company
Glenview, Illinois
Dallas, Tex.
Oakland, N.J.
Palo Alto, Cal.
Tucker, Ga.
London

Library of Congress Cataloging in Publication Data

Main entry under title:

American voices.

1. United States—History—Sources. I. Marcus, Robert D., 1936– II. Burner, David, 1937–
E173.A759 973 78-17850
ISBN 0-673-15172-7 (v. 1)

1 2 3 4 5 6 7-RRC-84 83 82 81 80 79 78

Acknowledgements

John Smith. "A Generall Historie of Virginia" from CAPTAIN JOHN SMITH, WORKS, 1608–1631, ed. Edward Arber, The English Scholar's Library, No. 16, (Birmingham, 1884).

Cotton Mather. THE WONDERS OF THE INVISIBLE WORLD. (London: John Russell Smith), 1862.

Jonathan Edwards. "Sinners in the Hands of an Angry God" from THE WORKS OF PRESIDENT EDWARDS, Vol. IV. (New York: Jonathan Leavitt and John F. Trow), 1843.

Francis Parkman. MONTCALM AND WOLFE: FRANCE AND ENGLAND IN NORTH AMERICA. (Boston: Little, Brown, and Company), 1898.

Benjamin Franklin. THE AUTOBIOGRAPHY OF BENJAMIN FRANKLIN. (Philadelphia: J. B. Lippincott & Co.), 1868.

Thomas Paine. "Common Sense" from THE POLITICAL WRITINGS OF THOMAS PAINE, Vol. I. (Granville, Middletown, N. J.: George H. Evans), 1844.

M. G. St. Jean de Crèvecoeur. LETTERS FROM AN AMERICAN FARMER, 1770–81. London, 1782.

Thomas Jefferson. NOTES ON VIRGINIA (Philadelphia, 1801).

Hamilton, Jay, Madison. THE FEDERALIST And Other Contemporary Papers on the Constitution of the United States. (Chicago: Scott, Foresman and Company), 1894.

M. L. Weems. THE LIFE OF GEORGE WASHINGTON; with CURIOUS ANECDOTES. (Philadelphia: J. B. Lippincott & Co.), 1860.

Washington Irving. "The Legend of Sleepy Hollow" from THE SKETCH-BOOK OF GEOFFREY CRAYON, Gent., Revised edition. (New York: G. P. Putnam; Hurd & Houghton), 1865.

Alexis de Tocqueville. DEMOCRACY IN AMERICA translated from the French, 2 Vols. (London, 1835 and 1840).

Red Jacket. "Reply to Missionary Cram at Buffalo, N. Y. 1805" from LIVES OF CELEBRATED AMERICAN INDIANS ed. by Samuel Griswold Goodrich. (New York: J. M. Allen), 1843.

George Catlin. LETTERS AND NOTES ON THE MANNERS, CUSTOMS, AND CONDITION OF THE NORTH AMERICAN INDIANS, Vol. I. (London: published by the author, at the Egyptian Hall, Piccadilly.), 1841.

Ralph Waldo Emerson. "The American Scholar" from THE COMPLETE WORKS OF RALPH WALDO EMERSON, Centenary Edition, 12 vols., Boston, 1904.

Margaret Fuller. WOMAN IN THE NINETEENTH CENTURY. (Boston: Brown, Taggard and Chase), 1860.

Frederick Douglass. MY BONDAGE AND MY FREEDOM. (New York and Auburn: Miller, Orton & Mulligan), 1855.

Mark Twain. ADVENTURES OF HUCKLEBERRY FINN. (Charles L. Webster & Co.), 1884.

Harriet Beecher Stowe. UNCLE TOM'S CABIN. (1852).

Henry David Thoreau. A PLEA FOR CAPTAIN JOHN BROWN. (Boston: David R. Godine, Publisher), MCMLXIX.

Margaret Leech. "Arrival of a Westerner" (pp 33–45) from REVEILLE IN WASHINGTON. Copyright 1941 by Margaret Leech Pulitzer. Reprinted by permission of Harper & Row, Publishers, Inc.

Grateful acknowledgement is given here for the illustrative material appearing in the book.

xii: Library of Congress

10: Library of Congress

28: Scott, Foresman

42: Library of Congress

64: Library of Congress

80: Library of Congress

94: Abby Aldrich Rockefeller Folk Art Center

116: Library of Congress

142: Library of Congress

156: Courtesy, the Henry Francis du Pont Winterthur Museum

174: Library of Congress

200: The St. Louis Art Museum

220: Library of Congress

242: The Bettman Archive

260: Library of Congress

290: Library of Congress

308: Library of Congress

332: Courtesy of The New York Historical Society

358: Courtesy of Department of Administration, State of Kansas

378: Archives of the B. & O. Railroad Museum, Baltimore

Preface

This anthology has but a single aim: to provide selections that are genuinely worth reading for students of American history. It is not a collection of recent articles or documents, nor does it develop some special approach. Rather, it is an offering of authentic voices from the American past, men and women who speak for themselves, who in some particular way speak for their age, and who through their writings can speak as readily to us.

The selections are sufficiently long to allow students to hear these voices in a meaningful way. The material is varied in style and genre: speeches, historical narratives, fiction, essay, memoirs and more. Some are examples of great literature, others of popular culture or folk wisdom. Some are important for the mark they made on their age; others were little noted until a later generation. A few are the writings of historians who have achieved special success in linking past and present, in allowing the past to live. Some are from the writings of great political leaders. Several are classics in journalism. While a few are literary masterpieces, many are simply authentic distillations of some piece of American experience: what it was like to live among the Indians, to be a cowboy or a slave or a ward politician or a dispossessed farmer or a Rock fan.

The writers in this volume address virtually all the major themes of American history. John Smith views the native Americans through the Age of Exploration, confronting a "strange new world" which calls into question European values, tests the courage of a buccaneering age, and raises disturbing questions about the meaning of critical concepts in Western history such as "civilization" and "nobility."

Cotton Mather and Jonathan Edwards offer an aperture through which to view the world that English puritanism created in Massachusetts Bay and in the Connecticut Valley. Both lived in a society which felt threatened with destruction by the baser human impulses that so easily fly out of control in a wilderness nation. Mather seeks to apply rationalist models of "evidence" to deal with the awful reality—a reality he never questioned—of what he called witches and what we might describe as social deviance. Edwards, in measured prose, sought to both stir and control his parishioners, the endless strand across which succeeding American evangelists have trod.

Francis Parkman's classic account of the tragic meeting of Montcalm and Wolfe on the Plains of Abraham in 1759 is a nineteenth-century reconstruction of the eighteenth-century world in which England and France both fought futilely for an empire in the New World. In Benjamin Franklin, Tom Paine, St. Jean de Crèvecoeur, Thomas Jefferson, and James Madison we see why both of these two major world powers of the age failed to hold the treasure of the New World, that great temperate zone strip we now call the United States. These men trace the evolution of a new creature, a political animal called the American, a mixture of rejected British traditions of republican radicalism, the wealth and opportunity of the new environment, and an already lengthy history of political contention and personal freedom—at least for some. A blend of business savvy, political genius, vested interest, and revolutionary idealism would take advantage of the blunders of these cumbersome remote empires, creating a new nation with its own heroes and its own values, free to create its own empires, make its own blunders, and achieve its own destiny.

George Washington quickly emerged as a recognizable type in American popular culture and rapidly became the new nation's first full-fledged hero. Parson Weems caught the national mood in his *Life of Washington,* turning the old general and leader into a subject for moral exhortation. The model for American virtue, the image of public probity, the official classical style—still visible in federal architecture—was forever fixed early in our history.

Yet Americans, too bound by the European conventions of their age to recognize that several of the founding fathers—Jefferson, Franklin, Madison—were great writers, soon clamored for literary heroes to add to the splendor of the early republic. Washington Irving discovered in conversation with Sir Walter Scott, the most popular writer of his day, that American history and American folklore might provide the romantic background for a literature both acceptable to world opinion yet native to the United States. Suddenly an American writer had entered the ranks of world literature.

Americans remained provincials in the world of nineteenth-century culture, however, and their demands for a national literature which would be unique yet be recognized by their European critics, remained a major theme through the great age of New England literature, the age of Ralph Waldo Emerson, Margaret Fuller, Henry David Thoreau, and Nathaniel Hawthorne. Most Americans still sought assurance from across the Atlantic to confirm the worth of their own culture. American readers nervously scanned the comments of foreign visitors such as Tocqueville to understand or to defend the new "institutions" of which they so frequently boasted.

Few writers or artists could follow the direction of George Catlin, convinced that a pure concentration on a quintessentially American subject would document a world intrinsically worthy of remembrance while creating high art. Perhaps Thoreau came closest to duplicating this perception, but with the important difference that his concentration on the immediacy of life around him made no special claims for American experience and sought no unique American culture. Rather, Thoreau's transcendental perspective—shared by his contemporaries, but never expressed with such purity and force—insisted on the perfect equality of all experience directly perceived and directed an intensity under which any part of nature could flower into art.

Modern critics would quickly name as the great works of American literature of the 1850s, Hawthorne's *The Scarlet Letter,* Melville's *Moby Dick,* and Walt Whitman's *Leaves of Grass.* Contemporary perceptions were quite different. *Uncle Tom's Cabin* by Harriet Beecher Stowe was the great sensation of the age, a monumental literary and political event. The problem of America's minorities, particularly blacks but Indians as well, was as close to the core of public policy and debate for the first two centuries of American life as it has been in recent decades. The contradictory promises of national life and the tentative assertions of national identity confronted the painful realities of groups denied these promises and excluded from that identity, tentative as it was.

Crèvecoeur celebrated what was later to be called the "melting pot," but his Pennsylvania landscape had been cleared not only of forests but of Indians, and it was north of the fateful line that would separate slave and free states. Jefferson struggled with the dilemma of slavery, the wolf—his own metaphor—which he held by the ears. Thoreau's hero John Brown suffered none of Jefferson's hesitations: he saw the issues depicted by Mrs. Stowe and Frederick Douglass in as straightforward moral terms as Parson Weems had viewed Washington. But Lincoln, stealing into a frightened capital, carried with him Jefferson's ambiguous legacy: an "Empire for Liberty" which tolerated slavery in nearly half of its territory. Like Jefferson and unlike John Brown, Lincoln cared about that empire, the Union, more than he did about eradicating the hateful institution of slavery. Lincoln, of course, succeeded (although by terrible means of which he could scarcely dream in 1861) in saving the Union and in destroying slavery. And he, too, became a model for virtue but with more of the common touch than any biographer could muster for Washington. Lincoln's achievement in dealing with the problem of slavery served to reveal the deeper problems of racism and of many another arrangement of American life, problems that continue to shape the American experience.

This book explores the many ways of being an American. In that sense its theme is the American identity, or rather the many identities that make up a diverse history and nation. It offers one kind of answer to the question asked nearly two centuries ago by Crèvecoeur: "What then is this American, this new man?" It invites students to view the experiences of these new people, these Americans, through the eyes of a few of those who saw what happened, who were there, and who had the power to tell of it.

Contents

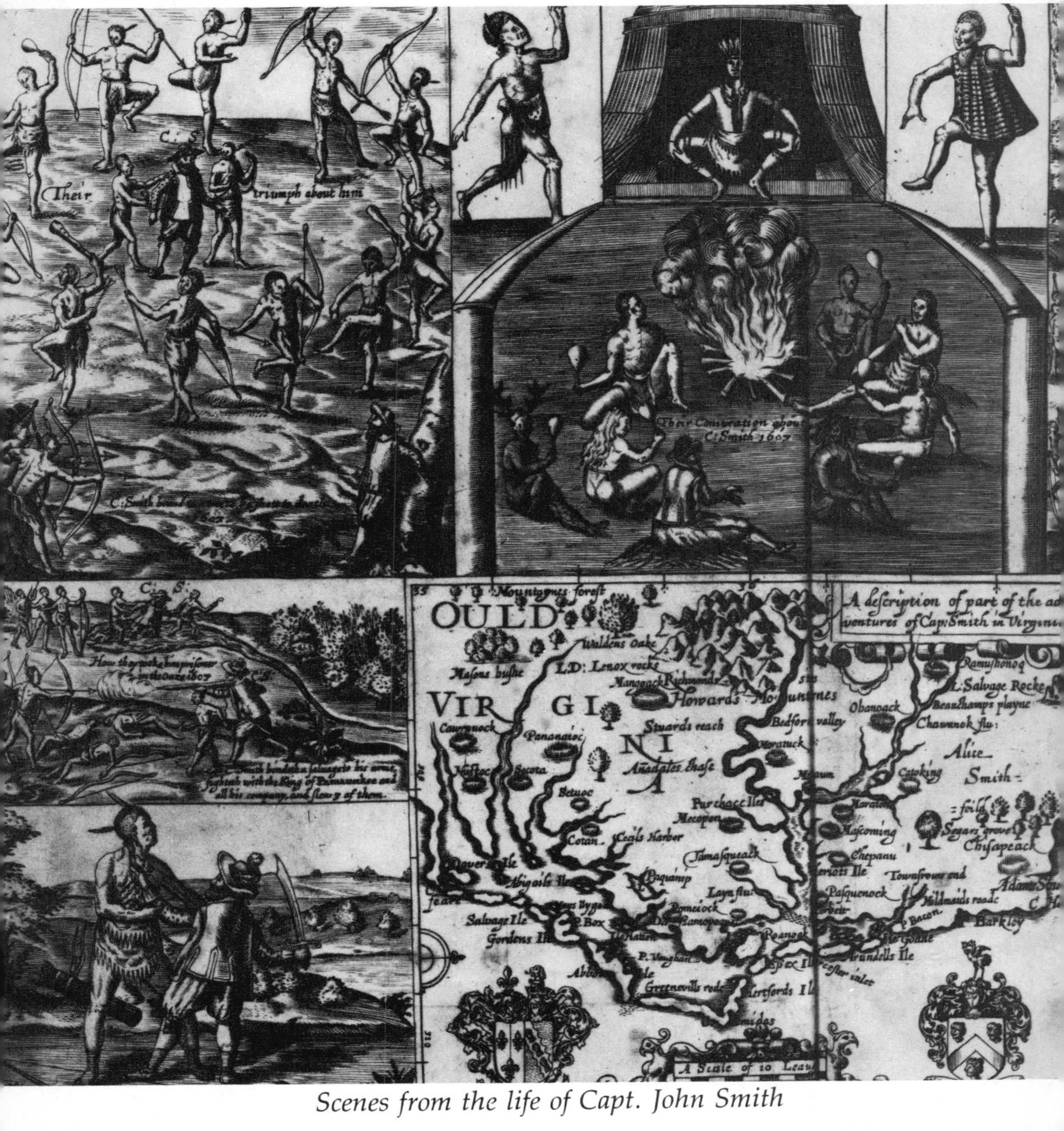

Scenes from the life of Capt. John Smith

JOHN SMITH

Of the Natural Inhabitants of Virginia

(1624)

Indians are the only people we can legitimately refer to as "Americans" in the first decades of the seventeenth century. Nonetheless, if one sought in that period for a prototype of the "historic American" the world now knows, Captain John Smith would be the man. He was a traveler and a man of action, a boaster and a braggart, a politician, a successful entrepreneur, and a public-relations man (his last book had a marvelous title: Advertisements for the Unexperienced Planters of

New England, or Anywhere). A third of a millenium ahead of Norman Mailer, he wrote advertisements for himself, and in an episode with the Indian maiden Pocahantas (which may even have occurred), upstaged every future American romantic. Living and dying an Englishman, Smith remains undeniably one of us.

Smith could never resist making himself the hero of his histories. Even so, behind the facade of heroism and leadership was at least a measure of reality and ample experience to write the history of his enterprises in Virginia and New England. The goals Smith set for himself and his colonies: the spread of civilization, religion, and English power; the acquisition of personal wealth and position; the achievement of political stability; the widening of useful knowledge about the world — all square remarkably well with the way future generations of Americans would understand their history. Smith caught much of the enterprising and imperial side of American dreams at their very inception.

Smith's views of the "Natural Inhabitants of Virginia" are in this tradition as well. No admirer of Indians, he nonetheless proved an able diplomat among them, serving the Virginia colony better than any of its other early leaders in maintaining good relations. And, as the selection indicates, he could appreciate parts of their culture even while dismissing them as heathens inferior to Englishmen. But then who, according to these Elizabethan imperialists, was not? There are few themes of later Indian-white relations (save the frequent but ineffectual sense of contrition over white misdeeds) that one cannot find in Smith's writings and career. Here too his story remains a piece of early Americana, a reminder of the adventurous Renaissance spirit that carved deep lines in the new world landscape.

The land is not populous, for the men be few; their far greater number is of women and children. Within sixty miles of Jamestown there are about some five thousand people, but of able men fit for their wars scarce fifteen hundred. To nourish so many together they have yet no means, because they make so small a benefit of their land, be it never so fertile.

Some being very great, as the Susquehannocks, others very little, as the Wighcocomocos; but generally tall and straight, of a comely proportion, and of a color brown when they are of any age, but they are born white. Their hair is generally black, but few have any beards. The men wear half their beards [heads] shaven, the other half long; for barbers they use their women, who with two shells will grate away the hair, of any fashion they please. The women ['s heads] are cut in many fashions, agreeable to their years, but ever some part remaineth long.

They are very strong, of an able body and full of agility, able to endure to lie in the woods under a tree by the fire in the worst of winter, or in the weeds and grass in ambuscado in the summer.

They are inconstant in everything but what fear constraineth them to keep. Crafty, timorous, quick of apprehension, and very ingenuous. Some are of disposition fearful, some bold, some cautelous [deceitful], all savage. They are covetous of copper, beads, and such like trash. They are soon moved to anger, and so malicious that they seldom forget an injury. They seldom steal one from another, lest their conjurers should reveal it and so they be pursued and punished. That they are thus feared is certain, but that any can reveal their offenses by conjuration I am doubtful. Their women are careful not to be suspected of dishonesty without the leave of their husbands.

Each household knoweth their own lands and gardens, and most live off their own labors.

For their apparel they are sometimes covered with the skins of wild beasts, which in winter are dressed with the hair but in summer without. The better sort use large mantles of deerskins, not much differing in fashion from the Irish mantles—some embroidered with white beads, some with copper, others painted after their manner. But the common sort have scarce to cover their nakedness but with grass, the leaves of trees, or such like. We have seen some use mantles made of turkey feathers, so prettily wrought and woven with threads that nothing could be discerned but the feathers. But the women are always covered about their middle with a skin, and very shamefast to be seen bare.

They adorn themselves most with copper beads and paintings. Their women, some have their legs, hands, breasts, and face cunningly embroidered with diverse works, as beasts, serpents, artificially wrought into their flesh with black spots. In each ear commonly they have three great holes, whereat they hang chains, bracelets, or copper. Some of their men wear in those holes a small green and yellow colored snake near half a yard in length, which, crawling and lapping herself about his neck, oftentimes familiarly would kiss his lips. Others wear a dead rat tied by the tail. Some on their heads wear the wing of a bird or some large feather with a rattle. Those rattles are somewhat like the shape of a rapier but less, which they take from the tail of a snake. Many have the whole skin of a hawk or some strange fowl stuffed with wings abroad, others a broad piece of copper, and some the hand of their enemy dried. Their heads and shoulders are painted red with the root puccoon [bloodroot] brayed to powder, mixed with oil; this they hold in summer to preserve them from the heat, and in winter from the cold. Many other forms of paintings they use, but he is the most gallant that is the most monstrous to behold.

Their buildings and habitations are for the most part by the rivers, or not far distant from some fresh spring. Their houses are built like our arbors, of small young sprigs bowed and tied and so close covered with mats or the barks of trees very handsomely that notwithstanding either wind, rain, or weather, they are as warm as stoves but very smoky; yet at the top of the house there is a hole made for the smoke to go into right over the fire.

Against the fire they lie on little hurdles of reeds covered with a mat, borne from the ground a foot and more by a hurdle of wood. On these round about the house they lie heads and points one by th'other against the fire, some covered with mats, some with skins, and some stark naked lie on the ground, from six to twenty in a house.

Their houses are in the midst of their fields or gardens, which are small plots of ground—some twenty acres, some forty, some one hundred, some two hundred, some more, some less. In some places from two to fifty of those houses [lie] together or but a little separated by groves of trees. Near their habitations is little small wood or old trees on the ground by reason of their burning of them for fire. So that a man may gallop a horse amongst those woods any way but where the creeks or rivers shall hinder.

Men, women, and children have their several names according to the several humors of their parents. Their women (they say) are easily delivered of child, yet do they love children very dearly. To make them hardy, in the coldest mornings they wash them in the rivers, and by painting and ointments so tan their skins that after a year or two no weather will hurt them.

The men bestow their time in fishing, hunting, wars, and such man-like exercises, scorning to be seen in any woman-like exercise, which is the cause that the women be very painful [toiling] and the men often idle. The women and children do the rest of the work. They make mats, baskets, pots, mortars, pound their corn, make their bread, prepare their victuals, plant their corn, gather their corn, bear all kind of burdens, and such like.

Their fire they kindle presently by chafing a dry pointed stick in a hole of a little square piece of wood, that firing itself will so fire moss, leaves, or any such like dry thing that will quickly burn.

In March and April they live much upon their fishing weirs, and feed on fish, turkeys, and squirrels. In May and June they plant their fields and live most off acorns, walnuts, and fish. But to amend their diet, some disperse themselves in small companies and live upon fish, beasts, crabs, oysters, land tortoises, strawberries, mulberries, and such like. In June, July, and August they feed upon the roots of tuckahoe, berries, fish, and green wheat.

It is strange to see how their bodies alter with their diet; even as the deer and wild beasts, they seem fat and lean, strong and weak. Powhatan, their great king, and some others that are provident, roast their fish and flesh upon hurdles and keep it till scarce times.

For fishing, hunting, and wars they use much their bow and arrows. They bring their bows to the form of ours by the scraping of a shell. Their arrows are made, some of straight young sprigs, which they head with bone some two or three inches long. These they use to shoot at squirrels on trees. Another sort of arrows they use is made of reeds. These are pieced with wood, headed with splinters of crystal or some sharp stone, the spurs of a turkey, or the bill of some bird. For his knife he hath the splinter of a reed to cut his feathers in form. With this knife also he will joint a deer or any beast, shape his shoes, buskins, mantles, etc. To make the notch of his arrow he hath the tooth of a beaver set in a stick, wherewith he grateth it by degrees. His arrow head he quickly maketh with a little bone, which he ever weareth at his bracer, of any splint of a stone or glass in the form of a heart, and these they glue to the end of their arrows. With the sinews of deer and the tops of deer horns boiled to a jelly, they make a glue that will not dissolve in cold water.

For their wars also they use targets [shields] that are round and made of the barks of trees, and a sword of wood [carried] at their backs, but oftentimes they use for swords the horn of a deer put through a piece of wood in form of a pickax. Some [prefer] a long stone sharpened at both ends, used in the same manner. This they were wont to use also for hatchets, but now by trucking [trading] they have plenty of the same form of iron. And those are their chief instruments and arms.

Their fishing is much in boats. These they make of one tree by burning and scratching away the coals with stones and shells, till they have made it in form of a trough. Some of them are an ell deep and forty or fifty foot in length, and some will bear forty men, but the most ordinary are smaller and will bear ten, twenty, or thirty, according to their bigness. Instead of oars, they use paddles and sticks, with which they will row faster than our barges.

Betwixt their hands and thighs their women use to spin the barks of trees, deer sinews, or a kind of grass they call pemmenaw; of these they make a thread very even and readily. This thread serveth for many uses, as about their housing, apparel, as also they make nets for fishing, for the quantity as formally [properly] braided as ours. They make also with it lines for angles.

Their hooks are either a bone grated as they notch their arrows, in the form of a crooked pin or fishhook, or of the splinter of a bone tied to the cleft of a little stick, and with the end of the line they tie on the bait.

They use also long arrows tied on a line, wherewith they shoot at fish in the rivers. But they of Accomac use staves like unto javelins headed with bone. With these they dart fish swimming in the water. They have also many artificial weirs in which they get abundance of fish.

In their hunting and fishing they take extreme pains; yet it being their ordinary exercise from their infancy, they esteem it a pleasure and are very proud to be expert therein. And by their continual ranging and travel they know all the advantages and places most frequented with deer, beasts, fish, fowl, roots, and berries. At their huntings they leave their habitations and reduce themselves into companies, as the Tartars do, and go to the most desert places [treeless plains] with their families, where they spend their time in hunting and fowling up towards the mountains, by the heads of their rivers, where there is plenty of game. For betwixt the rivers the grounds are so narrow that little cometh here which they devour not. It is a marvel they can so directly pass these deserts some three or four days' journey without habitation. Their hunting houses are like unto arbors covered with mats. These their women bear after them, with corn, acorns, mortars, and all bag and baggage they use. When they come to the place of exercise, every man doth his best to show his dexterity, for by their excelling in those qualities they get their wives. Forty yards will they shoot level [accurately] or very near the mark, and one hundred and twenty is their best at random.

At their huntings in the deserts they are commonly two or three hundred together. Having found the deer, they environ them with many fires, and betwixt the fires they place themselves. And some take their stands in the midsts. The deer being thus feared by the fires and their voices, they chase them so long within that circle that many times they kill six, eight, ten, or fifteen at a hunting. They use also to drive them into some narrow point of land when they find that advantage, and so force them into the river, where with their boats they have ambuscados to kill them. When they have shot a deer by land, they follow him like bloodhounds by the blood and strain, and oftentimes so take them. Hares, partridges, turkeys, or eggs, fat or lean, young or old, they devour all they can catch in their power.

(In one of these huntings they found me in the discovery of the head of the river of Chickahominy, where they slew my men and took me prisoner in a bogmire; where I saw those exercises and gathered these observations.)

One savage hunting alone useth the skin of a deer slit on the one side, and so put in his arm through the neck, so that his hand comes to the head which is stuffed, and the horns, head, eyes, ears, and every part as artificially counterfeited as they can devise. Thus shrouding his body in the skin, by stalking he approacheth the deer, creeping on the ground from one tree to another. If the deer chance to find fault, or stand at gaze, he turneth his head with his hand to his best advantage to seem like a deer also gazing and licking himself. So watching his best advantage to approach, having shot him, he chaseth him by his blood and strain till he get him.

When they intend any wars, the werowances usually have the advice of their priests and conjurers, and their allies, and ancient friends; but chiefly the priests determine their resolution. Every werowance, or some lusty fellow, they appoint captain over every nation. They seldom make war for lands or goods, but for women and children, and principally for revenge. They have many enemies, namely, all their westernly countries beyond the mountains and the heads of the rivers. Upon the head of the Powhatan's [river] are the Monacans, whose chief habitation is at Rassawek; unto whom the Mowhemchoes, the Massinacacks, the Monahassanughs, the Monasickapanoughs, and other nations pay tribute.

Upon the head of the river of Rappahannock is a people called Manahoacs. To these are contributors the Tauxanias, the Shackakonias, the Ontponeas, the Tegninateos, the Whonkentaes, the Stegarakes, the Hassinungaes, and diverse others, all confederates with the Monacans, though many different in language, and be very barbarous, living for the most part off wild beasts and fruits.

Beyond the mountains from whence is the head of the river Potomac the savages report inhabit their most mortal enemies, the Massawomekes, upon a great salt water, which by all likelihood is either some part of Canada, some great lake, or some inlet of some sea that falleth into the South Sea. These Massawomekes are a great nation and very populous. For the [people at] heads of all those rivers, especially the Potomacs, the Pautuxents, the Susquehannocks, the Tockwoughs, are continually tormented by them of whose cruelty they generally complained, and very importunate they were with me and my company to free them from these tormentors. To this purpose they offered food, conduct, assistance, and continual subjection.

(Which I concluded to effect. But the Council then present emulating [jealous of] my success, would not think it fit to spare me forty men to be hazarded in those unknown regions, and so was lost that opportunity.)

Seven boats full of these Massawomekes we encountered at the head of the Bay; whose targets, baskets, swords, tobacco pipes, platters [drums], bows and arrows, and everything showed they much exceeded them of our parts. And their dexterity in their small boats, made of the barks of trees sewed with bark and well luted with gum, argueth that they are seated upon some great water.

Against all these enemies the Powhatans are constrained sometimes to fight. Their chief attempts are by strategems, treacheries, or surprisals. Yet the werowances, women, and children they put not to death but keep them captives. They have a method in war, and for our pleasures they showed it us, and it was in this manner performed at Mattaponi.

Having painted and disguised themselves in the fiercest manner they could devise, they divided themselves into two companies, near a hundred in a company; the one company called Monacans, the other Powhatans. Either army had their captain. These as enemies took their stands a musket shot one from another; ranked themselves fifteen abreast, and each rank from another four or five yards, not in file but in the opening betwixt their files, so the rear could shoot as conveniently as the front.

Having thus pitched the fields, from either part went a messenger with these conditions: that whosoever were vanquished, such as escape upon their submission in two days after should live, but their wives and children should be prize for the conquerors.

The messengers were no sooner returned but they approached in their orders, on each flank a sergeant and in the rear an officer for lieutenant, all duly keeping their orders, yet leaping and singing after their accustomed tune, which they only use in wars. Upon the first flight of arrows they gave such horrible shouts and screeches as so many infernal hellhounds could not have made them more terrible.

When they had spent their arrows, they joined together prettily, charging and retiring, every rank seconding the other. As they got advantage, they catched their enemies by the hair of the head, and down he came that was taken. His enemy with his wooden sword seemed to beat out his brains, and still they crept to the rear to maintain the skirmish.

The Monacans decreasing, the Powhatans charged them in the form of a half moon. They, unwilling to be enclosed, fled all in a troop to their ambuscados, on whom they led them very cunningly. The Monacans disperse themselves among the fresh men, whereupon the Powhatans retired with all speed to their seconds; which the Monacans seeing, took that advantage to retire again to their own battle, and so each returned to their own quarter.

All their actions, voices, and gestures both in charging and retiring were so strained to the height of their quality and nature that the strangeness thereof made it seem very delightful.

For their music they use a thick cane on which they pipe as on a recorder. For their wars they have a great deep platter of wood. They cover the mouth thereof with a skin; at each corner they tie a walnut, which, meeting on the backside near the bottom, with a small rope they twitch them together till it be so taut and stiff that they may beat upon it as upon a drum. But their chief instruments are rattles made of small gourds or pumpkin shells. Of these they have bass, tenor, countertenor, mean, and treble. These mingled with their voices, sometimes twenty or thirty together, make such a terrible noise as would rather affright than delight any man.

If any great commander arrive at the habitation of a werowance, they spread a mat, as the Turks do a carpet, for him to sit upon. Upon another right opposite they sit themselves. Then do all with a tunable voice of shouting bid him welcome. After this do two or more of their chiefest men make an oration, testifying their love. Which they do with such vehemency and so great passions that they sweat till they drop and are so out of breath they can scarce speak, so that a man would take them to be exceeding angry or stark mad. Such victual as they have they spend freely; and at night where his lodging is appointed they set a woman fresh painted red with puccoon and oil to be his bedfellow.

Their manner of trading is for copper, beads, and such like, for which they give such commodities as they have, as skins, fowl, fish, flesh, and their country corn. But their victuals are their chiefest riches.

Every spring they make themselves sick with drinking the juice of a root they call wighsacan and water. Whereof they pour so great a quantity that it purgeth them in a very violent manner, so that in three or four days after they scarce recover their former health.

Sometimes they are troubled with dropsies, swellings, aches, and such like diseases. For cure whereof they build a stove in the form of a dove-house, with mats so close that a few coals therein covered with a pot will make the patient sweat extremely. For swellings also they use small pieces of touchwood, in the form of cloves, which pricking on the grief they burn close to the flesh, and from thence draw the corruption with their mouth. With this root wighsacan they ordinarily heal green wounds. But [to] scarify a swelling or make incision, their best instruments are some splinted stone. Old ulcers or putrefied hurts are seldom seen cured amongst them.

They have many professed physicians who with their charms and rattles, with an infernal rout of words and actions, will seem to suck their inward grief from their navels or their grieved places; but of our surgeons they were so conceited [admiring] that they believed any plaster would heal any hurt.

"The Witch, No. 1," a Salem trial scene

COTTON MATHER

The Wonders of the Invisible World

(1693)

The Salem witchcraft epidemic of 1692 has ever been the brush tarring New England Puritanism's historical reputation. The very word "Puritan" continues to carry connotations of intolerance, superstition, and a sour joy in making people miserable. Like most historical stereotypes, this one is unfair. Salem, a small isolated seacoast town, was not Boston, and the witchcraft episode was not representative of Puritan life. Rather, it was a low point in which provincial spite and superstition overcame the judgment of people who should have known better, and social tensions let a minor incident tumble into a massive tragedy.

In the seventeenth century most people—not just Puritans—believed in witches. When in 1688 four Boston children were seized with fits, they—reflecting their culture—blamed an old woman who in fact did believe that she was a witch and had equipped herself with the traditional paraphernalia of rag dolls to pinch and poke. Having confessed her witchcraft, she was hanged according to established law. Cotton Mather, the foremost Puritan intellectual and the first important figure in the history of American science, took the oldest of the young girls into his house and studied her closely, finally curing the psychosomatic ailment. His book describing her cure had an ill effect in Salem. Its clinical details somehow passed into the folklore, and a few years later several teen-aged girls in Salem began manifesting the same symptoms. Accusations uncovered other accusations, and all gained a spurious plausibility from the existence of some who thought themselves witches. The courts trying the accused lost all capacity to limit the debacle when they began, against the standard seventeenth-century rules of evidence, to find people guilty on the basis of "spectral" evidence—testimony that people had seen visions resembling the alleged witches. Before the hysteria ended, nineteen people and two dogs hanged, and one man was pressed to death for refusing to plead either guilty or not guilty.

The Salem witchcraft trials unquestionably say something about Puritanism. Arthur Miller, the distinguished modern playwright, wrote about the incident in The Crucible, which obliquely compared Salem to the anticommunist hysteria of the 1950s. The comparison was in many ways a reasonable one: the United States cannot be encapsulated in anticommunist witch hunts, but they reveal something which we must learn about the nation. Salem in 1692 must be seen the same way: a terrible question about Puritan society, not a damning conclusion.

§ II. The *New-Englanders* are a People of God settled in those, which were once the *Devil's* Territories; and it may easily be supposed that the *Devil* was exceedingly disturbed, when he perceived such a People here accomplishing the Promise of old made unto our Blessed Jesus, *That He should have the Utmost parts of the Earth for his Possession*. There was not a greater Uproar among the *Ephesians*, when the Gospel was first brought among them, than there was among, *The Powers of the Air* (after whom those *Ephesians* walked) when first the *Silver Trumpets* of the Gospel here made the *Joyful Sound*. The Devil thus Irritated, immediately try'd all sorts of Methods to overturn this poor Plantation: and so much of the Church, as was *Fled into this Wilderness*, immediately found, *The Serpent cast out of his Mouth a Flood for the carrying of it away*. I believe, that never were more *Satanical Devices* used for the Unsetling of any People under the Sun, than what have been Employ'd for the Extirpation of the *Vine* which God has here *Planted, Casting out the Heathen, and preparing a Room before it, and causing it to take deep Root, and fill the Land, so that it sent its Boughs unto the* Atlantic *Sea* Eastward, *and its Branches unto the* Connecticut *River* Westward, *and the Hills were covered with the shadow thereof*. But, All those Attempts of Hell, have hitherto been Abortive, many an *Ebenezer* has been Erected unto the Praise of God, by his Poor People here; and, *Having obtained Help from God, we continue to this Day*. Wherefore the Devil is now making one Attempt more upon us; an Attempt more Difficult, more Surprizing, more snarl'd with unintelligible Circumstances than any that we have hitherto Encountred; an Attempt so *Critical*, that if we get well through, we shall soon enjoy *Halcyon* Days with all the *Vultures* of Hell *Trodden under our Feet*. He has wanted his *Incarnate Legions* to Persecute us, as the People of God have in the other Hemisphere been Persecuted: he has therefore drawn forth his more *Spiritual* ones to make an Attacque upon us. We have been advised by some Credible Christians yet alive, that a Malefactor, accused of *Witchcraft* as well as *Murder*, and Executed in this place more than Forty Years ago, did then give Notice of, *An Horrible* PLOT *against the Country by* WITCHCRAFT, *and a Foundation of* WITCHCRAFT *then laid, which if it were not seasonably discovered, would probably Blow up, and pull down all the Churches in the Country*. And we have now with Horror seen the *Discovery* of such a *Witchcraft!* An Army of *Devils* is horribly broke in upon the place which is the *Center*, and after a sort, the *First-born* of our *English* Settlements: and the Houses of the Good People there are fill'd with the doleful Shrieks of their Children and Servants, Tormented by Invisible Hands, with Tortures altogether preternatural. After the Mischiefs there Endeavoured, and since in part Conquered, the terrible Plague, of *Evil Angels*, hath made its Progress into some other places, where other Persons have been in like manner Diabolically handled. These our poor Afflicted Neighbours, quickly after they become *Infected* and *Infested* with these *Dæmons*, arrive to a Capacity of Discerning those which they conceive the *Shapes* of their Troublers; and notwithstanding the Great and Just Suspicion, that the *Dæmons* might Impose the *Shapes* of Innocent Persons in their *Spectral Exhibitions* upon the Sufferers, (which may perhaps prove no small part of the *Witch-Plot* in the issue) yet many of the Persons thus Represented, being Examined, several of them have been Convicted of a very Damnable *Witchcraft:* yea, more than One *Twenty* have *Confessed,* that they have Signed unto a *Book,* which the Devil show'd them, and Engaged in his Hellish Design of *Bewitching,* and *Ruining* our Land. *We* know not, at least *I* know not, how far the *Delusions* of Satan may be Interwoven into some Circumstances of the *Confessions;* but one would think, all the Rules of Understanding Humane Affairs are at an end, if after so many most Voluntary Harmonious *Confessions,* made by Intelligent Persons of all Ages, in sundry Towns, at several Times, we must not Believe the *main strokes* wherein those *Confessions* all agree: especially when we have a thousand preternatural Things every day before our eyes, wherein the *Confessors* do acknowledge their Concernment, and give Demonstration of their being so Concerned. If the Devils now can strike the minds of men with any *Poisons* of so fine a Composition and Operation, that Scores of Innocent People shall Unite, in *Confessions* of a Crime, which we see actually committed, it is a thing prodigious, beyond the Wonders of the former Ages, and it threatens no less than a sort of a Dissolution upon the World. Now, by these *Confessions* 'tis Agreed, *That* the Devil has made a dreadful Knot of *Witches* in the Country, and by the help of *Witches* has dreadfully increased that Knot: *That* these *Witches* have driven a Trade of Commissioning their *Confederate Spirits,* to do all sorts of Mischiefs to the Neighbours, whereupon there have ensued such Mischievous consequences upon the Bodies and Estates of the Neighbourhood, as could not otherwise be accounted for: yea, *That* at prodigious *Witch-Meetings,* the Wretches have proceeded so far, as to Concert and Consult the Methods of Rooting out the Christian Religion from this Country, and setting up instead of it, perhaps a more gross *Diabolism,* than ever the World saw before. And yet it will be a thing little short of *Miracle,* if in so *spread* a Business as this, the Devil should not get in some of his Juggles, to confound the Discovery of all the rest.

§ III. Doubtless, the Thoughts of many will receive a great Scandal against *New-England,* from the Number of Persons that have been Accused, or Suspected, for *Witchcraft,* in this Country: But it were easie to offer many things, that may Answer and Abate the Scandal. If the Holy God should any where permit the Devils to hook two or three wicked *Scholars* into *Witchcraft,* and then by their Assistance to Range with their *Poisonous Insinuations* among Ignorant, Envious, Discontented People, till they have cunningly decoy'd them into some sudden *Act,* whereby the Toyls of Hell shall be perhaps inextricably cast over them: what Country in the World would not afford

Witches, numerous to a Prodigy? Accordingly, The Kingdoms of *Sweden, Denmark, Scotland,* yea and *England* it self, as well as the Province of *New-England,* have had their Storms of *Witchcrafts* breaking upon them, which have made most Lamentable Devastations: which also I wish, may be *The Last.* And it is not uneasie to be imagined, That God has not brought out all the *Witchcrafts* in many other Lands with such a speedy, dreadful, destroying *Jealousie,* as burns forth upon such *High Treasons,* committed here in A *Land of Uprightness:* Transgressors may more quickly here than elsewhere become a Prey to the Vengeance of Him, *Who has Eyes like a Flame of Fire,* and, *who walks in the midst of the Golden Candlesticks.* Moreover, There are many parts of the World, who if they do upon this Occasion insult over this People of God, need only to be told the Story of what happen'd at *Loim,* in the Dutchy of *Gulic,* where a Popish Curate having ineffectually try'd many Charms to Eject the Devil out of a Damsel there possessed, he passionately bid the Devil come out of her into himself; but the Devil answered him, *Quid mihi Opus, est eum tentare, quem Novissimo die, Jure Optimo, sum possessurus?* That is, *What need I meddle with one whom I am sure to have, and hold at the Last-day as my own for ever!*

* * *

§ VII. I was going to make one Venture more; that is, to offer some safe Rules, for the finding out of the Witches, which are at this day our accursed Troublers: but this were a Venture too *Presumptuous* and *Icarian* for me to make; I leave that unto those Excellent and Judicious Persons, with whom I am not worthy to be numbred: All that I shall do, shall be to lay before my Readers, a brief *Synopsis* of what has been written on that Subject, by a Triumvirate of as Eminent Persons as have ever handled it. I will begin with, . . .

AN ABSTRACT OF MR. PERKINS'S WAY FOR THE DISCOVERY OF WITCHES.

I. THERE *are* Presumptions, *which do at least probably and conjecturally note one to be a* Witch. *These give occasion to Examine, yet they are no sufficient Causes of Conviction.*

II. *If any Man or Woman be notoriously defamed for a* Witch, *this yields a strong Suspition. Yet the Judge ought carefully to look, that the Report be made by* Men *of Honesty and Credit.*

III. *If a* Fellow-Witch, *or* Magician, *give Testimony of any Person to be a* Witch; *this indeed is not sufficient for Condemnation; but it is a fit Presumption to cause a strait Examination.*

IV. *If after Cursing there follow Death, or at least some mischief: for* Witches *are wont to practise their mischievous Facts, by Cursing and Banning: This also is a sufficient matter of Examination, tho' not of Conviction.*

V. *If after Enmity, Quarrelling, or Threatning, a present mischief does follow; that also is a great Presumption.*

VI. *If the Party suspected be the Son or Daughter, the man-servant or maid-servant, the Familiar Friend, near Neighbor, or old Companion, of a known and convicted Witch; this may be likewise a Presumption; for Witchcraft is an Art that may be learned, and conveyed from man to man.*

VII. *Some add this for a Presumption: If the Party suspected be found to have the Devil's mark; for it is commonly thought, when the Devil makes his Covenant with them, he alwaies leaves his mark behind them, whereby he knows them for his own:—a mark whereof no evident Reason in Nature can be given.*

VIII. *Lastly, If the party examined be Unconstant, or contrary to himself, in his deliberate Answers, it argueth a Guilty Conscience, which stops the freedom of Utterance. And yet there are causes of Astonishment, which may befal the Good, as well as the Bad.*

IX. *But then there is a* Conviction, *discovering the* Witch, *which must proceed from just and sufficient proofs, and not from bare presumptions.*

X. *Scratching of the suspected party, and Recovery thereupon, with several other such weak Proofs; as also, the fleeting of the suspected Party, thrown upon the Water; these Proofs are so far from being sufficient, that some of them are, after a sort, practices of Witchcraft.*

XI. *The Testimony of some Wizzard, tho' offering to shew the Witches Face in a Glass: This, I grant, may be a good Presumption, to cause a strait Examination; but a sufficient Proof of Conviction it cannot be. If the Devil tell the Grand Jury, that the person in question is a Witch, and offers withal to confirm the same by Oath, should the Inquest receive his Oath or Accusation to condemn the man? Assuredly no. And yet, that is as much as the Testimony of another Wizzard, who only by the Devil's help reveals the Witch.*

XII. *If a man, being dangerously sick, and like to dye, upon Suspicion, will take it on his Death, that such a one hath bewitched him, it is an Allegation of the same nature, which may move the Judge to examine the Party, but it is of no moment for Conviction.*

XIII. *Among the sufficient means of Conviction, the first is, the free and voluntary Confession of the Crime, made by the party suspected and accused, after Examination. I say not, that a bare confession is sufficient, but a Confession after due Examination, taken upon pregnant presumptions. What needs now more witness or further Enquiry?*

XIV. *There is a second sufficient Conviction, by the Testimony of two Witnesses, of good and honest Report, avouching before the Magistrate, upon their own Knowledge, these two things: either that the party accused hath made a League with the Devil, or hath done some known practice of witchcraft. And,* all Arguments that do necessarily prove either of these, *being brought by two sufficient Witnesses, are of force fully to convince the party suspected.*

XV. *If it can be proved, that the party suspected hath called upon the* Devil, *or desired his Help, this is a pregnant proof of a League formerly made between them.*

XVI. *If it can be proved, that the party hath entertained a Familiar Spirit, and had Conference with it, in the likeness of some visible Creatures; here is Evidence of witchcraft.*

XVII. *If the witnesses affirm upon Oath, that the suspected person hath done any action or work which necessarily infers a Covenant made, as, that he hath used Enchantments, divined things before they come to pass, and that peremptorily, raised Tempests, caused the Form of a dead man to appear; it proveth sufficiently, that he or she is a* Witch. This is the Substance of Mr. *Perkins*.

* * *

And now, O *Thou Hope of* New-England, *and the Saviour thereof in the Time of Trouble; Do thou look mercifully down upon us, & Rescue us, out of the Trouble which at this time do's threaten to swallow us up. Let Satan be shortly bruised under our Feet, and Let the Covenanted Vassals of Satan, which have Traiterously brought him in upon us, be Gloriously Conquered, by thy Powerful and Gracious Presence in the midst of us. Abhor us not, O God, but cleanse us, but heal us, but save us, for the sake of thy Glory. Enwrapped in our Salvations. By thy Spirit, Lift up a standard against our infernal adversaries, Let us quickly find thee making of us glad, according to the Days wherein we have been afflicted. Accept of all our Endeavours to glorify thee, in the Fires that are upon us; and among the rest, Let these my poor and weak essays, composed with what Years, what Cares, what Prayers, thou* only *knowest, not want the Acceptance of the Lord.*

* * *

The Tryal of G. B. at a Court of Oyer and Terminer, Held in Salem, 1692.

Glad should I have been, if I had never known the Name of this Man: or never had this occasion to mention so much as the first Letters of his Name. But the Government requiring some Account of his Trial to be inserted in this Book, it becomes me with all Obedience to submit unto the Order.

I. This *G. B.* Was Indicted for Witch-craft, and in the prosecution of the Charge against him, he was Accused by five or six of the Bewitched, as the Author of their Miseries; he was Accused by Eight of the Confessing Witches, as being an head Actor at some of their Hellish Randezvouzes, and one who had the promise of being a King in Satan's Kingdom, now going to be Erected: He was accused by Nine Persons for extraordinary Lifting, and such feats of Strength as could not be done without a Diabolical Assistance. And for other such things he was Accused, until about thirty Testimonies were brought in against him; nor were these judg'd the half of what might have been considered for his Conviction: However they were enough to fix the Character of a Witch upon him according to the Rules of Reasoning, by the Judicious *Gaule,* in that Case directed.

II. The Court being sensible, that the Testimonies of the Parties Bewitched, use to have a Room among the *Suspicions* or *Presumptions,* brought in against one Indicted for Witch-craft; there were now heard the Testimonies of several Persons, who were most notoriously Bewitched, and every day Tortured by Invisible Hands, and these now all charged the Spectres of *G. B.* to have a share in their Torments. At the Examination of this *G. B.* the Bewitched People were grievously harrassed with Preternatural Mischiefs, which could not possibly be Dissembled; and they still ascribed it unto the endeavours of *G. B.* to Kill them. And now upon the Tryal of one of the Bewitched Persons, testified, that in her Agonies, a little black Hair'd Man came to her, saying his Name was *B.* and bidding her set her hand to a Book which he shewed unto her; and bragging that he was a *Conjurer,* above the ordinary Rank of Witches; That he often Persecuted her with the offer of that Book, saying, *She should be well, and need fear nobody, if she would but Sign it;* But he inflicted cruel Pains and Hurts upon her, because of her denying so to do. The Testimonies of the other Sufferers concurred with these; and it was remarkable, that whereas *Biting* was one of the ways which the Witches used for the vexing of the Sufferers; when they cry'd out of *G. B.* Biting them, the print of the Teeth would be seen on the Flesh of the Complainers, and just such a Set of Teeth as *G. B's* would then appear upon them, which could be distinguished from those of some other Mens. Others of them testified, That in their Torments, *G. B.* tempted them to go unto a Sacrament, unto which they perceived him with a Sound of Trumpet, Summoning of other Witches, who quickly after the Sound, would come from all Quarters unto the Rendezvouz. One of them falling into a kind of Trance, affirmed, that *G. B.* had carried her away into a very high Mountain, where he shewed her mighty and glorious Kingdoms, and said, *He would give them all to her, if she would write in his Book;* But she told him, *They were none of his to give;* and refused the Motions; enduring of much Misery for that refusal.

It cost the Court a wonderful deal of Trouble, to hear the Testimonies of the Sufferers; for when they were going to give in their Depositions, they would for a long time be taken with Fits, that made them uncapable of saying any thing. The Chief Judge asked the Prisoner, who he thought hindered these Witnesses from giving their *Testimonies?* And he answered, *He supposed it was the Devil.* That Honourable Person replied, *How comes the Devil then to be so loath to have any Testimony born against you?* Which cast him into very great Confusion.

III. It has been a frequent thing for the Bewitched People to be entertained with Apparitions of *Ghosts* of Murdered People, at the same time that the *Spectres* of the Witches trouble them. These Ghosts do always affright the Beholders more than all the other spectral Representations; and when they exhibit themselves, they cry out, of being Murthered by the Witch-crafts or other Violences of the Persons who are then in Spectre present. It is further considered, that once or twice, these *Apparitions* have been seen by others, at the very same time they have shewn themselves to the Bewitched; and seldom have there been these *Apparitions,* but when something unusual or suspected, have attended the Death of the Party thus Appearing. Some that have been accused by these *Apparitions* accosting of the Bewitched People, who had never heard a word of any such Persons ever being in the World, have upon a fair Examination, freely and fully confessed the Murthers of those very Persons, altho' these also did not know how the Apparitions had complained of them. Accordingly several of the Bewitched, had given in their Testimony, that they had been troubled with the Apparitions of two Women, who said, that they were *G. B's* two Wives, and that he had been the Death of them; and that the Magistrates must be told of it, before whom if *B.* upon his Tryal denied it, they did not know but that they should appear again in Court. Now, *G. B.* had been Infamous for the Barbarous usage of his two late Wives, all the Country over. Moreover, it was testified, the Spectre of *G. B.* threatning of the Sufferers, told them, he had Killed (besides others) Mrs. *Lawson* and her Daughter *Ann.* And it was noted, that these were the Vertuous Wife and Daughter of one at whom this *G. B.* might have a prejudice for his being serviceable at *Salem Village,* from whence himself had in ill Terms removed some Years before: And that when they dy'd, which was long since, there were some odd Circumstances about them, which made some of the Attendents there suspect something of Witch-craft, tho none Imagined from what Quarter it should come.

Well, *G. B.* being now upon his Tryal, one of the Bewitched Persons was cast into Horror at the Ghost of *B's* two Deceased Wives then appearing before him, and crying for *Vengeance* against him. Hereupon several of the Bewitched Persons were successively called in, who all not knowing what the former had seen and said, concurred in their Horror of the Apparition, which they affirmed that he had before him. But he, tho much appalled, utterly deny'd that he discerned any thing of it; nor was it any part of his *Conviction.*

IV. Judicious Writers have assigned it a great place in the Conviction of *Witches, when Persons are Impeached by other notorious Witches, to be as ill as themselves; especially, if the Persons have been much noted for neglecting the Worship of God.* Now, as there might have been Testimonies enough of *G. B's* Antipathy to *Prayer,* and the other Ordinances of God, tho by his Profession, singularly Obliged thereunto; so, there now came in against the Prisoner, the Testimonies of several Persons, who confessed their own having been horrible *Witches,* and ever since their Confessions, had been themselves terribly Tortured by the Devils and other Witches, even like the other Sufferers; and therein undergone the Pains of many *Deaths* for their Confessions.

These now testified, that *G. B.* had been at Witch-meetings with them; and that he was the Person who had Seduc'd, and Compell'd them into the snares of Witch-craft: That he promised them *Fine Cloaths,* for doing it; that he brought Poppets to them, and Thorns to stick into those Poppets, for the Afflicting of other People; and that he exhorted them with the rest of the Crew, to Bewitch all *Salem Village,* but besure to do it Gradually, if they would prevail in what they did.

When the *Lancashire Witches* were Condemn'd, I don't remember that there was any considerable further Evidence, than that of he Bewitched, and than that of some that confessed. We see so much already against *G. B.* But this being indeed not enough, there were other things to render what had been already produced *credible.*

V. A famous Divine recites this among the Convictions of a Witch; *The Testimony of the party Bewitched, whether Pining or Dying; together with the joint Oaths of sufficient Persons that have seen certain Prodigious Pranks or Feats wrought by the Party Accused.* Now, God had been pleased so to leave this *G. B.* that he had ensnared himself by several Instances, which he had formerly given of a Preternatural Strength, and which were now produced against him. He was a very Puny Man, yet he had often done things beyond the strength of a Giant. A Gun of about seven foot Barrel, and so heavy that strong Men could not steadily hold it out with both hands; there were several Testimonies, given in by Persons of Credit and Honor, that he made nothing of taking up such a Gun behind the Lock, with but one hand, and holding it out like a Pistol, at Arms-end. *G. B.* in his Vindication, was so foolish as to say, That *an* Indian *was there, and held it out at the same time:* Whereas none of the Spectators ever saw any such *Indian;* but they supposed, the *Black Man,* (as the Witches call the Devil; and they generally say he resembles an *Indian*) might give him that Assistance. There was Evidence likewise brought in, that he made nothing of taking up whole Barrels fill'd with *Molasses* or *Cider,* in very disadvantageous Postures, and Carrying of them through the difficultest Places out of a Canoo to the Shore.

Yea, there were two Testimonies, that *G. B.* with only putting the Fore Finger of his Right Hand into the Muzzle of an heavy Gun, a Fowling-piece of about six or seven foot Barrel, did lift up the Gun, and hold it out at Arms-end; a Gun which the Deponents thought strong Men could not with both hands lift up, and hold out at the But-end, as is usual. Indeed, one of these Witnesses was overperswaded by some Persons, to be out of the way upon *G. B's* Tryal; but he came afterwards with Sorrow for his withdraw, and gave in his Testimony. Nor were either of these Witnesses made use of as Evidences in the Trial.

VI. There came in several Testimonies relating to the Domestick Affairs of *G. B.* which had a very hard Aspect upon him; and not only prov'd him a very ill Man; but also confirmed the belief of the Character, which had been already fastned on him.

'Twas testified, that keeping his two Successive Wives in a strange kind of Slavery, he would when he came home from abroad, pretend to tell the Talk which any had with them; That he has brought them to the point of Death, by his harsh Dealings with his Wives, and then made the People about him, to promise that in case Death should happen, they would say nothing of it; That he used all means to make his Wives Write, Sign, Seal, and Swear a Covenant, never to reveal any of his Secrets; That his Wives had privately complained unto the Neighbours about frightful Apparitions of Evil Spirits, with which their House was sometimes infested; and that many such things have been whispered among the Neighbourhood. There were also some other Testimonies relating to the Death of People whereby the Consciences of an Impartial Jury were convinced that *G. B.* had Bewitched the Persons mentioned in the Complaints. But I am forced to omit several passages, in this, as well as in all the succeeding Tryals, because the Scribes who took notice of them, have not supplyed me.

VII. One Mr. *Ruck,* Brother-in-Law to this *G. B.* testified, that *G. B.* and himself, and his Sister, who was *G. B's* Wife, going out for two or three Miles to gather Straw-berries, *Ruck* with his Sister, the Wife of *G. B.* Rode home very Softly, with *G. B.* on Foot in their Company, *G. B.* stept aside a little into the Bushes; whereupon they halted and Halloo'd for him. He not answering, they went away homewards, with a quickened pace, without expectation of seeing him in a considerable while; and yet when they were got near home, to their Astonishment, they found him on foot with them, having a Basket of Straw-berries. *G. B.* immediately then fell to Chiding his Wife, on the account of what she had been speaking to her Brother, of him, on the Road: which when they wondred at, he said, *He knew their thoughts. Ruck* being startled at that, made some Reply, intimating, that the Devil himself did not know so far; but *G. B.* answered, *My God makes known your Thoughts unto me.* The Prisoner now at the Bar had nothing to answer, unto what was thus witnessed against him, that was worth considering. Only he said, *Ruck, and his Wife left a Man with him, when they left him.* Which *Ruck* now affirm'd to be false; and when the Court asked *G. B. What the Man's Name was?* his Countenance was much altered; nor could he say, who 'twas. But the Court began to think, that he then step'd aside, only that by the assistance of the *Black Man,* he might put on his *Invisibility,* and in that *Fascinating Mist,* gratifie his own Jealous Humour, to hear what they said of him. Which trick of rendring themselves *Invisible,* our Witches do in their Confessions pretend, that they sometimes are Masters of; and it is the more credible, because there is Demonstration, that they often render many other things utterly *Invisible.*

VIII. *Faltring, faulty, unconstant, and contrary Answers upon judicial and deliberate Examination,* are counted some unlucky Symptoms of Guilt, in all Crimes, especially in Witchcrafts. Now there never was a Prisoner more eminent for them, than *G. B.* both at his Examination and on his Trial. His *Tergiversations, Contradictions,* and *Falshoods* were very sensible: he had little to say, but that he had heard some things that he could not prove, Reflecting upon the Reputation of some of the Witnesses. Only he gave in a Paper to the Jury; wherein, altho' he had many times before, granted, not only that there are *Witches,* but also, that the present Sufferings of the Country are the effects of *horrible Witchcrafts,* yet he now goes to evince it, *That there neither are, nor ever were Witches, that having made a Compact with the Devil, can send a Devil to Torment other people at a distance.* This Paper was Transcribed out of *Ady;* which the Court presently knew, as soon as they heard it. But he said, he had taken none of it out of any Book; for which, his Evasion afterwards, was, That a Gentleman gave him the Discourse in a Manuscript, from whence he Transcribed it.

IX. The Jury brought him in *Guilty:* But when he came to Die, he utterly deni'd the Fact, whereof he had been thus convicted.

* * *

The Tryal of Susanna Martin, at the Court of Oyer and Terminer,

Held by Adjournment at Salem, June 29, 1692.

Susanna Martin, pleading *Not Guilty* to the Indictment of *Witchcraft*, brought in against her, there were produced the Evidences of many Persons very sensibly and grievously Bewitched; who all complained of the Prisoner at the Bar, as the Person whom they believed the cause of their Miseries. And now, as well as in the other Trials, there was an extraordinary Endeavour by *Witchcrafts,* with Cruel and frequent Fits, to hinder the poor Sufferers from giving in their Complaints, which the Court was forced with much Patience to obtain, by much waiting and watching for it.

II. There was now also an account given of what passed at her first Examination before the Magistrates. The Cast of her *Eye,* then striking the afflicted People to the Ground, whether they saw that Cast or no; there were these among other Passages between the Magistrates and the Examinate.

Magistrate. Pray, what ails these People?

Martin. I don't know.

Magistrate. But what do you think ails them?

Martin. I don't desire to spend my Judgment upon it.

Magistrate. Don't you think they are bewitch'd?

Martin. No, I do not think they are.

Magistrate. Tell us your Thoughts about them then.

Martin. No, my thoughts are my own, when they are in, but when they are out they are anothers. Their Master——

Magistrate. Their Master? who do you think is their Master?

Martin. If they be dealing in the Black Art, you may know as well as I.

Magistrate. Well, what have you done towards this?

Martin. Nothing at all.

Magistrate. Why, 'tis you or your Appearance.

Martin. I cannot help it.

Magistrate. Is it not *your* Master? How comes your Appearance to hurt these?

Martin. How do I know? He that appeared in the Shape of *Samuel,* a glorified Saint, may appear in any ones Shape.

It was then also noted in her, as in others like her, that if the Afflicted went to approach her, they were flung down to the Ground. And, when she was asked the reason of it, she said, *I cannot tell; it may be, the Devil bears me more Malice than another.*

III. The Court accounted themselves, alarum'd by these Things, to enquire further into the Conversation of the Prisoner; and see what there might occur, to render these Accusations further credible. Whereupon, *John Allen* of *Salisbury,* testify'd, That he refusing, because of the weakness of his Oxen, to Cart some Staves at the request of this *Martin,* she was displeased at it; and said, *It had been as good that he had; for his Oxen should never do him much more Service.* Whereupon, this Deponent said, *Dost thou threaten me, thou old Witch? I'l throw thee into the Brook:* Which to avoid, she flew over the Bridge, and escaped. But, as he was going home, one of his Oxen tired, so that he was forced to Unyoke him, that he might get him home. He then put his Oxen, with many more, upon *Salisbury* Beach, where Cattle did use to get *Flesh.* In a few days, all the Oxen upon the Beach were found by their Tracks, to have run unto the Mouth of *Merrimack-River,* and not returned; but the next day they were found come ashore upon *Plum-Island.* They that sought them, used all imaginable gentleness, but they would still run away with a violence, that seemed wholly Diabolical, till they came near the mouth of *Merrimack-River;* when they ran right into the Sea, swimming as far as they could be seen. One of them then swam back again, with a swiftness, amazing to the Beholders, who stood ready to receive him, and help up his tired Carcass: But the Beast ran furiously up into the Island, and from thence, thorough the Marshes, up into *Newbury* Town, and so up into the Woods; and there after a while found near *Amesbury.* So that, of fourteen good Oxen, there was only this saved: The rest were all cast up, some in one place, and some in another, Drowned.

IV. *John Atkinson* testifi'd, That he exchanged a Cow with a Son of *Susanna Martin's,* whereat she muttered, and was unwilling he should have it. Going to receive this Cow, tho he Hamstring'd her, and Halter'd her, she, of a Tame Creature, grew so mad, that they could scarce get her along. She broke all the Ropes that were fastned unto her, and though she were ty'd fast unto a Tree, yet she made her escape, and gave them such further trouble, as they could ascribe to no cause but Witchcraft.

V. *Bernard Peache* testifi'd, That being in Bed, on the Lord's-day Night, he heard a scrabbling at the Window, whereat he then saw *Susanna Martin* come in, and jump down upon the Floor. She took hold of this Deponent's Feet, and drawing his Body up into an Heap, she lay upon him near Two Hours; in all which time he could neither speak nor stir. At length, when he could begin to move, he laid hold on her Hand, and pulling it up to his Mouth, he bit three of her Fingers, as he judged, unto the Bone. Whereupon she went from the Chamber, down the Stairs, out at the Door. This Deponent thereupon called unto the People of the House, to advise them of what passed; and he himself did follow her. The People saw her not; but there being a Bucket at the Left-hand of the Door, there was a drop of Blood found upon it; and several more drops of Blood upon the Snow newly fallen abroad: There was likewise the print of her 2 Feet just without the Threshold; but no more sign of any Footing further off.

At another time this Deponent was desired by the Prisoner, to come unto an Husking of Corn, at her House; and she said, *If he did not come, it were better that he did!* He went not; but the Night following, *Susanna Martin,* as he judged, and another came towards him. One of them said, *Here he is!* but he having a Quarter-staff, made a Blow at them. The Roof of the Barn, broke his Blow; but following them to the Window, he made another Blow at them, and struck them down; yet they got up, and got out, and he saw no more of them.

About this time, there was a Rumour about the Town, that *Martin* had a Broken Head; but the Deponent could say nothing to that.

The said *Peache* also testifi'd the Bewitching the Cattle to Death, upon *Martin's* Discontents.

VI. *Robert Downer* testified, That this Prisoner being some Years ago prosecuted at Court for a Witch, he then said unto her, *He believed she was a Witch.* Whereat she being dissatisfied, said, *That some She-Devil would shortly fetch him away!* Which words were heard by others, as well as himself. The Night following, as he lay in his Bed, there came in at the Window, the likeness of a *Cat,* which flew upon him, took fast hold of his Throat, lay on him a considerable while, and almost killed him. At length he remembred what *Susanna Martin* had threatned the Day before; and with much striving he cried out, *Avoid, thou She-Devil! In the Name of God the Father, the Son, and the Holy Ghost, Avoid!* Whereupon it left him, leap'd on the Floor, and flew out at the Window.

And there also came in several Testimonies, that before ever *Downer* spoke a word of this Accident, *Susanna Martin* and her Family had related, *How this* Downer *had been handled!*

VII. *John Kembal* testified, that *Susanna Martin,* upon a Causeless Disgust, had threatned him, about a certain Cow of his, *That she should never do him any more Good:* and it came to pass accordingly. For soon after the Cow was found stark dead on the dry Ground, without any Distemper to be discerned upon her. Upon which he was followed with a strange Death upon more of his Cattle, whereof he lost in one Spring to the value of Thirty Pounds. But the said *John Kembal* had a further Testimony to give in against the Prisoner which was truly admirable.

Being desirous to furnish himself with a Dog, he applied himself to buy one of this *Martin,* who had a Bitch with Whelps in her House. But she not letting him have his choice, he said, he would supply himself then at one *Blezdels.* Having mark'd a Puppy, which he lik'd at *Blezdels,* he met *George Martin,* the Husband of the Prisoner, going by, who asked him, *Whether he would not have one of his Wife's Puppies?* and he answered, *No.* The same Day, one *Edmond Elliot,* being at *Martin's* House, heard *George Martin* relate, where this *Kembal* had been, and what he had said. Whereupon *Susanna Martin* replied, *If I live, I'll give him Puppies enough!* Within a few days after, this *Kembal,* coming out of the Woods, there arose a little Black Cloud in the N.W. and *Kembal* immediately felt a force upon him, which made him not able to avoid running upon the stumps of Trees, that were before him, albeit he had a broad, plain Cart-way, before him; but tho' he had his Ax also on his Shoulder to endanger him in his Falls, he could not forbear going out of his way to tumble over them. When he came below the Meeting House, there appeared unto him, a little thing like a *Puppy,* of a Darkish Colour; and it shot backwards and forwards between his Legs. He had the Courage to use all possible Endeavours of Cutting it with his Ax; but he could not Hit it: the Puppy gave a jump from him, and went, as to him it seem'd, into the Ground. Going a little further, there appeared unto him a Black Puppy, somewhat bigger than the first, but as Black as a Cole. Its Motions were quicker than those of his Ax; it flew at his Belly, and away; then at his Throat; so, over his Shoulder one way, and then over his Shoulder another way. His Heart now began to fail him, and he thought the Dog would have tore his Throat out. But he recovered himself, and called upon God in his Distress; and naming the Name of JESUS CHRIST, it vanished away at once. The Deponent spoke not one Word of these Accidents, for fear of affrighting his Wife. But the next Morning, *Edmond Eliot,* going into *Martin's* House, this Woman asked him where *Kembal* was? He replied, *At home, a Bed, for ought he knew.* She returned, *They say, he was frighted last Night. Eliot* asked, *With what?* She answered, *With Puppies. Eliot* asked, *Where she heard of it, for he had heard nothing of it?* She rejoined, *About the Town.* Altho' *Kembal* had mentioned the Matter to no Creature living.

VIII. *William Brown* testifi'd, That Heaven having blessed him with a most Pious and Prudent Wife, this Wife of his, one day met with *Susanna Martin;* but when she approach'd just unto her, *Martin* vanished out of sight, and left her extreamly affrighted. After which time, the said *Martin* often appear'd unto her, giving her no little trouble; and when she did come, she was visited with Birds, that sorely peck'd and prick'd her; and sometimes, a Bunch, like a Pullet's Egg, would rise in her Throat, ready to choak her, till she cry'd out, *Witch, you shan't choak me!* While this good Woman was in this extremity, the Church appointed a Day of Prayer, on her behalf; whereupon her Trouble ceas'd; she saw not *Martin* as formerly; and the Church, instead of their Fast, gave Thanks for her Deliverance. But a considerable while after, she being Summoned to give in some Evidence at the Court, against this *Martin,* quickly thereupon, this *Martin* came behind her, while she was milking her Cow, and said unto her, *For thy defaming her at Court, I'll make thee the miserablest Creature in the World.* Soon after which, she fell into a strange kind of distemper, and became horribly frantick, and uncapable of any reasonable Action; the Physicians declaring, that her Distemper was preternatural, and that some Devil had certainly bewitched her; and in that condition she now remained.

IX. *Sarah Atkinson* testify'd, That *Susanna Martin* came from *Amesbury* to their House at *Newbury,* in an extraordinary Season, when it was not fit for any to Travel. She came (as she said, unto *Atkinson*) all that long way on Foot. She brag'd and shew'd how dry she was; nor could it be perceived that so much as the Soles of her Shoes were wet. *Atkinson* was amazed at it; and professed, that she should her self have been wet up to the knees, if she had then come so far; but *Martin* reply'd, *She scorn'd to be Drabbled!* It was noted, that this Testimony upon her Trial, cast her in a very singular Confusion.

X. *John Pressy* testify'd, That being one Evening very unaccountably Bewildred, near a Field of *Martins,* and several times, as one under an Enchantment, returning to the place he had left, at length he saw a marvellous Light, about the bigness of an Half-bushel, near two Rod, out of the way. He went, and struck at it with a Stick, and laid it on with all his might. He gave it near forty blows; and felt it a palpable substance. But going from it, his Heels were struck up, and he was laid with his Back on the Ground, sliding, as he thought, into a Pit; from whence he recover'd by taking hold on the Bush; altho' afterwards he could find no such Pit in the place. Having, after his Recovery, gone five or six Rod, he saw *Susanna Martin* standing on his Left-hand, as the Light had done before; but they changed no words with one another. He could scarce find his House in his Return; but at length he got home extreamly affrighted. The next day, it was upon Enquiry understood, that *Martin* was in a miserable condition by pains and hurts that were upon her.

It was further testify'd by this Deponent, That after he had given in some Evidence against *Susanna Martin,* many years ago, she gave him foul words about it; and said, *He should never prosper more;* particularly, *That he should never have more than two Cows; that tho' he was never so likely to have more, yet he should never have them.* And that from that very day to this, namely for twenty years together, he could never exceed that number; but some strange thing or other still prevented his having any more.

XI. *Jervis Ring* testify'd, That about seven years ago, he was oftentimes and grievously oppressed in the Night, but saw not who troubled him; until at last he Lying perfectly Awake, plainly saw *Susanna Martin* approach him. She came to him, and forceably bit him by the

Finger; so that the Print of the bite is now, so long after, to be seen upon him.

XII. But besides all of these Evidences, there was a most wonderful Account of one *Joseph Ring,* produced on this occasion.

This Man has been strangely carried about by *Dæmons,* from one *Witch-meeting* to another, for near two years together; and for one quarter of this time, they have made him, and keep him Dumb, tho' he is now again able to speak. There was one *T. H.* who having, as 'tis judged, a design of engaging this *Joseph Ring* in a snare of Devillism, contrived a while, to bring this *Ring* two Shillings in Debt unto him.

Afterwards, this poor Man would be visited with unknown shapes, and this *T. H.* sometimes among them; which would force him away with them, unto unknown Places, where he saw Meetings, Feastings, Dancings; and after his return, wherein they hurried him along through the Air, he gave Demonstrations to the Neighbours, that he had indeed been so transported. When he was brought until these hellish Meetings, one of the first Things they still did unto him, was to give him a knock on the Back, whereupon he was ever as if bound with Chains, uncapable of stirring out of the place, till they should release him. He related, that there often came to him a Man, who presented him a *Book,* whereto he would have him set his Hand; promising to him, that he should then have even what he would; and presenting him with all the delectable Things, Persons, and Places, that he could imagin. But he refusing to subscribe, the business would end with dreadful Shapes, Noises and Screeches, which almost scared him out of his Wits. Once with the Book, there was a Pen offered him, and an Ink-horn with Liquor in it, that seemed like Blood: But he never toucht it.

This Man did now affirm, That he saw the Prisoner at several of those hellish Randezvouzes.

Note, this Woman was one of the most impudent, scurrilous, wicked Creatures in the World; and she did now throughout her whole Tryal, discover her self to be such an one. Yet when she was asked, what she had to say for her self? Her chief Plea was, *That she had lead a most virtuous and holy Life.*

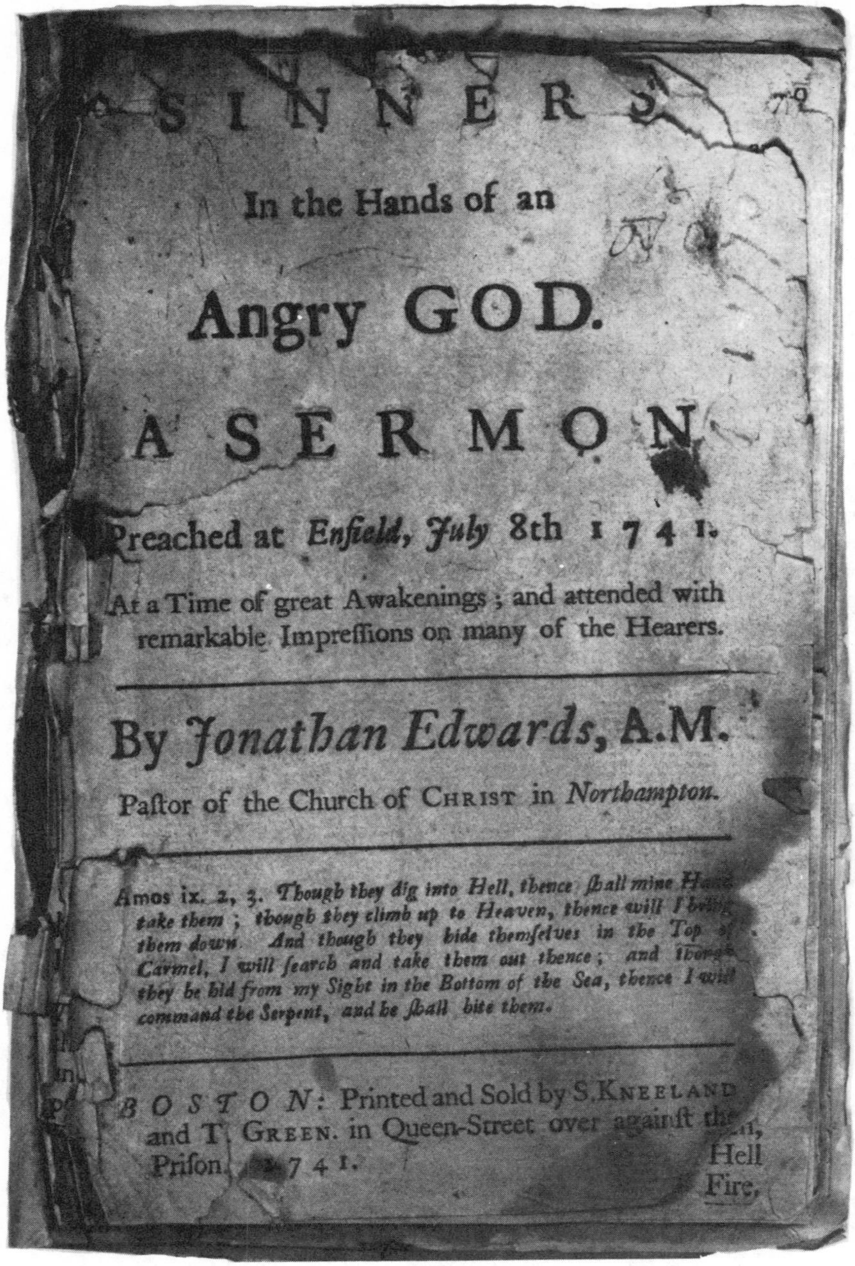

SINNERS

In the Hands of an

Angry GOD.

A SERMON

Preached at *Enfield, July* 8th 1741.

At a Time of great Awakenings; and attended with remarkable Impressions on many of the Hearers.

By *Jonathan Edwards*, A.M.

Pastor of the Church of CHRIST in *Northampton*.

Amos ix. 2, 3. *Though they dig into Hell, thence shall mine Hand take them; though they climb up to Heaven, thence will I bring them down. And though they hide themselves in the Top of Carmel, I will search and take them out thence; and though they be hid from my Sight in the Bottom of the Sea, thence I will command the Serpent, and he shall bite them.*

BOSTON: Printed and Sold by S. KNEELAND and T. GREEN. in Queen-Street over against the Prison. 1741.

JONATHAN EDWARDS

Sinners in the Hands of an Angry God

(1741)

This sermon, delivered in the little village of Enfield, Massachusetts, on a hot July Sunday in 1741, has become the model for a type of oratory that runs through American religious history: the sermon designed literally to scare the hell out of parishioners. This one did. The hysteria and religious enthusiasm it produced at Enfield that morning were part of the "Great Awakening," an outburst of revivalism that created enduring techniques for strengthening individual piety at the expense of divided religious institutions. Beginning in the 1720s in New Jersey and carried into New England by Edwards during the 1730s, the revival had touched all the mainland colonies by the 1740s. In its wake, new ideas and social attitudes spilled forth; new colleges arose to train ministers defending or opposing the revival; and in the works of Jonathan Edwards, the Great Awakening produced a system of theology that influenced American intellectual life for a century.

The "hell-fire and brimstone" sermon has become one of the standard clichés of American religion, so widely caricatured that it is difficult to recapture either Jonathan Edwards's goals or his method. We think of camp meetings with hymns loudly sung, the booming voice and theatrical gestures of the hot gospeler. But Edwards spoke in a flat tone, with few movements of hand or body and scarcely a glance at his audience. He had no desire for his parishioners' emotions to overwhelm their reason. Perhaps one of the greatest theologians America has known, he had complex ideas to communicate, and all his imagery was put to the service of making those ideas clear to his listeners. Edwards wished, he wrote, "to extricate all questions from the least confusion or ambiguity of words, so that the ideas shall be left naked."

Naked they are indeed: Edwards was, as the learned student of his work Perry Miller has written, "a revolutionary artist." One need not be sitting in a hot little church buried in the Connecticut River valley on a July day to feel, resting like some intolerable burden, the pressure of Edwards's carefully structured imagery of heat and weight. Nor need the reader be versed in Edwards's theology to respond with relief when, at the close of his sermon, he turns to the "extraordinary opportunity" offered so many "daily coming from the east, west, north and south" for the "feasting," "rejoicing," and "singing for joy of heart" that his message holds forth for those who will listen.

Sermon XV:

Sinners in the Hands of an Angry God.

Deuteronomy xxxii. 35.—Their foot shall slide in due time.

In this verse is threatened the vengeance of God on the wicked unbelieving Israelites, that were God's visible people, and lived under means of grace; and that notwithstanding all God's wonderful works that he had wrought towards that people, yet remained, as is expressed verse 28, void of counsel, having no understanding in them; and that, under all the cultivations of heaven, brought forth bitter and poisonous fruit; as in the two verses next preceding the text.

The expression that I have chosen for my text, *their foot shall slide in due time,* seems to imply the following things relating to the punishment and destruction that these wicked Israelites were exposed to.

1. That they were always exposed to destruction; as one that stands or walks in slippery places is always exposed to fall. This is implied in the manner of their destruction's coming upon them, being represented by their foot's sliding. The same is expressed, Psalm lxxiii. 18: "Surely thou didst set them in slippery places; thou castedst them down into destruction."

2. It implies, that they were always exposed to sudden, unexpected destruction. As he that walks in slippery places is every moment liable to fall, he cannot foresee one moment whether he shall stand or fall the next; and when he does fall, he falls at once, without warning, which is also expressed in that Psalm lxxiii. 18, 19: "Surely thou didst set them in slippery places; thou castedst them down into destruction: how are they brought into desolation as in a moment."

3. Another thing implied is, that they are liable to fall of themselves, without being thrown down by the hand of another; as he that stands or walks on slippery ground needs nothing but his own weight to throw him down.

4. That the reason why they are not fallen already, and do not fall now, is only that God's appointed time is not come. For it is said that when that due time, or appointed time comes, *their feet shall slide.* Then they shall be left to fall, as they are inclined by their own weight. God will not hold them up in these slippery places any longer, but will let them go; and then, at that very instant, they shall fall into destruction; as he that stands in such slippery declining ground on the edge of a pit that he cannot stand alone, when he is let go he immediately falls and is lost.

The observation from the words that I would now insist upon is this.

There is nothing that keeps wicked men at any one moment out of hell, but the mere pleasure of God.

By the mere pleasure of God, I mean his sovereign pleasure, his arbitrary will, restrained by no obligation, hindered by no manner of difficulty, any more than if nothing else but God's mere will had in the least degree or in any respect whatsoever, any hand in the preservation of wicked men one moment.

The truth of this observation may appear by the following considerations.

1. There is no want of power in God to cast wicked men into hell at any moment. Men's hands cannot be strong when God rises up: the strongest have no power to resist him, nor can any deliver out of his hands.

He is not only able to cast wicked men into hell, but he can most easily do it. Sometimes an earthly prince meets with a great deal of difficulty to subdue a rebel, that has found means to fortify himself, and has made himself strong by the number of his followers. But it is not so with God. There is no fortress that is any defence against the power of God. Though hand join in hand, and vast multitudes of God's enemies combine and associate themselves, they are easily broken in pieces: they are as great heaps of light chaff before the whirlwind; or large quantities of dry stubble before devouring flames. We find it easy to tread on and crush a worm that we see crawling on the earth; so it is easy for us to cut or singe a slender thread that any thing hangs by; thus easy is it for God, when he pleases, to cast his enemies down to hell. What are we, that we should think to stand before him, at whose rebuke the earth trembles, and before whom the rocks are thrown down!

2. They deserve to be cast into hell; so that divine justice never stands in the way, it makes no objection against God's using his power at any moment to destroy them. Yea, on the contrary, justice calls aloud for an infinite punishment of their sins. Divine justice says of the tree that brings forth such grapes of Sodom, "Cut it down, why cumbereth it the ground?" Luke xiii. 7. The sword of divine justice is every moment brandished over their heads, and it is nothing but the hand of arbitrary mercy, and God's mere will, that holds it back.

3. They are already under a sentence of condemnation to hell. They do not only justly deserve to be cast down thither, but the sentence of the law of God, that eternal and immutable rule of righteousness that God has fixed between him and mankind, is gone out against them; and stands against them; so that they are bound over already to hell: John iii. 18, "He that believeth not is condemned already." So that every unconverted man properly belongs to hell; that is his place; from thence he is: John viii. 23, "Ye are from beneath:" and thither he is bound; it is the place that justice, and God's word, and the sentence of his unchangeable law, assign to him.

4. They are now the objects of that very same anger and wrath of God, that is expressed in the torments of hell: and the reason why they do not go down to hell at each moment, is not because God, in whose power they are, is not then very angry with them; as angry, as

he is with many of those miserable creatures that he is now tormenting in hell, and do there feel and bear the fierceness of his wrath. Yea, God is a great deal more angry with great numbers that are now on earth; yea, doubtless, with many that are now in this congregation, that, it may be, are at ease and quiet, than he is with many of those that are now in the flames of hell.

So that it is not because God is unmindful of their wickedness, and does not resent it, that he does not let loose his hand and cut them off. God is not altogether such a one as themselves, though they may imagine him to be so. The wrath of God burns against them; their damnation does not slumber; the pit is prepared; the fire is made ready; the furnace is now hot; ready to receive them; the flames do now rage and glow. The glittering sword is whet, and held over them, and the pit hath opened her mouth under them.

5. The devil stands ready to fall upon them, and seize them as his own, at what moment God shall permit him. They belong to him; he has their souls in his possession, and under his dominion. The Scripture represents them as his goods, Luke xi. 21. The devils watch them; they are ever by them, at their right hand; they stand waiting for them, like greedy hungry lions that see their prey, and expect to have it, but are for the present kept back; if God should withdraw his hand by which they are restrained, they would in one moment fly upon their poor souls. The old serpent is gaping for them; hell opens its mouth wide to receive them; and if God should permit it, they would be hastily swallowed up and lost.

6. There are in the souls of wicked men those hellish principles reigning, that would presently kindle and flame out into hell-fire, if it were not for God's restraints. There is laid in the very nature of carnal men, a foundation for the torments of hell: there are those corrupt principles, in reigning power in them, and in full possession of them, that are the beginnings of hell-fire. These principles are active and powerful, exceeding violent in their nature, and if it were not for the restraining hand of God upon them, they would soon break out, they would flame out after the same manner as the same corruptions, the same enmity does in the hearts of damned souls, and would beget the same torments in them as they do in them. The souls of the wicked are in Scripture compared to the troubled sea, Isaiah lvii. 20. For the present God restrains their wickedness by his mighty power, as he does the raging waves of the troubled sea, saying, "Hitherto shalt thou come, and no further;" but if God should withdraw that restraining power, it would soon carry all before it. Sin is the ruin and misery of the soul; it is destructive in its nature; and if God should leave it without restraint, there would need nothing else to make the soul perfectly miserable. The corruption of the heart of man is a thing that is immoderate and boundless in its fury; and while wicked men live here, it is like fire pent up by God's restraints, whereas if it were

let loose, it would set on fire the course of nature; and as the heart is now a sink of sin, so, if sin was not restrained, it would immediately turn the soul into a fiery oven, or a furnace of fire and brimstone.

7. It is no security to wicked men for one moment, that there are no visible means of death at hand. It is no security to a natural man, that he is now in health, and that he does not see which way he should now immediately go out of the world by any accident, and that there is no visible danger in any respect in his circumstances. The manifold and continual experience of the world in all ages, shows that this is no evidence that a man is not on the very brink of eternity, and that the next step will not be into another world. The unseen, unthought of ways and means of persons' going suddenly out of the world are innumerable and inconceivable. Unconverted men walk over the pit of hell on a rotten covering, and there are innumerable places in this covering so weak that they will not bear their weight, and these places are not seen. The arrows of death fly unseen at noonday; the sharpest sight cannot discern them. God has so many different, unsearchable ways of taking wicked men out of the world and sending them to hell, that there is nothing to make it appear, that God had need to be at the expense of a miracle, or go out of the ordinary course of his providence, to destroy any wicked man, at any moment. All the means that there are of sinners' going out of the world, are so in God's hands, and so absolutely subject to his power and determination, that it does not depend at all less on the mere will of God, whether sinners shall at any moment go to hell, than if means were never made use of, or at all concerned in the case.

8. Natural men's prudence and care to preserve their own lives, or the care of others to preserve them, do not secure them a moment. This, divine providence and universal experience do also bear testimony to. There is this clear evidence that men's own wisdom is no security to them from death; that if it were otherwise we should see some difference between the wise and politic men of the world, and others, with regard to their liableness to early and unexpected death; but how is it in fact? Eccles. ii. 16, "How dieth the wise man? As the fool."

9. All wicked men's pains and contrivance they use to escape hell, while they continue to reject Christ, and so remain wicked men, do not secure them from hell one moment. Almost every natural man that hears of hell, flatters himself that he shall escape it; he depends upon himself for his own security; he flatters himself in what he has done, in what he is now doing, or what he intends to do; every one lays out matters in his own mind how he shall avoid damnation, and flatters himself that he contrives well for himself, and that his schemes will not fail. They hear indeed that there are but few saved, and that the bigger part of men that have died heretofore are gone to hell; but each one imagines that he lays out matters better for his own escape than others have done: he does not intend to come to that

place of torment; he says within himself, that he intends to take care that shall be effectual, and to order matters so for himself as not to fail.

But the foolish children of men do miserably delude themselves in their own schemes, and in their confidence in their own strength and wisdom, they trust to nothing but a shadow. The bigger part of those that heretofore have lived under the same means of grace, and are now dead, are undoubtedly gone to hell; and it was not because they were not as wise as those that are now alive; it was not because they did not lay out matters as well for themselves to secure their own escape. If it were so that we could come to speak with them, and could inquire of them, one by one, whether they expected, when alive, and when they used to hear about hell, ever to be subjects of that misery, we, doubtless, should hear one and another reply, "No, I never intended to come here: I had laid out matters otherwise in my mind; I thought I should contrive well for myself: I thought my scheme good: I intended to take effectual care; but it came upon me unexpectedly; I did not look for it at that time, and in that manner; it came as a thief: death outwitted me: God's wrath was too quick for me: O my cursed foolishness! I was flattering myself, and pleasing myself with vain dreams of what I would do hereafter; and when I was saying peace and safety, then sudden destruction came upon me."

10. God has laid himself under no obligation, by any promise, to keep any natural man out of hell one moment: God certainly has made no promises either of eternal life, or of any deliverance or preservation from eternal death, but what are contained in the covenant of grace, the promises that are given in Christ, in whom all the promises are yea and amen. But surely they have no interest in the promises of the covenant of grace that are not the children of the covenant, and that do not believe in any of the promises of the covenant, and have no interest in the Mediator of the covenant.

So that, whatever some have imagined and pretended about promises made to natural men's earnest seeking and knocking, it is plain and manifest, that whatever pains a natural man takes in religion, whatever prayers he makes, till he believes in Christ, God is under no manner of obligation to keep him a moment from eternal destruction.

So that thus it is, that natural men are held in the hand of God over the pit of hell; they have deserved the fiery pit, and are already sentenced to it; and God is dreadfully provoked, his anger is as great towards them as to those that are actually suffering the executions of the fierceness of his wrath in hell, and they have done nothing in the least, to appease or abate that anger, neither is God in the least bound by any promise to hold them up one moment; the devil is waiting for them, hell is gaping for them, the flames gather and flash about them, and would fain lay hold on them and swallow them up; the fire pent up in their own hearts is struggling to break out; and they have no interest in any Mediator, there are no means within reach that can be any security to them. In short, they have no refuge, nothing to take hold of; all that preserves them every moment is the mere arbitrary will, and uncovenanted, unobliged forbearance of an incensed God.

APPLICATION.

The use may be of awakening to unconverted persons in this congregation. This that you have heard is the case of every one of you that are out of Christ. That world of misery, that lake of burning brimstone, is extended abroad under you. There is the dreadful pit of the glowing flames of the wrath of God; there is hell's wide gaping mouth open; and you have nothing to stand upon, nor any thing to take hold of. There is nothing between you and hell but the air; it is only the power and mere pleasure of God that holds you up.

You probably are not sensible of this; you find you are kept out of hell, but do not see the hand of God in it; but look at other things, as the good state of your bodily constitution, your care of your own life, and the means you use for your own preservation. But indeed these things are nothing; if God should withdraw his hand, they would avail no more to keep you from falling, than the thin air to hold up a person that is suspended in it.

Your wickedness makes you as it were heavy as lead, and to tend downwards with great weight and pressure towards hell; and if God should let you go, you would immediately sink and swiftly descend and plunge into the bottomless gulf, and your healthy constitution, and your own care and prudence, and best contrivance, and all your righteousness, would have no more influence to uphold you and keep you out of hell, than a spider's web would have to stop a falling rock. Were it not that so is the sovereign pleasure of God, the earth would not bear you one moment; for you are a burden to it; the creation groans with you; the creature is made subject to the bondage of your corruption, not willingly; the sun does not willingly shine upon you to give you light to serve sin and Satan; the earth does not willingly yield her increase to satisfy your lusts; nor is it willingly a stage for your wickedness to be acted upon; the air does not willingly serve you for breath to maintain the flame of life in your vitals, while you spend your life in the service of God's enemies. God's creatures are good, and were made for men to serve God with, and do not willingly subserve to any other purpose, and groan when they are abused to purposes so directly contrary to their nature and end. And the world would spew you out, were it not for the sovereign hand of him who hath subjected it in hope. There are the black clouds of God's wrath now hanging directly over your heads, full of the dreadful storm, and big with thunder; and were it not for the restraining hand of God, it would immediately burst forth upon you. The sovereign pleasure of God, for the present, stays his rough wind;

otherwise it would come with fury, and your destruction would come like a whirlwind, and you would be like the chaff of the summer threshing floor.

The wrath of God is like great waters that are dammed for the present; they increase more and more, and rise higher and higher, till an outlet is given; and the longer the stream is stopped, the more rapid and mighty is its course, when once it is let loose. It is true, that judgment against your evil work has not been executed hitherto; the floods of God's vengeance have been withheld; but your guilt in the mean time is constantly increasing, and you are every day treasuring up more wrath; the waters are continually rising, and waxing more and more mighty; and there is nothing but the mere pleasure of God, that holds the waters back, that are unwilling to be stopped, and press hard to go forward. If God should only withdraw his hand from the floodgate, it would immediately fly open, and the fiery floods of the fierceness and wrath of God, would rush forth with inconceivable fury, and would come upon you with omnipotent power; and if your strength were ten thousand times greater than it is, yea, ten thousand times greater than the strength of the stoutest, sturdiest devil in hell, it would be nothing to withstand or endure it.

The bow of God's wrath is bent, and the arrow made ready on the string, and justice bends the arrow at your heart, and strains the bow, and it is nothing but the mere pleasure of God, and that of an angry God, without any promise or obligation at all, that keeps the arrow one moment from being made drunk with your blood.

Thus are all you that never passed under a great change of heart, by the mighty power of the Spirit of God upon your souls; all that were never born again, and made new creatures, and raised from being dead in sin, to a state of new, and before altogether unexperienced light and life, (however you may have reformed your life in many things, and may have had religious affections, and may keep up a form of religion in your families and closets, and in the houses of God, and may be strict in it,) you are thus in the hands of an angry God; it is nothing but his mere pleasure that keeps you from being this moment swallowed up in everlasting destruction.

However unconvinced you may now be of the truth of what you hear, by and by you will be fully convinced of it. Those that are gone from being in the like circumstances with you, see that it was so with them; for destruction came suddenly upon most of them; when they expected nothing of it, and while they were saying, Peace and safety: now they see, that those things that they depended on for peace and safety were nothing but thin air and empty shadows.

The God that holds you over the pit of hell, much as one holds a spider, or some loathsome insect, over the fire, abhors you, and is dreadfully provoked; his wrath towards you burns like fire; he looks upon you as worthy of nothing else, but to be cast into the fire; he is of purer eyes than to bear to have you in his sight; you are ten thousand times so abominable in his eyes, as the most hateful and venomous serpent is in ours. You have offended him infinitely more than ever a stubborn rebel did his prince: and yet it is nothing but his hand that holds you from falling into the fire every moment: it is ascribed to nothing else, that you did not go to hell the last night; that you was suffered to awake again in this world, after you closed your eyes to sleep; and there is no other reason to be given, why you have not dropped into hell since you arose in the morning, but that God's hand has held you up: there is no other reason to be given why you have not gone to hell, since you have sat here in the house of God, provoking his pure eyes by your sinful wicked manner of attending his solemn worship: yea, there is nothing else that is to be given as a reason why you do not this very moment drop down into hell.

O sinner! consider the fearful danger you are in: it is a great furnace of wrath, a wide and bottomless pit, full of the fire of wrath, that you are held over in the hand of that God, whose wrath is provoked and incensed as much against you, as against many of the damned in hell: you hang by a slender thread, with the flames of divine wrath flashing about it, and ready every moment to singe it, and burn it asunder; and you have no interest in any Mediator, and nothing to lay hold of to save yourself, nothing to keep off the flames of wrath, nothing of your own, nothing that you ever have done, nothing that you can do, to induce God to spare you one moment.

And consider here more particularly several things concerning that wrath that you are in such danger of.

1. Whose wrath it is. It is the wrath of the infinite God. If it were only the wrath of man, though it were of the most potent prince, it would be comparatively little to be regarded. The wrath of kings is very much dreaded, especially of absolute monarchs, that have the possessions and lives of their subjects wholly in their power, to be disposed of at their mere will. Prov. xx. 2, "The fear of a king is as the roaring of a lion: whoso provoketh him to anger, sinneth against his own soul." The subject that very much enrages an arbitrary prince, is liable to suffer the most extreme torments that human art can invent, or human power can inflict. But the greatest earthly potentates, in their greatest majesty and strength, and when clothed in their greatest terrors, are but feeble, despicable worms of the dust, in comparison of the great and almighty Creator and King of heaven and earth: it is but little that they can do, when most enraged, and when they have exerted the utmost of their fury. All the kings of the earth before God, are as grasshoppers; they are nothing, and less than nothing: both their love and their hatred is to be despised. The wrath of the great King of kings, is as much more terrible than theirs, as his majesty is greater. Luke xii. 4, 5, "And I say unto you, my friends, Be not afraid of them that kill the body, and after that have no more that they can do. But I will forewarn you whom you shall fear: fear him, which after he hath killed, hath power to cast into hell; yea, I say unto you, Fear him."

2. It is the fierceness of his wrath that you are exposed to. We often read of the fury of God; as in Isaiah lix. 18: "According to their deeds, accordingly he will repay fury to his adversaries." So Isaiah lxvi. 15, "For behold, the Lord will come with fire, and with his chariots like a whirlwind, to render his anger with fury, and his rebuke with flames of fire." And so in many other places. So we read of God's fierceness, Rev. xix. 15. There we read of "the wine-press of the fierceness and wrath of Almighty God." The words are exceedingly terrible: if it had only been said, "the wrath of God," the words would have implied that which is infinitely dreadful: but it is not only said so, but "the fierceness and wrath of God:" the fury of God! the fierceness of Jehovah! Oh how dreadful must that be! Who can utter or conceive what such expressions carry in them! But it is not only said so, but "the fierceness and wrath of Almighty God." As though there would be a very great manifestation of his almighty power in what the fierceness of his wrath should inflict, as though omnipotence should be as it were enraged, and exerted, as men are wont to exert their strength in the fierceness of their wrath. Oh! then, what will be the consequence! What will become of the poor worm that shall suffer it! Whose hands can be strong! And whose heart endure! To what a dreadful, inexpressible, inconceivable depth of misery must the poor creature be sunk who shall be the subject of this!

Consider this, you that are here present, that yet remain in an unregenerate state. That God will execute the fierceness of his anger, implies, that he will inflict wrath without any pity: when God beholds the ineffable extremity of your case, and sees your torment so vastly disproportioned to your strength, and sees how your poor soul is crushed, and sinks down, as it were, into an infinite gloom; he will have no compassion upon you, he will not forbear the executions of his wrath, or in the least lighten his hand; there shall be no moderation or mercy, nor will God then at all stay his rough wind; he will have no regard to your welfare, nor be at all careful lest you should suffer too much in any other sense, than only that you should not suffer beyond what strict justice requires: nothing shall be withheld, because it is so hard for you to bear. Ezek. viii. 18, "Therefore will I also deal in fury; mine eye shall not spare, neither will I have pity; and though they cry in mine ears with a loud voice, yet will I not hear them." Now God stands ready to pity you; this is a day of mercy; you may cry now with some encouragement of obtaining mercy: but when once the day of mercy is past, your most lamentable and dolorous cries and shrieks will be in vain; you will be wholly lost and thrown away of God, as to any regard to your welfare; God will have no other use to put you to, but only to suffer misery; you shall be continued in being to no other end; for you will be a vessel of wrath fitted to destruction; and there will be no other use of this vessel, but only to be filled full of wrath: God will be so far from pitying you when you cry to him, that it is said he will only "laugh and mock," Prov. i. 25, 26, &c.

How awful are those words, Isaiah lxiii. 3, which are the words of the great God: "I will tread them in mine anger, and trample them in my fury, and their blood shall be sprinkled upon my garments, and I will stain all my raiment." It is perhaps impossible to conceive of words that carry in them greater manifestations of these three things, viz., contempt and hatred, and fierceness of indignation. If you cry to God to pity you, he will be so far from pitying you in your doleful case, or showing you the least regard or favor, that instead of that he will only tread you under foot: and though he will know that you cannot bear the weight of omnipotence treading upon you, yet he will not regard that, but he will crush you under his feet without mercy; he will crush out your blood, and make it fly, and it shall be sprinkled on his garments, so as to stain all his raiment. He will not only hate you, but he will have you in the utmost contempt; no place shall be thought fit for you but under his feet, to be trodden down as the mire in the streets.

3. The misery you are exposed to is that which God will inflict to that end, that he might show what that wrath of Jehovah is. God hath had it on his heart to show to angels and men, both how excellent his love is, and also how terrible his wrath is. Sometimes earthly kings have a mind to show how terrible their wrath is, by the extreme punishments they would execute on those that provoke them. Nebuchadnezzar, that mighty and haughty monarch of the Chaldean empire, was willing to show his wrath when enraged with Shadrach, Meshech, and Abednego; and accordingly gave order that the burning fiery furnace should be heated seven times hotter than it was before; doubtless, it was raised to the utmost degree of fierceness that human art could raise it; but the great God is also willing to show his wrath, and magnify his awful Majesty and mighty power in the extreme sufferings of his enemies. Rom. ix. 22, "What if God, willing to show his wrath, and to make his power known, endured with much long-suffering, the vessels of wrath fitted to destruction?" And seeing this is his design, and what he has determined, to show how terrible the unmixed, unrestrained wrath, the fury, and fierceness of Jehovah is, he will do it to effect. There will be something accomplished and brought to pass that will be dreadful with a witness. When the great and angry God hath risen up and executed his awful vengeance on the poor sinner, and the wretch is actually suffering the infinite weight and power of his indignation, then will God call upon the whole universe to behold that awful majesty and mighty power that is to be seen in it. Isa. xxxiii. 12, 13, 14, "And the people shall be as the burnings of lime, as thorns cut up shall they be burnt in the fire. Hear, ye that are afar off, what I have done; and ye that are near, acknowledge my might. The sinners in Zion are afraid; fearfulness hath surprised the hypocrites," &c.

Thus it will be with you that are in an unconverted state, if you continue in it; the infinite might, and majesty, and terribleness, of the Omnipotent God shall be magnified upon you in the ineffable strength of your torments: you shall be tormented in the presence of the holy angels, and in the presence of the Lamb; and when you shall be in this state of suffering, the glorious inhabitants of heaven shall go forth and look on the awful spectacle, that they may see what the wrath and fierceness of the Almighty is; and when they have seen it, they will fall down and adore that great power and majesty. Isa. lxvi. 23, 24, "And it shall come to pass, that from one moon to another, and from one Sabbath to another, shall all flesh come to worship before me, saith the Lord. And they shall go forth and look upon the carcasses of the men that have transgressed against me; for their worm shall not die, neither shall their fire be quenched, and they shall be an abhorring unto all flesh."

4. It is everlasting wrath. It would be dreadful to suffer this fierceness and wrath of Almighty God one moment; but you must suffer it to all eternity: there will be no end to this exquisite, horrible misery: when you look forward, you shall see a long forever, a boundless duration before you, which will swallow up your thoughts, and amaze your soul; and you will absolutely despair of ever having any deliverance, any end, any mitigation, any rest at all; you will know certainly that you must wear out long ages, millions of millions of ages, in wrestling and conflicting with this Almighty merciless vengeance; and then when you have so done, when so many ages have actually been spent by you in this manner, you will know that all is but a point to what remains. So that your punishment will indeed be infinite. Oh, who can express what the state of a soul in such circumstances is! All that we can possibly say about it, gives but a very feeble, faint representation of it; it is inexpressible and inconceivable: for "who knows the power of God's anger?"

How dreadful is the state of those that are daily and hourly in danger of this great wrath and infinite misery! But this is the dismal case of every soul in this congregation that has not been born again, however moral and strict, sober and religious, they may otherwise be. Oh that you would consider it, whether you be young or old! There is reason to think, that there are many in this congregation now hearing this discourse, that will actually be the subjects of this very misery to all eternity. We know not who they are, or in what seats they sit, or what thoughts they now have. It may be they are now at ease, and hear all these things without much disturbance, and are now flattering themselves that they are not the persons; promising themselves that they shall escape. If we knew that there was one person, and but one, in the whole congregation, that was to be the subject of this misery, what an awful thing it would be to think of! If we knew who it was, what an awful sight would it be to see such a person! How might all the rest of the congregation lift up a lamentable and bitter cry over him! But alas! Instead of one, how many is it likely will remember this discourse in hell! And it would be a wonder, if some that are now present should not be in hell in a very short time, before this year is out. And it would be no wonder if some persons, that now sit here in some seats of this meeting-house in health, and quiet and secure, should be there before to-morrow morning.

"The Death of Wolfe" by Benjamin West

FRANCIS PARKMAN

Montcalm and Wolfe

(1884)

Do great men and dramatic moments determine the course of history? If the battle in 1759 that Parkman describes on the Heights of Abraham in the war between France and Great Britain had gone differently, would North America have been dominated by French instead of British culture? Few historians would comfortably endorse such assertions. There were twenty British settlers in the New World to every Frenchman. Yet the slow accumulation of trends and events that move history can never grasp the imagination the way stirring events do. There are points on which history turns—pivots, not levers—symbols of vast social processes if not causes of subsequent events. Inevitably they are magnets attracting the historical imagination.

The confrontation on the plains above Montreal was the symbolic focus for Parkman's entire life's work, the vast history of the struggle between France and England for control of North America. Parkman—in a series of volumes ranging over a century-and-a-half of diplomacy, exploration, and war—traced the story of French exploration and settlement, of both cultures' interaction with the Indians, of the world of wilderness riches each sought. There is no work of American historiography to match it in scope or in literary excellence. Towards the end of his life, Parkman abruptly moved out of sequence in telling his story for fear that he would die before he could present the culminating moment of French defeat and English victory. That task completed, he returned to finish the story before his health—always fragile—finally broke.

Parkman's chief interest was ever and always heroism. The author recounts exploits of moral and physical heroism by French, English, and Indians across an entire continent. He wrote with the specific intention of offering his own tamer nineteenth-century world earlier images of heroic virtue, men who endured great suffering in the wilderness to achieve great imperial missions, or to struggle and fail in glorious effort. Parkman's heroes, however larger than life they are, remain convincing because their suffering is described so vividly. Wilderness living meant illness and defeat, struggle with the limits of the human body and will. There are no easy victories in Parkman's narrative, as there were none in the historian's life. For he is one of the great intellectual heroes, a rare figure who could demonstrate more courage in a library than most humans are capable of in battle. Parkman, throughout the nearly half-century during which he wrote his histories, suffered from severe disabilities. A nervous condition prevented him from working for more than short periods of time and left him almost blind. To write his voluminous histories, he constructed a wooden frame across which he stretched wires so that he could make notes and write his manuscripts without looking at the paper. His massive research was carried out largely by having sources read to him. His life, like those of the heroes about whom he wrote, was a constant test of will. Just as his books offered nineteenth-century Americans a gallery of heroes to emulate, his life—about which he was philosophical and even good humored—suggests a model of heroic endeavor suitable even for a modern world without heroes.

Wolfe was deeply moved by the disaster at the heights of Montmorenci, and in a General Order on the next day he rebuked the grenadiers for their precipitation. "Such impetuous, irregular, and unsoldierlike proceedings destroy all order, make it impossible for the commanders to form any disposition for an attack, and put it out of the general's power to execute his plans. The grenadiers could not suppose that they could beat the French alone."

The French were elated by their success. "Everybody," says the commissary Berniers, "thought that the campaign was as good as ended, gloriously for us." They had been sufficiently confident even before their victory; and the bearer of a flag of truce told the English officers that he had never imagined they were such fools as to attack Quebec with so small a force. Wolfe, on the other hand, had every reason to despond. At the outset, before he had seen Quebec and learned the nature of the ground, he had meant to begin the campaign by taking post on the Plains of Abraham, and thence laying siege to the town; but he soon discovered that the Plains of Abraham were hardly more within his reach than was Quebec itself. Such hope as was left him lay in the composition of Montcalm's army. He respected the French commander, and thought his disciplined soldiers not unworthy of the British steel; but he held his militia in high scorn, and could he but face them in the open field, he never doubted the result. But Montcalm also distrusted them, and persisted in refusing the coveted battle.

Wolfe, therefore, was forced to the conviction that his chances were of the smallest. It is said that, despairing of any decisive stroke, he conceived the idea of fortifying Isle-aux-Coudres, and leaving a part of his troops there when he sailed for home, against another attempt in the spring. The more to weaken the enemy and prepare his future conquest, he began at the same time a course of action which for his credit one would gladly wipe from the record; for, though far from inhuman, he threw himself with extraordinary intensity into whatever work he had in hand, and, to accomplish it, spared others scarcely more than he spared himself. About the middle of August he issued a third proclamation to the Canadians, declaring that as they had refused his offers of protection and "had made such ungrateful returns in practising the most unchristian barbarities against his troops on all occasions, he could no longer refrain in justice to himself and his army from chastising them as they deserved." The barbarities in question consisted in the frequent scalping and mutilating of sentinels and men on outpost duty, perpetrated no less by Canadians than by Indians. Wolfe's object was twofold: first, to cause the militia to desert, and, secondly, to exhaust the colony. Rangers, light infantry, and Highlanders were sent to waste the settlements far and wide. Wherever resistance was offered, farmhouses and villages were laid in ashes, though churches were generally spared. St. Paul, far below Quebec, was sacked and burned, and the settlements of the opposite shore were partially destroyed. The parishes of L'Ange Gardien, Château Richer, and St. Joachim were wasted with fire and sword.

Night after night the garrison of Quebec could see the light of burning houses as far down as the mountain of Cape Tourmente. Near St. Joachim there was a severe skirmish, followed by atrocious cruelties. Captain Alexander Montgomery, of the forty-third regiment, who commanded the detachment, and who has been most unjustly confounded with the revolutionary general, Richard Montgomery, ordered the prisoners to be shot in cold blood, to the indignation of his own officers. Robineau de Portneuf, curé of St. Joachim, placed himself at the head of thirty parishioners and took possession of a large stone house in the adjacent parish of Château Richer, where for a time he held the English at bay. At length he and his followers were drawn out into an ambush, where they were surrounded and killed; and, being disguised as Indians, the rangers scalped them all.

Most of the French writers of the time mention these barbarities without much comment, while Vaudreuil loudly denounces them. Yet he himself was answerable for atrocities incomparably worse, and on a far larger scale. He had turned loose his savages, red and white, along a frontier of six hundred miles, to waste, burn, and murder at will. "Women and children," such were the orders of Wolfe, "are to be treated with humanity; if any violence is offered to a woman, the offender shall be punished with death." These orders were generally obeyed. The English, with the single exception of Montgomery, killed none but armed men in the act of resistance or attack; Vaudreuil's war-parties spared neither age nor sex.

Montcalm let the parishes burn, and still lay fast intrenched in his lines of Beauport. He would not imperil all Canada to save a few hundred farmhouses; and Wolfe was as far as ever from the battle that he coveted. Hitherto, his attacks had been made chiefly below the town; but, these having failed, he now changed his plan and renewed on a larger scale the movements begun above it in July. With every fair wind, ships and transports passed the batteries of Quebec, favored by a hot fire from Point Levi, and generally succeeded, with more or less damage, in gaining the upper river. A fleet of flatboats was also sent thither, and twelve hundred troops marched overland to embark in them, under Brigadier Murray. Admiral Holmes took command of the little fleet now gathered above the town, and operations in that quarter were systematically resumed.

To oppose them, Bougainville was sent from the camp at Beauport with fifteen hundred men. His was a most arduous and exhausting duty. He must watch the shores for fifteen or twenty miles, divide his force into detachments, and subject himself and his followers to the strain of incessant vigilance and incessant marching. Murray made a descent at Pointe-aux-Trembles, and was repulsed with loss. He tried a second time at another place, was met before landing by a body of ambushed Canadians, and was again driven back, his foremost boats full of dead and wounded. A third time he succeeded, landed at Deschambault, and burned a large building filled with stores and all the spare baggage of the French regular officers. The blow was so alarming that Montcalm hastened from Beauport to take command in person; but when he arrived the English were gone.

Vaudreuil now saw his mistake in sending the French frigates up the river out of harm's way, and withdrawing their crews to serve the batteries of Quebec. Had these ships been there, they might have overpowered those of the English in detail as they passed the town. An attempt was made to retrieve the blunder. The sailors were sent to man the frigates anew and attack the squadron of Holmes. It was too late. Holmes was already too strong for them, and they were recalled. Yet the difficulties of the English still seemed insurmountable. Dysentery and fever broke out in their camps, the number of their effective men was greatly reduced, and the advancing season told them that their work must be done quickly, or not done at all.

On the other side, the distress of the French grew greater every day. Their army was on short rations. The operations of the English above the town filled the camp of Beauport with dismay, for troops and Canadians alike dreaded the cutting off of their supplies. These were all drawn from the districts of Three Rivers and Montreal; and, at best, they were in great danger, since when brought down in boats at night they were apt to be intercepted, while the difficulty of bringing them by land was extreme, through the scarcity of cattle and horses. Discipline was relaxed, disorder and pillage were rife, and the Canadians deserted so fast, that towards the end of August two hundred of them, it is said, would sometimes go off in one night. Early in the month the disheartening news came of the loss of Ticonderoga and Crown Point, the retreat of Bourlamaque, the fall of Niagara, and the expected advance of Amherst on Montreal. It was then that Lévis was despatched to the scene of danger; and Quebec was deplorably weakened by his absence. About this time the Lower Town was again set on fire by the English batteries, and a hundred and sixty-seven houses were burned in a night. In the front of the Upper Town nearly every building was a ruin. At the General Hospital, which was remote enough to be safe from the bombardment, every barn, shed, and garret, and even the chapel itself, were crowded with sick and wounded, with women and children from the town, and the nuns of the Ursulines and the Hôtel-Dieu, driven thither for refuge. Bishop Pontbriand, though suffering from a mortal disease, came almost daily to visit and console them from his lodging in the house of the curé at Charlesbourg.

Towards the end of August the sky brightened again. It became known that Amherst was not moving on Montreal, and Bourlamaque wrote that his position at Isle-aux-Noix was impregnable. On the twenty-seventh a deserter from Wolfe's army brought the welcome assurance that the invaders despaired of success, and would soon sail for home; while there were movements in the English camps and fleet that seemed to confirm what he said. Vaudreuil breathed more freely, and renewed hope and confidence visited the army of Beauport.

Meanwhile a deep cloud fell on the English. Since the siege began,

Wolfe had passed with ceaseless energy from camp to camp, animating the troops, observing everything, and directing everything; but now the pale face and tall lean form were seen no more, and the rumor spread that the general was dangerously ill. He had in fact been seized by an access of the disease that had tortured him for some time past; and fever had followed. His quarters were at a French farmhouse in the camp at Montmorenci; and here, as he lay in an upper chamber, helpless in bed, his singular and most unmilitary features haggard with disease and drawn with pain, no man could less have looked the hero. But as the needle, though quivering, points always to the pole, so through torment and languor and the heats of fever, the mind of Wolfe dwelt on the capture of Quebec. His illness, which began before the twentieth of August, had so far subsided on the twenty-fifth that Knox wrote in his Diary of that day: "His Excellency General Wolfe is on the recovery, to the inconceivable joy of the whole army." On the twenty-ninth he was able to write or dictate a letter to the three brigadiers, Monckton, Townshend, and Murray: "That the public service may not suffer by the General's indisposition, he begs the brigadiers will meet and consult together for the public utility and advantage, and consider of the best method to attack the enemy." The letter then proposes three plans, all bold to audacity. The first was to send a part of the army to ford the Montmorenci eight or nine miles above its mouth, march through the forest, and fall on the rear of the French at Beauport, while the rest landed and attacked them in front. The second was to cross the ford at the mouth of the Montmorenci and march along the strand, under the French intrenchments, till a place could be found where the troops might climb the heights. The third was to make a general attack from boats at the Beauport flats. Wolfe had before entertained two other plans, one of which was to scale the heights at St. Michel, about a league above Quebec; but this he had abandoned on learning that the French were there in force to receive him. The other was to storm the Lower Town; but this also he had abandoned, because the Upper Town, which commanded it, would still remain inaccessible.

The brigadiers met in consultation, rejected the three plans proposed in the letter, and advised that an attempt should be made to gain a footing on the north shore above the town, place the army between Montcalm and his base of supply, and so force him to fight or surrender. The scheme was similar to that of the heights of St. Michel. It seemed desperate, but so did all the rest; and if by chance it should succeed, the gain was far greater than could follow any success below the town. Wolfe embraced it at once.

Not that he saw much hope in it. He knew that every chance was against him. Disappointment in the past and gloom in the future, the pain and exhaustion of disease, toils, and anxieties "too great," in the words of Burke, "to be supported by a delicate constitution, and a body unequal to the vigorous and enterprising soul that it lodged," threw him at times into deep dejection. By those intimate with him he was heard to say that he would not go back defeated, "to be exposed to the censure and reproach of an ignorant populace." In other moods he felt that he ought not to sacrifice what was left of his diminished army in vain conflict with hopeless obstacles. But his final resolve once taken, he would not swerve from it. His fear was that he might not be able to lead his troops in person. "I know perfectly well you cannot cure me," he said to his physician; "but pray make me up so that I may be without pain for a few days, and able to do my duty: that is all I want."

In a despatch which Wolfe had written to Pitt, Admiral Saunders conceived that he had ascribed to the fleet more than its just share in the disaster at Montmorenci; and he sent him a letter on the subject. Major Barré kept it from the invalid till the fever had abated. Wolfe then wrote a long answer, which reveals his mixed dejection and resolve. He affirms the justice of what Saunders had said, but adds: "I shall leave out that part of my letter to Mr. Pitt which you object to. I am sensible of my own errors in the course of the campaign, see clearly wherein I have been deficient, and think a little more or less blame to a man that must necessarily be ruined, of little or no consequence. I take the blame of that unlucky day entirely upon my own shoulders, and I expect to suffer for it." Then, speaking of the new project of an attack above Quebec, he says despondingly: "My ill state of health prevents me from executing my own plan; it is of too desperate a nature to order others to execute." He proceeds, however, to give directions for it. "It will be necessary to run as many small craft as possible above the town, with provisions for six weeks, for about five thousand, which is all I intend to take. My letters, I hope, will be ready to-morrow, and I hope I shall have strength to lead these men to wherever we can find the enemy."

On the next day, the last of August, he was able for the first time to leave the house. It was on this same day that he wrote his last letter to his mother: "My writing to you will convince you that no personal evils worse than defeats and disappointments have fallen upon me. The enemy puts nothing to risk, and I can't in conscience put the whole army to risk. My antagonist has wisely shut himself up in inaccessible intrenchments, so that I can't get at him without spilling a torrent of blood, and that perhaps to little purpose. The Marquis de Montcalm is at the head of a great number of bad soldiers, and I am at the head of a small number of good ones, that wish for nothing so much as to fight him; but the wary old fellow avoids an action, doubtful of the behavior of his army. People must be of the profession to understand the disadvantages and difficulties we labor under, arising from the uncommon natural strength of the country."

On the second of September a vessel was sent to England with his last despatch to Pitt. It begins thus: "The obstacles we have met with in the operations of the campaign are much greater than we had reason to expect or could foresee; not so much from the number of the enemy (though superior to us) as from the natural strength of the country, which the Marquis of Montcalm seems wisely to depend upon. When I learned that succors of all kinds had been thrown into Quebec; that five battalions of regular troops, completed from the best inhabitants of the country, some of the troops of the colony, and every Canadian that was able to bear arms, besides several nations of savages, had taken the field in a very advantageous situation,—I could not flatter myself that I should be able to reduce the place. I sought, however, an occasion to attack their army, knowing well that with these troops I was able to fight, and hoping that a victory might disperse them." Then, after recounting the events of the campaign with admirable clearness, he continues: "I found myself so ill, and am still so weak, that I begged the general officers to consult together for the general utility. They are all of opinion that, as more ships and provisions are now got above the town, they should try, by conveying up a corps of four or five thousand men (which is nearly the whole strength of the army after the Points of Levi and Orleans are left in a proper state of defence), to draw the enemy from their present situation and bring them to an action. I have acquiesced in the proposal, and we are preparing to put it into execution." The letter ends thus: "By the list of disabled officers, many of whom are of rank, you may perceive that the army is much weakened. By the nature of the river, the most formidable part of this armament is deprived of the power of acting; yet we have almost the whole force of Canada to oppose. In this situation there is such a choice of difficulties that I own myself at a loss how to determine. The affairs of Great Britain, I know, require the most vigorous measures; but the courage of a handful of brave troops should be exerted only when there is some hope of a favorable event; however, you may be assured that the small part of the campaign which remains shall be employed, as far as I am able, for the honor of His Majesty and the interest of the nation, in which I am sure of being well seconded by the Admiral and by the generals; happy if our efforts here can contribute to the success of His Majesty's arms in any other parts of America."

Some days later, he wrote to the Earl of Holdernesse: "The Marquis of Montcalm has a numerous body of armed men (I cannot call it an army), and the strongest country perhaps in the world. Our fleet blocks up the river above and below the town, but can give no manner of aid in an attack upon the Canadian army. We are now here [*off Cap-Rouge*] with about thirty-six hundred men, waiting to attack them when and wherever they can best be got at. I am so far recovered as to do business; but my constitution is entirely ruined, without the consolation of doing any considerable service to the state, and without any prospect of it." He had just learned, through the letter brought from Amherst by Ensign Hutchins, that he could expect no help from that quarter.

Perhaps he was as near despair as his undaunted nature was capable of being. In his present state of body and mind he was a hero without the light and cheer of heroism. He flattered himself with no illusions, but saw the worst and faced it all. He seems to have been entirely without excitement. The languor of disease, the desperation of the chances, and the greatness of the stake may have wrought to tranquillize him. His energy was doubly tasked: to bear up his own sinking frame, and to achieve an almost hopeless feat of arms.

Audacious as it was, his plan cannot be called rash if we may accept the statement of two well-informed writers on the French side. They say that on the tenth of September the English naval commanders held a council on board the flagship, in which it was resolved that the lateness of the season required the fleet to leave Quebec without delay. They say further that Wolfe then went to the admiral, told him that he had found a place where the heights could be scaled, that he would send up a hundred and fifty picked men to feel the way, and that if they gained a lodgement at the top, the other troops should follow; if, on the other hand, the French were there in force to oppose them, he would not sacrifice the army in a hopeless attempt, but embark them for home, consoled by the thought that all had been done that man could do. On this, concludes the story, the admiral and his officers consented to wait the result.

As Wolfe had informed Pitt, his army was greatly weakened. Since the end of June his loss in killed and wounded was more than eight hundred and fifty, including two colonels, two majors, nineteen captains, and thirty-four subalterns; and to these were to be added a greater number disabled by disease.

The squadron of Admiral Holmes above Quebec had now increased to twenty-two vessels, great and small. One of the last that went up was a diminutive schooner, armed with a few swivels, and jocosely named the "Terror of France." She sailed by the town in broad daylight, the French, incensed at her impudence, blazing at her from all their batteries; but she passed unharmed, anchored by the admiral's ship, and saluted him triumphantly with her swivels.

Wolfe's first move towards executing his plan was the critical one of evacuating the camp at Montmorenci. This was accomplished on the third of September. Montcalm sent a strong force to fall on the rear of the retiring English. Monckton saw the movement from Point Levi, embarked two battalions in the boats of the fleet, and made a feint of landing at Beauport. Montcalm recalled his troops to repulse the threatened attack; and the English withdrew from Montmorenci unmolested, some to the Point of Orleans, others to Point Levi. On the night of the fourth a fleet of flatboats passed above the town with the baggage and stores. On the fifth, Murray, with four battalions, marched up the river Etechemin, and forded it under a hot fire from the French batteries at Sillery. Monckton and Townshend followed with three more battalions, and the united force, of about thirty-six hundred men, was embarked on board the ships of Holmes, where Wolfe joined them on the same evening.

These movements of the English filled the French commanders with mingled perplexity, anxiety, and hope. A deserter told them that Admiral Saunders was impatient to be gone. Vaudreuil grew confident. "The breaking up of the camp at Montmorenci," he says, "and the abandonment of the intrenchments there, the re-embarkation on board the vessels above Quebec of the troops who had encamped on the south bank, the movements of these vessels, the removal of the heaviest pieces of artillery from the batteries of Point Levi,—these and the lateness of the season all combined to announce the speedy departure of the fleet, several vessels of which had even sailed down the river already. The prisoners and the deserters who daily came in told us that this was the common report in their army." He wrote to Bourlamaque on the first of September: "Everything proves that the grand design of the English has failed."

Yet he was ceaselessly watchful. So was Montcalm; and he, too, on the night of the second, snatched a moment to write to Bourlamaque from his headquarters in the stone house, by the river of Beauport: "The night is dark; it rains; our troops are in their tents, with clothes on, ready for an alarm; I in my boots; my horses saddled. In fact, this is my usual way. I wish you were here; for I cannot be everywhere, though I multiply myself, and have not taken off my clothes since the twenty-third of June." On the eleventh of September he wrote his last letter to Bourlamaque, and probably the last that his pen ever traced. "I am overwhelmed with work, and should often lose temper, like you, if I did not remember that I am paid by Europe for not losing it. Nothing new since my last. I give the enemy another month, or something less, to stay here." The more sanguine Vaudreuil would hardly give them a week.

Meanwhile, no precaution was spared. The force under Bougainville above Quebec was raised to three thousand men. He was ordered to watch the shore as far as Jacques-Cartier, and follow with his main body every movement of Holmes's squadron. There was little fear for the heights near the town; they were thought inaccessible. Even Montcalm believed them safe, and had expressed himself to that effect some time before. "We need not suppose," he wrote to Vaudreuil, "that the enemy have wings;" and again, speaking of the very place where Wolfe afterwards landed, "I swear to you that a hundred men posted there would stop their whole army." He was right. A hundred watchful and determined men could have held the position long enough for reinforcements to come up.

The hundred men were there. Captain de Vergor, of the colony troops, commanded them, and reinforcements were within his call; for the battalion of Guienne had been ordered to encamp close at hand on the Plains of Abraham. Vergor's post, called Anse du Foulon, was a mile and a half from Quebec. A little beyond it, by the brink of the cliffs, was another post, called Samos, held by seventy men with four cannon; and, beyond this again, the heights of Sillery were guarded by a hundred and thirty men, also with cannon. These were outposts of Bougainville, whose headquarters were at Cap-Rouge, six miles above Sillery, and whose troops were in continual movement along the intervening shore. Thus all was vigilance; for while the French were strong in the hope of speedy delivery, they felt that there was no safety till the tents of the invader had vanished from their shores and his ships from their river. "What we knew," says one of them, "of the character of M. Wolfe, that impetuous, bold, and intrepid warrior, prepared us for a last attack before he left us."

Wolfe had been very ill on the evening of the fourth. The troops knew it, and their spirits sank; but, after a night of torment, he grew better, and was soon among them again, rekindling their ardor, and imparting a cheer that he could not share. For himself he had no pity; but when he heard of the illness of two officers in one of the ships, he sent them a message of warm sympathy, advised them to return to Point Levi, and offered them his own barge and an escort. They thanked him, but replied that, come what might, they would see the enterprise to an end. Another officer remarked in his hearing that one of the invalids had a very delicate constitution. "Don't tell me of constitution," said Wolfe; "he has good spirit, and good spirit will carry a man through everything." An immense moral force bore up his own frail body and forced it to its work.

Major Robert Stobo, who, five years before, had been given as a hostage to the French at the capture of Fort Necessity, arrived about this time in a vessel from Halifax. He had long been a prisoner at Quebec, not always in close custody, and had used his opportunities to acquaint himself with the neighborhood. In the spring of this year he and an officer of rangers named Stevens had made their escape with extraordinary skill and daring; and he now returned to give his countrymen the benefit of his local knowledge. His biographer says that it was he who directed Wolfe in the choice of a landing-place. Be this as it may, Wolfe in person examined the river and the shores as far as Pointe-aux-Trembles; till at length, landing on the south side a little above Quebec, and looking across the water with a telescope, he descried a path that ran with a long slope up the face of the woody precipice, and saw at the top a cluster of tents. They were those of Vergor's guard at the Anse du Foulon, now called Wolfe's Cove. As he could see but ten or twelve of them, he thought that the guard could not be numerous, and might be overpowered. His hope would have been stronger if he had known that Vergor had once been tried for misconduct and cowardice in the surrender of Beauséjour, and saved from merited disgrace by the friendship of Bigot and the protection of Vaudreuil.

The morning of the seventh was fair and warm, and the vessels of Holmes, their crowded decks gay with scarlet uniforms, sailed up the river to Cap-Rouge. A lively scene awaited them; for here were the headquarters of Bougainville, and here lay his principal force, while the rest watched the banks above and below. The cove into which the little river runs was guarded by floating batteries; the surrounding shore was defended by breastworks; and a large body of regulars, militia, and mounted Canadians in blue uniforms moved to and fro, with restless activity, on the hills behind. When the vessels came to anchor, the horsemen dismounted and formed in line with the infantry; then, with loud shouts, the whole rushed down the heights to man their works at the shore. That true Briton, Captain Knox, looked on with a critical eye from the gangway of his ship, and wrote that night in his Diary that they had made a ridiculous noise. "How different!" he exclaims, "how nobly awful and expressive of true valor is the customary silence of the British troops!"

In the afternoon the ships opened fire, while the troops entered the boats and rowed up and down as if looking for a landing-place. It was but a feint of Wolfe to deceive Bougainville as to his real design. A heavy easterly rain set in on the next morning, and lasted two days without respite. All operations were suspended, and the men suffered greatly in the crowded transports. Half of them were therefore landed on the south shore, where they made their quarters in the village of St. Nicolas, refreshed themselves, and dried their wet clothing, knapsacks, and blankets.

For several successive days the squadron of Holmes was allowed to drift up the river with the flood tide and down with the ebb, thus passing and repassing incessantly between the neighborhood of Quebec on one hand, and a point high above Cap-Rouge on the other; while Bougainville, perplexed, and always expecting an attack, followed the ships to and fro along the shore, by day and by night, till his men were exhausted with ceaseless forced marches.

At last the time for action came. On Wednesday, the twelfth, the troops at St. Nicolas were embarked again, and all were told to hold themselves in readiness. Wolfe, from the flagship "Sutherland," issued his last general orders. "The enemy's force is now divided, great scarcity of provisions in their camp, and universal discontent among the Canadians. Our troops below are in readiness to join us; all the light artillery and tools are embarked at the Point of Levi; and the troops will land where the French seem least to expect it. The first body that gets on shore is to march directly to the enemy and drive them from any little post they may occupy; the officers must be careful that the succeeding bodies do not by any mistake fire on those who go before them. The battalions must form on the upper ground with expedition, and be ready to charge whatever presents itself. When the artillery and troops are landed, a corps will be left to secure the landing-place, while the rest march on and endeavor to bring the Canadians and French to a battle. The officers and men will remember what their country expects from them, and what a determined body of soldiers inured to war is capable of doing against five weak French battalions mingled with a disorderly peasantry."

The spirit of the army answered to that of its chief. The troops loved and admired their general, trusted their officers, and were ready for any attempt. "Nay, how could it be otherwise," quaintly asks honest Sergeant John Johnson, of the fifty-eighth regiment, "being at the heels of gentlemen whose whole thirst, equal with their general, was for glory? We had seen them tried, and always found them sterling. We knew that they would stand by us to the last extremity."

Wolfe had thirty-six hundred men and officers with him on board the vessels of Holmes; and he now sent orders to Colonel Burton at Point Levi to bring to his aid all who could be spared from that place and the Point of Orleans. They were to march along the south bank, after nightfall, and wait further orders at a designated spot convenient for embarkation. Their number was about twelve hundred, so that the entire force destined for the enterprise was at the utmost forty-eight hundred. With these, Wolfe meant to climb the heights of Abraham in the teeth of an enemy who, though much reduced, were still twice as numerous as their assailants.

Admiral Saunders lay with the main fleet in the Basin of Quebec. This excellent officer, whatever may have been his views as to the necessity of a speedy departure, aided Wolfe to the last with unfailing energy and zeal. It was agreed between them that while the general made the real attack, the admiral should engage Montcalm's attention by a pretended one. As night approached, the fleet ranged itself along the Beauport shore; the boats were lowered and filled with sailors, marines, and the few troops that had been left behind; while ship signalled to ship, cannon flashed and thundered, and shot ploughed the beach, as if to clear a way for assailants to land. In the gloom of the evening the effect was imposing. Montcalm, who thought that the movements of the English above the town were only a feint, that their main force was still below it, and that their real attack would be made there, was completely deceived, and massed his troops in front of Beauport to repel the expected landing. But while in the fleet of Saunders all was uproar and ostentatious menace, the danger was ten miles away, where the squadron of Holmes lay tranquil and silent at its anchorage off Cap-Rouge.

It was less tranquil than it seemed. All on board knew that a blow would be struck that night, though only a few high officers knew where. Colonel Howe, of the light infantry, called for volunteers to lead the unknown and desperate venture, promising, in the words of one of them, "that if any of us survived we might depend on being recommended to the general." As many as were wanted—twenty-four in all—soon came forward. Thirty large bateaux and some boats belonging to the squadron lay moored alongside the vessels; and late in the evening the troops were ordered into them, the twenty-four volunteers taking their place in the foremost. They held in all about seventeen hundred men. The rest remained on board.

Bougainville could discern the movement, and misjudged it, thinking that he himself was to be attacked. The tide was still flowing; and, the better to deceive him, the vessels and boats were allowed to drift upward with it for a little distance, as if to land above Cap-Rouge.

The day had been fortunate for Wolfe. Two deserters came from the camp of Bougainville with intelligence that, at ebb tide on the next night, he was to send down a convoy of provisions to Montcalm. The necessities of the camp at Beauport, and the difficulties of transportation by land, had before compelled the French to resort to this perilous means of conveying supplies; and their boats, drifting in darkness under the shadows of the northern shore, had commonly passed in safety. Wolfe saw at once that, if his own boats went down in advance of the convoy, he could turn the intelligence of the deserters to good account.

He was still on board the "Sutherland." Every preparation was made, and every order given; it only remained to wait the turning of the tide. Seated with him in the cabin was the commander of the sloop-of-war "Porcupine," his former school-fellow, John Jervis, afterwards Earl St. Vincent. Wolfe told him that he expected to die in the battle of the next day; and taking from his bosom a miniature of Miss Lowther, his betrothed, he gave it to him with a request that he would return it to her if the presentiment should prove true.

Towards two o'clock the tide began to ebb, and a fresh wind blew down the river. Two lanterns were raised into the maintop shrouds of the "Sutherland." It was the appointed signal; the boats cast off and fell down with the current, those of the light infantry leading the way. The vessels with the rest of the troops had orders to follow a little later.

To look for a moment at the chances on which this bold adventure hung. First, the deserters told Wolfe that provision-boats were ordered to go down to Quebec that night; secondly, Bougainville countermanded them; thirdly, the sentries posted along the heights were told of the order, but not of the countermand; fourthly, Vergor at the Anse du Foulon had permitted most of his men, chiefly Canadians from Lorette, to go home for a time and work at their harvesting, on condition, it is said, that they should afterwards work in a neighboring field of his own; fifthly, he kept careless watch, and went quietly to bed; sixthly, the battalion of Guienne, ordered to take post on the Plains of Abraham, had, for reasons unexplained, remained encamped by the St. Charles; and lastly, when Bougainville saw Holmes's vessels drift down the stream, he did not tax his weary troops to follow them, thinking that they would return as usual with the flood tide. But for these conspiring circumstances New France might have lived a little longer, and the fruitless heroism of Wolfe would have passed, with countless other heroisms, into oblivion.

For full two hours the procession of boats, borne on the current, steered silently down the St. Lawrence. The stars were visible, but the night was moonless and sufficiently dark. The general was in one of the foremost boats, and near him was a young midshipman, John Robison, afterwards professor of natural philosophy in the University of Edinburgh. He used to tell in his later life how Wolfe, with a low voice, repeated Gray's "Elegy in a Country Churchyard" to the officers about him. Probably it was to relieve the intense strain of his thoughts. Among the rest was the verse which his own fate was soon to illustrate,—

"The paths of glory lead but to the grave."

"Gentlemen," he said, as his recital ended, "I would rather have written those lines than take Quebec." None were there to tell him that the hero is greater than the poet.

As they neared their destination, the tide bore them in towards the shore, and the mighty wall of rock and forest towered in darkness on their left. The dead stillness was suddenly broken by the sharp *Qui vive!* of a French sentry, invisible in the thick gloom. *France!* answered a Highland officer of Fraser's regiment from one of the boats of the light infantry. He had served in Holland, and spoke French fluently.

À quel régiment?

De la Reine, replied the Highlander. He knew that a part of that corps was with Bougainville. The sentry, expecting the convoy of provisions, was satisfied, and did not ask for the password.

Soon after, the foremost boats were passing the heights of Samos, when another sentry challenged them, and they could see him through the darkness running down to the edge of the water, within range of a pistol-shot. In answer to his questions, the same officer replied, in French: "Provision-boats. Don't make a noise; the English will hear us." In fact, the sloop-of-war "Hunter" was anchored in the stream not far off. This time, again, the sentry let them pass. In a few moments they rounded the headland above the Anse du Foulon. There was no sentry there. The strong current swept the boats of the light infantry a little below the intended landingplace. They disembarked on a narrow strand at the foot of heights as steep as a hill covered with trees can be. The twenty-four volunteers led the way, climbing with what silence they might, closely followed by a much larger body. When they reached the top they saw in the dim light a cluster of tents at a short distance, and immediately made a dash at them. Vergor leaped from bed and tried to run off, but was shot in the heel and captured. His men, taken by surprise, made little resistance. One or two were caught, and the rest fled.

The main body of troops waited in their boats by the edge of the strand. The heights near by were cleft by a great ravine choked with forest trees; and in its depths ran a little brook called Ruisseau St.-Denis, which, swollen by the late rains, fell splashing in the stillness over a rock. Other than this no sound could reach the strained ear of Wolfe but the gurgle of the tide and the cautious climbing of his advance-parties as they mounted the steeps at some little distance from where he sat listening. At length from the top came a sound of musket-shots, followed by loud huzzas, and he knew that his men were masters of the position. The word was given; the troops leaped from the boats and scaled the heights, some here, some there, clutching at trees and bushes, their muskets slung at their backs. Tradition still points out the place, near the mouth of the ravine, where the foremost reached the top. Wolfe said to an officer near him: "You can try it, but I don't think you'll get up." He himself, however, found strength to drag himself up with the rest. The narrow slanting path on the face of the heights had been made impassable by trenches and abattis; but all obstructions were soon cleared away, and then the ascent was easy. In the gray of the morning the long file of red-coated soldiers moved quickly upward, and formed in order on the plateau above.

Before many of them had reached the top, cannon were heard close on the left. It was the battery at Samos firing on the boats in the rear and the vessels descending from Cap-Rouge. A party was sent to silence it; this was soon effected, and the more distant battery at Sillery was next attacked and taken. As fast as the boats were emptied they returned for the troops left on board the vessels and for those waiting on the southern shore under Colonel Burton.

The day broke in clouds and threatening rain. Wolfe's battalions were drawn up along the crest of the heights. No enemy was in sight, though a body of Canadians had sallied from the town and moved along the strand towards the landing-place, whence they were quickly driven back. He had achieved the most critical part of his enterprise; yet the success that he coveted placed him in imminent danger. On one side was the garrison of Quebec and the army of Beauport, and Bougainville was on the other. Wolfe's alternative was victory or ruin; for if he should be overwhelmed by a combined attack, retreat would be hopeless. His feelings no man can know; but it would be safe to say that hesitation or doubt had no part in them.

He went to reconnoitre the ground, and soon came to the Plains of Abraham, so called from Abraham Martin, a pilot known as Maître Abraham, who had owned a piece of land here in the early times of the colony. The Plains were a tract of grass, tolerably level in most parts, patched here and there with cornfields, studded with clumps of bushes, and forming a part of the high plateau at the eastern end of which Quebec stood. On the south it was bounded by the declivities along the St. Lawrence; on the north, by those along the St. Charles, or rather along the meadows through which that lazy stream crawled like a writhing snake. At the place that Wolfe chose for his battle-field the plateau was less than a mile wide.

Thither the troops advanced, marched by files till they reached the ground, and then wheeled to form their line of battle, which stretched across the plateau and faced the city. It consisted of six battalions and the detached grenadiers from Louisbourg, all drawn up in ranks three deep. Its right wing was near the brink of the heights along the St. Lawrence; but the left could not reach those along the St. Charles. On this side a wide space was perforce left open, and there was danger of being outflanked. To prevent this, Brigadier Townshend was stationed here with two battalions, drawn up at right angles with the rest, and fronting the St. Charles. The battalion of Webb's regiment, under Colonel Burton, formed the reserve; the third battalion of Royal Americans was left to guard the landing; and Howe's light infantry occupied a wood far in the rear. Wolfe, with Monckton and Murray, commanded the front line, on which the heavy fighting was to fall, and which, when all the troops had arrived, numbered less than thirty-five hundred men.

Quebec was not a mile distant, but they could not see it; for a ridge of broken ground intervened, called Buttes-à-Neveu, about six hundred paces off. The first division of troops had scarcely come up when, about six o'clock, this ridge was suddenly thronged with white uniforms. It was the battalion of Guienne, arrived at the eleventh hour from its camp by the St. Charles. Some time after there was hot firing in the rear. It came from a detachment of Bougainville's command attacking a house where some of the light infantry were posted. The assailants were repulsed, and the firing ceased. Light showers fell at intervals, besprinkling the troops as they stood patiently waiting the event.

Montcalm had passed a troubled night. Through all the evening the cannon bellowed from the ships of Saunders, and the boats of the fleet hovered in the dusk off the Beauport shore, threatening every moment to land. Troops lined the intrenchments till day, while the general walked the field that adjoined his headquarters till one in the morning, accompanied by the Chevalier Johnstone and Colonel Poulariez. Johnstone says that he was in great agitation, and took no rest all night. At daybreak he heard the sound of cannon above the town. It was the battery at Samos firing on the English ships. He had sent an officer to the quarters of Vaudreuil, which were much nearer Quebec, with orders to bring him word at once should anything unusual happen. But no word came, and about six o'clock he mounted and rode thither with Johnstone. As they advanced, the country behind the town opened more and more upon their sight; till at length, when opposite Vaudreuil's house, they saw across the St. Charles, some two miles away, the red ranks of British soldiers on the heights beyond.

"This is a serious business," Montcalm said; and sent off Johnstone at full gallop to bring up the troops from the centre and left of the camp. Those of the right were in motion already, doubtless by the governor's order. Vaudreuil came out of the house. Montcalm stopped for a few words with him; then set spurs to his horse, and rode over the bridge of the St. Charles to the scene of danger. He rode with a fixed look, uttering not a word.

The army followed in such order as it might, crossed the bridge in hot haste, passed under the northern rampart of Quebec, entered at the Palace Gate, and pressed on in headlong march along the quaint narrow streets of the warlike town: troops of Indians in scalp-locks and war-paint, a savage glitter in their deep-set eyes; bands of Canadians whose all was at stake,—faith, country, and home; the colony regulars; the battalions of Old France, a torrent of white uniforms and gleaming bayonets, La Sarre, Languedoc, Roussillon, Béarn,—victors of Oswego, William Henry, and Ticonderoga. So they swept on, poured out upon the plain, some by the gate of St. Louis, and some by that of St. John, and hurried, breathless, to where the banners of Guienne still fluttered on the ridge.

Montcalm was amazed at what he saw. He had expected a detachment, and he found an army. Full in sight before him stretched the lines of Wolfe: the close ranks of the English infantry, a silent wall of red, and the wild array of the Highlanders, with their waving tartans, and bagpipes screaming defiance. Vaudreuil had not come; but not the less was felt the evil of a divided authority and the jealousy of the rival chiefs. Montcalm waited long for the forces he had ordered to join him from the left wing of the army. He waited in vain. It is said that the governor had detained them, lest the English should attack the Beauport shore. Even if they did so, and succeeded, the French might defy them, could they but put Wolfe to rout on the Plains of Abraham. Neither did the garrison of Quebec come to the aid of Montcalm. He sent to Ramesay, its commander, for twenty-five field-pieces which were on the Palace battery. Ramesay would give him only three, saying that he wanted them for his own defence. There were orders and counter-orders; misunderstanding, haste, delay, perplexity.

Montcalm and his chief officers held a council of war. It is said that he and they alike were for immediate attack. His enemies declare that he was afraid lest Vaudreuil should arrive and take command; but the governor was not a man to assume responsibility at such a crisis. Others say that his impetuosity overcame his better judgment; and of this charge it is hard to acquit him. Bougainville was but a few miles distant, and some of his troops were much nearer; a messenger sent by way of Old Lorette could have reached him in an hour and a half at most, and a combined attack in front and rear might have been concerted with him. If, moreover, Montcalm could have come to an understanding with Vaudreuil, his own force might have been strengthened by two or three thousand additional men from the town and the camp of Beauport; but he felt that there was no time to lose, for he imagined that Wolfe would soon be reinforced, which was impossible, and he believed that the English were fortifying themselves, which was no less an error. He has been blamed not only for fighting too soon, but for fighting at all. In this he could not choose. Fight he must, for Wolfe was now in a position to cut off all his supplies. His men were full of ardor, and he resolved to attack before their ardor cooled. He spoke a few words to them in his keen, vehement way. "I remember very well how he looked," one of the Canadians, then a boy of eighteen, used to say in his old age; "he rode a black or dark bay horse along the front of our lines, brandishing his sword, as if to excite us to do our duty. He wore a coat with wide sleeves, which fell back as he raised his arm, and showed the white linen of the wristband."

The English waited the result with a composure which, if not quite real, was at least well feigned. The three field-pieces sent by Ramesay plied them with canister-shot, and fifteen hundred Canadians and Indians fusilladed them in front and flank. Over all the plain, from behind bushes and knolls and the edge of cornfields, puffs of smoke sprang incessantly from the guns of these hidden marksmen. Skirmishers were thrown out before the lines to hold them in check, and the soldiers were ordered to lie on the grass to avoid the shot. The firing was liveliest on the English left, where bands of sharpshooters got under the edge of the declivity, among thickets, and behind scattered houses, whence they killed and wounded a considerable number of Townshend's men. The light infantry were called up from the rear. The houses were taken and retaken, and one or more of them was burned.

Wolfe was everywhere. How cool he was, and why his followers loved him, is shown by an incident that happened in the course of the morning. One of his captains was shot through the lungs; and on recovering consciousness he saw the general standing at his side. Wolfe pressed his hand, told him not to despair, praised his services, promised him early promotion, and sent an aide-de-camp to Monckton to beg that officer to keep the promise if he himself should fall.

It was towards ten o'clock when, from the high ground on the right of the line, Wolfe saw that the crisis was near. The French on the ridge had formed themselves into three bodies, regulars in the centre, regulars and Canadians on right and left. Two field-pieces, which had been dragged up the heights at Anse du Foulon, fired on them with grape-shot, and the troops, rising from the ground, prepared to receive them. In a few moments more they were in motion. They came on rapidly, uttering loud shouts, and firing as soon as they were within range. Their ranks, ill ordered at the best, were further confused by a number of Canadians who had been mixed among the regulars, and who, after hastily firing, threw themselves on the ground to reload. The British advanced a few rods; then halted and stood still. When the French were within forty paces the word of command rang out, and a crash of musketry answered all along the line. The volley was delivered with remarkable precision. In the battalions of the centre, which had suffered least from the enemy's bullets, the simultaneous explosion was afterwards said by French officers to have sounded like a cannon-shot. Another volley followed, and then a furious clattering fire that lasted but a minute or two. When the smoke rose, a miserable sight was revealed: the ground cumbered with dead and wounded, the advancing masses stopped short and turned into a frantic mob, shouting, cursing, gesticulating. The order was given to charge. Then over the field rose the British cheer, mixed with the fierce yell of the Highland slogan. Some of the corps pushed forward with the bayonet; some advanced firing. The clansmen drew their broadswords and dashed on, keen and swift as bloodhounds. At the English right, though the attacking column was broken to pieces, a fire was still kept up, chiefly, it seems, by sharpshooters from the bushes and cornfields, where they had lain for an hour or more. Here Wolfe himself led the charge, at the head of the Louisbourg grenadiers. A shot shattered his wrist. He wrapped his handkerchief about it and kept on. Another shot struck him, and he still advanced, when a third lodged in his breast. He staggered, and sat on the ground. Lieutenant Brown, of the grenadiers, one Henderson, a volunteer in the same company, and a private soldier, aided by an officer of artillery who ran to join them, carried him in their arms to the rear. He begged them to lay him down. They did so, and asked if he would have a surgeon. "There's no need," he answered; "it's all over with me." A moment after, one of them cried out: "They run; see how they run!" "Who run?" Wolfe demanded, like a man roused from sleep. "The enemy, sir. Egad, they give way everywhere!" "Go, one of you, to Colonel Burton," returned the dying man; "tell him to march Webb's regiment down to Charles River, to cut off their retreat from the bridge." Then, turning on his side, he murmured, "Now, God be praised, I will die in peace!" and in a few moments his gallant soul had fled.

Montcalm, still on horseback, was borne with the tide of fugitives towards the town. As he approached the walls a shot passed through his body. He kept his seat; two soldiers supported him, one on each side, and led his horse through the St. Louis Gate. On the open space within, among the excited crowd, were several women, drawn, no doubt, by eagerness to know the result of the fight. One of them recognized him, saw the streaming blood, and shrieked, *"O mon Dieu! mon Dieu! le Marquis est tué!"* "It's nothing, it's nothing," replied the death-stricken man; "don't be troubled for me, my good friends." *("Ce n'est rien, ce n'est rien; ne vous affligez pas pour moi, mes bonnes amies.")*

*Note.—There are several contemporary versions of the dying words of Wolfe. The report of Knox, given above, is by far the best attested. Knox says that he took particular pains at the time to learn them accurately from those who were with Wolfe when they were uttered.

The anecdote of Montcalm is due to the late Hon. Malcolm Fraser, of Quebec. He often heard it in his youth from an old woman, who, when a girl, was one of the group who saw the wounded general led by, and to whom the words were addressed.

Force of the English and French at the Battle of Quebec.—The tabular return given by Knox shows the number of officers and men in each corps engaged. According to this, the battalions as they stood on the Plains of Abraham before the battle varied in strength from 322 (Monckton's) to 683 (Webb's), making a total of 4,828, including officers. But another return, less specific, signed *George Townshend, Brigadier,* makes the entire number only 4,441. Townshend succeeded Wolf in the command; and this return, which is preserved in the Public Record Office, was sent to London a few days after the battle. Some French writers present put the number lower, perhaps for the reason that Webb's regiment and the third battalion of Royal Americans took no part in the fight, the one being in the rear as a reserve, and the other also invisible, guarding the landing-place. Wolfe's front line, which alone met and turned the French attack, was made up as follows, the figures including officers and men:—

Thirty-fifth Regiment	519	Twenty-eighth Regiment	421
Fifty-eighth "	335	Forty-seventh "	360
Seventy-eighth "	662	Forty-third "	327
Louisbourg Grenadiers	241	Light Infantry	400

Making a total of 3,265.

The French force engaged cannot be precisely given. Knox, on information received from "an intelligent Frenchman," states the number, corps by corps, the aggregate being 7,520. This, on examination, plainly appears exaggerated. Fraser puts it at 5,000; Townshend at 4,470, including militia. Bigot says, 3,500, which may perhaps be as many as actually advanced to the attack, since some of the militia held back. Including Bougainville's command, the militia and artillerymen left in the Beauport camp, the sailors at the town batteries, and the garrison of Quebec, at least as many of the French were out of the battle as were in it; and the numbers engaged on each side seem to have been about equal.

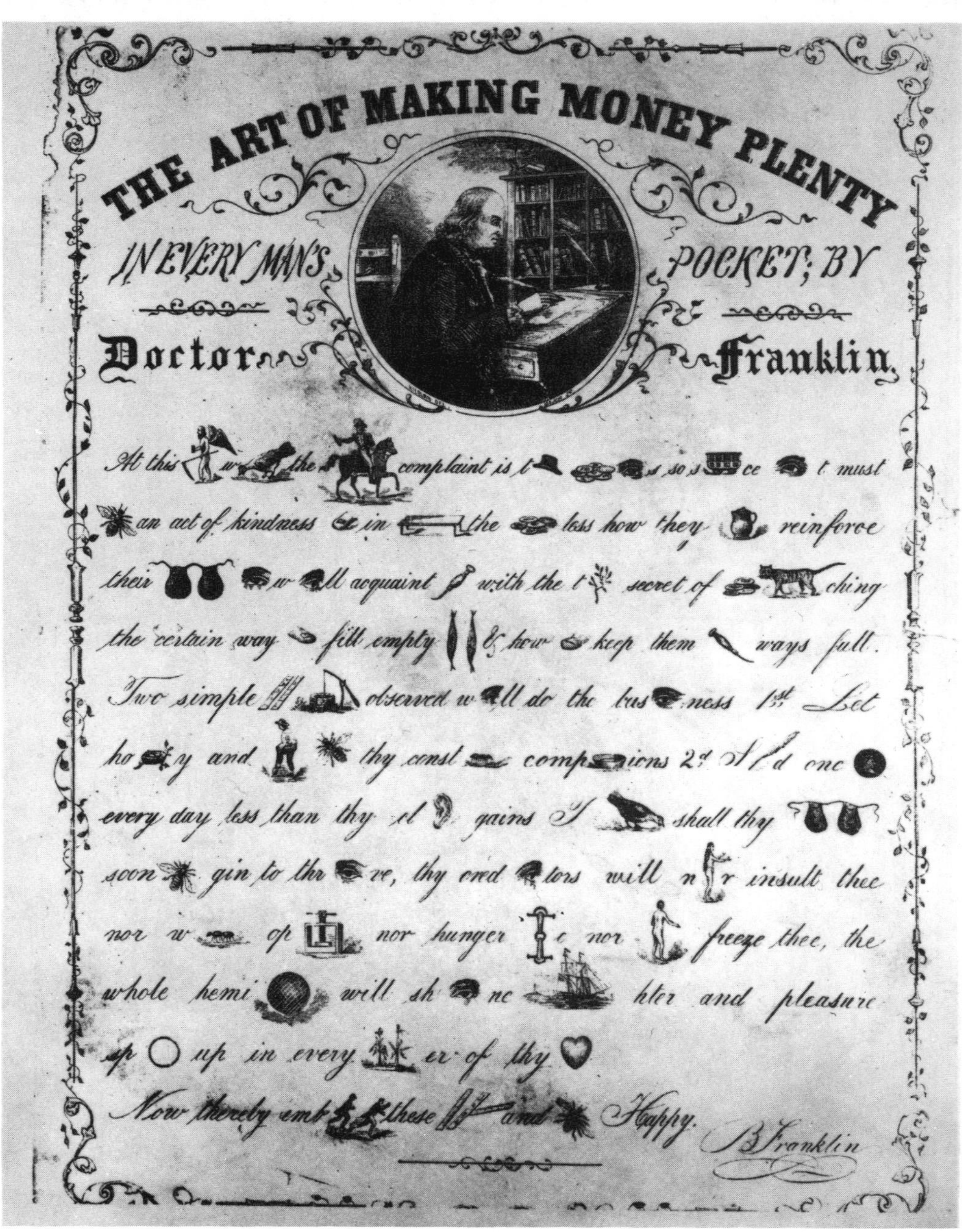
THE ART OF MAKING MONEY PLENTY
IN EVERY MAN'S POCKET; BY
Doctor Franklin
B Franklin

BENJAMIN FRANKLIN

Autobiography

(1868)

Carl Van Doren described Benjamin Franklin as "a scientist, a diplomat, a statesman, a businessman, an economist, a printer, a humorist and wit, a great writer, a sage, and a landmark in the history of human speech about the common ways of life." He was something of a hypocrite and very much a paradox—American all over.

As Poor Richard the moralist, Franklin directly reflected the Puritan virtues of temperance, silence, order, resolution, frugality, industry, sincerity, justice, and the like; but he freed these qualities from their theological background and frankly set them to serve the uses of man, not the glory of God. A utilitarian, he offered means of living which fit perfectly with the spirit of developing capitalism, like abstinence in order to create capital, and working with small reward for a future goal. Only when this behavior becomes the end of life does it appear materialistic, petty, and dull. Then it becomes classic Philistinism, the eternal dominance of means over ends, the continual postponement of every satisfaction, the rhetoric of the booster. D. H. Lawrence, who hated this side of Americans, angrily blamed it on Franklin, calling him a "snuff-colored little man."

While it is easy to take just such trivial lessons from Franklin, his life indicates something more. He remained poor as short a time as possible, and Richard little longer. Retiring from business at age 42 after innumerable public services in addition to making money, he took the next 42 years to exercise his intellectual curiosity (another Puritan inheritance perhaps), to serve mankind (certainly a Puritan legacy), and to enjoy himself. As Poor Richard, he had married a plain practical woman – he likened her shape to that of a beer mug! But his later life was given over to an English mistress and a series of flirtations in France. His cautious hedonism was a model for successful Americans down to the present.

Franklin's achievements in life were huge; his pleasure in it perhaps as great. The American success story is older than the American nation, and Franklin's legacy to his country was, very much, his success: the capitalist ethic, the tradition of self-help and voluntary community service, and, above all, the application of rationality and science – quietly and with a bow toward tradition – to every avenue of life.

At the time I established myself in Pennsylvania, there was not a good bookseller's shop in any of the Colonies to the southward of Boston. In New York and Philadelphia the printers were indeed stationers; they sold only paper, etc., almanacs, ballads, and a few common schoolbooks. Those who loved reading were obliged to send for their books from England. The members of the Junto had each a few. We had left the alehouse where we first met and hired a room to hold our club in. I proposed that we should all of us bring our books to that room, where they would not only be ready to consult in our conferences but become a common benefit, each of us being at liberty to borrow such as he wished to read at home. This was accordingly done and for some time contented us. Finding the advantage of this little collection, I proposed to render the benefit from books more common by commencing a public subscription library. I drew a sketch of the plan and rules that would be necessary, and got a skillful conveyancer, Mr. Charles Brockden, to put the whole in form of articles of agreement to be subscribed, by which each subscriber engaged to pay a certain sum down for the first purchase of books and an annual contribution for encreasing them. So few were the readers at that time in Philadelphia and the majority of us so poor that I was not able with great industry to find more than fifty persons, mostly young tradesmen, willing to pay down for this purpose forty shillings each and ten shillings per annum. With this little fund we began. The books were imported. The library was open one day in the week for lending them to the subscribers, on their promissory notes to pay double the value if not duly returned. The institution soon manifested its utility, was imitated by other towns and in other provinces; the libraries were augmented by donations; reading became fashionable; and our people, having no public amusements to divert their attention from study, became better acquainted with books, and in a few years were observed by strangers to be better instructed and more intelligent than people of the same rank generally are in other countries.

When we were about to sign the above-mentioned articles, which were to be binding on us, our heirs, etc., for fifty years, Mr. Brockden, the scrivener, said to us, "You are young men, but it is scarce probable that any of you will live to see the expiration of the term fixed in this instrument." A number of us, however, are yet living; but the instrument was after a few years rendered null by a charter that incorporated and gave perpetuity to the company.

The objections and reluctances I met with in soliciting the subscriptions made me soon feel the impropriety of presenting one's self as the proposer of any useful project that might be supposed to raise one's reputation in the smallest degree above that of one's neighbours when one has need of their assistance to accomplish that project. I therefore put myself as much as I could out of sight, and stated it as a scheme of a "number of friends" who had requested me to go about and propose it to such as they thought lovers of reading. In this way my affair went on more smoothly, and I ever after practised it on such occasions, and from my frequent successes can heartily recommend it. The present little sacrifice of your vanity will afterwards be amply repaid. If it remains a while uncertain to whom the merit belongs, someone more vain than yourself will be encouraged to claim it, and then even envy will be disposed to do you justice by plucking those assumed feathers and restoring them to their right owner.

This library afforded me the means of improvement by constant study, for which I set apart an hour or two each day, and thus repaired in some degree the loss of the learned education my father once intended for me. Reading was the only amusement I allowed myself. I spent no time in taverns, games, or frolics of any kind. And my industry in my business continued as indefatigable as it was necessary. I was in debt for my printing house, I had a young family coming on to be educated, and I had two competitors to contend with for business, who were established in the place before me. My circumstances, however, grew daily easier—my original habits of frugality continuing, and my father having among his instructions to me when a boy frequently repeated a proverb of Solomon, "Seest thou a man diligent in his calling, he shall stand before kings, he shall not stand before mean men." I from thence considered industry as a means of obtaining wealth and distinction, which encouraged me, tho' I did not think that I should ever literally stand before kings, which, however, has since happened; for I have stood before five, and even had the honour of sitting down with one, the king of Denmark, to dinner.

We have an English proverb that says;

He that would thrive
Must ask his wife.

It was lucky for me that I had one as much disposed to industry and frugality as myself. She assisted me cheerfully in my business, folding and stitching pamphlets, tending shop, purchasing old linen rags for the papermakers, etc. We kept no idle servants, our table was plain and simple, our furniture of the cheapest. For instance, my breakfast was for a long time bread and milk, (no tea), and I ate it out of a twopenny earthen porringer with a pewter spoon. But mark how luxury will enter families and make a progress, in spite of principle. Being called one morning to breakfast, I found it in a china bowl, with a spoon of silver. They had been bought for me without my knowledge by my wife, and had cost her the enormous sum of three-and-twenty shillings, for which she had no other excuse or apology to make but that she thought *her* husband deserved a silver spoon and china bowl as well as any of his neighbours. This was the first appearance of plate and china in our house, which afterwards in a course of years as our wealth increased, augmented gradually to several hundred pounds in value.

I had been religiously educated as a Presbyterian; and tho' some of the dogmas of that persuasion, such as the eternal decrees of God, election, reprobation, etc., appeared to me unintelligible, others doubtful, and I early absented myself from the public assemblies of the sect, Sunday being my studying-day, I never was without some religious principles. I never doubted, for instance, the existence of the Deity, that he made the world and governed it by his providence, that the most acceptable service of God was the doing good to man, that our souls are immortal, and that all crime will be punished and virtue rewarded either here or hereafter. These I esteemed the essentials of every religion, and being to be found in all the religions we had in our country, I respected them all, tho' with different degrees of respect as I found them more or less mixed with other articles which without any tendency to inspire, promote, or confirm morality, served principally to divide us and make us unfriendly to one another. This respect to all, with an opinion that the worst had some good effects, induced me to avoid all discourse that might tend to lessen the good opinion another might have of his own religion; and as our province increased in people and new places of worship were continually wanted and generally erected by voluntary contribution, my mite for such purpose, whatever might be the sect, was never refused.

Tho' I seldom attended any public worship, I had still an opinion of its propriety and of its utility when rightly conducted, and I regularly paid my annual subscription for the support of the only Presbyterian minister or meeting we had in Philadelphia. He used to visit me sometimes as a friend and admonish me to attend his administrations, and I was now and then prevailed on to do so, once for five Sundays successively. Had he been, *in my opinion*, a good preacher, perhaps I might have continued, notwithstanding the occasion I had for the Sunday's leisure in my course of study; but his discourses were chiefly either polemic arguments or explications of the peculiar doctrines of our sect, and were all to me very dry, uninteresting, and unedifying since not a single moral principle was inculcated or enforced, their aim seeming to be rather to make us Presbyterians than good citizens. At length he took for his text that verse of the fourth chapter of Philippians, "Finally, brethren, whatsoever things are true, honest, just, pure, lovely, or of good report, if there be any virtue, or any praise, think on these things"; and I imagined, in a sermon on such a text, we could not miss of having some morality. But he confined himself to five points only as meant by the apostle; viz., 1. Keeping holy the Sabbath day, 2. Being diligent in reading the Holy Scriptures, 3. Attending duly the public worship, 4. Partaking of the sacrament, 5. Paying a due respect to God's ministers. These might be all good things, but as they were not the kind of good things that I expected from that text, I despaired of ever meeting with them from any other, was disgusted, and attended his preaching no more. I had some years before composed a little liturgy or form of prayer for my own private use; viz., in 1728, entitled *Articles of Belief and Acts of Religion.* I returned to the use of this and went no more to the public assemblies. My conduct might be blamable, but I leave it without attempting further to excuse it, my present purpose being to relate facts and not to make apologies for them.

It was about this time I conceived the bold and arduous project of arriving at moral perfection. I wished to live without committing any fault at any time; I would conquer all that either natural inclination, custom, or company might lead me into. As I knew, or thought I knew, what was right and wrong, I did not see why I might not *always* do the one and avoid the other. But I soon found I had undertaken a task of more difficulty than I had imagined. While my attention was taken up and care employed in guarding against one fault, I was often surprized by another. Habit took the advantage of inattention. Inclination was sometimes too strong for reason. I concluded at length that the mere speculative conviction that it was our interest to be completely virtuous was not sufficient to prevent our slipping, and that the contrary habits must be broken and good ones acquired and established before we can have any dependence on a steady, uniform rectitude of conduct. For this purpose I therefore contrived the following method.

In the various enumerations of the moral virtues I had met with in my reading, I found the catalogue more or less numerous, as different writers included more or fewer ideas under the same name. Temperance, for example, was by some confined to eating and drinking, while by others it was extended to mean the moderating every other pleasure, appetite, inclination, or passion—bodily or mental, even to our avarice and ambition. I proposed to myself, for the sake of clearness, to use rather more names with fewer ideas annexed to each than a few names with more ideas; and I included under thirteen names of virtues all that at that time occurred to me as necessary or desirable, and annexed to each a short precept which fully expressed the extent I gave to its meaning.

These names of virtues with their precepts were

1. Temperance

Eat not to dulness. Drink not to elevation.

2. Silence

Speak not but what may benefit others or yourself. Avoid trifling conversation.

3. Order

Let all your things have their places. Let each part of your business have its time.

4. Resolution

Resolve to perform what you ought. Perform without fail what you resolve.

5. Frugality

Make no expence but to do good to others or yourself; i.e., waste nothing.

6. Industry

Lose no time. Be always employed in something useful. Cut off all unnecessary actions.

7. Sincerity

Use no hurtful deceit. Think innocently and justly; and, if you speak, speak accordingly.

8. Justice

Wrong none by doing injuries or omitting the benefits that are your duty.

9. Moderation

Avoid extremes. Forbear resenting injuries so much as you think they deserve.

10. Cleanliness

Tolerate no uncleanness in body, clothes or habitation.

11. Tranquillity

Be not disturbed at trifles or at accidents common or unavoidable.

12. Chastity

Rarely use venery but for health or offspring—never to dulness, weakness, or the injury of your own or another's peace or reputation.

13. Humility

Imitate Jesus and Socrates.

My intention being to acquire the *habitude* of all these virtues, I judged it would be well not to distract my attention by attempting the whole at once but to fix it on one of them at a time, and when I should be master of that, then to proceed to another, and so on till I should have gone thro' the thirteen. And as the previous acquisition of some might facilitate the acquisition of certain others, I arranged them with that view as they stand above. *Temperance* first, as it tends to procure that coolness and clearness of head which is so necessary where constant vigilance was to be kept up, and guard maintained, against the unremitting attraction of ancient habits, and the force of perpetual temptations. This being acquired and established, *Silence* would be more easy, and my desire being to gain knowledge at the same time that I improved in virtue, and considering that in conversation it was obtained rather by the use of the ear than of the tongue, and therefore wishing to break a habit I was getting into of prattling, punning, and joking, which only made me acceptable to trifling company, I gave *Silence* the second place. This and the next, *Order,* I expected would allow me more time for attending to my project and my studies. *Resolution,* once become habitual, would keep me firm in my endeavours to obtain all the subsequent virtues; *Frugality* and *Industry,* freeing me from my remaining debt and, producing affluence and independence, would make more easy the practice of *Sincerity* and *Justice,* etc., etc. Conceiving then that agreeable to the advice of Pythagoras in his golden verses, daily examination would be necessary, I contrived the following method for conducting that examination.

I made a little book in which I allotted a page for each of the virtues. I ruled each page with red ink so as to have seven columns, one for each day of the week, marking each column with a letter for the day. I crossed these columns with thirteen red lines, marking the beginning of each line with the first letter of one of the virtues, on which line and in its proper column I might mark by a little black spot every fault I found upon examination to have been committed respecting that virtue upon that day.

I determined to give a week's strict attention to each of the virtues successively. Thus in the first week my great guard was to avoid even the least offence against temperance, leaving the other virtues to their ordinary chance, only marking every evening the faults of the day. Thus if in the first week I could keep my first line marked "T." clear of spots, I supposed the habit of that virtue so much strengthened and its opposite weakened that I might venture extending my attention to include the next, and for the following week keep both lines clear of spots. Proceeding thus to the last, I could go thro' a course complete in thirteen weeks, and four courses in a year. And like him who, having a garden to weed, does not attempt to eradicate all the bad herbs at once, which would exceed his reach and his strength, but works on one of the beds at a time, and having accomplished the first, proceeds to a second; so I should have (I hoped) the encouraging pleasure of seeing on my pages the progress I made in virtue by clearing successively my lines of their spots, till in the end by a number of courses, I should be happy in viewing a clean book after a thirteen weeks' daily examination.

Thus my little book had for its motto these lines from Addison's *Cato;*

Here will I hold: if there is a power above us,
(And that there is, all Nature cries aloud
Thro' all her works) he must delight in virtue,
And that which he delights in must be happy.

Another from Cicero,

O vitae philosophia dux! O virtutum indagatrix, expultrixque vitiorum! Unus dies bene et ex preceptis tuis actus, peccanti immortalitati est anteponendus.

Another from the proverbs of Solomon speaking of wisdom or virtue;

Form of the Pages

TEMPERANCE

Eat not to dulness.
Drink not to elevation.

	S	M	T	W	T	F	S
T							
S	• •	•		•		•	
O	•	•	•		•	•	•
R			•			•	
F		•			•		
I			•				
S							
J							
M							
Cl.							
T							
Ch							
H							

Length of days is in her right hand, and in her left hand riches and honours; her ways are ways of pleasantness, and all her paths are peace (III, 16, 17).

And conceiving God to be the fountain of wisdom, I thought it right and necessary to solicit his assistance for obtaining it; to this end I formed the following little prayer, which was prefixed to my tables of examination, for daily use.

O powerful Goodness, bountiful Father, merciful Guide! Increase in me that wisdom which discovers my truest interests; strengthen my resolutions to perform what that wisdom dictates. Accept my kind offices to thy other children, as the only return in my power for thy continual favours to me.

I used also sometimes a little prayer which I took from Thomson's *Poems;* viz.,

Father of light and life, thou Good supreme,
Oh, teach me what is good, teach me thy self!
Save me from folly, vanity and vice,
From every low pursuit, and fill my soul
With knowledge, conscious peace, and virtue pure,
Sacred, substantial, never-fading bliss!

The precept of *Order* requiring that *every part of my business should have its allotted time,* one page in my little book contained the following scheme of employment for the twenty-four hours of a natural day.

I entered upon the execution of this plan for self-examination and continued it with occasional intermissions for some time. I was surprized to find myself so much fuller of faults than I had imagined, but I had the satisfaction of seeing them diminish. To avoid the trouble of renewing now and then my little book, which by scraping out the marks on the paper of old faults to make room for new ones in a new course became full of holes, I transferred my tables and precepts to the ivory leaves of a memorandum book on which the lines were drawn with red ink that made a durable stain, and on those lines I marked my faults with a black lead pencil, which marks I could easily wipe out with a wet sponge. After a while I went thro' one course only in a year, and afterwards only one in several years, till at length I omitted them entirely, being employed in voyages and business abroad with a multiplicity of affairs that interfered; but I always carried my little book with me. My scheme of *Order* gave me the most trouble, and I found that tho' it might be practicable where a man's business was such as to leave him the disposition of his time, that of a

The morning question, What good shall I do this day?	5	Rise, wash, and address *Powerful Goodness;* contrive day's business and take the resolution of the day; prosecute the present study; and breakfast.
	6	
	7	
	8	Work.
	9	
	10	
	11	
	12	Read or overlook my accounts, and dine.
	1	
	2	Work.
	3	
	4	
	5	
	6	Put things in their places, supper, music, or diversion, or conversation; examination of the day.
	7	
	8	
	9	
Evening question, What good have I done today?	10	Sleep.
	11	
	12	
	1	
	2	
	3	
	4	

journeyman printer for instance, it was not possible to be exactly observed by a master, who must mix with the world and often receive people of business at their own hours. Order, too, with regard to places for things, papers, etc., I found extremely difficult to acquire. I had not been early accustomed to *method,* and having an exceeding good memory, I was not so sensible of the inconvenience attending want of method. This article therefore cost me so much painful attention, and my faults in it vexed me so much, and I made so little progress in amendment and had such frequent relapses, that I was almost ready to give up the attempt and content myself with a faulty character in that respect. Like the man who in buying an ax of a smith my neighbour, desired to have the whole of its surface as bright as the edge; the smith consented to grind it bright for him if he would turn the wheel. He turned while the smith pressed the broad face of the ax hard and heavily on the stone, which made the turning of it very fatiguing. The man came every now and then from the wheel to see how the work went on; and at length would take his ax as it was, without further grinding. "No," says the smith, "turn on, turn on; we shall have it bright by and by; as yet 'tis only speckled." "Yes," says the man, *"but I think I like a speckled ax best."* And I believe this may have been the case with many who having, for want of some such means as I employed, found the difficulty of obtaining good and breaking bad habits in other points of vice and virtue, have given up the struggle and concluded that "a speckled ax was best." For something that pretended to be reason was every now and then suggesting to me that such extreme nicety as I exacted of myself might be a kind of foppery in morals, which if it were known would make me ridiculous; that a perfect character might be attended with the inconvenience of being envied and hated; and that a benevolent man should allow a few faults in himself, to keep his friends in countenance. In truth, I found myself incorrigible with respect to *Order;* and now I am old and my memory bad, I feel very sensibly the want of it. But on the whole, tho' I never arrived at the perfection I had been so ambitious of obtaining but fell far short of it, yet I was by the endeavour a better and a happier man than I otherwise should have been if I had not attempted it; as those who aim at perfect writing by imitating the engraved copies, tho' they never reach the wished-for excellence of those copies, their hand is mended by the endeavour and is tolerable while it continues fair and legible.

It may be well my posterity should be informed that to this little artifice, with the blessing of God, their ancestor owed the constant felicity of his life down to his seventy-ninth year, in which this is written. What reverses may attend the remainder is in the hand of providence; but if they arrive, the reflection on past happiness enjoyed ought to help his bearing them with more resignation. To *Temperance* he ascribes his long-continued health and what is still left to him of a good constitution; to *Industry* and *Frugality,* the early easiness of his circumstances and acquisition of his fortune with all that knowledge which enabled him to be an useful citizen and obtained for him some degree of reputation among the learned. To *Sincerity* and *Justice,* the confidence of his country and the honourable employs it conferred upon him; and to the joint influence of the whole mass of the virtues, even in the imperfect state he was able to acquire them, all that evenness of temper and that cheerfulness in conversation which makes his company still sought for and agreeable even to his younger acquaintance. I hope, therefore, that some of my descendants may follow the example and reap the benefit.

It will be remarked that, tho' my scheme was not wholly without religion, there was in it no mark of any of the distinguishing tenets of any particular sect. I had purposely avoided them; for being fully persuaded of the utility and excellency of my method, and that it might be serviceable to people in all religions, and intending sometime or other to publish it, I would not have anything in it that should prejudice anyone of any sect against it. I purposed writing a little comment on each virtue, in which I would have shown the advantages of possessing it and the mischiefs attending its opposite vice; I should have called my book *The Art of Virtue* because it would have shown the means and manner of obtaining virtue, which would have distinguished it from the mere exhortation to be good, that does not instruct and indicate the means, but is like the apostle's man of verbal charity, who only, without showing to the naked and hungry how or where they might get clothes or victuals, exhorted them to be fed and clothed (*James* II: 15, 16).

But it so happened that my intention of writing and publishing this comment was never fulfilled. I did, indeed, from time to time put down short hints of the sentiments, reasonings, etc., to be made use of in it, some of which I have still by me; but the necessary close attention to private business in the earlier part of life and public business since, have occasioned my postponing it. For it being connected in my mind with *a great and extensive project* that required the whole man to execute, and which an unforeseen succession of employs prevented my attending to, it has hitherto remained unfinished.

In this piece it was my design to explain and enforce this doctrine: That vicious actions are not hurtful because they are forbidden, but forbidden because they are hurtful, the nature of man alone considered; that it was therefore everyone's interest to be virtuous who wished to be happy even in this world. And I should from this circumstance, there being always in the world a number of rich merchants, nobility, states, and princes who have need of honest instruments for the management of their affairs, and such being so rare have endeavoured to convince young persons, that no qualities are so likely to make a poor man's fortune as those of probity and integrity.

My list of virtues contained at first but twelve. But a Quaker friend having kindly informed me that I was generally thought proud, that my pride showed itself frequently in conversation, that I was not content with being in the right when discussing any point, but was overbearing and rather insolent—of which he convinced me by mentioning several instances—I determined endeavouring to cure myself if I could of this vice or folly among the rest, and I added *Humility* to my list, giving an extensive meaning to the word. I cannot boast of much success in acquiring the *reality* of this virtue, but I had a good deal with regard to the *appearance* of it. I made it a rule to forbear all direct contradiction to the sentiments of others and all positive assertion of my own. I even forbade myself agreeable to the old laws of our Junto, the use of every word or expression in the language that imported a fixed opinion, such as "certainly," "undoubtedly," etc.; and I adopted instead of them, "I conceive," "I apprehend," or "I imagine" a thing to be so or so, or "It so appears to me at present." When another asserted something that I thought an error, I denied myself the pleasure of contradicting him abruptly and of showing immediately some absurdity in his proposition; and in answering I began by observing that in certain cases or circumstances his opinion would be right, but that in the present case there "appeared" or "seemed to me" some difference, etc. I soon found the advantage of this change in my manners: The conversations I engaged in went on more pleasantly; the modest way in which I proposed my opinions procured them a readier reception and less contradiction; I had less mortification when I was found to be in the wrong, and I more easily prevailed with others to give up their mistakes and join with me when I happened to be in the right. And this mode, which I at first put on with some violence to natural inclination, became at length so easy and so habitual to me that perhaps for these fifty years past no one has ever heard a dogmatical expression escape me. And to this habit (after my character of integrity) I think it principally owing that I had early so much weight with my fellow citizens when I proposed new institutions or alterations in the old, and so much influence in public councils when I became a member. For I was but a bad speaker, never eloquent, subject to much hesitation in my choice of words, hardly correct in language, and yet I generally carried my point.

In reality there is perhaps no one of our natural passions so hard to subdue as *pride:* disguise it, struggle with it, beat it down, stifle it, mortify it as much as one pleases, it is still alive and will every now and then peep out and show itself. You will see it perhaps often in this history. For even if I could conceive that I had completely overcome it, I should probably be proud of my humility.

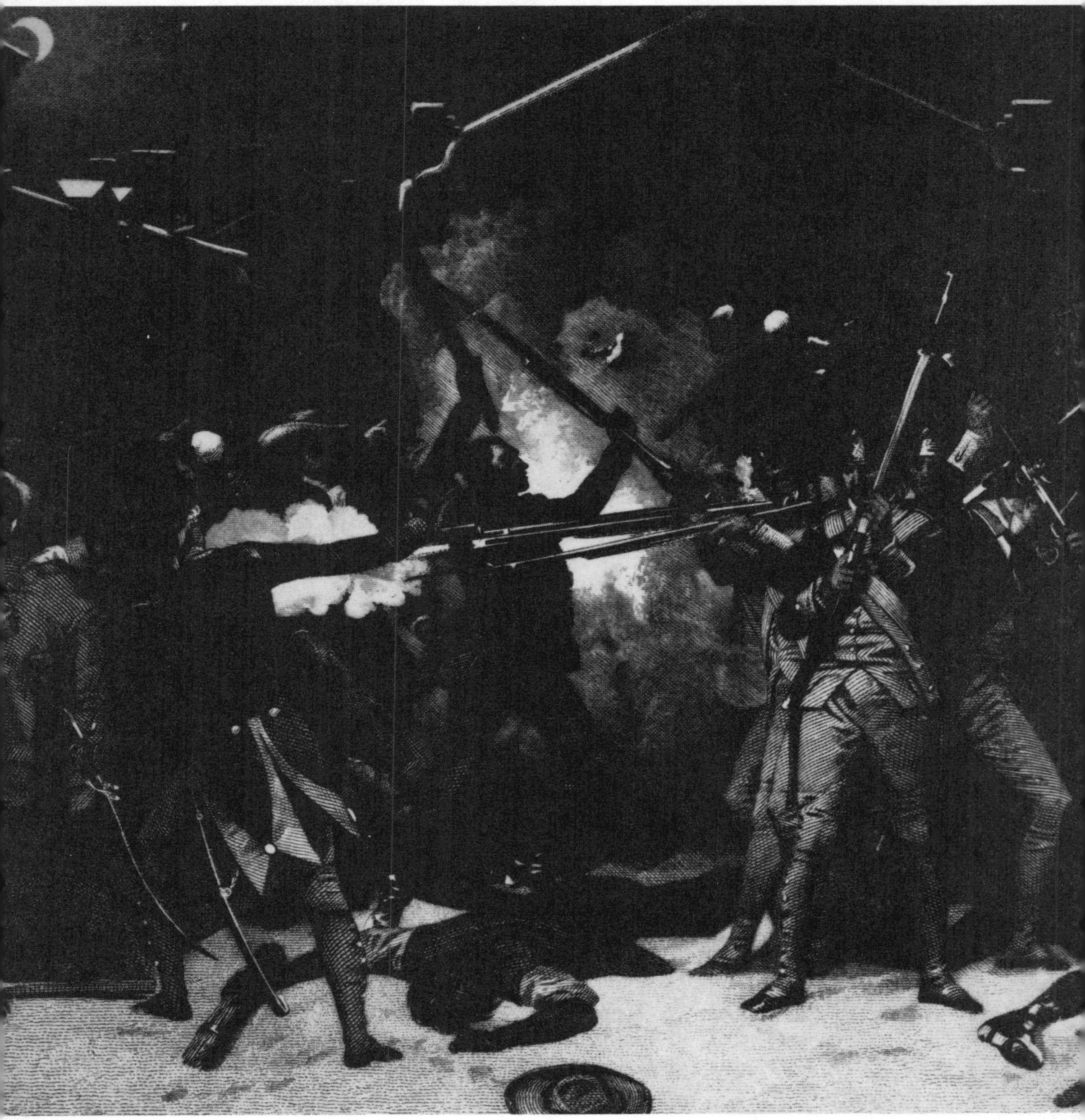

"Boston Massacre" by Alonzo Chappel

THOMAS PAINE

Common Sense

(1776)

Published anonymously in January 1776, Thomas Paine's Common Sense touched chords of public response that no other revolutionary pamphlet had reached. In a nation of some three million inhabitants, 300,000 copies of Paine's tract circulated in the later 1770s. This transplanted Englishman had written the American best-seller of his age, suggesting that only a fine line separated American and English culture. Paine, in fact, wrote from a tradition of English dissent which was a minor voice in England but the dominant note of American political rhetoric: the radical republican view of natural rights that considered every instance of executive power as a sign of "corruption" or "privilege." Earlier writers had limited their assaults to the king's ministers alone; but after coming to America, Paine felt free to attack monarchy outright. The example of this Englishman who denounced George III as a "royal brute" could only intoxicate Americans already in arms against the British government.

Paine's writing was of great immediate importance in the independence movement, but his thought also had wider ranging significance. His plain style and vigorous polemic offered a model of political writing for succeeding generations, and Paine became the fountainhead of the tradition of free thought in the United States. His later The Age of Reason scandalized John Adams, who called Paine a "transcendant libeller of all that is sacred." And finally, Paine's forthright isolationism offered the first full-scale argument that the American people could best prosper and be a model to the world by remaining as separate as possible from the nations of Europe.

Thoughts on the Present State of American Affairs

In the following pages I offer nothing more than simple facts, plain arguments, and common sense: and have no other preliminaries to settle with the reader, than that he will divest himself of prejudice and prepossession, and suffer his reason and his feelings to determine for themselves: that he will put on, or rather that he will not put off, the true character of a man, and generously enlarge his views beyond the present day.

Volumes have been written on the subject of the struggle between England and America. Men of all ranks have embarked in the controversy, from different motives, and with various designs; but all have been ineffectual, and the period of debate is closed. Arms as the last resource decide the contest; the appeal was the choice of the king, and the continent has accepted the challenge.

It hath been reported of the late Mr. Pelham (who though an able minister was not without his faults) that on his being attacked in the House of Commons on the score that his measures were only of a temporary kind, replied, *"they will last my time."* Should a thought so fatal and unmanly possess the colonies in the present contest, the name of ancestors will be remembered by future generations with detestation.

The sun never shone on a cause of greater worth. 'Tis not the affair of a city, a county, a province, or a kingdom; but of a continent—of at least one eighth part of the habitable globe. 'Tis not the concern of a day, a year, or an age; posterity are virtually involved in the contest, and will be more or less affected even to the end of time, by the proceedings now. Now is the seed-time of continental union, faith and honor. The least fracture now will be like a name engraved with the point of a pin on the tender rind of a young oak; the wound would enlarge with the tree, and posterity read it in full grown characters.

By referring the matter from argument to arms, a new era for politics is struck—a new method of thinkings has arisen. All plans, proposals, &c. prior to the nineteenth of April, *i.e.* to the commencement of hostilities, are like the almanacks of the last year; which though proper then, are superceded and useless now. Whatever was advanced by the advocates on either side of the question then, terminated in one and the same point, *viz.* a union with Great Britain; the only difference between the parties was the method of effecting it; the one proposing force, the other friendship; but it has so far happened that the first has failed, and the second has withdrawn her influence.

As much has been said of the advantages of reconciliation, which, like an agreeable dream, has passed away and left us as we were, it is but right that we should examine the contrary side of the argument, and inquire into some of the many material injuries which these colonies sustain, and always will sustain, by being connected with and dependant on Great Britain. To examine that connection and dependance, on the principles of nature and common sense, to see what we have to trust to, if separated, and what we are to expect, if dependant.

I have heard it asserted by some, that as America has flourished under her former connection with Great Britain, the same connection is necessary towards her future happiness, and will always have the same effect. Nothing can be more fallacious than this kind of argument. We may as well assert that because a child has thrived upon milk, that it is never to have meat, or that the first twenty years of our lives is to become a precedent for the next twenty. But even this is admitting more than is true; for I answer roundly, that America would have flourished as much, and probably much more, had no European power taken any notice of her. The commerce by which she hath enriched herself are the necessaries of life, and will always have a market while eating is the custom of Europe.

But she has protected us, say some. That she hath engrossed us is true, and defended the continent at our expense as well as her own, is admitted; and she would have defended Turkey from the same motive, *viz.* for the sake of trade and dominion.

Alas! we have been long led away by ancient prejudices and made large sacrifices to superstition. We have boasted the protection of Great Britain, without considering, that her motive was *interest* not *attachment;* and that she did not protect us from *our enemies* on *our account;* but from *her enemies* on *her own account,* from those who had no quarrel with us on any *other account,* and who will always be our enemies on the *same account.* Let Britain waive her pretensions to the continent, or the continent throw off the dependance, and we should be at peace with France and Spain, were they at war with Britain. The miseries of Hanover's last war ought to warn us against connections.

It hath lately been asserted in Parliament, that the colonies have no relation to each other but through the parent country, *i.e.* that Pennsylvania and the Jerseys, and so on for the rest, are sister colonies by the way of England; this is certainly a very roundabout way of proving relationship, but it is the nearest and only true way of proving enmity (or enemyship, if I may so call it). France and Spain never were, nor perhaps ever will be, our enemies as *Americans,* but as our being the *subjects of Great Britain.*

But Britain is the parent country, say some. Then the more shame upon her conduct. Even brutes do not devour their young, nor savages make war upon their families; wherefore, the assertion, if true, turns to her reproach; but it happens not to be true, or only partly so, and the phrase *parent* or *mother country* hath been jesuitically adopted by the king and his parasites, with a low papistical design of gaining an unfair bias on the credulous weakness of our minds. Europe, and not England, is the parent country of America. This new world hath been the asylum for the persecuted lovers of civil and religious liberty from *every part* of Europe. Hither have they fled, not from the tender embraces of the mother, but from the cruelty of the monster; and it is so far true of England, that the same tyranny which drove the first emigrants from home, pursues their descendants still.

In this extensive quarter of the globe, we forget the narrow limits of three hundred and sixty miles (the extent of England) and carry our friendship on a larger scale; we claim brotherhood with every European Christian, and triumph in the generosity of the sentiment.

It is pleasant to observe by what regular gradations we surmount the force of local prejudices, as we enlarge our acquaintance with the world. A man born in any town in England divided into parishes, will naturally associate most with his fellow parishioners (because their interests in many cases will be common) and distinguish him by the name of *neighbor;* if he meet him but a few miles from home, he drops the narrow idea of a street, and salutes him by the name of *townsman;* if he travel out of the county and meet him in any other, he forgets the minor divisions of street and town, and calls him *countryman, i.e. countyman;* but if in their foreign excursions they should associate in France, or any other part of *Europe,* their local remembrance would be enlarged into that of *Englishman.* And by a just parity of reasoning, all Europeans meeting in America, or any other quarter of the globe, are *countrymen;* for England, Holland, Germany, or Sweden, when compared with the whole, stand in the same places on the larger scale, which the divisions of street, town, and county do on the smaller ones; distinctions too limited for continental minds. Not one third of the inhabitants, even of this province, [Pennsylvania], are of English descent. Wherefore, I reprobate the phrase of parent or mother country applied to England only, as being false, selfish, narrow and ungenerous.

But, admitting that we were all of English descent, what does it amount to? Nothing. Britain, being now an open enemy, extinguishes every other name and title: and to say that reconciliation is our duty, is truly farcical. The first king of England, of the present line (William the Conqueror) was a Frenchman, and half the peers of England are descendants from the same country; wherefore, by the same method of reasoning, England ought to be governed by France.

Much hath been said of the united strength of Britain and the colonies, that in conjunction they might bid defiance to the world. But this is mere presumption; the fate of war is uncertain, neither do the expressions mean any thing; for this continent would never suffer itself to be drained of inhabitants, to support the British arms in either Asia, Africa or Europe.

Besides, what have we to do with setting the world at defiance? Our plan is commerce, and that, well attended to, will secure us the peace and friendship of all Europe; because it is the interest of all Europe to have America a free port. Her trade will always be a protection, and her barrenness of gold and silver secure her from invaders.

I challenge the warmest advocate for reconciliation to show a single advantage that this continent can reap by being connected with Great Britain. I repeat the challenge; not a single advantage is derived. Our corn will fetch its price in any market in Europe, and our imported goods must be paid for, buy them where we will.

But the injuries and disadvantages which we sustain by that connection, are without number; and our duty to mankind at large, as well as to ourselves, instruct us to renounce the alliance: because, any submission to, or dependence on, Great Britain, tends directly to involve this continent in European wars and quarrels, and set us at variance with nations who would otherwise seek our friendship, and against whom we have neither anger nor complaint. As Europe is our market for trade, we ought to form no partial connection with any part of it. It is the true interest of America to steer clear of European contentions, which she never can do, while, by her dependence on Britain, she is made the makeweight in the scale of British politics.

Europe is too thickly planted with kingdoms to be long at peace, and whenever a war breaks out between England and any foreign power, the trade of America goes to ruin, *because of her connection with Britain*. The next war may not turn out like the last, and should it not, the advocates for reconciliation now will be wishing for separation then, because neutrality in that case would be a safer convoy than a man of war. Every thing that is right or reasonable pleads for separation. The blood of the slain, the weeping voice of nature cries, 'TIS TIME TO PART. Even the distance at which the Almighty hath placed England and America is a strong and natural proof that the authority of the one over the other, was never the design of heaven. The time likewise at which the continent was discovered, adds weight to the argument, and the manner in which it was peopled, encreases the force of it. The Reformation was preceded by the discovery of America: As if the Almighty graciously meant to open a sanctuary to the persecuted in future years, when home should afford neither friendship nor safety.

The authority of Great Britain over this continent, is a form of government, which sooner or later must have an end. And a serious mind can draw no true pleasure by looking forward, under the painful and positive conviction that what he calls "the present constitution" is merely temporary. As parents, we can have no joy, knowing that this government is not sufficiently lasting to insure any thing which we may bequeath to posterity. And by a plain method of argument, as we are running the next generation into debt, we ought to do the work of it, otherwise we use them meanly and pitifully. In order to discover the line of our duty rightly, we should take our children in our hand, and fix our station a few years farther into life; that eminence will present a prospect which a few present fears and prejudices conceal from our sight.

Though I would carefully avoid giving unnecessary offence, yet I am inclined to believe, that all those who espouse the doctrine of reconciliation, may be included within the following descriptions.

Interested men, who are not to be trusted, weak men who *cannot* see, prejudiced men who will not see, and a certain set of moderate men who think better of the European world than it deserves; and this last class, by an ill-judged deliberation, will be the cause of more calamities to this continent than all the other three.

It is the good fortune of many to live distant from the scene of present sorrow; the evil is not sufficiently brought to their doors to make them feel the precariousness with which all American property is possessed. But let our imaginations transport us a few moments to Boston; that seat of wretchedness will teach us wisdom, and instruct us for ever to renounce a power in whom we can have no trust. The inhabitants of that unfortunate city who but a few months ago were in ease and affluence, have now no other alternative than to stay and starve, or turn out to beg. Endangered by the fire of their friends if they continue within the city, and plundered by the soldiery if they leave it, in their present situation they are prisoners without the hope of redemption, and in a general attack for their relief they would be exposed to the fury of both armies.

Men of passive tempers look somewhat lightly over the offences of Great Britain, and, still hoping for the best, are apt to call out, *Come, come, we shall be friends again for all this.* But examine the passions and feelings of mankind: bring the doctrine of reconciliation to the touchstone of nature, and then tell me whether you can hereafter love, honor, and faithfully serve the power that hath carried fire and sword into your land? If you cannot do all these, then are you only deceiving yourselves, and by your delay bringing ruin upon posterity. Your future connection with Britain, whom you can neither love nor honor, will be forced and unnatural, and being formed only on the plan of present convenience, will in a little time fall into a relapse more wretched than the first. But if you say, you can still pass the violations over, then I ask, hath your house been burnt? Hath your property been destroyed before your face? Are your wife and children destitute of a bed to lie on, or bread to live on? Have you lost a parent or a child by their hands, and yourself the ruined and wretched survivor? If you have not, then are you not a judge of those who have. But if you have, and can still shake hands with the murderers, then are you unworthy the name of husband, father, friend, or lover, and whatever may be your rank or title in life, you have the heart of a coward, and the spirit of a sycophant.

This is not inflaming or exaggerating matters, but trying them by those feelings and affections which nature justifies, and without which we should be incapable of discharging the social duties of life, or enjoying the felicities of it. I mean not to exhibit horror for the purpose of provoking revenge, but to awaken us from fatal and unmanly slumbers, that we may pursue determinately some fixed object. 'Tis not in the power of Britain or of Europe to conquer America, if she doth not conquer herself by delay and timidity. The present winter is worth an age if rightly employed, but if lost or neglected the whole continent will partake of the misfortune; and there is no punishment which that man doth not deserve, be he who, or what, or where he will, that may be the means of sacrificing a season so precious and useful.

'Tis repugnant to reason, to the universal order of things, to all examples from former ages, to suppose that this continent can long remain subject to any external power. The most sanguine in Britain doth not think so. The utmost stretch of human wisdom cannot, at this time, compass a plan, short of separation, which can promise the continent even a year's security. Reconciliation is *now* a fallacious dream. Nature has deserted the connection, and art cannot supply her place. For, as Milton wisely expresses, "never can true reconcilement grow where wounds of deadly hate have pierced so deep."

Every quiet method for peace hath been ineffectual. Our prayers have been rejected with disdain; and hath tended to convince us that nothing flatters vanity or confirms obstinacy in kings more than repeated petitioning—and nothing hath contributed more than that very measure to make the kings of Europe absolute. Witness Denmark and Sweden. Wherefore, since nothing but blows will do, for God's sake let us come to a final separation, and not leave the next generation to be cutting throats under the violated unmeaning names of parent and child.

To say they will never attempt it again is idle and visionary; we thought so at the repeal of the Stamp Act, yet a year or two undeceived us; as well may we suppose that nations which have been once defeated will never renew the quarrel.

As to government matters, 'tis not in the power of Britain to do this continent justice: the business of it will soon be too weighty and intricate to be managed with any tolerable degree of convenience, by a power so distant from us, and so very ignorant of us; for if they cannot conquer us, they cannot govern us. To be always running three or four thousand miles with a tale or a petition, waiting four or five months for an answer, which, when obtained, requires five or six more to explain it in, will in a few years be looked upon as folly and childishness. There was a time when it was proper, and there is a proper time for it to cease.

Small islands not capable of protecting themselves are the proper objects for government to take under their care; but there is something absurd, in supposing a Continent to be perpetually governed by an island. In no instance hath nature made the satellite larger than its primary planet; and as England and America, with respect to each other, reverse the common order of nature, it is evident that they belong to different systems. England to Europe: America to itself.

I am not induced by motives of pride, party or resentment to espouse the doctrine of separation and independence; I am clearly, positively, and conscientiously persuaded that it is the true interest of this continent to be so; that everything short of *that* is mere patchwork, that it can afford no lasting felicity,—that it is leaving the sword to our children, and shrinking back at a time when a little more, a little further, would have rendered this continent the glory of the earth.

As Britain hath not manifested the least inclination towards a compromise, we may be assured that no terms can be obtained worthy the acceptance of the continent, or any ways equal to the expence of blood and treasure we have been already put to.

The object contended for, ought always to bear some just proportion to the expence. The removal of North, or the whole detestable junto, is a matter unworthy the millions we have expended. A temporary stoppage of trade was an inconvenience, which would have sufficiently balanced the repeal of all the acts complained of, had such repeals been obtained; but if the whole continent must take up arms, if every man must be a soldier, 'tis scarcely worth our while to fight against a contemptible ministry only. Dearly, dearly do we pay for the repeal of the acts, if that is all we fight for; for, in a just estimation 'tis as great a folly to pay a Bunker Hill price for law as for land. As I have always considered the independency of this continent, as an event which sooner or later must arrive, so from the late rapid progress of the continent to maturity, the event cannot be far off. Wherefore, on the breaking out of hostilities, it was not worth the while to have disputed a matter which time would have finally redressed, unless we meant to be in earnest: otherwise it is like wasting an estate on a suit at law, to regulate the trespasses of a tenant whose lease is just expiring. No man was a warmer wisher for a reconciliation than myself, before the fatal nineteenth of April, 1775, but the moment the event of that day was made known, I rejected the hardened, sullen-tempered Pharaoh of England for ever; and disdain the wretch, that with the pretended title of FATHER OF HIS PEOPLE can unfeelingly hear of their slaughter, and composedly sleep with their blood upon his soul.

But admitting that matters were now made up, what would be the event? I answer, the ruin of the continent. And that for several reasons.

First. The powers of governing still remaining in the hands of the king, he will have a negative over the whole legislation of this continent. And as he hath shown himself such an inveterate enemy to liberty, and discovered such a thirst for arbitrary power, is he, or is he not, a proper person to say to these colonies, *You shall make no laws but what I please!?* And is there any inhabitant of America so ignorant as not to know, that according to what is called the *present Constitution,* this continent can make no laws but what the king gives leave to; and is there any man so unwise as not to see, that (considering what has happened) he will suffer no law to be made here but such as suits *his* purpose? We may be as effectually enslaved by the want of laws in America, as by submitting to laws made for us in England. After matters are made up (as it is called) can there be any doubt, but the whole power of the crown will be exerted to keep this continent as low and humble as possible? Instead of going forward we shall go backward, or be perpetually quarrelling, or ridiculously petitioning. We are already greater than the king wishes us to be, and will he not hereafter endeavor to make us less? To bring the matter to one point, Is the power who is jealous of our prosperity, a proper power to govern us? Whoever says *No,* to this question, is an independent for independency means no more than this, whether we shall make our own laws, or, whether the king, the greatest enemy this continent hath, or can have, shall tell us *there shall be no laws but such as I like.*

But the king, you will say, has a negative in England; the people there can make no laws without his consent. In point of right and good order, it is something very ridiculous that a youth of twenty-one (which hath often happened) shall say to several millions of people older and wiser than himself, "I forbid this or that act of yours to be law." But in this place I decline this sort of reply, though I will never cease to expose the absurdity of it, and only answer that England being the king's residence, and America not so, makes quite another case. The king's negative here is ten times more dangerous and fatal than it can be in England; for there he will scarcely refuse his consent to a bill for putting England into as strong a state of defense as possible, and in America he would never suffer such a bill to be passed.

America is only a secondary object in the system of British politics. England consults the good of this country no further than it answers her own purpose. Wherefore, her own interest leads her to suppress the growth of ours in every case which doth not promote her advantage, or in the least interferes with it. A pretty state we should soon be in under such a second hand government, considering what has happened! Men do not change from enemies to friends by the alteration of a name: And in order to show that reconciliation now is a dangerous doctrine, I affirm, *that it would be policy in the king at this time to repeal the acts, for the sake of reinstating himself in the government of the provinces;* In order that HE MAY ACCOMPLISH BY CRAFT AND SUBTLETY, IN THE LONG RUN, WHAT HE CANNOT DO BY FORCE AND VIOLENCE IN THE SHORT ONE. Reconciliation and ruin are nearly related.

Secondly. That as even the best terms which we can expect to obtain can amount to no more than a temporary expedient, or a kind of government by guardianship, which can last no longer than till the colonies come of age, so the general face and state of things in the interim will be unsettled and unpromising. Emigrants of property will not choose to come to a country whose form of government hangs but by a thread, and who is every day tottering on the brink of commotion and disturbance; and numbers of the present inhabitants would lay hold of the interval to dispose of their effects, and quit the continent.

But the most powerful of all arguments is, that nothing but independence, *i.e.* a continental form of government, can keep the peace of the continent and preserve it inviolate from civil wars. I dread the event of a reconciliation with Britain now, as it is more than probable that it will be followed by a revolt some where or other, the consequences of which may be far more fatal than all the malice of Britain.

Thousands are already ruined by British barbarity; (thousands more will probably suffer the same fate). Those men have other feelings than us who have nothing suffered. All they now possess is liberty; what they before enjoyed is sacrificed to its service, and having nothing more to lose they disdain submission. Besides, the general temper of the colonies, towards a British government will be like that of a youth who is nearly out of his time; they will care very little about her: And a government which cannot preserve the peace is no government at all, and in that case we pay our money for nothing; and pray what is it that Britain can do, whose power will be wholly on paper, should a civil tumult break out the very day after reconciliation? I have heard some men say, many of whom I believe spoke without thinking, that they dreaded an independence, fearing that it would produce civil wars: It is but seldom that our first thoughts are truly correct, and that is the case here; for there is ten times more to dread from a patched up connection than from independence. I make the sufferer's case my own, and I protest, that were I driven from house and home, my property destroyed, and my circumstances ruined, that as a man, sensible of injuries, I could never relish the doctrine of reconciliation, or consider myself bound thereby.

The colonies have manifested such a spirit of good order and obedience to continental government, as is sufficient to make every reasonable person easy and happy on that head. No man can assign the least pretence for his fears, on any other grounds, than such as are truly childish and ridiculous, *viz.*, that one colony will be striving for superiority over another.

Where there are no distinctions there can be no superiority; perfect equality affords no temptation. The Republics of Europe are all (and we may say always) in peace. Holland and Switzerland are without wars, foreign or domestic: Monarchical governments, it is true, are never long at rest: the crown itself is a temptation to enterprising ruffians at home; and that degree of pride and insolence ever attendant on regal authority, swells into a rupture with foreign powers in instances where a republican government, by being formed on more natural principles, would negociate the mistake.

* * *

But where, say some, is the king of America? I'll tell you, friend, he reigns above, and doth not make havoc of mankind like the royal brute of Great Britain. Yet that we may not appear to be defective even in earthly honors, let a day be solemnly set apart for proclaiming the charter; let it be brought forth placed on the divine law, the Word of God; let a crown be placed thereon, by which the world may know, that so far as we approve of monarchy, that in America the law is king. For as in absolute governments the king is law, so in free countries the law ought to be king; and there ought to be no other. But lest any ill use should afterwards arise, let the crown at the conclusion of the ceremony be demolished, and scattered among the people whose right it is.

A prosperous American farm of the late 1700's

HECTOR ST. JEAN de CRÈVECOEUR

What is an American?

(1782)

Crèvecoeur's Letters From An American Farmer, which appeared in 1782, was perhaps the most persuasive social portrait of eighteenth-century America. Popular both here and in Europe, it fixed an ideal picture that nearly two centuries later remains close to what Americans want their nation to be. Virtually all the themes since developed of what is American receive expression in Crèvecoeur's clear prose: land of opportunity and sturdy, independent, prosperous farmers; melting pot; refuge from the decadence and class-ridden society of Europe; simple republic; government of laws. Such is the society which, in Crèvecoeur's vision, makes "the American, this new man."

Crèvecoeur was in a position to know. Born in France, he had served his crown in the wars of mid-century, exploring the lands about the Great Lakes and down into Ohio. After years of travel, he settled in New York, received citizenship, married an American girl, and became the American farmer of his book's title, working land in Orange County, New York. There he viewed with admiration the society about him, looked realistically at the frontiers beyond, and came to his classically optimistic view of the American experiment.

Yet all is not so clean and simple as Crèvecoeur's brisk Enlightenment style makes it appear. This celebrator of America was a Tory in the Revolution, served the French government in the 1780s, and in 1790 returned to his native country to close out his life. Neither the first nor the last to find the land easier to sing than to settle, Crèvecoeur reveals in places the doubts that his grand conclusions sweep over: the violence and degeneracy of the frontier; the arrogance and imbalance of men suddenly freed from limited lives; the uneasy awareness that some immigrants melt into the American environment better than others. The reader must judge what in Crèvecoeur's portrait of America describes the scene he witnessed, what expresses the aspirations of his neighbors, and what assumptions he shared with other Enlightenment thinkers.

I wish I could be acquainted with the feelings and thoughts which must agitate the heart and present themselves to the mind of an enlightened Englishman, when he first lands on this continent. He must greatly rejoice that he lived at a time to see this fair country discovered and settled; he must necessarily feel a share of national pride, when he views the chain of settlements which embellishes these extended shores. When he says to himself, this is the work of my countrymen, who, when convulsed by factions, afflicted by a variety of miseries and wants, restless and impatient, took refuge here. They brought along with them their national genius, to which they principally owe what liberty they enjoy, and what substance they possess. Here he sees the industry of his native country displayed in a new manner, and traces in their works the embrios of all the arts, sciences, and ingenuity which flourish in Europe. Here he beholds fair cities, substantial villages, extensive fields, an immense country filled with decent houses, good roads, orchards, meadows, and bridges, where an hundred years ago all was wild, woody and uncultivated! What a train of pleasing ideas this fair spectacle must suggest; it is a prospect which must inspire a good citizen with the most heartfelt pleasure. The difficulty consists in the manner of viewing so extensive a scene. He is arrived on a new continent; a modern society offers itself to his contemplation, different from what he had hitherto seen. It is not composed, as in Europe, of great lords who possess every thing, and of a herd of people who have nothing. Here are no aristocratical families, no courts, no kings, no bishops, no ecclesiastical dominion, no invisible power giving to a few a very visible one; no great manufacturers employing thousands, no great refinements of luxury. The rich and the poor are not so far removed from each other as they are in Europe. Some few towns excepted, we are all tillers of the earth, from Nova Scotia to West Florida. We are a people of cultivators, scattered over an immense territory, communicating with each other by means of good roads and navigable rivers, united by the silken bands of mild government, all respecting the laws, without dreading their power, because they are equitable. We are all animated with the spirit of an industry which is unfettered and unrestrained, because each person works for himself. If he travels through our rural districts he views not the hostile castle, and the haughty mansion, contrasted with the clay-built hut and miserable cabbin, where cattle and men help to keep each other warm, and dwell in meanness, smoke, and indigence. A pleasing uniformity of decent competence appears throughout our habitations. The meanest of our log-houses is a dry and comfortable habitation. Lawyer or merchant are the fairest titles our towns afford; that of a farmer is the only appellation of the rural inhabitants of our country. It must take some time ere he can reconcile himself to our dictionary, which is but short in words of dignity, and names of honour. There, on a Sunday, he sees a congregation of respectable farmers and their wives, all clad in neat homespun, well mounted, or riding in their own humble waggons. There is not among them an esquire, saving the unlettered magistrate. There he sees a parson as simple as his flock, a farmer who does not riot on the labour of others. We have no princes, for whom we toil, starve, and bleed: we are the most perfect society now existing in the world. Here man is free as he ought to be; nor is this pleasing equality so transitory as many others are. Many ages will not see the shores of our great lakes replenished with inland nations, nor the unknown bounds of North America entirely peopled. Who can tell how far it extends? Who can tell the millions of men whom it will feed and contain? for no European foot has as yet travelled half the extent of this mighty continent!

The next wish of this traveller will be to know whence came all these people? they are a mixture of English, Scotch, Irish, French, Dutch, Germans, and Swedes. From this promiscuous breed, that race now called Americans have arisen. The eastern provinces must indeed be excepted, as being the unmixed descendents of Englishmen. I have heard many wish that they had been more intermixed also: for my part, I am no wisher, and think it much better as it has happened. They exhibit a most conspicuous figure in this great and variegated picture; they too enter for a great share in the pleasing perspective displayed in these thirteen provinces. I know it is fashionable to reflect on them, but I respect them for what they have done; for the accuracy and wisdom with which they have settled their territory; for the decency of their manners; for their early love of letters; their ancient college, the first in this hemisphere; for their industry; which to me who am but a farmer, is the criterion of everything. There never was a people, situated as they are, who with so ungrateful a soil have done more in so short a time. Do you think that the monarchical ingredients which are more prevalent in other governments, have purged them from all foul stains? Their histories assert the contrary.

In this great American asylum, the poor of Europe have by some means met together, and in consequence of various causes; to what purpose should they ask one another what countrymen they are? Alas, two thirds of them had no country. Can a wretch who wanders about, who works and starves, whose life is a continual scene of sore affliction or pinching penury; can that man call England or any other kingdom his country? A country that had no bread for him, whose fields procured him no harvest, who met with nothing but the frowns of the rich, the severity of the laws, with jails and punishments; who owned not a single foot of the extensive surface of this planet? No! urged by a variety of motives, here they came. Every thing has tended to regenerate them; new laws, a new mode of living, a new social system; here they are become men: in Europe they were as so many useless plants, wanting vegetative mould, and refreshing showers; they withered, and were mowed down by want, hunger, and war;

but now by the power of transplantation, like all other plants they have taken root and flourished! Formerly they were not numbered in any civil lists of their country, except in those of the poor; here they rank as citizens. By what invisible power has this surprising metamorphosis been performed? By that of the laws and that of their industry. The laws, the indulgent laws, protect them as they arrive, stamping on them the symbol of adoption; they receive ample rewards for their labours; these accumulated rewards procure them lands; those lands confer on them the title of freemen, and to that title every benefit is affixed which men can possibly require. This is the great operation daily performed by our laws. From whence proceed these laws? From our government. Whence the government? It is derived from the original genius and strong desire of the people ratified and confirmed by the crown. This is the great chain which links us all, this is the picture which every province exhibits, Nova Scotia excepted. There the crown has done all; either there were no people who had genius, or it was not much attended to: the consequence is, that the province is very thinly inhabited indeed; the power of the crown in conjunction with the musketos has prevented men from settling there. Yet some parts of it flourished once, and it contained a mild harmless set of people. But for the fault of a few leaders, the whole were banished. The greatest political error the crown ever committed in America, was to cut off men from a country which wanted nothing but men!

What attachment can a poor European emigrant have for a country where he had nothing? The knowledge of the language, the love of a few kindred as poor as himself, were the only cords that tied him: his country is now that which gives him land, bread, protection, and consequence: *Ubi panis ibi patria,* is the motto of all emigrants. What then is the American, this new man? He is either an European, or the descendant of an European, hence that strange mixture of blood, which you will find in no other country. I could point out to you a family whose grandfather was an Englishman, whose wife was Dutch, whose son married a French woman, and whose present four sons have now four wives of different nations. *He* is an American, who leaving behind him all his ancient prejudices and manners, receives new ones from the new mode of life he has embraced, the new government he obeys, and the new rank he holds. He becomes an American by being received in the broad lap of our great *Alma Mater*. Here individuals of all nations are melted into a new race of men, whose labours and posterity will one day cause great changes in the world. Americans are the western pilgrims, who are carrying along with them that great mass of arts, sciences, vigour, and industry which began long since in the east; they will finish the great circle. The Americans were once scattered all over Europe; here they are incorporated into one of the finest systems of population which has ever appeared, and which will hereafter become distinct by the power of the different climates they inhabit. The American ought therefore to love this country much better than that wherein either he or his forefathers were born. Here the rewards of his industry follow with equal steps the progress of his labour; his labour is founded on the basis of nature, *self-interest;* can it want a stronger allurement? Wives and children, who before in vain demanded of him a morsel of bread, now, fat and frolicsome, gladly help their father to clear those fields whence exuberant crops are to arise to feed and to clothe them all; without any part being claimed, either by a despotic prince, a rich abbot, or a mighty lord. Here religion demands but little of him; a small voluntary salary to the minister, and gratitude to God; can he refuse these? The American is a new man, who acts upon new principles; he must therefore entertain new ideas, and form new opinions. From involuntary idleness, servile dependence, penury, and useless labour, he has passed to toils of a very different nature, rewarded by ample subsistence.—This is an American.

British America is divided into many provinces, forming a large association, scattered along a coast 1500 miles extent and about 200 wide. This society I would fain examine, at least such as it appears in the middle provinces; if it does not afford that variety of tinges and gradations which may be observed in Europe, we have colours peculiar to ourselves. For instance, it is natural to conceive that those who live near the sea, must be very different from those who live in the woods; the intermediate space will afford a separate and distinct class.

Men are like plants; the goodness and flavour of the fruit proceeds from the peculiar soil and exposition in which they grow. We are nothing but what we derive from the air we breathe, the climate we inhabit, the government we obey, the system of religion we profess, and the nature of our employment. Here you will find but few crimes; these have acquired as yet no root among us. I wish I were able to trace all my ideas; if my ignorance prevents me from describing them properly, I hope I shall be able to delineate a few of the outlines, which are all I propose.

Those who live near the sea, feed more on fish than on flesh, and often encounter that boisterous element. This renders them more bold and enterprising; this leads them to neglect the confined occupations of the land. They see and converse with a variety of people; their intercourse with mankind becomes extensive. The sea inspires them with a love of traffic, a desire of transporting produce from one place to another; and leads them to a variety of resources which supply the place of labour. Those who inhabit the middle settlements, by far the most numerous, must be very different; the simple cultivation of the earth purifies them, but the indulgences of the government, the soft remonstrances of religion, the rank of independent freeholders, must necessarily inspire them with sentiments, very little known in Europe among people of the same class. What do I say? Europe has no such class of men; the early knowledge they acquire, the early bargains they make, give them a great degree of sagacity. As freemen they will be litigious; pride and obstinacy are often the cause of law suits; the nature of our laws and governments may be another. As citizens it is easy to imagine, that they will carefully read the newspapers, enter into every political disquisition, freely blame or censure governors and others. As farmers they will be careful and anxious to get as much as they can, because what they get is their own. As northern men they will love the chearful cup. As Christians, religion curbs them not in their opinions; the general indulgence leaves every one to think for themselves in spiritual matters; the laws inspect our actions, our thoughts are left to God. Industry, good living, selfishness, litigiousness, country politics, the pride of freemen, religious indifference, are their characteristics. If you recede still farther from the sea, you will come into more modern settlements; they exhibit the same strong lineaments, in a ruder appearance. Religion seems to have still less influence, and their manners are less improved.

Now we arrive near the great woods, near the last inhabited districts; there men seem to be placed still farther beyond the reach of government, which in some measure leaves them to themselves. How can it pervade every corner; as they were driven there by misfortunes, necessity of beginnings, desire of acquiring large tracks of land, idleness, frequent want of economy, ancient debts; the re-union of such people does not afford a very pleasing spectacle. When discord, want of unity and friendship; when either drunkenness or idleness prevail in such remote districts; contention, inactivity, and wretchedness must ensue. There are not the same remedies to these evils as in a long established community. The few magistrates they have, are in general little better than the rest; they are often in a perfect state of war; that of man against man, sometimes decided by blows, sometimes by means of the law; that of man against every wild inhabitant of these venerable woods, of which they are come to dispossess them. There men appear to be no better than carnivorous animals of a superior rank, living on the flesh of wild animals when they can catch them, and when they are not able, they subsist on grain. He who would wish to see America in its proper light, and have a true idea of its feeble beginnings and barbarous rudiments, must visit our extended line of frontiers where the last settlers dwell, and where he may see the first labours of settlement, the mode of clearing the earth, in all their different appearances; where men are wholly left dependent on their native tempers, and on the spur of uncertain industry, which often fails when not sanctified by the efficacy of a few moral rules. There, remote from the power of example, and check of shame, many families exhibit the most hideous parts of our society. They are a kind of forlorn hope, preceding by ten or twelve years the most respectable army of veterans which come after them. In that space, prosperity will polish some, vice and the law will drive off the rest, who uniting again with others like themselves will recede still farther; making room for more industrious people, who will finish their improvements, convert the loghouse into a convenient habitation, and rejoicing that the first heavy labours are finished, will change in a few years that hitherto barbarous country into a fine fertile, well regulated district. Such is our progress, such is the march of the Europeans toward the interior parts of this continent. In all societies there are off-casts; this impure part serves as our precursors or pioneers; my father himself was one of that class, but he came upon honest principles, and was therefore one of the few who held fast; by good conduct and temperance, he transmitted to me his fair inheritance, when not above one in fourteen of his contemporaries had the same good fortune.

Forty years ago this smiling country was thus inhabited; it is now purged, a general decency of manners prevails throughout, and such has been the fate of our best countries.

Exclusive of those general characteristics, each province has its own, founded on the government, climate, mode of husbandry, customs, and peculiarity of circumstances. Europeans submit insensibly to these great powers, and become, in the course of a few generations, not only Americans in general, but either Pennsylvanians, Virginians, or provincials under some other name. Whoever traverses the continent must easily observe those strong differences, which will grow more evident in time. The inhabitants of Canada, Massachuset, the middle provinces, the southern ones will be as different as their climates; their only points of unity will be those of religion and language.

As I have endeavoured to shew you how Europeans become Americans; it may not be disagreeable to shew you likewise how the various Christian sects introduced, wear out, and how religious indifference becomes prevalent. When any considerable number of a particular sect happen to dwell contiguous to each other, they immediately erect a temple, and there worship the Divinity agreeably to their own peculiar ideas. Nobody disturbs them. If any new sect springs up in Europe, it may happen that many of its professors will come and settle in America. As they bring their zeal with them, they are at liberty to make proselytes if they can, and to build a meeting and to follow the dictates of their consciences; for neither the government nor any other power interferes. If they are peaceable subjects, and are industrious, what is it to their neighbours how and in what manner they think fit to address their prayers to the Supreme Being? But if the sectaries are not settled close together, if they are mixed with other denominations, their zeal will cool for want of fuel, and will be extinguished in a little time. Then the Americans become as to religion, what they are as to country, allied to all. In them the name of Englishman, Frenchman, and European is lost, and in like manner, the strict modes of Christianity as practised in Europe are lost also.

This effect will extend itself still farther hereafter, and though this may appear to you as a strange idea, yet it is a very true one. I shall be able perhaps hereafter to explain myself better, in the meanwhile, let the following example serve as my first justification.

Let us suppose you and I to be travelling; we observe that in this house, to the right, lives a Catholic, who prays to God as he has been taught, and believes in transubstantiation; he works and raises wheat, he has a large family of children, all hale and robust; his belief, his prayers offend nobody. About one mile farther on the same road, his next neighbour may be a good honest plodding German Lutheran, who addresses himself to the same God, the God of all, agreeably to the modes he has been educated in, and believes in consubstantiation; by so doing he scandalizes nobody; he also works in his fields, embellishes the earth, clears swamps, &c. What has the world to do with his Lutheran principles? He persecutes nobody, and nobody persecutes him, he visits his neighbours, and his neighbours visit him. Next to him lives a seceder, the most enthusiastic of all sectaries; his zeal is hot and fiery, but separated as he is from others of the same complexion, he has no congregation of his own to resort to, where he might cabal and mingle religious pride with worldly obstinacy. He likewise raises good crops, his house is handsomely painted, his orchard is one of the fairest in the neighbourhood. How does it concern the welfare of the country, or of the province at large, what this man's religious sentiments are, or really whether he has any at all? He is a good farmer, he is a sober, peaceable, good citizen: William Penn himself would not wish for more. This is the visible character, the invisible one is only guessed at, and is nobody's business. Next again lives a Low Dutchman, who implicitly believes the rules laid down by the synod of Dort. He conceives no other idea of a clergyman than that of an hired man; if he does his work well he will pay him the stipulated sum; if not he will dismiss him, and do without his sermons, and let his church be shut up for years. But notwithstanding this coarse idea, you will find his house and farm to be the neatest in all the country; and you will judge by his waggon and fat horses, that he thinks more of the affairs of this world than of those of the next. He is sober and laborious, therefore he is all he ought to be as to the affairs of this life; as for those of the next, he must trust to the great Creator. Each of these people instruct their children as well as they can, but these instructions are feeble compared to those which are given to the youth of the poorest class in Europe. Their children will therefore grow up less zealous and more indifferent in matters of religion than their parents. The foolish vanity, or rather the fury of making Proselytes, is unknown here; they have no time, the seasons call for all their attention, and thus in a few years, this mixed neighbourhood will exhibit a strange religious medley, that will be neither pure Catholicism nor pure Calvinism. A very perceptible indifference even in the first generation, will become apparent; and it may happen that the daughter of the Catholic will marry the son of the seceder, and settle by themselves at a distance from their parents. What religious education will they give their children? A very imperfect one. If there happens to be in the neighbourhood any place of worship, we will suppose a Quaker's meeting; rather than not shew their fine clothes, they will go to it, and some of them may perhaps attach themselves to that society. Others will remain in a perfect state of indifference; the children of these zealous parents will not be able to tell what their religious principles are, and their grandchildren still less. The neighbourhood of a place of worship generally leads them to it, and the action of going thither, is the strongest evidence they can give of their attachment to any sect. The Quakers are the only people who retain a fondness for their own mode of worship; for be they ever so far separated from each other, they hold a sort of communion with the society, and seldom depart from its rules, at least in this country. Thus all sects are mixed as well as all nations; thus religious indifference is imperceptibly disseminated from one end of the continent to the other; which is at present one of the strongest characteristics of the Americans. Where this will reach no one can tell, perhaps it may leave a vacuum fit to receive other systems. Persecution, religious pride, the love of contradiction, are the food of what the world commonly calls religion. These motives have ceased here: zeal in Europe is confined; here it evaporates in the great distance it has to travel; there it is a grain of powder inclosed, here it burns away in the open air, and consumes without effect.

But to return to our back-settlers. I must tell you, that there is something in the proximity of the woods, which is very singular. It is with men as it is with the plants and animals that grow and live in the forests; they are entirely different from those that live in the plains. I will candidly tell you all my thoughts but you are not to expect that I shall advance any reasons. By living in or near the woods, their actions are regulated by the wildness of the neighbourhood. The deer often come to eat their grain, the wolves to destroy their sheep, the bears to kill their hogs, the foxes to catch their poultry. This surrounding hostility, immediately puts the gun into their hands; they watch these animals, they kill some; and thus by defending their property, they soon become professed hunters; this is the progress; once hunters, farewell to the plough. The chase renders them ferocious, gloomy, and unsociable; a hunter wants no neighbour, he rather hates them, because he dreads the competition. In a little time their success in the woods makes them neglect their tillage. They trust to the natural fecundity of the earth, and therefore do little; carelessness in fencing, often exposes what little they sow to destruction; they are not at home to watch; in order therefore to make up the deficiency, they go oftener to the woods. That new mode of life brings along with it a new set of manners, which I cannot easily describe.

These new manners being grafted on the old stock, produce a strange sort of lawless profligacy, the impressions of which are indelible. The manners of the Indian natives are respectable, compared with this European medley. Their wives and children live in sloth and inactivity; and having no proper pursuits, you may judge what education the latter receive. Their tender minds have nothing else to contemplate but the example of their parents; like them they grow up a mongrel breed, half civilized, half savage, except nature stamps on them some constitutional propensities. That rich, that voluptuous sentiment is gone that struck them so forcibly; the possession of their freeholds no longer conveys to their minds the same pleasure and pride. To all these reasons you must add, their lonely situation, and you cannot imagine what an effect on manners the great distances they live from each other has! Consider one of the last settlements in its first view: of what is it composed? Europeans who have not that sufficient share of knowledge they ought to have, in order to prosper; people who have suddenly passed from oppression, dread of government, and fear of laws, into the unlimited freedom of the woods. This sudden change must have a very great effect on most men, and on that class particularly. Eating of wild meat, whatever you may think, tends to alter their temper: though all the proof I can adduce, is, that I have seen it: and having no place of worship to resort to, what little society this might afford, is denied them. The Sunday meetings, exclusive of religious benefits, were the only social bonds that might have inspired them with some degree of emulation in neatness. Is it then surprising to see men thus situated, immersed in great and heavy labours, degenerate a little? It is rather a wonder the effect is not more diffusive. The Moravians and the Quakers are the only instances in exception to what I have advanced. The first never settle singly, it is a colony of the society which emigrates; they carry with them their forms, worship, rules, and decency: the others never begin so hard, they are always able to buy improvements, in which there is a great advantage, for by that time the country is recovered from its first barbarity. Thus our bad people are those who are half cultivators and half hunters; and the worst of them are those who have degenerated altogether into the hunting state. As old ploughmen and new men of the woods, as Europeans and new made Indians, they contract the vices of both; they adopt the moroseness and ferocity of a native, without his mildness, or even his industry at home. If manners are not refined, at least they are rendered simple and inoffensive by tilling the earth; all our wants are supplied by it, our time is divided between labour and rest, and leaves none for the commission of great misdeeds. As hunters it is divided between the toil of the chase, the idleness of repose, or the indulgence of inebriation. Hunting is but a licentious idle life, and if it does not always pervert good dispositions; yet, when it is united with bad luck, it leads to want: want stimulates that propensity to rapacity and injustice, too natural to needy men, which is the fatal gradation. After this explanation of the effects which follow by living in the woods, shall we yet vainly flatter ourselves with the hope of converting the Indians? We should rather begin with converting our back-settlers; and now if I dare mention the name of religion, its sweet accents would be lost in the immensity of these woods. Men thus placed, are not fit either to receive or remember its mild instructions; they want temples and ministers, but as soon as men cease to remain at home, and begin to lead an erratic life, let them be either tawny or white, they cease to be its disciples.

Thus have I faintly and imperfectly endeavoured to trace our society from the sea to our woods! yet you must not imagine that every person who moves back, acts upon the same principles, or falls into the same degeneracy. Many families carry with them all their decency of conduct, purity of morals, and respect of religion; but these are scarce, the power of example is sometimes irresistible. Even among these back-settlers, their depravity is greater or less, according to what nation or province they belong. Were I to adduce proofs of this, I might be accused of partiality. If there happens to be some rich intervals, some fertile bottoms, in those remote districts, the people will there prefer tilling the land to hunting, and will attach themselves to it; but even on these fertile spots you may plainly perceive the inhabitants to acquire a great degree of rusticity and selfishness.

It is in consequence of this straggling situation, and the astonishing power it has on manners, that the back-settlers of both the Carolinas, Virginia, and many other parts, have been long a set of lawless people; it has been even dangerous to travel among them. Government can do nothing in so extensive a country, better it should wink at these irregularities, than that it should use means inconsistent with its usual mildness. Time will efface those stains: in proportion as the great body of population approaches them they will reform, and become polished and subordinate. Whatever has been said of the four New-England provinces, no such degeneracy of manners has ever tarnished their annals; their back-settlers have been kept within the bounds of decency, and government, by means of wise laws, and by the influence of religion. What a detestable idea such people must have given to the natives of the Europeans! They trade with them, the worst of people are permitted to do that which none but persons of the best characters should be employed in. They get drunk with them, and often defraud the Indians. Their avarice, removed from the eyes of their superiors, knows no bounds; and aided by a little superiority of knowledge, these traders deceive them, and even sometimes shed blood. Hence those shocking violations, those sudden devastations which have so often stained our frontiers, when hundreds of innocent people have been sacrificed for the crimes of a few. It was in consequence of such behaviour, that the Indians took the hatchet against the Virginians in 1774. Thus are our first steps trod, thus are our first trees felled, in general, by the most vicious of our people; and thus the path is opened for the arrival of a second and better class, the true American freeholders; the most respectable set of people in this part of the world: respectable for their industry, their happy independence, the great share of freedom they possess, the good regulation of their families, and for extending the trade and the dominion of our mother country.

Europe contains hardly any other distinctions but lords and tenants; this fair country alone is settled by freeholders, the possessors of the soil they cultivate, members of the government they obey, and the framers of their own laws, by means of their representatives. This is a thought which you have taught me to cherish; our difference from Europe, far from diminishing, rather adds to our usefulness and consequence as men and subjects. Had our forefathers remained there, they would only have crouded it, and perhaps prolonged those convulsions which had shook it so long. Every industrious European who transports himself here, may be compared to a sprout growing at the foot of a great tree; it enjoys and draws but a little portion of sap; wrench it from the parent roots, transplant it, and it will become a tree bearing fruit also. Colonists are therefore entitled to the consideration due to the most useful subjects; a hundred families barely existing in some parts of Scotland, will here in six years, cause an annual exportation of 10,000 bushels of wheat: 100 bushels being but a common quantity for an industrious family to sell, if they cultivate good land. It is here then that the idle may be employed, the useless become useful, and the poor become rich; but by riches I do not mean gold and silver, we have but little of those metals; I mean a better sort of wealth, cleared lands, cattle, good houses, good cloaths, and an increase of people to enjoy them.

There is no wonder that this country has so many charms, and presents to Europeans so many temptations to remain in it. A traveller in Europe becomes a stranger as soon as he quits his own kingdom; but it is otherwise here. We know, properly speaking, no strangers; this is every person's country; the variety of our soils, situations, climates, governments, and produce, hath something which must please every body. No sooner does an European arrive, no matter of what condition, than his eyes are opened upon the fair prospect; he hears his language spoke, he retraces many of his own country manners, he perpetually hears the names of families and towns with which he is acquainted; he sees happiness and prosperity in all places disseminated; he meets with hospitality, kindness, and plenty every where; he beholds hardly any poor, he seldom hears of punishments and executions; and he wonders at the elegance of our towns, those miracles of industry and freedom. He cannot admire enough our rural districts, our convenient roads, good taverns, and our many accommodations; he involuntarily loves a country where every thing is so lovely. When in England, he was a mere Englishman; here he stands on a larger portion of the globe, not less than its fourth part, and may see the productions of the north, in iron and naval stores; the provisions of Ireland, the grain of Egypt, the indigo, the rice of China. He does not find, as in Europe, a crouded society, where every place is over-stocked; he does not feel that perpetual collision of parties, that difficulty of beginning, that contention which oversets so many. There is room for every body in America; has he any particular talent, or industry? he exerts it in order to procure a livelihood, and it succeeds. Is he a merchant? the avenues of trade are infinite; is he eminent in any respect? he will be employed and respected. Does he love a country life? pleasant farms present themselves; he may purchase what he wants, and thereby become an American farmer. Is he a labourer, sober and industrious? he need not go many miles, nor receive many informations before he will be hired, well fed at the table of his employer, and paid four or five times more than he can get in Europe. Does he want uncultivated lands? thousands of acres present themselves, which he may purchase cheap. Whatever be his talents or inclinations, if they are moderate, he may satisfy them. I do not mean that every one who comes will grow rich in a little time; no, but he may procure an easy, decent maintenance, by his industry. Instead of starving he will be fed, instead of being idle he will have employment; and these are riches enough for such men as come over here. The rich stay in Europe, it is only the middling and the poor that emigrate. Would you wish to travel in independent idleness, from north to south, you will find easy access, and the most chearful reception at every house; society without ostentation, good cheer without pride, and every decent diversion which the country affords, with little expence. It is no wonder that the European who has lived here a few years, is desirous to remain; Europe with all its pomp, is not to be compared to this continent, for men of middle stations, or labourers.

An European, when he first arrives, seems limited in his intentions, as well as in his views; but he very suddenly alters his scale; two hundred miles formerly appeared a very great distance, it is now but a trifle; he no sooner breathes our air than he forms schemes, and embarks in designs he never would have thought of in his own country. There the plenitude of society confines many useful ideas, and often extinguishes the most laudable schemes which here ripen into maturity. Thus Europeans become Americans.

But how is this accomplished in that croud of low, indigent people, who flock here every year from all parts of Europe? I will tell you; they no sooner arrive than they immediately feel the good effects of that plenty of provisions we possess: they fare on our best food, and are kindly entertained; their talents, character, and peculiar industry are immediately inquired into; they find countrymen every where disseminated, let them come from whatever part of Europe. Let me select one as an epitome of the rest; he is hired, he goes to work, and works moderately; instead of being employed by a haughty person, he finds himself with his equal, placed at the substantial table of the farmer, or else at an inferior one as good; his wages are high, his bed is not like that bed of sorrow on which he used to lie: if he behaves with propriety, and is faithful, he is caressed, and becomes as it were a member of the family. He begins to feel the effects of a sort of resurrection; hitherto he had not lived, but simply vegetated; he now feels himself a man, because he is treated as such; the laws of his own country had overlooked him in his insignificancy; the laws of this cover him with their mantle. Judge what an alteration there must arise in the mind and thoughts of this man; he begins to forget his former servitude and dependence, his heart involuntarily swells and glows; this first swell inspires him with those new thoughts which constitute an American. What love can he entertain for a country where his existence was a burthen to him; if he is a generous good man, the love of this new adoptive parent will sink deep into his heart. He looks around, and sees many a prosperous person, who but a few years before was as poor as himself. This encourages him much, he begins to form some little scheme, the first, alas, he ever formed in his life. If he is wise he thus spends two or three years, in which time he acquires knowledge, the use of tools, the modes of working the lands, felling trees, &c. This prepares the foundation of a good name, the most useful acquisition he can make. He is encouraged, he has gained friends; he is advised and directed, he feels bold, he purchases some land; he gives all the money he has brought over, as well as what he has earned, and trusts to the God of harvests for the discharge of the rest. His good name procures him credit. He is now possessed of the deed, conveying to him and his posterity the fee simple and absolute property of two hundred acres of land, situated on such a river. What an epocha in this man's life! He is become a freeholder, from perhaps a German boor—he is now an American, a Pennsylvanian, an English subject. He is naturalized, his name is enrolled with those of the other citizens of the province. Instead of being a vagrant, he has a place of residence; he is called the inhabitant of such a county, or of such a district, and for the first time in his life counts for something; for hitherto he has been a cypher. I only repeat what I have heard many say, and no wonder their hearts should glow, and be agitated with a multitude of feelings, not easy to describe. From nothing to start into being; from a servant to the rank of a master; from being the slave of some despotic prince, to become a free man, invested with lands, to which every municipal blessing is annexed! What a change indeed! It is in consequence of that change that he becomes an American. This great metamorphosis has a double effect, it extinguishes all his European prejudices, he forgets that mechanism of subordination, that servility of disposition which poverty had taught him; and sometimes he is apt to forget too much, often passing from one extreme to the other. If he is a good man, he forms schemes of future prosperity, he proposes to educate his children better than he has been educated himself; he thinks of future modes of conduct, feels an ardor to labour he never felt before. Pride steps in and leads him to every thing that the laws do not forbid: he respects them; with a heartfelt gratitude he looks toward the east, toward that insular government from whose wisdom all his new felicity is derived, and under whose wings and protection he now lives. These reflections constitute him the good man and the good subject. Ye poor Europeans, ye, who sweat, and work for the great—ye, who are obliged to give so many sheaves to the church, so many to your lords, so many to your government, and have hardly any left for yourselves—ye, who are held in less estimation than favourite hunters or useless lap-dogs—ye, who only breathe the air of nature, because it cannot be withheld from you; it is here that ye can conceive the possibility of those feelings I have been describing; it is here the laws of naturalization invite every one to partake of our great labours and felicity, to till unrented, untaxed lands! Many, corrupted beyond the power of amendment, have brought with them all their vices, and disregarding the advantages held to them, have gone on in their former career of iniquity, until they have been overtaken and punished by our laws. It is not every emigrant who succeeds; no, it is only the sober, the honest, and industrious: happy those to whom this transition has served as a powerful spur to labour, to prosperity, and to the good establishment of children, born in the days of their poverty; and who had no other portion to expect but the rags of their parents, had it not been for their happy emigration. Others again, have been led astray by this enchanting scene; their new pride, instead of leading them to the fields, has kept them in idleness; the idea of possessing lands is all that satisfies them—though surrounded with fertility, they have mouldered away their time in inactivity, misinformed husbandry, and ineffectual endeavours. How much wiser, in general, the honest Germans than almost all other Europeans; they hire themselves to some of their wealthy landsmen, and in that apprenticeship learn every thing that is necessary. They attentively consider the prosperous industry of others, which imprints in their minds a strong desire of possessing the same advantages. This forcible idea never quits them, they launch forth, and by dint of sobriety, rigid parsimony, and the most persevering industry, they commonly succeed. Their astonishment at their first arrival from Germany is very great—it is to them a dream; the contrast must be powerful indeed; they observe their countrymen flourishing in every place; they travel through whole counties where not a word of English is spoken; and in the names and the language of the people, they retrace Germany. They have been an useful acquisition to this continent, and to Pennsylvania in particular; to them it owes some share of its prosperity: to their mechanical knowledge and patience, it owes the finest mills in all America, the best teams of horses, and many other advantages. The recollection of their former poverty and slavery never quits them as long as they live.

The Scotch and the Irish might have lived in their own country perhaps as poor, but enjoying more civil advantages, the effects of their new situation do not strike them so forcibly, nor has it so lasting an effect. From whence the difference arises I know not, but out of twelve families of emigrants of each country, generally seven Scotch will succeed, nine German, and four Irish. The Scotch are frugal and laborious, but their wives cannot work so hard as German women, who on the contrary vie with their husbands, and often share with them the most severe toils of the field, which they understand better. They have therefore nothing to struggle against, but the common casualties of nature. The Irish do not prosper so well; they love to drink and to quarrel; they are litigious, and soon take to the gun, which is the ruin of every thing; they seem beside to labour under a greater degree of ignorance in husbandry than the others; perhaps it is that their industry had less scope, and was less exercised at home. I have heard many relate, how the land was parcelled out in that kingdom; their ancient conquest has been a great detriment to them, by over-setting their landed property. The lands possessed by a few, are leased down *ad infinitum,* and the occupiers often pay five guineas an acre. The poor are worse lodged there than any where else in Europe; their potatoes, which are easily raised, are perhaps an inducement to laziness: their wages are too low and their whisky too cheap.

There is no tracing observations of this kind, without making at the same time very great allowances, as there are every where to be found, a great many exceptions. The Irish themselves, from different parts of that kingdom, are very different. It is difficult to account for this surprising locality, one would think on so small an island an Irishman must be an Irishman: yet it is not so, they are different in their aptitude to, and in their love of labour.

The Scotch on the contrary are all industrious and saving; they want nothing more than a field to exert themselves in, and they are commonly sure of succeeding. The only difficulty they labour under is, that technical American knowledge which requires some time to obtain; it is not easy for those who seldom saw a tree, to conceive how it is to be felled, cut up, and split into rails and posts.

As I am fond of seeing and talking of prosperous families, I intend to finish this letter by relating to you the history of an honest Scotch Hebridean, who came here in 1774, which will shew you in epitome, what the Scotch can do, wherever they have room for the exertion of their industry. Whenever I hear of any new settlement, I pay it a visit once or twice a year, on purpose to observe the different steps each settler takes, the gradual improvements, the different tempers of each family, on which their prosperity in a great nature depends; their different modifications of industry, their ingenuity, and contrivance; for being all poor, their life requires sagacity and prudence. In an evening I love to hear them tell their stories, they furnish me with new ideas; I sit still and listen to their ancient misfortunes, observing in many of them a strong degree of gratitude to God, and the government. Many a well meant sermon have I preached to some of them. When I found laziness and inattention to prevail, who could refrain from wishing well to these new countrymen; after having undergone so many fatigues. Who could withhold good advice? What a happy change it must be, to descend from the high, sterile, bleak lands of Scotland, where every thing is barren and cold, to rest on some fertile farms in these middle provinces! Such a transition must have afforded the most pleasing satisfaction.

The following dialogue passed at an out-settlement, where I lately paid a visit:

Well, friend, how do you do now; I am come fifty odd miles on purpose to see you; how do you go on with your new cutting and slashing? Very well, good Sir, we learn the use of the axe bravely, we shall make it out; we have a belly full of victuals every day, our cows run about, and come home full of milk, our hogs get fat of themselves in the woods: Oh, this is a good country! God bless the king, and William Penn; we shall do very well by and by, if we keep our healths. Your loghouse looks neat and light, where did you get these shingles? One of our neighbours is a New-England man, and he shewed us how to split them out of chestnut-trees. Now for a barn, but all in good time, here are fine trees to build with. Who is to frame it, sure you don't understand that work yet? A country-man of ours who has been in America these ten years, offers to wait for his money until the second crop is lodged in it. What did you give for your land? Thirty-five shillings per acre, payable in seven years. How many acres have you got? An hundred and fifty. That is enough to begin with; is not your land pretty hard to clear? Yes, Sir, hard enough, but it would be harder still if it was ready cleared, for then we should have no timber, and I love the woods much; the land is nothing without them. Have not you found out any bees yet? No, Sir; and if we had we should not know what to do with them. I will tell you by and by. You are very kind. Farewell, honest man, God prosper you; whenever you travel toward **, enquire for J. S. he will entertain you kindly, provided you bring him good tidings from your family and farm. In this manner I often visit them, and carefully examine their houses, their modes of ingenuity, their different ways; and make them all relate all they know, and describe all they feel. These are scenes which I believe you would willingly share with me. I well remember your philanthropic turn of mind. Is it not better to contemplate under these humble roofs, the rudiments of future wealth and population, than to behold the accumulated bundles of litigious papers in the office of a lawyer? To examine how the world is gradually settled, how the howling swamp is converted into a pleasing meadow, the rough ridge into a fine field; and to hear the chearful whistling, the rural song, where there was no sound heard before, save the yell of the savage, the screech of the owl, or the hissing of the snake? Here an European, fatigued with luxury, riches, and pleasures, may find a sweet relaxation in a series of interesting scenes, as affecting as they are new. England, which now contains so many domes, so many castles, was once like this; a place woody and marshy; its inhabitants, now the favourite nation for arts and commerce, were once painted like our neighbours. The country will flourish in its turn, and the same observations will be made which I have just delineated. Posterity will look back with avidity and pleasure, to trace, if possible, the æra of this or that particular settlement.

Pray, what is the reason that the Scots are in general more religious, more faithful, more honest, and industrious than the Irish? I do not mean to insinuate national reflections, God forbid! It ill becomes any man, and much less an American; but as I know men are nothing of themselves, and that they owe all their different modifications either to government or other local circumstances, there must be some powerful causes which constitute this great national difference.

Agreeable to the account which severale Scotchmen have given me of the north of Britain, of the Orkneys, and the Hebride Islands, they seem, on many accounts, to be unfit for the habitation of men; they appear to be calculated only for great sheep pastures. Who then can blame the inhabitants of these countries for transporting themselves hither? This great continent must in time absorb the poorest part of Europe; and this will happen in proportion as it becomes better known; and as war, taxation, oppression, and misery increase there. The Hebrides appear to be fit only for the residence of malefactors, and it would be much better to send felons there than either to Virginia or Maryland. What a strange compliment has our mother country paid to two of the finest provinces in America! England has entertained in that respect very mistaken ideas; what was intended as a punishment, is become the good fortune of several; many of those who have been transported as felons, are now rich, and strangers to the stings of those wants that urged them to violations of the law: they are become industrious, exemplary, and useful citizens. The English government should purchase the most northern and barren of those islands; it should send over to us the honest, primitive Hebrideans, settle them here on good lands, as a reward for their virtue and ancient poverty; and replace them with a colony of her wicked sons. The severity of the climate, the inclemency of the seasons, the sterility of the soil, the tempestuousness of the sea, would afflict and punish enough. Could there be found a spot better adapted to retaliate the injury it had received by their crimes? Some of those islands might be considered as the hell of Great Britain, where all evil spirits should be sent. Two essential ends would be answered by this simple operation. The good people, by emigration, would be rendered happier; the bad ones would be placed where they ought to be. In a few years the dread of being sent to that wintry region would have a much stronger effect, than that of transportation.—This is no place of punishment; were I a poor hopeless, breadless Englishman, and not restrained by the power of shame, I should be very thankful for the passage. It is of very little importance how, and in what manner an indigent man arrives; for if he is but sober, honest, and industrious, he has nothing more to ask of heaven. Let him go to work, he will have opportunities enough to earn a comfortable support, and even the means of procuring some land; which ought to be the utmost wish of every person who has health and hands to work. I knew a man who came to this country, in the literal sense of the expression, stark naked; I think he was a Frenchman, and a sailor on board an English man of war. Being discontented, he had stripped himself and swam ashore; where finding clothes and friends, he settled afterwards at Maraneck, in the county of Chester, in the province of New-York: he married and left a good farm to each of his sons. I knew another person who was but twelve years old when he was taken on the frontiers of Canada, by the Indians; at his arrival at Albany he was purchased by a gentleman, who generously bound him apprentice to a taylor. He lived to the age of ninety, and left behind him a fine estate and a numerous family, all well settled; many of them I am acquainted with.—Where is then the industrious European who ought to despair?

After a foreigner from any part of Europe is arrived, and become a citizen; let him devoutly listen to the voice of our great parent, which says to him, "Welcome to my shores, distressed European; bless the hour in which thou didst see my verdant fields, my fair navigable rivers, and my green mountains!—If thou wilt work, I have bread for thee; if thou wilt be honest, sober, and industrious, I have greater rewards to confer on thee—ease and independence. I will give thee fields to feed and cloath thee; a comfortable fire-side to sit by, and tell thy children by what means thou hast prospered; and a decent bed to repose on. I shall endow thee beside with the immunities of a freeman. If thou wilt carefully educate thy children, teach them gratitude to God, and reverence to that government, that philanthropic government, which has collected here so many men and made them happy. I will also provide for thy progeny; and to every good man this ought to be the most holy, the most powerful, the most earnest wish he can possibly form, as well as the most consolatory prospect when he dies. Go thou and work and till; thou shalt prosper, provided thou be just, grateful and industrious."

View of the Natural Bridge in Virginia

THOMAS JEFFERSON

Notes on the State of Virginia

(1785)

In addition to all his other accomplishments, Thomas Jefferson was one of the great prose stylists in American history. The glittering phrases of the Declaration of Independence and the first Inaugural Address, the brilliant arguments with John Adams in their famous correspondence, the many state papers and letters—all etch a personality and literary mind as sharply as do the novels of Nathaniel Hawthorne or the poetry of Robert Frost. Had Jefferson somehow failed to become President, we would still in all likelihood have a thriving industry of scholars studying his life and thought, and editing and annotating his writings.

Although the writings of Jefferson have filled some fifty volumes, Notes on the State of Virginia is the only full-length book that Jefferson wrote and published. The title is too modest: Jefferson is defending the entire Anglo-American civilization — of which he is a part — as well as the natural environment of the New World. Anti-American theories such as those of the Count de Buffon argued that the New World was an inferior environment to that of Europe, producing smaller, less developed animal species and degrading the Europeans who settled there. Jefferson carefully analyzes the natural history of Virginia, defends the virtues of the Native Americans as well as of the European-based civilization forming in the United States, and presents a picture of evolving social institutions which clearly aims at establishing not just America's parity with but its superiority to European life and customs. The Notes set forth the vision of an "Empire for Liberty" based on democratic institutions, public education, religious toleration, intellectual enlightenment, and an agrarian economy which has since been closely identified with Jefferson. The argument of the Notes gains peculiar power from its detail and its matter-of-fact scientific tone. The reader readily infers the unstated contrasts drawn between Europe and America: ignorance, superstition, despotism, and the decadence of cities are no model for the new republic. The nation has a separate destiny from that of Europe. It also has problems of its own: the one deeply disturbing connection to an older world has little to do with European civilization. It is the link with Africa that torments Jefferson, that raises questions for his theories of human nature, that poses social problems he cannot solve. That Jeffersonianism, one of the great philosophies of liberty in human history, was founded on slavery — an institution Jefferson abhored — is a paradox. That it was also founded on racism is more than a paradox: it is the central tragedy of American history.

On American Animals

The opinion advanced by the Count de Buffon, is 1. That the animals common both to the old and new world, are smaller in the latter. 2. That those peculiar to the new, are on a smaller scale. 3. That those which have been domesticated in both, have degenerated in America: and 4. That on the whole it exhibits fewer species. And the reason he thinks is, that the heats of America are less; that more waters are spread over its surface by nature, and fewer of these drained off by the hand of man. In other words, that *heat* is friendly, and *moisture* adverse to the production and developement of large quadrupeds. I will not meet this hypothesis on its first doubtful ground, whether the climate of America be comparatively more humid? Because we are not furnished with observations sufficient to decide this question. And though, till it be decided, we are as free to deny, as others are to affirm the fact, yet for a moment let it be supposed. The hypothesis, after this supposition, proceeds to another; that *moisture* is unfriendly to animal growth. The truth of this is inscrutable to us by reasonings a priori. Nature has hidden from us her modus agendi. Our only appeal on such questions is to experience; and I think that experience is against the supposition. It is by the assistance of *heat* and *moisture* that vegetables are elaborated from the elements of earth, air, water, and fire. We accordingly see the more humid climates produce the greater quantity of vegetables. Vegetables are mediately or immediately the food of every animal: and in proportion to the quantity of food, we see animals not only multiplied in their numbers, but improved in their bulk, as far as the laws of their nature will admit. Of this opinion is the Count de Buffon himself in another part of his work: "in general it seems that somewhat cold countries are better suited to our oxen than hot countries, and they are the heavier and bigger in proportion as the climate is damper and more abounding in pasture lands. The oxen of Denmark, of Podolie, of the Ukraine, and of Tartary which is inhabited by the Calmouques, are the largest of all." Here then a race of animals, and one of the largest too, has been increased in its dimensions by *cold* and *moisture,* in direct opposition to the hypothesis, which supposes that these two circumstances diminish animal bulk, and that it is their contraries *heat* and *dryness* which enlarge it. But when we appeal to experience, we are not to rest satisfied with a single fact. Let us therefore try our question on more general ground. Let us take two portions of the earth, Europe and America for instance, sufficiently extensive to give operation to general causes; let us consider the circumstances peculiar to each, and observe their effect on animal nature. America, running through the torrid as well as temperate zone, has more *heat,* collectively taken, than Europe. But Europe, according to our hypothesis, is the *dryest.* They are equally adapted then to animal productions; each being endowed with one of those causes which befriend animal growth, and with one which opposes it. If it be thought unequal to compare Europe with America, which is so much larger, I answer, not more so than to compare America with the whole world. Besides, the purpose of the comparison is to try an hypothesis, which makes the size of animals depend on the *heat* and *moisture* of climate. If therefore we take a region, so extensive as to comprehend a sensible distinction of climate, and so extensive too as that local accidents, or the intercourse of animals on its borders, may not materially affect the size of those in its interior parts, we shall comply with those conditions which the hypothesis may reasonably demand. The objection would be the weaker in the present case, because any intercourse of animals which may take place on the confines of Europe and Asia, is to the advantage of the former, Asia producing certainly larger animals than Europe.

* * *

He tells us too that on examining a bear from America, he remarked no difference "in the *shape* of this American bear compared with that of Europe." But adds from Bartram's journal, that an American bear weighed 400 lb. English, equal to 367 lb. French: whereas we find the European bear examined by Mons. D'Aubenton weighed but 141 lb. French. Kalm tells us that the Moose, (Orignal) or (palmated Elk) of America, is as high as a tall horse; and Catesby, that it is about the bigness of a middle sized ox. (I have seen a skeleton 7 feet high, and from good information believe they are often considerably higher. The Elk of Europe is not two-thirds of his height). The wesel is larger in America than in Europe, as may be seen by comparing its dimensions as reported by Mons. D'Aubenton and Kalm. The latter tells us, that the lynx, badger, red fox, and flying squirrel, are the *same* in America as in Europe: by which expression I understand, they are the same in all material circumstances, in size as well as others: for if they were smaller, they would differ from the European. Our grey fox is, by Catesby's account, little different in size and shape from the European fox. I presume he means the red fox of Europe, as does Kalm, where he says, that in size "they do not quite come up to our foxes." For proceeding next to the red fox of America, he says "they are entirely the same with the European sort." Which shews he had in view one European sort only, which was the red. So that the result of their testimony is, that the American grey fox is somewhat less than the European red; which is equally true of the grey fox of Europe, as may be seen by comparing the measures of the Count de Buffon and Mons. D'Aubenton. The white bear of America is as large as that of Europe. The bones of the Mammoth which have been found in America, are as large as those found in the old world. It may be asked, why I insert the Mammoth, as if it still existed? I ask in return, why I should omit it, as if it did not exist? Such is the œconomy of nature, that no instance can be produced of her having permitted any one race of her animals to become extinct; of her having formed any link in her great work so weak as to be broken. To add to this, the traditionary testimony of the Indians, that this animal still exists in the northern and western parts of America, would be adding the light of a taper to that of the meridian sun. Those parts still remain in their aboriginal state, unexplored and undisturbed by us, or by others for us. He may as well exist there now, as he did formerly where we find his bones. If he be a carnivorous animal, as some Anatomists have conjectured, and the Indians affirm, his early retirement may be accounted for from the general destruction of the wild game by the Indians, which commences in the first instant of their connection with us, for the purpose of purchasing matchcoats, hatchets, and fire locks, with their skins. There remain then the buffalo, red deer, fallow deer, wolf, (the renne), glutton, wild cat, monax, vison, hedgehog, martin, and water rat, of the comparative sizes of which we have not sufficient testimony. It does not appear that Messrs. de Buffon and D'Aubenton have measured, weighed, or seen those of America. It is said of some of them, by some travellers, that they are smaller than the European. But who were these travellers? Have they not been men of a very different description from those who have laid open to us the other three quarters of the world? Was natural history the object of their travels? Did they measure or weigh the animals they speak of? or did they not judge of them by sight, or perhaps even from report only? Were they acquainted with the animals of their own country, with which they undertake to compare them? Have they not been so ignorant as often to mistake the species? A true answer to these questions would probably lighten their authority, so as to render it insufficient for the foundation of an hypothesis. How unripe we yet are, for an accurate comparison of the animals of the two countries, will appear from the work of Mons. de Buffon. The ideas we should have formed of the sizes of some animals, from the information he had received at his first publications concerning them, are very different from what his subsequent communications give us. And indeed his candour in this can never be too much praised. One sentence of his book must do him immortal honour. "I love as much a person who corrects me in an error as another who teaches me a truth, because in effect an error corrected is a truth." He seems to have thought the Cabiai he first examined wanted little of its full growth. "It was not yet fully grown." Yet he weighed but 46½ lb. and he found afterwards, that these animals, when full grown, weigh 100 lb. He had supposed, from the examination of a jaguar, said to be two years old, which weighed but 16 lb. 12 oz. that, when he should have acquired his full growth, he would not be larger than a middle sized dog. But a subsequent account raises his weight to 200 lb. Further information will, doubtless, produce further corrections. The wonder is, not that there is yet something in this great work to correct, but that there is so little. The result of this view then is, that of 26 quadrupeds common to both countries, 7 are said to be larger in America, 7 of equal size, and 12 not sufficiently examined. So that the first table impeaches the first member of the assertion, that of the animals common to both countries, the American are smallest, "and that without any exception." It shews it not just, in all the latitude in which its author has advanced it, and probably not to such a degree as to found a distinction between the two countries.

* * *

. . . [of] quadrupeds . . . which are domestic in both countries. That some of these, in some parts of America, have become less than their original stock, is doubtless true; and the reason is very obvious. In a thinly peopled country, the spontaneous productions of the forests and waste fields are sufficient to support indifferently the domestic animals of the farmer, with a very little aid from him in the severest and scarcest season. He therefore finds it more convenient to receive them from the hand of nature in that indifferent state, than to keep up their size by a care and nourishment which would cost him much labour. If, on this low fare, these animals dwindle, it is no more than they do in those parts of Europe where the poverty of the soil, or poverty of the owner, reduces them to the same scanty subsistance. It is the uniform effect of one and the same cause, whether acting on this or that side of the globe. It would be erring therefore against that rule of philosophy, which teaches us to ascribe like effects to like causes, should we impute this diminution of size in America to any imbecility or want of uniformity in the operations of nature. It may be affirmed with truth that, in those countries, and with those individuals of America, where necessity or curiosity has produced equal attention as in Europe to the nourishment of animals, the horses, cattle, sheep, and hogs of the one continent are as large as those of the other. There are particular instances, well attested, where individuals of this country have imported good breeders from England, and have improved their size by care in the course of some years. To make a fair comparison between the two countries, it will not answer to bring together animals of what might be deemed the middle or ordinary size of their species; because an error in judging of that middle or ordinary size would vary the result of the comparison. Thus Monsieur D'Aubenton considers a horse of 4 feet 5 inches high and 400 lb. weight French, equal to 4 feet 8.6 inches and 436 lb. English, as a middle sized horse. Such a one is deemed a small horse in America. The extremes must therefore be resorted to. The same anatomist dissected a horse of 5 feet 9 inches height, French measure, equal to 6 feet 1.7 English. This is near 6 inches higher than any horse I have seen: and could it be supposed that I had seen the largest horses in America, the conclusion would be, that ours have diminished, or that we have bred from a smaller stock. In Connecticut and Rhode-Island, where the climate is favorable to the production of grass, bullocks have been slaughtered which weighed 2500, 2200, and 2100 lb. nett; and those of 1800 lb. have been frequent. I have seen a hog weigh

1050 lb. after the blood, bowels, and hair had been taken from him. Before he was killed an attempt was made to weigh him with a pair of steel-yards, graduated to 1200 lb. but he weighed more. Yet this hog was probably not within fifty generations of the European stock. I am well informed of another which weighed 1100 lb. gross. Asses have been still more neglected than any other domestic animal in America. They are neither fed nor housed in the most rigorous season of the year. Yet they are larger than those measured by Mons. D'Aubenton, of 3 feet 7¼ inches, 3 feet 4 inches, and 3 feet 2½ inches, the latter weighing only 215.8 lb. These sizes, I suppose, have been produced by the same negligence in Europe, which has produced a like diminution here. Where care has been taken of them on that side of the water, they have been raised to a size bordering on that of the horse; not by the *heat* and *dryness* of the climate, but by good food and shelter. Goats have been also much neglected in America. Yet they are very prolific here, bearing twice or three times a year, and from one to five kids at a birth. Mons. de Buffon has been sensible of a difference in this circumstance in favour of America. But what are their greatest weights I cannot say. A large sheep here weights 100 lb. I observe Mons. D'Aubenton calls a ram of 62 lb. one of the middle size. But to say what are the extremes of growth in these and the other domestic animals of America, would require information of which no one individual is possessed. The weights actually known and stated in the third table preceding will suffice to shew, that we may conclude, on probable grounds, that, with equal food and care, the climate of America will preserve the races of domestic animals as large as the European stock from which they are derived; and consequently that the third member of Mons. de Buffon's assertion, that the domestic animals are subject to degeneration from the climate of America, is as probably wrong as the first and second were certainly so.

* * *

On Indians

Hitherto I have considered this hypothesis as applied to brute animals only, and not in its extension to the man of America, whether aboriginal or transplated. It is the opinion of Mons. de Buffon that the former furnishes no exception to it: "Although the savage of the new world is about the same height as man in our world, this does not suffice for him to constitute an exception to the general fact that all living nature has become smaller on that continent. The savage is feeble, and has small organs of generation; he has neither hair nor beard, and no ardor whatever for his female; although swifter than the European because he is better accustomed to running, he is, on the other hand, less strong in body; he is also less sensitive, and yet more timid and cowardly; he has no vivacity, no activity of mind; the activity of his body is less an exercise, a voluntary motion, than a necessary action caused by want; relieve him of hunger and thirst, and you deprive him of the active principle of all his movements; he will rest stupidly upon his legs or lying down entire days. There is no need for seeking further the cause of the isolated mode of life of these savages and their repugnance for society: the most precious spark of the fire of nature has been refused to them; they lack ardor for their females, and consequently have no love for their fellow men: not knowing this strongest and most tender of all affections, their other feelings are also cold and languid; they love their parents and children but little; the most intimate of all ties, the family connection, binds them therefore but loosely together; between family and family there is no tie at all; hence they have no communion, no commonwealth, no state of society. Physical love constitues their only morality; their heart is icy, their society cold, and their rule harsh. They look upon their wives only as servants for all work, or as beasts of burden, which they load without consideration with the burden of their hunting, and which they compel without mercy, without gratitude, to perform tasks which are often beyond their strength. They have only few children, and they take little care of them. Everywhere the original defect appears: they are indifferent because they have little sexual capacity, and this indifference to the other sex is the fundamental defect which weakens their nature, prevents its development, and—destroying the very germs of life—uproots society at the same time. Man is here no exception to the general rule. Nature, by refusing him the power of love, has treated him worse and lowered him deeper than any animal." An afflicting picture indeed, which, for the honor of human nature, I am glad to believe has no original. Of the Indian of South America I know nothing; for I would not honor with the appelation of knowledge, what I derive from the fables published of them. These I believe to be just as true as the fables of Æsop. This belief is founded on what I have seen of man, white, red, and black, and what has been written of him by authors, enlightened themselves, and writing amidst an enlightened people. The Indian of North America being more within our reach, I can speak of him somewhat from my own knowledge, but more from the information of others better acquainted with him, and on whose truth and judgment I can rely. From these sources I am able to say, in contradiction to this representation, that he is neither more defective in ardor, nor more impotent with his female, than the white reduced to the same diet and exercise: that he is brave, when an enterprize depends on bravery; education with him making the point of honor consist in the destruction of an enemy by stratagem, and in the preservation of his own person free from injury; or perhaps this is nature; while it is education which teaches us to honor force more than finesse; that he will defend himself against an host of enemies, always chusing to be killed, rather than to surrender, though it be to the whites, who he knows will treat him well: that in other situations also he meets death with more deliberation, and endures tortures with a firmness unknown almost to religious enthusiasm with us: that he is affectionate to his children, careful of them, and indulgent in the extreme: that his affections comprehend his other connections, weakening, as with us, from circle to circle, as they recede from the center: that his friendships are strong and faithful to the uttermost extremity: that his sensibility is keen, even the warriors weeping most bitterly on the loss of their children, though in general they endeavour to appear superior to human events: that his vivacity and activity of mind is equal to ours in the same situation; hence his eagerness for hunting, and for games of chance. The women are submitted to unjust drudgery. This I believe is the case with every barbarous people. With such, force is law. The stronger sex therefore imposes on the weaker. It is civilization alone which replaces women in the enjoyment of their natural equality. That first teaches us to subdue the selfish passions, and to respect those rights in others which we value in ourselves. Were we in equal barbarism, our females would be equal drudges. The man with them is less strong than with us, but their woman stronger than ours; and both for the same obvious reason; because our man and their woman is habituated to labour, and formed by it. With both races the sex which is indulged with ease is least athletic. An Indian man is small in the hand and wrist for the same reason for which a sailor is large and strong in the arms and shoulders, and a porter in the legs and thighs.—They raise fewer children than we do. The causes of this are to be found, not in a difference of nature, but of circumstance. The women very frequently attending the men in their parties of war and of hunting, child-bearing becomes extremely inconvenient to them. It is said, therefore, that they have learnt the practice of procuring abortion by the use of some vegetable; and that it even extends to prevent conception for a considerable time after. During these parties they are exposed to numerous hazards, to excessive exertions, to the greatest extremities of hunger. Even at their homes the nation depends for food, through a certain part of every year, on the gleanings of the forest: that is, they experience a famine once in every year. With all animals, if the female be badly fed, or not fed at all, her young perish: and if both male and female be reduced to like want, generation becomes less active, less productive. To the obstacles then of want and hazard, which nature has opposed to the multiplication of wild animals, for the purpose of restraining their numbers within certain bounds, those of labour and of voluntary abortion are added with the Indian. No wonder then if they multiply less than we do. Where food is regularly supplied, a single farm will shew more of cattle, than a whole country of forests can of buffaloes. The same Indian women, when married to white traders, who feed them and their children plentifully and regularly, who exempt them from excessive drudgery, who keep them stationary and unexposed to accident, produce and raise as many children as the white women. Instances are known, under these circumstances, of their rearing a dozen children. An inhuman practice once prevailed in this country of making slaves of the Indians. (This practice commenced with the Spaniards with the first discovery of America). It is a fact well known with us, that the Indian women so enslaved produced and raised as numerous families as either the whites or blacks among whom they lived.—It has been said, that Indians have less hair than the whites, except on the head. But this is a fact of which fair proof can scarcely be had. With them it is disgraceful to be hairy on the body. They say it likens them to hogs. They therefore pluck the hair as fast as it appears. But the traders who marry their women, and prevail on them to discontinue this practice, say, that nature is the same with them as with the whites. Nor, if the fact be true, is the consequence necessary which has been drawn from it. Negroes have notoriously less hair than the whites; yet they are more ardent. But if cold and moisture be the agents of nature for diminishing the races of animals, how comes she all at once to suspend their operation as to the physical man of the new world, whom the Count acknowledges to be "about the same size as the man of our hemisphere," and to let loose their influence on his moral faculties? How has this "combination of the elements and other physical causes, so contrary to the enlargement of animal nature in this new world, these obstacles to the developement and formation of great germs," been arrested and suspended, so as to permit the human body to acquire its just dimensions, and by what inconceivable process has their action been directed on his mind alone? To judge of the truth of this, to form a just estimate of their genius and mental powers, more facts are wanting, and great allowance to be made for those circumstances of their situation which call for a display of particular talents only. This done, we shall probably find that they are formed in mind as well as in body, on the same module with the "Homo sapiens Europæus." The principles of their society forbidding all compulsion, they are to be led to duty and to enterprize by personal influence and persuasion. Hence eloquence in council, bravery and address in war, become the foundations of all consequence with them. To these acquirements all their faculties are directed. Of their bravery and address in war we have multiplied proofs, because we have been the subjects on which they were exercised. Of their eminence in oratory we have fewer examples, because it is displayed chiefly in their own councils. Some, however, we have of very superior lustre. I may challange the whole orations of Demosthenes and Cicero, and of any more eminent orator, if Europe has furnished more eminent, to produce a single passage, superior to the speech of Logan, a Mingo chief, to Lord Dunmore, when governor of this state. And, as a testimony of their talents in this line, I beg leave to introduce it, first stating the incidents necessary for understanding it. In the spring of the year

1774, a robbery was committed by some Indians on certain land-adventurers on the river Ohio. The whites in that quarter, according to their custom, undertook to punish this outrage in a summary way. Captain Michael Cresap, and a certain Daniel Great-house, leading on these parties, surprized, at different times, travelling and hunting parties of the Indians, having their women and children with them, and murdered many. Among these were unfortunately the family of Logan, a chief celebrated in peace and war, and long distinguished as the friend of the whites. This unworthy return provoked his vengeance. He accordingly signalized himself in the war which ensued. In the autumn of the same year a decisive battle was fought at the mouth of the Great Kanhaway, between the collected forces of the Shawanese, Mingoes, and Delawares, and a detachment of the Virginia militia. The Indians were defeated, and sued for peace. Logan however disdained to be seen among the suppliants. But, lest the sincerity of a treaty should be distrusted, from which so distinguished a chief absented himself, he sent by a messenger the following speech to be delivered to Lord Dunmore.

"I appeal to any white man to say, if ever he entered Logan's cabin hungry, and he gave him not meat; if ever he came cold and naked, and he clothed him not. During the course of the last long and bloody war, Logan remained idle in his cabin, an advocate for peace. Such was my love for the whites, that my countrymen pointed as they passed, and said, 'Logan is the friend of white men.' I had even thought to have lived with you, but for the injuries of one man. Col. Cresap, the last spring, in cold blood, and unprovoked, murdered all the relations of Logan, not sparing even my women and children. There runs not a drop of my blood in the veins of any living creature. This called on me for revenge. I have sought it: I have killed many: I have fully glutted my vengeance. For my country, I rejoice at the beams of peace. But do not harbour a thought that mine is the joy of fear. Logan never felt fear. He will not turn on his heel to save his life. Who is there to mourn for Logan?—Not one."

Before we condemn the Indians of this continent as wanting genius, we must consider that letters have not yet been introduced among them. Were we to compare them in their present state with the Europeans North of the Alps, when the Roman arms and arts first crossed those mountains, the comparison would be unequal, because, at that time, those parts of Europe were swarming with numbers; because numbers produce emulation, and multiply the chances of improvement, and one improvement begets another. Yet I may safely ask, How many good poets, how many able mathematicians, how many great inventors in arts or sciences, had Europe North of the Alps then produced? And it was sixteen centuries after this before a Newton could be formed. I do not mean to deny, that there are varieties in the race of man, distinguished by their powers both of body and mind. I believe there are, as I see to be the case in the races of other animals. I only mean to suggest a doubt, whether the bulk and faculties of animals depend on the side of the Atlantic on which their food happens to grow, or which furnishes the elements of which they are compounded? Whether nature has enlisted herself as a Cis or Trans-Atlantic partisan? I am induced to suspect, there has been more eloquence than sound reasoning displayed in support of this theory; that it is one of those cases where the judgment has been seduced by a glowing pen: and whilst I render every tribute of honor and esteem to the celebrated Zoologist, who has added, and is still adding, so many precious things to the treasures of science, I must doubt whether in this instance he has not cherished error also, by lending her for a moment his vivid imagination and bewitching language.

So far the Count de Buffon has carried this new theory of the tendency of nature to belittle her productions on this side of the Atlantic. Its application to the race of whites, transplanted from Europe, remained for the Abbé Raynal. "One must be astonished (he says) that America has not yet produced one good poet, one able mathematician, one man of genius in a single art or a single science." "America has not yet produced one good poet." When we shall have existed as a people as long as the Greeks did before they produced a Homer, the Romans a Virgil, the French a Racine and Voltaire, the English a Shakespeare and Milton, should this reproach be still true, we will enquire from what unfriendly causes it has proceeded, that the other countries of Europe and quarters of the earth shall not have inscribed any name in the roll of poets. But neither has America produced "one able mathematician, one man of genius in a single art or a single science." In war we have produced a Washington, whose memory will be adored while liberty shall have votaries, whose name will triumph over time, and will in future ages assume its just station among the most celebrated worthies of the world, when that wretched philosophy shall be forgotten which would have arranged him among the degeneracies of nature. In physics we have produced a Franklin, than whom no one of the present age has made more important discoveries, nor has enriched philosophy with more, or more ingenious solutions of the phænomena of nature. We have supposed Mr. Rittenhouse second to no astronomer living: that in genius he must be the first, because he is self-taught. As an artist he has exhibited as great a proof of mechanical genius as the world has ever produced. He has not indeed made a world; but he has by imitation approached nearer its Maker than any man who has lived from the creation to this day. As in philosophy and war, so in government, in oratory, in painting, in the plastic art, we might shew that America, though but a child of yesterday, has already given hopeful proofs of genius, as well of the nobler kinds, which arouse the best feelings of man, which call him into action, which substantiate his freedom, and conduct him to happiness, as of the subordinate, which serve to amuse him only. We therefore suppose, that this reproach is as unjust as it is unkind; and that, of the geniuses which adorn the present age, America contributes its full share. For comparing it with those countries, where genius is most cultivated, where are the most excellent models for art, and scaffoldings for the attainment of science, as France and England for instance, we calculate thus. The United States contain three millions of inhabitants; France twenty millions; and the British islands ten. We produce a Washington, a Franklin, a Rittenhouse. France then should have half a dozen in each of these lines, and Great-Britain half that number, equally eminent. It may be true, that France has: we are but just becoming acquainted with her, and our acquaintance so far gives us high ideas of the genius of her inhabitants. It would be injuring too many of them to name particularly a Voltaire, a Buffon, the constellation of Encyclopedists, the Abbé Raynal himself, &c. &c. We therefore have reason to believe she can produce her full quota of genius. The present war having so long cut off all communication with Great-Britain, we are not able to make a fair estimate of the state of science in that country. The spirit in which she wages war is the only sample before our eyes, and that does not seem the legitimate offspring either of science or of civilization. The sun of her glory is fast descending to the horizon. Her philosophy has crossed the Channel, her freedom the Atlantic, and herself seems passing to that awful dissolution, whose issue is not given human foresight to scan.

* * *

On Blacks

It will probably be asked, Why not retain and incorporate the blacks into the state, and thus save the expence of supplying, by importation of white settlers, the vacancies they will leave? Deep rooted prejudices entertained by the whites; ten thousand recollections, by the blacks, of the injuries they have sustained; new provocations; the real distinctions which nature has made; and many other circumstances, will divide us into parties, and produce convulsions which will probably never end but in the extermination of the one or the other race.—To these objections, which are political, may be added others, which are physical and moral. The first difference which strikes us is that of colour. Whether the black of the negro resides in the reticular membrane between the skin and scarf-skin, or in the scarf-skin itself; whether it proceeds from the colour of the blood, the colour of the bile, or from that of some other secretion, the difference is fixed in nature, and is as real as if its seat and cause were better known to us. And is this difference of no importance? Is it not the foundation of a greater or less share of beauty in the two races? Are not the fine mixtures of red and white, the expressions of every passion by greater or less suffusions of colour in the one, preferable to that eternal monotony, which reigns in the countenances, that immoveable veil of black which covers all the emotions of the other race? Add to these, flowing hair, a more elegant symmetry of form, their own judgment in favour of the whites, declared by their preference of them, as uniformly as is the preference of the Oran-ootan for the black women over those of his own species. The circumstance of superior beauty, is thought worthy attention in the propagation of our horses, dogs, and other domestic animals; why not in that of man? Besides those of colour, figure, and hair, there are other physical distinctions proving a difference of race. They have less hair on the face and body. They secrete less by the kidnies, and more by the glands of the skin, which gives them a very strong and disagreeable odour. This greater degree of transpiration renders them more tolerant of heat, and less so of cold, than the whites. Perhaps too a difference of structure in the pulmonary apparatus, which a late ingenious experimentalist has discovered to be the principal regulator of animal heat, may have disabled them from extricating, in the act of inspiration, so much of that fluid from the outer air, or obliged them in expiration, to part with more of it. They seem to require less sleep. A black, after hard labour through the day, will be induced by the slightest amusements to sit up till midnight, or later, though knowing he must be out with the first dawn of the morning. They are at least as brave, and more adventuresome. But this may perhaps proceed from a want of forethought, which prevents their seeing a danger till it be present. When present, they do not go through it with more coolness or steadiness than the whites. They are more ardent after their female: but love seems with them to be more an eager desire, than a tender delicate mixture of sentiment and sensation. Their griefs are transient. Those numberless afflictions, which render it doubtful whether heaven has given life to us in mercy or in wrath, are less felt, and sooner forgotten with them. In general, their existence appears to participate more of sensation than reflection. To this must be ascribed their disposition to sleep when abstraced from their diversions, and unemployed in labour. An animal whose body is at rest, and who does not reflect, must be disposed to sleep of course. Comparing them by their faculties of memory, reason, and imagination, it appears to me, that in memory they are equal to the whites; in reason much inferior, as I think one could scarcely be found capable of tracing and comprehending the investigations of Euclid; and that in imagination they are dull, tasteless, and anomalous. It would be unfair to follow them to Africa for this investigation. We will consider them here, on the same stage with the whites, and where the facts are not apocryphal on which a judgment is to be formed. It will be right to make great allowances for the difference of condition, of education, of conversation, of the sphere in which they move. Many millions of them have been brought to, and born in America. Most of them indeed have been confined to tillage, to their own homes, and their own society: yet many have been so situated, that they might have availed themselves of the conversation of their masters; many have been brought up to the handicraft arts, and from that circumstance have always been associated with the whites. Some have been liberally educated, and all have lived in countries where the arts and sciences are cultivated to a considerable degree, and have had before their eyes samples of the best works from abroad. The Indians, with no advantages of this kind, will often carve figures on their pipes not destitute of design and merit. They will crayon out an animal, a plant, or a country, so as to prove the existence of a germ in their minds which only wants cultivation. They astonish you with strokes of the most sublime oratory; such as prove their reason and sentiment strong, their imagination glowing and elevated. But never yet could I find that a black had uttered a thought above the level of plain narration; never see even an elementary trait of painting or sculpture. In music they are more generally gifted than the whites with accurate ears for tune and time, and they have been found capable of imagining a small catch. Whether they will be equal to the composition of a more extensive run of melody, or of complicated harmony, is yet to be proved. Misery is often the parent of the most affecting touches in poetry.—Among the blacks is misery enough, God knows, but no poetry. Love is the peculiar œstrum of the poet. Their love is ardent, but it kindles the senses only, not the imagination. Religion indeed has produced a Phyllis Whately; but it could not produce a poet. The compositions published under her name are below the dignity of criticism. The heroes of the Dunciad are to her, as Hercules to the author of that poem. Ignatius Sancho has approached nearer to merit in composition; yet his letters do more honour to the heart than the head. They breathe the purest effusions of friendship and general philanthropy, and shew how great a degree of the latter may be compounded with strong religious zeal. He is often happy in the turn of his compliments, and his stile is easy and familiar, except when he affects a Shandean fabrication of words. But his imagination is wild and extravagant, escapes incessantly from every restraint of reason and taste, and, in the course of its vagaries, leaves a tract of thought as incoherent and eccentric, as is the course of a meteor through the sky. His subjects should often have led him to a process of sober reasoning: yet we find him always substituting sentiment for demonstration. Upon the whole, though we admit him to the first place among those of his own colour who have presented themselves to the public judgment, yet when we compare him with the writers of the race among whom he lived, and particularly with the epistolary class, in which he has taken his own stand, we are compelled to enroll him at the bottom of the column. This criticism supposes the letters published under his name to be geniune, and to have received amendment from no other hand; points which would not be of easy investigation. The improvement of the blacks in body and mind, in the first instance of their mixture with the whites, has been observed by every one, and proves that their inferiority is not the effect merely of their condition of life. We know that among the Romans, about the Augustan age especially, the condition of their slaves was much more deplorable than that of the blacks on the continent of America. The two sexes were confined in separate apartments, because to raise a child cost the master more than to buy one. Cato, for a very restricted indulgence to his slaves in this particular, took from them a certain price. But in this country the slaves multiply as fast as the free inhabitants. Their situation and manners place the commerce between the two sexes almost without restraint.—The same Cato, on a principle of œconomy, always sold his sick and superannuated slaves. He gives it as a standing precept to a master visiting his farm, to sell his old oxen, old waggons, old tools, old and diseased servants, and every thing else become useless. "Vendat boves vetulos, plaustrum vetus, ferramenta, vetera, servum senem, servum morbosum, & si quid aliud supersit vendat." The American slaves cannot enumerate this among the injuries and insults they receive. It was the common practice to expose in the island of Æsculapius, in the Tyber, diseased slaves, whose cure was like to become tedious. The Emperor Claudius, by an edict, gave freedom to such of them as should recover, and first declared, that if any person chose to kill rather than to expose them, it should be deemed homicide. The exposing them is a crime of which no instance has existed with us; and were it to be followed by death, it would be punished capitally. We are told of a certain Vedius Pollio, who, in the presence of Augustus, would have given a slave as food to his fish, for having broken a glass. With the Romans, the regular method of taking the evidence of their slaves was under torture. Here it has been thought better never to resort to their evidence. When a master was murdered, all his slaves, in the same house, or within hearing, were condemned to death. Here punishment falls on the guilty only, and as precise proof is required against him as against a freeman. Yet notwithstanding these and other discouraging circumstances among the Romans, their slaves were often their rarest artists. They excelled too in science, insomuch as to be usually employed as tutors to their master's children. Epictetus, (Diogenes, Phaedon), Terence, and Phædrus, were slaves. But they were of the race of whites. It is not their condition then, but nature, which has produced the distinction.—Whether further observation will or will not verify the conjecture, that nature has been less bountiful to them in the endowments of the head, I believe that in those of the heart she will be found to have done them justice. That disposition to theft with which they have been branded, must be ascribed to their situation, and not to any depravity of the moral sense. The man, in whose favour no laws of property exist, probably feels himself less bound to respect those made in favour of others. When arguing for ourselves, we lay it down as a fundamental, that laws, to be just, must give a reciprocation of right: that, without this, they are mere arbitrary rules of conduct, founded in force, and not in conscience: and it is a problem which I give to the master to solve, whether the religious precepts against the violation of property were not framed for him as well as his slave? And whether the slave may not as justifiably take a little from one, who has taken all from him, as he may slay one who would slay him? That a change in the relations in which a man is placed should change his ideas of moral right and wrong, is neither new, nor peculiar to the colour of the blacks. Homer tells us it was so 2600 years ago.

'Ημισυ, γαζ τ' ἀρετῆς ἀποαίνυΰιαι εὐρύθπα Ζεὺς
'Ανεροs, ευτ' ἄν μιν κατὰ δέλιον ἦμαζ ἔλησιν. *Od.* 17. 323.

Jove fix'd it certain, that whatever day
Makes man a slave, takes half his worth away.

But the slaves of which Homer speaks were whites. Notwithstanding these considerations which must weaken their respect for the laws of property, we find among them numerous instances of the most rigid integrity, and as many as among their better instructed masters, of benevolence, gratitude, and unshaken fidelity.—The opinion, that they are inferior in the faculties of reason and imagination, must be hazarded with great diffidence. To justify a general conclusion, requires many observations, even where the subject may be submitted to the Anatomical knife, to Optical glasses, to analysis by fire, or by solvents. How much more then where it is a faculty, not a substance, we are examining; where it eludes the research of all the senses; where the conditions of its existence are various and variously combined; where the effects of those which are present or absent bid defiance to calculation; let me add too, as a circumstance of great tenderness, where our conclusion would degrade a whole race of men from the rank in the scale of beings which their Creator may perhaps have given them. To our reproach it must be said, that though for a century and a half we have had under our eyes the races of black and of red men, they have never yet been viewed by us as subjects of natural history. I advance it therefore as a suspicion only, that the blacks, whether originally a distinct race, or made distinct by time and circumstances, are inferior to the whites in the endowments both of body and mind. It is not against experience to suppose, that different species of the same genus, or varieties of the same species, may possess different qualifications. Will not a lover of natural history then, one who views the gradations in all the races of animals with the eye of philosophy, excuse an effort to keep those in the department of man as distinct as nature has formed them? This unfortunate difference of colour, and perhaps of faculty, is a powerful obstacle to the emancipation of these people. Many of their advocates, while they wish to vindicate the liberty of human nature, are anxious also to preserve its dignity and beauty. Some of these, embarrassed by the question "What further is to be done with them?" join themselves in opposition with those who are actuated by sordid avarice only. Among the Romans emancipation required but one effort. The slave, when made free, might mix with, without staining the blood of his master. But with us a second is necessary, unknown to history. When freed, he is to be removed beyond the reach of mixture.

* * *

On Education

Another object of the revisal is, to diffuse knowledge more generally through the mass of the people. This bill proposes to lay off every county into small districts of five or six miles square, called hundreds, and in each of them to establish a school for teaching reading, writing, and arithmetic. The tutor to be supported by the hundred, and every person in it entitled to send their children three years gratis, and as much longer as they please, paying for it. These schools to be under a visitor, who is annually to chuse the boy, of best genius in the school, of those whose parents are too poor to give them further education, and to send him forward to one of the grammar schools, of which twenty are proposed to be erected in different parts of the country, for teaching Greek, Latin, geography, and the higher branches of numerical arithmetic. Of the boys thus sent in any one year, trial is to be made at the grammar schools one or two years, and the best genius of the whole selected, and continued six years, and the residue dismissed. By this means twenty of the best geniusses will be raked from the rubbish annually, and be instructed, at the public expence, so far as the grammar schools go. At the end of six years instruction, one half are to be discontinued (from among whom the grammar schools will probably be supplied with future masters); and the other half, who are to be chosen for the superiority of their parts and disposition, are to be sent and continued three years in the study of such sciences as they shall chuse, at William and Mary college, the plan of which is proposed to be enlarged, as will be hereafter explained, and extended to all the useful sciences. The ultimate result of the whole scheme of education would be the teaching all children of the state reading, writing, and common arithmetic: turning out ten annually of superior genius, well taught in Greek, Latin, geography, and the higher branches of arithmetic: turning out ten others annually, of still superior parts, who, to those branches of learning, shall have added such of the sciences as their genius shall have led them to: the furnishing to the wealthier part of the people convenient schools, at which their children may be educated, at their own expence.—The general objects of this law are to provide an education adapted to the years, to the capacity, and the condition of every one, and directed to their freedom and happiness. Specific details were not proper for the law. These must be the business of the visitors entrusted with its execution. The first stage of this education being the schools of the hundreds, wherein the great mass of the people will receive their instruction, the principal foundations of future order will be laid here. Instead therefore of putting the Bible and Testament into the hands of the children, at an age when their judgments are not sufficiently matured for religious enquiries, their memories may here be stored with the most useful facts from Grecian, Roman, European and American history. The first elements of morality too may be instilled into their minds; such as, when further developed as their judgments advance in strength, may teach them how to work out their own greatest happiness, by shewing them that it does not depend on the condition of life in which chance has placed them, but is always the result of a good conscience, good health, occupation, and freedom in all just pursuits.—Those whom either the wealth of their parents or the adoption of the state shall destine to higher degrees of learning, will go on to the grammar schools, which constitute the next stage, there to be instructed in the languages. The learning Greek and Latin, I am told, is going into disuse in Europe. I know not what their manners and occupations may call for: but it would be very ill-judged in us to follow their example in this instance. There is a certain period of life, say from eight to fifteen or sixteen years of age, when the mind, like the body, is not yet firm enough for laborious and close operations. If applied to such, it falls an early victim to premature exertion; exhibiting indeed at first, in these young and tender subjects, the flattering appearance of their being men while they are yet children, but ending in reducing them to be children when they should be men. The memory is then most susceptible and tenacious of impressions; and the learning of languages being chiefly a work of memory, it seems precisely fitted to the powers of this period, which is long enough too for acquiring the most useful languages ancient and modern. I do not pretend that language is science. It is only an instrument for the attainment of science. But that time is not lost which is employed in providing tools for future operation: more especially as in this case the books put into the hands of the youth for this purpose may be such as will at the same time impress their minds with useful facts and good principles. If this period be suffered to pass in idleness, the mind becomes lethargic and impotent, as would the body it inhabits of unexercised during the same time. The sympathy between body and mind during their rise, progress and decline, is too strict and obvious to endanger our being misled while we reason from the one to the other.—As soon as they are of sufficient age, it is supposed they will be sent on from the grammar schools to the university, which constitutes our third and last stage, there to study those sciences which may be adapted to their views.—By that part of our plan which prescribes the selection of the youths of genius from among the classes of the poor, we hope to avail the state of those talents which nature has sown as liberally among the poor as the rich, but which perish without use, if not sought for and cultivated.—But of all the views of this law none is more important, none more legitimate, than that of rendering the people the safe, as they are the ultimate, guardians of their own liberty. For this purpose the reading in the first stage, where *they* will receive their whole education, is proposed, as has been said, to be chiefly historical. History by apprising them of the past will enable them to judge of the future; it will avail them of the experience of other times and other nations; it will qualify them as judges of the actions and designs of men; it will enable them to know ambition under every disguise it may assume; and knowing it, to defeat its views. In every government on earth is some trace of human weakness, some germ of corruption and degeneracy, which cunning will discover and wickedness insensibly open, cultivate, and improve. Every government degenerates when trusted to the rulers of the people alone. The people themselves therefore are its only safe depositories. And to render even them safe their minds must be improved to a certain degree. This indeed is not all that is necessary, though it be essentially necessary. An amendment of our constitution must here come in aid of the public education. The influence over government must be shared among all the people. If every individual which composes their mass participates of the ultimate authority, the government will be safe; because the corrupting the whole mass will exceed any private resources of wealth: and public ones cannot be provided but by levies on the people. In this case every man would have to pay his own price. The government of Great-Britain has been corrupted, because but one man in ten has a right to vote for members of parliament. The sellers of the government therefore get nine-tenths of their price clear. It has been thought that corruption is restrained by confining the right of suffrage to a few of the wealthier of the people: but it would be more effectually restrained by an extension of that right to such numbers as would bid defiance to the means of corruption.

Lastly, it is proposed, by a bill in this revisal, to begin a public library and gallery, by laying out a certain sum annually in books, paintings, and statues.

On Religion

The first settlers in this country were emigrants from England, of the English church, just at a point of time when it was flushed with complete victory over the religious of all other persuasions. Possessed, as they became, of the powers of making, administering, and executing the laws, they shewed equal intolerance in this country with their Presbyterian brethren, who had emigrated to the northern government. The poor Quakers were flying from persecution in England. They cast their eyes on these new countries as asylums of civil and religious freedom; but they found them free only for the reigning sect. Several acts of the Virginia assembly of 1659, 1662, and 1693, had made it penal in parents to refuse to have their children baptized; had prohibited the unlawful assembling of Quakers; had made it penal for any master of a vessel to bring a Quaker into the state; had ordered those already here, and such as should come thereafter, to be imprisoned till they should abjure the country; provided a milder punishment for their first and second return, but death for their third; had inhibited all persons from suffering their meetings in or near their houses, entertaining them individually, or disposing of books which supported their tenets. If no capital execution took place here, as did in New-England, it was not owing to the moderation of the church, or spirit of the legislature, as may be inferred from the law itself; but to historical circumstances which have not been handed down to us. The Anglicans retained full possession of the country about a century. Other opinions began then to creep in, and the great care of the government to support their own church, having begotten an equal degree of indolence in its clergy, two-thirds of the people had become dissenters at the commencement of the present revolution. The laws indeed were still oppressive on them, but the spirit of the one party had subsided into moderation, and of the other had risen to a degree of determination which commanded respect.

The present state of our laws on the subject of religion is this. The convention of May 1776, in their declaration of rights, declared it to be a truth, and a natural right, that the exercise of religion should be free; but when they proceeded to form on that declaration the ordinance of government, instead of taking up every principle declared in the bill of rights, and guarding it by legislative sanction, they passed over that which asserted our religious rights, leaving them as they found them. The same convention, however, when they met as a member of the general assembly in October 1776, repealed all *acts of parliament* which had rendered criminal the maintaining any opinions in matters of religion, the forbearing to repair to church, and the exercising any mode of worship; and suspended the laws giving salaries to the clergy, which suspension was made perpetual in October 1779. Statutory oppressions in religion being thus wiped away, we remain at present under those only imposed by the common law, or by our own acts of assembly. At the common law, *heresy* was a capital offence, punishable by burning. Its definition was left to the ecclesiastical judges, before whom the conviction was, till the statute of the I El. c. I. circumscribed it, by declaring, that nothing should be deemed heresy, but what had been so determined by authority of the canonical scriptures, or by one of the four first general councils, or by some other council having for the grounds of their declaration the express and plain words of the scriptures. Heresy, thus circumscribed, being an offence at the common law, our act of assembly of October 1777, c. 17. gives cognizance of it to the general court, by declaring, that the jurisdiction of that court shall be general in all matters at the common law. The execution is by the writ *De hæretico comburendo*. By our own act of assembly of 1705, c. 30, if a person brought up in the Christian religion denies the being of a God, or the Trinity, or asserts there are more Gods than one, or denies the Christian religion to be true, or the scriptures to be of divine authority, he is punishable on the first offence by incapacity to hold any office or employment ecclesiastical, civil, or military; on the second by disability to sue, to take any gift or legacy, to be guardian, executor, or administrator, and by three years imprisonment, without bail. A father's right to the custody of his own children being founded in law on his right of guardianship, this being taken away, they may of course be severed from him, and put, by the authority of a court, into more orthodox hands. This is a summary view of that religious slavery, under which a people have been willing to remain, who have lavished their lives and fortunes for the establishment of their civil freedom.

The error seems not sufficiently eradicated, that the operations of the mind, as well as the acts of the body, are subject to the coercion of the laws. But our rulers can have authority over such natural rights only as we have submitted to them. The rights of conscience we never submitted, we could not submit. We are answerable for them to our God. The legitimate powers of government extend to such acts only as are injurious to others. But it does me no injury for my neighbour to say there are twenty gods, or no god. It neither picks my pocket nor breaks my leg. If it be said, his testimony in a court of justice cannot be relied on, reject it then, and be the stigma on him. Constraint may make him worse by making him a hypocrite, but it will never make him a truer man. It may fix him obstinately in his errors, but will not cure them. Reason and free enquiry are the only effectual agents against error. Give a loose to them, they will support the true religion, by bringing every false one to their tribunal, to the test of their investigation. They are the natural enemies of error, and of error only. Had not the Roman government permitted free enquiry, Christianity could never have been introduced. Had not free enquiry been indulged, at the æra of the reformation, the corruptions of Christianity could not have been purged away. If it be restrained now, the present corruptions will be protected, and new ones encouraged. Was the government to prescribe to us our medicine and diet, our bodies would be in such keeping as our souls are now. Thus in France the emetic was once forbidden as a medicine, and the potatoe as an article of food. Government is just as infallible too when it fixes systems in physics. Galileo was sent to the inquisition for affirming that the earth was a sphere: the government had declared it to be as flat as a trencher, and Galileo was obliged to abjure his error. This error however at length prevailed, the earth became a globe, and Descartes declared it was whirled round its axis by a vortex. The government in which he lived was wise enough to see that this was no question of civil jurisdiction, or we should all have been involved by authority in vortices. In fact, the vortices have been exploded, and the Newtonian principle of gravitation is now more firmly established, on the basis of reason, than it would be were the government to step in, and to make it an article of necessary faith. Reason and experiment have been indulged, and error has fled before them. It is error alone which needs the support of government. Truth can stand by itself. Subject opinion to coercion: whom will you make your inquisitors? Fallible men; men governed by bad passions, by private as well as public reasons. And why subject it to coercion? To produce uniformity. But is uniformity of opinion desireable? No more than of face and stature. Introduce the bed of Procrustes then, and as there is danger that the large men may beat the small, make us all of a size, by lopping the former and stretching the latter. Difference of opinion is advantageous in religion. The several sects perform the office of a Censor morum over each other. Is uniformity attainable? Millions of innocent men, women, and children, since the introduction of Christianity, have been burnt, tortured, fined, imprisoned; yet we have not advanced one inch towards uniformity. What has been the effect of coercion? To make one half the world fools, and the other half hypocrites. To support roguery and error all over the earth. Let us reflect that it is inhabited by a thousand millions of people. That these profess probably a thousand different systems of religion. That ours is but one of that thousand. That if there be but one right, and ours that one, we should wish to see the 999 wandering sects gathered into the fold of truth. But against such a majority we cannot effect this by force. Reason and persuasion are the only practicable instruments. To make way for these, free enquiry must be indulged; and how can we wish others to indulge it while we refuse it ourselves. But every state, says an inquisitor, has established some religion. No two, say I, have established the same. Is this a proof of the infallibility of establishments? Our sister states of Pennsylvania and New York, however, have long subsisted without any establishment at all. The experiment was new and doubtful when they made it. It has answered beyond conception. They flourish infinitely. Religion is well supported; of various kinds, indeed, but all good enough; all sufficient to preserve peace and order: or if a sect arises, whose tenets would subvert morals, good sense has fair play, and reasons and laughs it out of doors, without suffering the state to be troubled with it. They do not hang more malefactors than we do. They are not more disturbed with religious dissensions. On the contrary, their harmony is unparalleled, and can be ascribed to nothing but their unbounded tolerance, because there is no other circumstance in which they differ from every nation on earth. They have made the happy discovery, that the way to silence religious disputes, is to take no notice of them. Let us too give this experiment fair play, and get rid, while we may, of those tyrannical laws. It is true, we are as yet secured against them by the spirit of the times. I doubt whether the people of this country would suffer an execution for heresy, or a three years imprisonment for not comprehending the mysteries of the Trinity. But is the spirit of the people an infallible, a permanent reliance? Is it government? Is this the kind of protection we receive in return for the rights we give up? Besides, the spirit of the times may alter, will alter. Our rulers will become corrupt, our people careless. A single zealot may commence persecutor, and better men be his victims. It can never be too often repeated, that the time for fixing every essential right on a legal basis is while our rulers are honest, and ourselves united. From the conclusion of this war we shall be going down hill. It will not then be necessary to resort every moment to the people for support. They will be forgotten, therefore, and their rights disregarded. They will forget themselves, but in the sole faculty of making money, and will never think of uniting to effect a due respect for their rights. The shackles, therefore, which shall not be knocked off at the conclusion of this war, will remain on us long, will be made heavier and heavier, till our rights shall revive or expire in a convulsion.

On Manufactures

We never had an interior trade of any importance. Our exterior commerce has suffered very much from the beginning of the present contest. During this time we have manufactured within our families the most necessary articles of cloathing. Those of cotton will bear some comparison with the same kinds of manufacture in Europe; but those of wool, flax and hemp are very coarse, unsightly, and unpleasant: and such is our attachment to agriculture, and such our preference for foreign manufactures, that be it wise or unwise, our people will certainly return as soon as they can, to the raising raw materials, and exchanging them for finer manufactures than they are able to execute themselves.

The political œconomists of Europe have established it as a principle that every state should endeavour to manufacture for itself: and this principle, like many others, we transfer to America, without calculating the difference of circumstance which should often produce a difference of result. In Europe the lands are either cultivated, or locked up against the cultivator. Manufacture must therefore be resorted to of necessity not of choice, to support the surplus of their people. But we have an immensity of land courting the industry of the husbandman. Is it best then that all our citizens should be employed in its improvement, or that one half should be called off from that to exercise manufactures and handicraft arts for the other? Those who labour in the earth are the chosen people of God, if ever he had a chosen people, whose breasts he has made his peculiar deposit for substantial and genuine virtue. It is the focus in which he keeps alive that sacred fire, which otherwise might escape from the face of the earth. Corruption of morals in the mass of cultivators is a phænomenon of which no age nor nation has furnished an example. It is the mark set on those, who not looking up to heaven, to their own soil and industry, as does the husbandman, for their subsistance, depend for it on the casualties and caprice of customers. Dependance begets subservience and venality, suffocates the germ of virtue, and prepares fit tools for the designs of ambition. This, the natural progress and consequence of the arts, has sometimes perhaps been retarded by accidental circumstances: but, generally speaking, the proportion which the aggregate of the other classes of citizens bears in any state to that of its husbandmen, is the proportion of its unsound to its healthy parts, and is a good-enough barometer whereby to measure its degree of corruption. While we have land to labour then, let us never wish to see our citizens occupied at a work-bench, or twirling a distaff. Carpenters, masons, smiths, are wanting in husbandry: but, for the general operations of manufacture, let our work-shops remain in Europe. It is better to carry provisions and materials to workmen there, than bring them to the provisions and materials, and with them their manners and principles. The loss by the transportation of commodities across the Atlantic will be made up in happiness and permanence of government. The mobs of great cities add just so much to the support of pure government, as sores do to the strength of the human body. It is the manners and spirit of a people which preserve a republic in vigour. A degeneracy in these is a canker which soon eats to the heart of its laws and constitution.

JAMES MADISON

The Federalist

(1787–1788)

The American republic was a political experiment of startling novelty. Since ancient times, political theorists had argued that a republic could only endure in a small state, that only the coercive force of a monarch could hold together an area of any size of a population of considerable heterogeneity. The Federalist Papers, written in 1787 and 1788 by Alexander Hamilton, James Madison, and John Jay, constituted the great rationale for a radical experiment in government, and they remain the leading American contribution to the history of political theory.

The tenth essay, written by Madison, gets to the crux of the problem: the danger of what eighteenth-century writers

called "faction." Free political expression arouses passions, passions create partisan divisions, and divisions always bring the death of republics. Madison's argument adroitly turns the tables on the traditional fear of faction. He accepts the problem of faction, but sees its solution only in a large **republic. His is, one might say, a theory of countervailing factions, a domestic balance of power based on the multiplication of different interests in a heterogeneous country. In a nation of many different minorities, in a political system of divided sovereignties, Madison claimed there was little danger of anyone putting together enough people to dominate so broad an area and such a diverse political system. Of course, the men who advanced this notion of politics achieved just what their theory said was not possible: they managed to press their ideas of a stronger federal union upon a population that most scholars agree opposed the greater centralization of power provided in the Federalist's constitution of 1787.**

The Federalist No. 10

To the People of the State of New York:

Among the numerous advantages promised by a well-constructed Union, none deserves to be more accurately developed than its tendency to break and control the violence of faction. The friend of popular governments never finds himself so much alarmed for their character and fate, as when he contemplates their propensity to this dangerous vice. He will not fail, therefore, to set a due value on any plan which, without violating the principles to which he is attached, provides a proper cure for it. The instability, injustice, and confusion introduced into the public councils, have, in truth, been the mortal diseases under which popular governments have everywhere perished; as they continue to be the favorite and fruitful topics from which the adversaries to liberty derive their most specious declamations. The valuable improvements made by the American constitutions on the popular models, both ancient and modern, cannot certainly be too much admired; but it would be an unwarrantable partiality, to contend that they have as effectually obviated the danger on this side, as was wished and expected. Complaints are everywhere heard from our most considerate and virtuous citizens, equally the friends of public and private faith, and of public and personal liberty, that our governments are too unstable, that the public good is disregarded in the conflicts of rival parties, and that measures are too often decided, not according to the rules of justice and the rights of the minor party, but by the superior force of an interested and overbearing majority. However anxiously we may wish that these complaints had no foundation, the evidence of known facts will not permit us to deny that they are in some degree true. It will be found, indeed, on a candid review of our situation, that some of the distresses under which we labor have been erroneously charged on the operation of our governments; but it will be found, at the same time, that other causes will not alone account for many of our heaviest misfortunes; and, particularly, for that prevailing and increasing distrust of public engagements, and alarm for private rights, which are echoed from one end of the continent to the other. These must be chiefly, if not wholly, effects of the unsteadiness and injustice with which a factious spirit has tainted our public administrations.

By a faction, I understand a number of citizens, whether amounting to a majority or minority of the whole, who are united and actuated by some common impulse of passion, or of interest, adverse to the rights of other citizens, or to the permanent and aggregate interests of the community.

There are two methods of curing the mischiefs of faction: the one, by removing its causes; the other, by controlling its effects.

There are again two methods of removing the causes of faction: the one, by destroying the liberty which is essential to its existence; the other, by giving to every citizen the same opinions, the same passions, and the same interests.

It could never be more truly said than of the first remedy, that it was worse than the disease. Liberty is to faction what air is to fire, an aliment without which it instantly expires. But it could not be less folly to abolish liberty, which is essential to political life, because it nourishes faction, than it would be to wish the annihilation of air, which is essential to animal life, because it imparts to fire its destructive agency.

The second expedient is as impracticable as the first would be unwise. As long as the reason of man continues fallible, and he is at liberty to exercise it, different opinions will be formed. As long as the connection subsists between his reason and his self-love, his opinions and his passions will have a reciprocal influence on each other; and the former will be objects to which the latter will attach themselves. The diversity in the faculties of men, from which the rights of property originate, is not less an insuperable obstacle to a uniformity of interests. The protection of these faculties is the first object of government. From the protection of different and unequal faculties of acquiring property, the possession of different degrees and kinds of property immediately results; and from the influence of these on the sentiments and views of the respective proprietors, ensues a division of the society into different interests and parties.

The latent causes of faction are thus sown in the nature of man; and we see them everywhere brought into different degrees of activity, according to the different circumstances of civil society. A zeal for different opinions concerning religion, concerning government, and many other points, as well of speculation as of practice; an attachment to different leaders ambitiously contending for pre-eminence and power; or to persons of other descriptions whose fortunes have been interesting to the human passions, have, in turn, divided mankind into parties, inflamed them with mutual animosity, and rendered them much more disposed to vex and oppress each other than to co-operate for their common good. So strong is this propensity of mankind to fall into mutual animosities, that where no substantial occasion presents itself, the most frivolous and fanciful distinctions have been sufficient to kindle their unfriendly passions and excite their most violent conflicts. But the most common and durable source of factions has been the various and unequal distribution of property. Those who hold and those who are without property have ever formed distinct interests in society. Those who are creditors, and those who are debtors, fall under a like discrimination. A landed interest, a manufacturing interest, a mercantile interest, a moneyed interest, with many lesser interests, grow up of necessity in civilized nations, and divide them into different classes, actuated by different sentiments and views. The regulation of these various and interfering interests forms the principal task of modern legislation, and involves the spirit of party and faction in the necessary and ordinary operations of the government.

No man is allowed to be a judge in his own cause, because his interest would certainly bias his judgment, and, not improbably, corrupt his integrity. With equal, nay with greater reason, a body of men are unfit to be both judges and parties at the same time; yet what are many of the most important acts of legislation, but so many judicial determinations, not indeed concerning the rights of single persons, but concerning the rights of large bodies of citizens? And what are the different classes of legislators but advocates and parties to the causes which they determine? Is a law proposed concerning private debts? It is a question to which the creditors are parties on one side and the debtors on the other. Justice ought to hold the balance between them. Yet the parties are, and must be, themselves the judges; and the most numerous party, or, in other words, the most powerful faction must be expected to prevail. Shall domestic manufactures be encouraged, and in what degree, by restrictions on foreign manufactures? are questions which would be differently decided by the landed and the manufacturing classes, and probably by neither with a sole regard to justice and the public good. The apportionment of taxes on the various descriptions of property is an act which seems to require the most exact impartiality; yet there is, perhaps, no legislative act in which greater opportunity and temptation are given to a predominant party to trample on the rules of justice. Every shilling with which they overburden the inferior number, is a shilling saved to their own pockets.

It is in vain to say that enlightened statesmen will be able to adjust these clashing interests, and render them all subservient to the public good. Enlightened statesmen will not always be at the helm. Nor, in many cases, can such an adjustment be made at all without taking into view indirect and remote considerations, which will rarely prevail over the immediate interest which one party may find in disregarding the rights of another or the good of the whole.

The inference to which we are brought is, that the *causes* of faction cannot be removed, and that relief is only to be sought in the means of controlling its *effects*.

If a faction consists of less than a majority, relief is supplied by the republican principle, which enables the majority to defeat its sinister views by regular vote. It may clog the administration, it may convulse the society; but it will be unable to execute and mask its violence under the forms of the Constitution. When a majority is included in a faction, the form of popular government, on the other hand, enables it to sacrifice to its ruling passion or interest both the public good and the rights of other citizens. To secure the public good and private rights against the danger of such a faction, and at the same time to preserve the spirit and the form of popular government, is then the great object to which our inquiries are directed. Let me add that it is the great desideratum by which this form of government can be rescued from the opprobrium under which it has so long labored, and be recommended to the esteem and adoption of mankind.

By what means is this object attainable? Evidently by one of two only. Either the existence of the same passion or interest in a majority at the same time must be prevented, or the majority, having such coexistent passion or interest, must be rendered, by their number and local situation, unable to concert and carry into effect schemes of oppression. If the impulse and the opportunity be suffered to coincide, we well know that neither moral nor religious motives can be relied on as an adequate control. They are not found to be such on the injustice and violence of individuals, and lose their efficacy in proportion to the number combined together, that is, in proportion as their efficacy becomes needful.

From this view of the subject it may be concluded that a pure democracy, by which I mean a society consisting of a small number of citizens, who assemble and administer the government in person, can admit of no cure for the mischiefs of faction. A common passion or interest will, in almost every case, be felt by a majority of the whole; a communication and concert result from the form of government itself; and there is nothing to check the inducements to sacrifice the weaker party or an obnoxious individual. Hence it is that such democracies have ever been spectacles of turbulence and contention; have ever been found incompatible with personal security or the rights of property; and have in general been as short in their lives as they have been violent in their deaths. Theoretic politicians, who have patronized this species of government, have erroneously supposed that by reducing mankind to a perfect equality in their political rights, they would, at the same time, be perfectly equalized and assimilated in their possessions, their opinions, and their passions.

A republic, by which I mean a government in which the scheme of representation takes place, opens a different prospect, and promises the cure for which we are seeking. Let us examine the points in which it varies from pure democracy, and we shall comprehend both the nature of the cure and the efficacy which it must derive from the Union.

The two great points of difference between a democracy and a republic are: first, the delegation of the government, in the latter, to a small number of citizens elected by the rest; secondly, the greater number of citizens, and greater sphere of country, over which the latter may be extended.

The effect of the first difference is, on the one hand, to refine and enlarge the public views, by passing them through the medium of a chosen body of citizens, whose wisdom may best discern the true interest of their country, and whose patriotism and love of justice will be least likely to sacrifice it to temporary or partial considerations.

Under such a regulation, it may well happen that the public voice, pronounced by the representatives of the people, will be more consonant to the public good than if pronounced by the people themselves, convened for the purpose. On the other hand, the effect may be inverted. Men of factious tempers, of local prejudices, or of sinister designs, may, by intrigue, by corruption, or by other means, first obtain the suffrages, and then betray the interests, of the people. The question resulting is, whether small or extensive republics are more favorable to the election of proper guardians of the public weal; and it is clearly decided in favor of the latter by two obvious considerations:

In the first place, it is to be remarked that, however small the republic may be, the representatives must be raised to a certain number, in order to guard against the cabals of a few; and that, however large it may be, they must be limited to a certain number, in order to guard against the confusion of a multitude. Hence, the number of representatives in the two cases not being in proportion to that of the two constituents, and being proportionally greater in the small republic, it follows that, if the proportion of fit characters be not less in the large than in the small republic, the former will present a greater option, and consequently a greater probability of a fit choice.

In the next place, as each representative will be chosen by a greater number of citizens in the large than in the small republic, it will be more difficult for unworthy candidates to practise with success the vicious arts by which elections are too often carried; and the suffrages of the people being more free, will be more likely to centre in men who possess the most attractive merit and the most diffusive and established characters.

It must be confessed that in this, as in most other cases, there is a mean, on both sides of which inconveniences will be found to lie. By enlarging too much the number of electors, you render the representative too little acquainted with all their local circumstances and lesser interests; as by reducing it too much, you render him unduly attached to these, and too little fit to comprehend and pursue great and national objects. The federal Consititution forms a happy combination in this respect; the great and aggregate interests being referred to the national, the local and particular to the State legislatures.

The other point of difference is, the greater number of citizens and extent of territory which may be brought within the compass of republican than of democratic government; and it is this circumstance principally which renders factious combinations less to be dreaded in the former than in the latter. The smaller the society, the fewer probably will be the distinct parties and interests composing it; the fewer the distinct parties and interests, the more frequently will a majority be found of the same party; and the smaller the number of individuals composing a majority, and the smaller the compass within which they are placed, the more easily will they concert and execute their plans of oppression. Extend the sphere, and you take in a greater variety of parties and interests; you make it less probable that a majority of the whole will have a common motive to invade the rights of other citizens; or if such a common motive exists, it will be more difficult for all who feel it to discover their own strength, and to act in unison with each other. Besides other impediments, it may be remarked that, where there is a consciousness of unjust or dishonorable purposes, communication is always checked by distrust in proportion to the number whose concurrence is necessary.

Hence, it clearly appears, that the same advantage which a republic has over a democracy, in controlling the effects of faction, is enjoyed by a large over a small republic,—is enjoyed by the Union over the States composing it. Does the advantage consist in the substitution of representatives whose enlightened views and virtuous sentiments render them superior to local prejudices and to schemes of injustice? It will not be denied that the representation of the Union will be most likely to possess these requisite endowments. Does it consist in the greater security afforded by a greater variety of parties, against the event of any one party being able to outnumber and oppress the rest? In an equal degree does the increased variety of parties comprised within the Union, increase this security. Does it, in fine, consist in the greater obstacles opposed to the concert and accomplishment of the secret wishes of an unjust and interested majority? Here, again, the extent of the Union gives it the most palpable advantage.

The influence of factious leaders may kindle a flame within their particular States, but will be unable to spread a general conflagration through the other States. A religious sect may degenerate into a political faction in a part of the Confederacy; but the variety of sects dispersed over the entire face of it must secure the national councils against any danger from that source. A rage for paper money, for an abolition of debts, for an equal division of property, or for any other improper or wicked project, will be less apt to pervade the whole body of the Union than a particular member of it; in the same proportion as such a malady is more likely to taint a particular county or district, than an entire State.

In the extent and proper structure of the Union, therefore, we behold a republican remedy for the diseases most incident to republican government. And according to the degree of pleasure and pride we feel in being republicans, ought to be our zeal in cherishing the spirit and supporting the character of Federalists.

PUBLIUS

The Federalist No. 39

To the People of the State of New York:

The last paper having concluded the observations which were meant to introduce a candid survey of the plan of government reported by the convention, we now proceed to the execution of that part of our undertaking.

The first question that offers itself is, whether the general form and aspect of the government be strictly republican. It is evident that no other form would be reconcilable with the genius of the people of America; with the fundamental principles of the Revolution; or with that honorable determination which animates every votary of freedom, to rest all our political experiments on the capacity of mankind for self-government. If the plan of the convention, therefore, be found to depart from the republican character, its advocates must abandon it as no longer defensible.

What, then, are the distinctive characters of the republican form? Were an answer to this question to be sought, not by recurring to principles, but in the application of the term by political writers, to the constitutions of different States, no satisfactory one would ever be found. Holland, in which no particle of the supreme authority is derived from the people, has passed almost universally under the denomination of a republic. The same title has been bestowed on Venice, where absolute power over the great body of the people is exercised, in the most absolute manner, by a small body of hereditary nobles. Poland, which is a mixture of aristocracy and of monarchy in their worst forms, has been dignified with the same appellation. The government of England, which has one republican branch only, combined with an hereditary aristocracy and monarchy, has, with equal impropriety, been frequently placed on the list of republics. These examples, which are nearly as dissimilar to each other as to a genuine republic, show the extreme inaccuracy with which the term has been used in political disquisitions.

If we resort for a criterion to the different principles on which different forms of government are established, we may define a republic to be, or at least may bestow that name on, a government which derives all its powers directly or indirectly from the great body of the people, and is administered by persons holding their offices during pleasure, for a limited period, or during good behavior. It is *essential* to such a government that it be derived from the great body of the society, not from an inconsiderable proportion, or a favored class of it; otherwise a handful of tyrannical nobles, exercising their oppressions by a delegation of their powers, might aspire to the rank of republicans, and claim for their government the honorable title of republic. It is *sufficient* for such a government that the persons administering it be appointed, either directly or indirectly, by the people; and that they hold their appointments by either of the tenures just specified; otherwise every government in the United States, as well as every other popular government that has been or can be well organized or well executed, would be degraded from the republican character. According to the constitution of every State in the Union, some or other of the officers of government are appointed indirectly only by the people. According to most of them, the chief magistrate himself is so appointed. And according to one, this mode of appointment is extended to one of the coördinate branches of the legislature. According to all the constitutions, also, the tenure of the highest offices is extended to a definite period, and in many instances, both within the legislative and executive departments, to a period of years. According to the provisions of most of the constitutions, again, as well as according to the most respectable and received opinions on the subject, the members of the judiciary department are to retain their offices by the firm tenure of good behavior.

On comparing the Constitution planned by the convention with the standard here fixed, we perceive at once that it is, in the most rigid sense, conformable to it. The House of Representatives, like that of one branch at least of all the State legislatures, is elected immediately by the great body of the people. The Senate, like the present Congress, and the Senate of Maryland, derives its appointment indirectly from the people. The President is indirectly derived from the choice of the people, according to the example in most of the States. Even the judges with all other officers of the Union, will, as in the several States, be the choice, though a remote choice, of the people themselves. The duration of the appointments is equally conformable to the republican standard, and to the model of State constitutions. The House of Representatives is periodically elective, as in all the States; and for the period of two years, as in the State of South Carolina. The Senate is elective, for the period of six years; which is but one year more than the period of the Senate of Maryland, and but two more than that of the Senates of New York and Virginia. The President is to continue in office for the period of four years; as in New York and Delaware the chief magistrate is elected for three years, and in South Carolina for two years. In the other States the election is annual. In several of the States, however, no constitutional provision is made for the impeachment of the chief magistrate. And in Delaware and Virginia he is not impeachable till out of office. The President of the United States is impeachable at any time during his continuance in office. The tenure by which the judges are to hold their places, is, as it unquestionably ought to be, that of good behavior. The tenure of the ministerial offices generally, will be a subject of legal regulation, conformably to the reason of the case and the example of the State constitutions.

Could any further proof be required of the republican complexion of this system, the most decisive one might be found in its absolute prohibition of titles of nobility, both under the federal and the State governments; and in its express guaranty of the republican form to each of the latter.

"But it was not sufficient," say the adversaries of the proposed Constitution, "for the convention to adhere to the republican form.

They ought, with equal care, to have preserved the *federal* form, which regards the Union as a *Confederacy* of sovereign states; instead of which, they have framed a *national* government, which regards the Union as a *consolidation* of the States." And it is asked by what authority this bold and radical innovation was undertaken? The handle which has been made of this objection requires that it should be examined with some precision.

Without inquiring into the accuracy of the distinction on which the objection is founded, it will be necessary to a just estimate of its force, first, to ascertain the real character of the government in question; secondly, to inquire how far the convention were authorized to propose such a government; and thirdly, how far the duty they owed to their country could supply any defect of regular authority.

First.—In order to ascertain the real character of the government, it may be considered in relation to the foundation on which it is to be established; to the sources from which its ordinary powers are to be drawn; to the operation of those powers; to the extent of them; and to the authority by which future changes in the government are to be introduced.

On examining the first relation, it appears, on one hand, that the Constitution is to be founded on the assent and ratification of the people of America, given by deputies elected for the special purpose; but, on the other, that this assent and ratification is to be given by the people, not as individuals composing one entire nation, but as composing the distinct and independent States to which they respectively belong. It is to be the assent and ratification of the several States, derived from the supreme authority in each State,—the authority of the people themselves. The act, therefore, establishing the Constitution, will not be a *national,* but a *federal* act.

That it will be a federal and not a national act, as these terms are understood by the objectors; the act of the people, as forming so many independent States, not as forming one aggregate nation, is obvious from this single consideration, that it is to result neither from the decision of a *majority* of the people of the Union, nor from that of a *majority* of the States. It must result from the *unanimous* assent of the several States that are parties to it, differing no otherwise from their ordinary assent than in its being expressed, not by the legislative authority, but by that of the people themselves. Were the people regarded in this transaction as forming one nation, the will of the majority of the whole people of the United States would bind the minority, in the same manner as the majority in each State must bind the minority; and the will of the majority must be determined either by a comparison of the individual votes, or by considering the will of the majority of the States as evidence of the will of a majority of the people of the United States. Neither of these rules has been adopted. Each State, in ratifying the Constitution, is considered as a sovereign body, independent of all others, and only to be bound by its own voluntary act. In this relation, then, the new Constitution will, if established, be a *federal,* and not a *national* constitution.

The next relation is, to the sources from which the ordinary powers of government are to be derived. The House of Representatives will derive its powers from the people of America; and the people will be represented in the same proportion, and on the same principle, as they are in the legislature of a particular State. So far the government is *national,* not *federal.* The Senate, on the other hand, will derive its powers from the States, as political and coequal societies; and these will be represented on the principle of equality in the Senate, as they now are in the existing Congress. So far the government is *federal,* not *national.* The executive power will be derived from a very compound source. The immediate election of the President is to be made by the States in their political characters. The votes allotted to them are in a compound ratio, which considers them partly as distinct and coequal societies, partly as unequal members of the same society. The eventual election, again, is to be made by that branch of the legislature which consists of the national representatives; but in this particular act they are to be thrown into the form of individual delegations, from so many distinct and coequal bodies politic. From this aspect of the government, it appears to be of a mixed character, presenting at least as many *federal* as *national* features.

The difference between a federal and national government, as it relates to the *operation of the government,* is supposed to consist in this, that in the former the powers operate on the political bodies composing the Confederacy, in their political capacities; in the latter, on the individual citizens composing the nation, in their individual capacities. On trying the Constitution by this criterion, it falls under the *national,* not the *federal* character; though perhaps not so completely as has been understood. In several cases, and particularly in the trial of controversies to which States may be parties, they must be viewed and proceeded against in their collective and political capacities only. So far the national countenance of the government on this side seems to be disfigured by a few federal features. But this blemish is perhaps unavoidable in any plan; and the operation of the government on the people, in their individual capacities, in its ordinary and most essential proceedings, may, on the whole, designate it, in this relation, a *national* government.

But if the government be national with regard to the *operation* of its powers, it changes its aspect again when we contemplate it in relation to the extent of its powers. The idea of a national government involves in it, not only an authority over the individual citizens, but an indefinite supremacy over all persons and things, so far as they are objects of lawful government. Among a people consolidated into one nation, this supremacy is completely vested in the national legislature. Among communities united for particular purposes, it is vested partly in the general and partly in the municipal legislatures. In the former case, all local authorities are subordinate to the supreme; and may be controlled, directed, or abolished by it at pleasure. In the latter, the local or municipal authorities form distinct and independent portions of the supremacy, no more subject, within their respective spheres, to the general authority, than the general authority is subject to them, within its own sphere. In this relation, then, the proposed government cannot be deemed a *national* one; since its jurisdiction extends to certain enumerated objects only, and leaves to the several States a residuary and inviolable sovereignty over all other objects. It is true that in controversies relating to the boundary between the two jurisdictions, the tribunal which is ultimately to decide, is to be established under the general government. But this does not change the principle of the case. The decision is to be impartially made, according to the rules of the Constitution; and all the usual and most effectual precautions are taken to secure this impartiality. Some such tribunal is clearly essential to prevent an appeal to the sword and a dissolution of the compact; and that it ought to be established under the general rather than under the local governments, or, to speak more properly, that it could be safely established under the first alone, is a position not likely to be combated.

If we try the Constitution by its last relation to the authority by which amendments are to be made, we find it neither wholly *national* nor wholly *federal.* Were it wholly national, the supreme and ultimate authority would reside in the *majority* of the people of the Union; and this authority would be competent at all times, like that of a majority of every national society, to alter or abolish its established government. Were it wholly federal, on the other hand, the concurrence of each State in the Union would be essential to every alteration that would be binding on all. The mode provided by the plan of the convention is not founded on either of these principles. In requiring more than a majority, and particularly in computing the proportion by *States,* not by *citizens,* it departs from the *national* and advances towards the *federal* character; in rendering the concurrence of less than the whole number of States sufficient, it loses again the *federal* and partakes of the *national* character.

The proposed Constitution, therefore, is, in strictness, neither a national nor a federal Constitution, but a composition of both. In its foundation it is federal, not national; in the sources from which the ordinary powers of the government are drawn, it is partly federal and partly national; in the operation of these powers, it is national, not federal; in the extent of them, again, it is federal, not national; and, finally, in the authoritative mode of introducing amendments, it is neither wholly federal nor wholly national.

PUBLIUS

PARSON WEEMS

The Life of George Washington

(1800)

The Life of George Washington; with Curious Anecdotes, Equally Honourable to Himself, and Exemplary to his Young Countrymen by Mason Locke Weems, "Formerly Rector of Mount Vernon Parish," was the basis for the schoolbook vision of Washington which nineteenth-century Americans absorbed and twentieth-century Americans have rejected. The anecdote of the cherry tree, reprinted in McGuffey's Readers for a century, confronts the modern reader with – in the words of a later, more scholarly biographer than Weems – "an impossible and intolerable prig." That a boy does not lie is commend-

able, but a boy who "can't tell a lie, Pa" cannot easily be forgiven. Weems's blend of moralism and patriotism obscures the real Washington, who delighted in pretty women and whose capacity for consumption of alcohol was well known to junior officers during the Revolutionary War. Somewhere between the moral claims of The Life of Washington and the realities can be found the values around which much of American life has always pivoted.

Weems's Washington was everything that Weems himself was not. The "Parson" had no trouble telling lies. Not only was he not the "Rector of Mount Vernon Parish," as he claimed, there was not even a Mount Vernon parish! The anecdote about the cherry tree may be "curious," but it surely is not true: Weems made it up sometime between the publication of the first edition in 1800 and the 5th edition in 1806. On the other hand, no one can accuse Weems of concocting the story of the cabbage seeds spelling Washington's name, which also appears first in the 5th edition: that tale he plagiarized from a recently published book. Weems's moralism was honest enough: he had already written a pioneering work about the dangers of masturbation (Onania, 1791 or 1792) and would later regale American sensitivities with treatises commending marriage (Hymen's Recruiting Sergeant [1805]) and condemning murder, gambling, alcohol, adultery (in two volumes), and dueling. His motivation in publishing The Life of Washington, however, was—to say the least—mixed:

> "I've something to whisper in your lug (he wrote to his publisher right after Washington's death). Washington, you know is gone! Millions are gaping to read something about him. I am very nearly primd and cockd for 'em. 6 months ago I set myself to collect anecdotes of him. . . . We may sell it with great rapidity for 25 or 37 Cents and it wd not cost 10 . . . it will be the first. I can send it on, half of it, immediately."

There was, as Weems wrote at another time, "a world of pence and popularity" in it. Indeed there was! This purveyor of "plagiarism and piety" as one writer describes him, this itinerant book peddler and literary charlatan remains intertwined with our vision of George Washington, first in war and first in the presidency, a chastening thought as we continue to wonder if behind every great man there is not in fact a great PR man.

I

Oh! as along the stream of time thy name
Expanded flies, and gathers all its fame;
May then these lines to future days descend,
And prove thy country's good thine only end!

"Ah, gentlemen!"—exclaimed Bonaparte—'twas just as he was about to embark for Egypt—some young Americans happening at Toulon, and anxious to see the mighty Corsican, had obtained the honour of an introduction to him. Scarcely were past the customary salutations, when he eagerly asked, "how fares your countryman, the great WASHINGTON?" "He was very well," replied the youths, brightening at the thought, that they were the countrymen of Washington; "he was very well, general, when we left America."—"Ah, gentlemen!" rejoined he, "Washington can never be otherwise than well.—The measure of his fame is full.—Posterity will talk of him with reverence as the founder of a great empire, when my name shall be lost in the vortex of Revolutions!"

Who, then, that has a spark of virtuous curiosity, but must wish to know the history of him whose name could thus awaken the sigh even of Bonaparte? But is not his history already known? Have not a thousand orators spread his fame abroad, bright as his own Potomac, when he reflects the morning sun, and flames like a sea of liquid gold, the wonder and delight of all the neighbouring shores? Yes, they have indeed spread his fame abroad. . . . his fame as Generalissimo of the armies, and first President of the councils of his nation. But this is not half his fame. . . . True, he has been seen in greatness: but it is only the greatness of public character, which is no evidence of true greatness; for a public character is often an artificial one. At the head of an army or nation, where gold and glory are at stake, and where a man feels himself the burning focus of unnumbered eyes; he must be a paltry fellow, indeed, who does not play his part pretty handsomely . . . even the common passions of pride, avarice, or ambition, will put him up to his mettle, and call forth his best and bravest doings. But let this heat and blaze of public situation and incitement be withdrawn; let him be thrust back into the shade of private life; and you shall see how soon, like a forced plant robbed of its hot-bed, he will drop his false foliage and fruit, and stand forth confessed in native stickweed sterility and worthlessness.—There was Benedict Arnold—while strutting a BRIGADIER GENERAL on the public state, he could play you the great man, on a handsome scale——he out-marched Hannibal, and out-fought Burgoyne——he chased the British like curlews, or cooped them up like chickens! and yet in the private walks of life, in Philadelphia, he could swindle rum from the commissary's stores, and, with the aid of loose women, retail it by the gill!!—And there was the great duke of Marlborough too—his public character, a thunderbolt in war! Britain's boast, and the terror of the French! But his private character, what? Why a swindler to whom Arnold's self could hold a candle; a perfect nondescript of baseness; a shaver of farthings from the poor sixpenny pay of his own brave soldiers!!

It is not, then, in the glare of public, but in the shade of private life, that we are to look for the man. Private life, is always real life. Behind the curtain, where the eyes of the million are not upon him, and where a man can have no motive but inclination, no incitement but honest nature, there he will always be sure to act himself: consequently, if he act greatly, he must be great indeed. Hence it has been justly said, that, "our private deeds, if noble, are noblest of our lives."

Of these private deeds of Washington very little has been said. In most of the elegant orations pronounced to his praise, you see nothing of Washington below the clouds—nothing of Washington the dutiful son—the affectionate brother—the cheerful school-boy—the diligent surveyor—the neat draftsman—the laborious farmer—the widow's husband—the orphan's father—the poor man's friend. No! this is not the Washington you see; 'tis only Washington, the HERO, and the Demigod—Washington the sunbeam in council, or the storm in war.

And in all the ensigns of character amidst which he is generally drawn, you see none that represent him what he really was, "the jupiter Conservator," the friend and benefactor of men. Where's his bright ploughshare that he loved—or his wheat-crowned fields, waving in yellow ridges before the wanton breeze—or his hills whitened over with flocks—or his clover covered pastures spread with innumerous herds—or his neat-clad servants with songs rolling the heavy harvest before them? Such were the scenes of peace, plenty, and happiness, in which Washington delighted. But his eulogists have denied him these, the only scenes which belong to man the GREAT; and have trick'd him up in the vile drapery of man the little. See! there he stands! with the port of Mars "the destroyer," dark frowning over the fields of war—the lightning of Potter's blade is by his side—the deep-mouthed cannon is before him, disgorging its flesh-mangling balls—his war-horse pants with impatience to bear him, a speedy thunderbolt, against the pale and bleeding ranks of Britain!—These are the drawings usually given of Washington; drawings masterly no doubt, and perhaps justly descriptive of him in some scenes of his life. But scenes they were, which I am sure his soul abhorred, and in which, at any rate, you see nothing of his private virtues. These old fashioned commodities are generally thrown into the back ground of the picture; and treated, as the grandees at the London and Paris routs, treat their good old aunts and grandmothers, huddling them together into the back rooms, there to wheeze and cough by themselves, and not depress the fine laudanum-raised spirits of the young sparklers. And yet it was to those old fashioned virtues that our hero owed every thing. For they in fact were the food of the great actions of him, whom men call Washington. It was they that enabled him, first to triumph over himself; then over the British; and uniformly to set such bright examples of human perfectibility and true greatness, that, compared therewith, the history of his capturing Cornwallis and Tarleton, with their buccaneering legions, sounds almost as small as the story of General Putnam's catching his wolf and her lamb-killing whelps.

Since then it is the private virtues that lay the foundation of all human excellence—since it was these that exalted Washington to be "Columbia's first and greatest Son," be it our first care to present these, in all their lustre, before the admiring eyes of our children. To them his private character is every thing; his public, hardly any thing. For how glorious soever it may have been in Washington to have undertaken the emancipation of his country; to have stemmed the long tide of adversity; to have baffled every effort of a wealthy and warlike nation; to have obtained for his countrymen the completest victory, and for himself the most unbounded power; and then to have returned that power, accompanied with all the weight of his own great character and advice to establish a government that should immortalize the blessings of liberty—however glorious, I say, all this may have been to himself, or instructive to future generals and presidents, yet does it but little concern our children. For who among us can hope that his son shall ever be called, like Washington, to direct the storm of war, or to ravish the ears of deeply listening Senates? To be constantly placing him then, before our children, in this high character, what is it but like springing in the clouds a golden Phoenix, which no mortal calibre can ever hope to reach? Or like setting pictures of the Mammoth before the mice, whom "not all the manna of Heaven" can ever raise to equality? Oh no! give us his private virtues! In these, every youth is interested, because in these every youth may become a Washington—a Washington in piety and patriotism,—in industry and honour—and consequently a Washington, in what alone deserves the name, SELF ESTEEM and UNIVERSAL RESPECT.

II

Birth and Education

"Children like tender osiers take the bow;
"And as they first are form'd, forever grow."

To this day numbers of good Christians can hardly find faith to believe that Washington was, bona fide, a Virginian! "What! a buckskin!" say they with a smile. "George Washington a buckskin! pshaw! impossible! he was certainly an European: So great a man could never have been born in America."

So great a man could never have been born in America!—why that's the very prince of reasons why he should have been born here! Nature, we know, is fond of harmonies; and paria paribus, that is, great things to great, is the rule she delights to work by. Where, for example, do we look for the whale, "the biggest born of nature?" not, I trow, in a mill-pond, but in the main ocean. "There go the great ships": and there are the spoutings of whales amidst their boiling foam.

By the same rule, where shall we look for Washington, the greatest among men, but in America—that greatest Continent, which, rising from beneath the frozen pole, stretches far and wide to the south, running almost "the whole length of this vast terrene," and sustaining on her ample sides the roaring shock of half the watery globe? And equal to its size is the furniture of this vast continent, where the Almighty has reared his cloud-capt mountains, and spread his sea-like lakes, and poured his mighty rivers, and hurled down his thundering cataracts in a style of the sublime, so far superior to any thing of the kind in the other continents, that we may fairly conclude that great men and great deeds are designed for America.

This seems to be the verdict of honest analogy; and accordingly we find America the honoured cradle of Washington, who was born on Pope's creek, in Westmoreland county, Virginia, the 22nd of February, 1732. His father, whose name was Augustin Washington, was also a Virginian: but his grandfather (John) was an Englishman, who came over and settled in Virginia in 1657.

His father, fully persuaded that a marriage of virtuous love comes nearest to angelic life, early stepped up to the altar with glowing cheeks and joy sparkling eyes, while by his side with soft warm hand, sweetly trembling in his, stood the angel-form of the lovely Miss Dandridge.

After several years of great domestic happiness Mr. Washington was separated by death from this excellent woman, who left him and two children to lament her early fate.

Fully persuaded still, that "it is not good for man to be alone," he renewed, for the second time, the chaste delights of matrimonial love. His consort was Miss Mary Ball, a young lady of fortune, and descended from one of the best families in Virginia.

From his intermarriage with this charming girl, it would appear that our hero's father must have possessed either a very pleasing person, or highly polished manners, or perhaps both; for, from what I can learn, he was at that time at least forty years old! while she, on the other hand, was universally toasted as the belle of the Northern Neck, and in the full bloom and freshness of love-inspiring sixteen. This I have from one who tells me that he has carried down many a sett dance with her; I mean that amiable and pleasant old gentleman, John Fitzhugh, Esq. of Stafford, who was, all his life, a neighbour and intimate of the Washington family. By his first wife, Mr. Washington had two children, both sons—Lawrence and Augustin. By his second wife, he had five children, four sons and a daughter—George, Samuel, John, Charles, and Elizabeth. Those over delicate folk, who are ready to faint at thought of a second marriage, might do well to remember, that the greatest man that ever lived was the son of this second marriage.

Little George had scarcely attained his fifth year, when his father left Pope's creek, and came up to a plantation which he had in Stafford, opposite to Fredericksburg. The house in which he lived is still to be seen. It lifts its low and modest front of faded red, over the turbid waters of Rappahannock; whither, to this day, numbers of people repair, and, with emotions unutterable, looking at the weather-beaten mansion, exclaim, "Here's the house where the great Washington was born!"

But it is all a mistake; for he was born, as I said, at Pope's creek, in Westmoreland county, near the margin of his own roaring Potomac.

The first place of education to which George was ever sent, was a little "old field school," kept by one of his father's tenants, named Hobby; an honest, poor old man, who acted in the double character of sexton and schoolmaster. On his skill as a grave-digger, tradition is silent; but for a teacher of youth, his qualifications were certainly of the humbler sort; making what is generally called an A. B. C. schoolmaster. Such was the preceptor who first taught Washington the knowledge of letters! Hobby lived to see his young pupil in all his glory, and rejoiced exceedingly. In his cups—for though a sexton, he would sometimes drink, particularly on the General's birth days—he used to boast that "'twas he, who, between his knees, had laid the foundation of George Washington's greatness."

But though George was early sent to a schoolmaster, yet he was not on that account neglected by his father. Deeply sensible of the loveliness and worth of which human nature is capable, through the virtues and graces early implanted in the heart, he never for a moment, lost sight of George in those all-important respects.

To assist his son to overcome that selfish spirit, which too often leads children to fret and fight about trifles, was a notable care of Mr. Washington. For this purpose, of all the presents, such as cakes, fruit, &c. he received, he was always desired to give a liberal part to his play-mates. To enable him to do this with more alacrity, his father would remind him of the love which he would thereby gain, and the frequent presents which would in return be made to him; and also would tell of that great and good God; who delights above all things to see children love one another, and will assuredly reward them for acting so amiable a part.

Some idea of Mr. Washington's plan of education in this respect, may be collected from the following anecdote, related to me twenty years ago by an aged lady, who was a distant relative, and, when a girl, spent much of her time in the family:

"On a fine morning," said she, "in the fall of 1737, Mr. Washington having little George by the hand, came to the door and asked my cousin Washington and myself to walk with him to the orchard, promising he would show us a fine sight. On arriving at the orchard, we were presented with a fine sight indeed. The whole earth, as far as we could see, was strewed with fruit: and yet the trees were bending under the weight of apples, which hung in clusters like grapes, and vainly strove to hide their blushing cheeks behind the green leaves. Now, George, said his father, look here, my son! don't you remember when this good cousin of yours brought you that fine large apple last spring, how hardly I could prevail on you to divide with your brothers and sisters; though I promised you that if you would but do it, God Almighty would give you plenty of apples this fall. Poor George could not say a word; but hanging down his head, looked quite confused, while with his little naked toes he scratched in the soft ground. Now look up, my son, continued his father, look up, George! and see there how richly the blessed God has made good my promise to you. Wherever you turn your eyes, you see the trees loaded with fine fruit; many of them indeed breaking down; while the ground is covered with mellow apples, more than you could eat, my son, in all your life time."

George looked in silence on the wide wilderness of fruit. He marked the busy humming bees, and heard the gay notes of birds; then lifting his eyes, filled with shining moisture, to his father, he softly said, "Well, Pa, only forgive me this time; and see if I ever be so stingy any more."

Some, when they look up to the oak, whose giant arms throw a darkening shade over distant acres, or whose single trunk lays the keel of a man of war, cannot bear to hear of the time when this mighty plant was but an acorn, which a pig could have demolished. But others, who know their value, like to learn the soil and situation which best produces such noble trees. Thus, parents that are wise, will listen, well pleased, while I relate how moved the steps of the youthful Washington, whose single worth far outweighs all the oaks of Bashan and the red spicy cedars of Lebanon. Yes, they will listen delighted while I tell of their Washington in the days of his youth, when his little feet were swift towards the nests of birds; or when, wearied in the chase of the butterfly, he laid him down on his grassy couch and slept, while ministering spirits, with their roseate wings, fanned his glowing cheeks, and kissed his lips of innocence with that fervent love which makes the Heaven!

Never did the wise Ulysses take more pains with his beloved Telemachus, than did Mr. Washington with George, to inspire him with an early love of truth. "Truth, George," said he, "is the loveliest quality of youth. I would ride fifty miles, my son, to see the little boy whose heart is so honest, and his lips so pure, that we may depend on every word he says. O how lovely does such a child appear in the eyes of every body! his parents doat on him. His relations glory in him. They are constantly praising him to their children, whom they beg to imitate him. They are often sending for him to visit them; and receive him, when he comes, with as much joy as if he were a little angel, come to set pretty examples to their children.

"But, Oh! how different, George, is the case with the boy who is so given to lying, that nobody can believe a word he says! He is looked at with aversion wherever he goes, and parents dread to see him come among their children. Oh, George! my son! rather than see you come to this pass, dear as you are to my heart, gladly would I assist to nail you up in your little coffin, and follow you to your grave. Hard, indeed, would it be to me to give up my son, whose little feet are always so ready to run about with me, and whose fondly looking eyes, and sweet prattle make so large a part of my happiness. But still I would give him up, rather than see him a common liar."

"Pa," said George very seriously, "do I ever tell lies?"

"No, George, I thank God you do not, my son; and I rejoice in the hope you never will. At least, you shall never, from me, have cause to be guilty of so shameful a thing. Many parents, indeed, even compel their children to this vile practice, by barbarously beating them for every little fault: hence, on the next offence, the little terrified creature slips out a lie! just to escape the rod. But as to yourself George, you know I have always told you, and now tell you again, that, whenever by accident, you do any thing wrong, which must often be the case, as you are but a poor little boy yet, without experience or knowledge, you must never tell a falsehood to conceal it; but come bravely up, my son, like a little man, and tell me of it: and, instead of beating you, George, I will but the more honour and love you for it, my dear."

This, you'll say, was sowing good seed!—Yes, it was: and the crop, thank God, was, as I believe it ever will be, where a man acts the true parent, that is, the Guardian Angel, by his child.

The following anecdote is a case in point. It is too valuable to be lost, and too true to be doubted; for it was communicated to me by the same excellent lady to whom I am indebted for the last.

"When George," said she, "was about six years old, he was made the wealthy master of a hatchet! of which, like most little boys, he was immoderately fond, and was constantly going about chopping every thing that came in his way. One day, in the garden, where he often amused himself hacking his mother's pea-sticks, he unluckily tried the edge of his hatchet on the body of a beautiful young English cherry-tree, which he barked so terribly, that I don't believe the tree ever got the better of it. The next morning the old gentleman, finding out what had befallen his tree, which, by the by, was a great favourite, came into the house; and with much warmth asked for the mischievous author, declaring at the same time, that he would not have taken five guineas for his tree. Nobody could tell him any thing about it. Presently George and his hatchet made their appearance.

"George," said his father, "do you know who killed that beautiful little cherry tree yonder in the garden?" This was a tough question; and George staggered under it for a moment; but quickly recovered himself: and looking at his father, with the sweet face of youth brightened with the inexpressible charm of all-conquering truth, he bravely cried out, "I can't tell a lie, Pa; you know I can't tell a lie. I did cut it with my hatchet." "Run to my arms, you dearest boy," cried his father in transports, "run to my arms. Glad am I, George, that you killed my tree; for you have paid me for it a thousand fold. Such an act of heroism in my son is more worth than a thousand trees, though blossomed with silver, and their fruits of purest gold."

It was in this way by interesting at once both his heart and head, that Mr. Washington conducted George with great ease and pleasure along the happy paths of virtue. But well knowing that his beloved charge, soon to be a man, would be left exposed to numberless temptations, both from himself and from others, his heart throbbed with the tenderest anxiety to make him acquainted with that great being, whom to know and love, is to possess the surest defence against vice, and the best of all motives to virtue and happiness. To startle George into a lively sense of his Maker, he fell upon the following very curious but impressive expedient:

One day he went into the garden, and prepared a little bed of finely pulverized earth, on which he wrote George's name at full, in large letters—then strewing in plenty of cabbage seed, he covered them up, and smoothed all over nicely with the roller.—This bed he purposely prepared close along side of a gooseberry walk, which happening at this time to be well hung with ripe fruit, he knew would be honoured with George's visits pretty regularly every day. Not many mornings had passed away before in came George, with eyes wild rolling, and his little cheeks ready to burst with great news.

"O Pa! come here! come here!"

"What's the matter, my son? what's the matter?"

"O come here, I tell you, Pa: come here! and I'll shew you such a sight as you never saw in all your life time."

The old gentleman suspecting what George would be at, gave him his hand, which he seized with great eagerness, and tugging him along through the garden, led him point blank to the bed whereon was inscribed, in large letters, and in all the freshness of newly sprung plants, the full name of

GEORGE WASHINGTON.

"There Pa?" said George, quite in an ecstacy of astonishment, "did you ever see such a sight in all your life time?"

"Why it seems like a curious affair, sure enough, George!"

"But, Pa, who did make it there? who did make it there?"

"It grew there by chance, I suppose, my son."

"By chance, Pa! O no! no! it never did grow here by chance, Pa. Indeed that it never did!"

"High! why not, my son?"

"Why, Pa, did you ever see any body's name in a plant bed before?"

"Well, but George, such a thing might happen, though you never saw it before."

"Yes, Pa; but I did never see the little plants grow up so as to make one single letter of my name before. Now, how could they grow up so as to make all the letters of my name! and then standing one after another, to spell my name so exactly!—and all so neat and even too, at top and bottom!! O Pa, you must not say chance did all this. Indeed somebody did it; and I dare say now, Pa, you did it just to scare me, because I am your little boy."

His father smiled; and said, "Well George, you have guessed right. I indeed did it; but not to scare you, my son; but to learn you a great thing which I wish you to understand. I want, my son, to introduce you to your true Father."

"High, Pa, an't you my true father, that has loved me, and been so good to me always?"

"Yes George, I am your father, as the world calls it: and I love you very dearly too. But yet with all my love for you, George, I am but a poor good-for-nothing sort of a father in comparison of one you have."

"Aye! I know, well enough whom you mean, Pa. You mean God Almighty; don't you?"

"Yes, my son, I mean him indeed. He is your true Father, George."

"But, Pa, where is God Almighty! I did never see him yet."

"True my son; but though you never saw him, yet he is always with you. You did not see me when ten days ago I made this little plant bed, where you see your name in such beautiful green letters: but though you did not see me here, yet you know I was here!!"

"Yes, Pa, that I do. I know you was here."

"Well then, and as my son could not believe that chance had made and put together so exactly the letters of his name, (though only sixteen) then how can he believe, that chance could have made and put together all those millions and millions of things that are now so exactly fitted to his good! That my son may look at every thing around him, see! what fine eyes he has got! and a little pug nose to smell the sweet flowers! and pretty ears to hear sweet sounds! and a lovely mouth for his bread and butter! and O, the little ivory teeth to cut it for him! and the dear little tongue to prattle with his father! and precious little hands and fingers to hold his play-things! and beautiful little feet for him to run about upon! and when my little rogue of a son is tired with running about, then the still night comes for him to lie down: and his mother sings, and the little crickets chirp him to sleep! and as soon as he has slept enough, and jumps up fresh and strong as a little buck, there the sweet golden light is ready for him! When he looks down into the water, there he sees the beautiful silver fishes for him! and up in the trees there are the apples, and peaches, and thousands of sweet fruits for him! and all, all around him, wherever my dear boy looks, he sees every thing just to his wants and wishes;—the bubbling springs with cool sweet water for him to drink! and the wood to make him sparkling fires when he is cold! and beautiful horses for him to ride! and strong oxen to work for him, and the good cow to give him milk! and bees to make sweet honey for his sweeter mouth! and the little lambs, with snowy wool, for beautiful clothes for him! Now, these and all the ten thousand thousand other good things more than my son can ever think of, and all so exactly fitted to his use and delight—Now how could chance ever have done all this for my little son? Oh George!—"

He would have gone on: but George, who had hung upon his father's words with looks and eyes of all-devouring attention, here broke out—

"Oh, Pa, that's enough! that's enough! It can't be chance, indeed—it can't be chance, that made and gave me all these things."

"What was it then, do you think, my son?"

"Indeed, Pa, I don't know unless it was God Almighty!"

"Yes, George, he it was, my son, and nobody else."

"Well, but Pa, (continued George) does God Almighty give me every thing? Don't you give me some things, Pa?"

"I give you something indeed! Oh how can I give you any thing, George! I who have nothing on earth that I can call my own, no, not even the breath I draw!"

"High, Pa! is'nt that great big house your house, and this garden, and the horses yonder, and oxen, and sheep, and trees, and every thing, is'nt all yours, Pa?"

"Oh no! my son! no! why you make me shrink into nothing, George, when you talk of all these belonging to me, who can't even make a grain of sand! Oh, how could I, my son, have given life to those great oxen and horses, when I can't give life even to a fly?—no! for if the poorest fly were killed, it is not your father, George, nor all the men in the world, that could ever make him alive again!"

At this, George fell into a profound silence, while his pensive looks showed that his youthful soul was labouring with some idea never felt before. Perhaps it was at that moment, that the good Spirit of God ingrafted on his heart that germ of piety, which filled his after life with so many of the precious fruits of morality.

* * *

XII

The Death of Washington

And when disease obstructs the labouring breath,
When the heart sickens and each pulse is death,

Even then Religion shall sustain the just;
Grace their last moments; nor desert their dust.

If the prayers of millions could have prevailed, Washington would have been immortal on earth. And if fulness of peace, riches, and honours could have rendered that immortality happy, Washington had been blessed indeed. But this world is not the place of true happiness. Though numberless are the satisfactions, which a prudence and virtue like Washington's may enjoy in this world, yet they fall short, infinite degrees, of that pure, unembittered felicity which the Almighty parent has prepared in heaven for the spirits of the just.

To prepare for this immensity of bliss, is the real errand on which God sent us into the world. Our preparation consists in acquiring those great virtues, purity and love, which alone can make us worthy companions of angels, and fit partakers of their exalted delights. Washington had wisely spent his life in acquiring the immortal virtues. "He had fought the good fight" against his own unreasonable affections. He had glorified God, by exemplifying the charms of virtue to men. He had borne the heat and burden of the day—his great day of duty: and the evening of old age being come, the servant of God must now go to receive his wages. Happy Washington! If crowns and kingdoms could have purchased such peace as thine, such hopes big with immortality, with what begging earnestness would crowns and kingdoms have been offered by the mighty conquerors of the earth, in their dying moments of terror and despair!

On the 14th of December, 1799, (when he wanted but nine weeks and two days of being sixty-eight years old,) he rode out to his mill, three miles distant. The day was raw and rainy. The following night he was attacked with a violent pain and inflammation of the throat. The lancet of one of his domestics was employed, but with no advantage. Early in the morning, Dr. Craik, the friend and physician of his youth and age, was sent for. Alarmed at the least appearance of danger threatening a life so dear to him, Dr. Craik advised to call in, immediately, the consulting assistance of his friends, the ingenious and learned Dr. Dick, of Alexandria, and Dr. Prown, of Port Tobacco. They came on the wings of speed. They felt the awfulness of their situation. The greatest of human beings was lying low. A life, of all others the most revered, the most beloved, was at stake. And if human skill could have saved—if the sword of genius, and the buckler of experience could have turned the stroke of death, Washington had still lived. But his hour was come.

It appears, that from the commencement of the attack, he was favored with a presentiment, that he was now laid down to rise no more. He took, however, the medicines that were offered him: but it was principally from a sense of duty.

It has been said that a man's death is generally a copy of his life. It was Washington's case exactly. In his last illness he behaved with the firmness of a soldier, and the resignation of a christian.

The inflammation in his throat was attended with great pain, which he bore with the fortitude that became him. He was, once or twice, heard to say that, had it pleased God, he should have been glad to die a little easier; but that he doubted not that it was for his good.

Every hour now spread a sadder gloom over the scene. Despair sat on the faces of the physicians; for they saw that their art had failed! The strength of the mighty was departing from him; and death, with his sad harbingers, chills and paleness, was coming on apace.

Mount Vernon, which had long shone the queen of elegant joys, was now about to suffer a sad eclipse! an eclipse, which would soon be mournfully visible, not only through the United States, but throughout the whole world.

Sons and daughters of Columbia, gather yourselves together around the bed of your expiring father—around the last bed of him to whom under God you and your children owe many of the best blessings of this life. When Joseph the prime minister of Egypt heard that his shepherd father was sick, he hastened up, to see him; and fell on his face, and kissed him and wept a long while. But Joseph had never received such services from Jacob as you have received from Washington. But we call you not to weep for Washington. We ask you not to view those eyes, now sunk hollow, which formerly darted their lightning flashes against your enemies—nor to feel that heart, now faintly laboring, which so often throbbed with more than mortal joys when he saw his young countrymen charging like lions, upon the foes of liberty. No! we call you not to weep, but to rejoice. Washington, who so often conquered himself, is now about to conquer the last enemy.

Silent and sad his physicians sat by his bedside, looking on him as he lay panting for breath. They thought on the past, and the tear swelled in their eyes. He marked it, and, stretching out his hand to them, and shaking his head, said, "O no! don't! don't!" then with a delightful smile added, "I am dying, gentlemen! but, thank God, I am not afraid to die."

Feeling that the hour of his departure out of this world was at hand, he desired that every body would quit the room. They all went out; and, according to his wish, left him—with his God.

There, by himself, like Moses alone on the top of Pisgah, he seeks the face of God. There, by himself, standing as on the awful boundary that divides time from eternity, that separates this world from the next, he cannot quit the long frequented haunts of the one, nor launch away into the untried regions of the other, until (in humble imitation of the world's great Redeemer,) he has poured forth, into the bosom of his God, those strong sensations which the solemnity of his situation naturally suggested.

With what angelic fervor did he adore that Almighty Love, which, though inhabiting the heaven of heavens, deigned to wake his sleeping dust—framed him so fearfully in the womb—nursed him on a tender mother's breast—watched his helpless infancy—guarded his heedless youth—preserved him from the dominion of his passions—inspired him with the love of virtue—led him safely up to man—and, from such low beginnings, advanced him to such unparalleled usefulness and glory among men! These, and ten thousand other precious gifts heaped on him, unasked—many of them long before he had the knowledge to ask—overwhelmed his soul with gratitude unutterable; exalted to infinite heights his ideas of eternal love; and bade him without fear resign his departing spirit into the arms of his Redeemer God, whose mercies are over all his works.

He is now about to leave the great family of man, in which he has so long sojourned! The yearnings of his soul are over his brethren! How fervently does he adore that goodness, which enabled him to be so serviceable to them! that grace, which preserved him from injuring them by violence or fraud! How fervently does he pray, that the unsuffering kingdom of God may come, and that the earth may be filled with the richest fruits of righteousness and peace!

He is now about to leave his country! that dear spot which gave him birth—that dear spot for which he has so long watched and prayed, so long toiled and fought; and whose beloved children he has so often sought to gather, "even as a hen gathereth her chickens under her wings." He sees them now spread abroad like flocks in goodly pastures; like favoured Israel in the land of promise. He remembers how God, by a mighty hand, and by an outstretched arm, brought their fathers into this good land, a land flowing with milk and honey; and blessed them with the blessings of heaven above, and the earth beneath; with the blessings of liberty and of peace, of religion and of laws, above all other people. He sees that, through the rich mercies of God, they have now the precious opportunity to continue their country the glory of the earth, and a refuge for the poor, and for the persecuted of all lands! The transporting sight of such a cloud of blessings, impending close over the heads of his countrymen, together with the distressing uncertainty whether they will put forth their hands and enjoy them, shakes the parent soul of Washington with feelings too strong for his dying frame! The last tear that he is ever to shed, now steals into his eye—the last groan that he is ever to heave, is about to issue from his faintly labouring heart.

Feeling that the silver cord of life is loosing, and that his spirit is ready to quit her old companion, the body, he extends himself on his bed—closes his eyes for the last time with his own hands—folds his arms decently on his breast, then breathing out "Father of mercies, take me to thyself,"—he fell asleep.

Swift on angel's wings the brightening saint ascended; while voices more than human were warbling through the happy regions, and hymning the great procession towards the gates of heaven. His glorious coming was seen afar off; and myriads of mighty angels hastened forth, with golden harps, to welcome the honoured stranger. High in front of the shouting hosts, were seen the beauteous forms of Franklin, Warren, Mercer, Scammel, and of him who fell at Quebec, with all the virtuous patriots, who, on the side of Columbia, toiled or bled for liberty and truth. But oh! how changed from what they were, when, in their days of flesh, bathed in sweat and blood, they fell at the parent feet of their weeping country! Not the homeliest infant suddenly springing into a soul-enchanting Hebe—not dreary winter suddenly brightening into spring, with all her bloom and fragrance, ravishing the senses, could equal such a glorious change. Oh! where are now their wrinkles and grey hairs? Where their ghastly wounds and clotted blood? Their forms are of the stature of angels—their robes like morning clouds streaked with gold—the stars of heaven, like crowns glitter on their heads—immortal youth, celestial rosy red, sits blooming on their cheeks, while infinite benignity and love beam from their eyes. Such were the forms of thy sons, O Columbia! such the brother band of thy martyred saints, that now poured forth from heaven's wide opening gates, to meet thy Washington; to meet their beloved chief, who, in the days of his mortality, had led their embattled squadrons to the war. At sight of him, even these blessed spirits seem to feel new raptures, and to look more dazzlingly bright. In joyous throngs they pour around him—they devour him with their eyes of love—they embrace him in transports of tenderness unutterable; while from their roseate cheeks, tears of joy, such as angels weep, roll down.

All that followed was too much for the overdazzled eye of imagination. She was seen to return, with the quick panting bosom and looks entranced of a fond mother, near swooning at sudden sight of a dear loved son, deemed lost, but now found, and raised to kingly honours! She was heard passionately to exclaim, with palms and eyes lifted to heaven, "O, who can count the stars of Jacob, or number the fourth part of the blessings of Israel!—Let me die the death of Washington! and may my latter end be like his!"

Let us now return to all that remained of Washington on earth. He had expressly ordered in his will, that he should be buried in a private manner, and without any parade. But this was impossible; for who could stay at home when it was said, "Today General Washington is to be buried!" On the morning of the 18th, which was fixed on for his funeral, the people poured in by thousands to pay him the last respect, and, as they said, to take their last look. And, while they looked on him, nature stirred that at their hearts, which quickly brought the best blood into their cheeks, and rolled down the tears from their eyes. About two o'clock they bore him to his long home, and buried him in his own family vault, near the banks of the great

Potomac. And to this day, often as the ships of war pass that way, they waken up the thunder of their loudest guns, pointed to the spot, as if to tell the sleeping hero, that he is not forgotten in his narrow dwelling.

The news of his death soon reached Philadelphia, where Congress was then in session. A question of importance being on the carpet that day, the house, as usual, was much interested. But soon as it was announced—"General Washington is dead"—an instant stop was put to all business—the tongue of the orator was struck dumb—and a midnight silence ensued, save when it was interrupted by deepest sighs of the members, as, with drooping foreheads rested on their palms, they sat, each absorbed in mournful cogitation. Presently, as utterly unfit for business, both houses adjourned; and the members retired slow and sad to their lodgings, like men who had suddenly heard of the death of a father.

For several days hardly any thing was done in Congress; hardly any thing thought of but to talk of and to praise the departed Washington. In this patriotic work all parties joined with equal alacrity and earnestness. In this all were federalists, all were republicans. Elegant addresses were exchanged between the two houses of Congress and the President, and all of them replete with genius and gratitude.

Then, by unanimous consent, Congress came to the following resolutions:

1st. That a grand marble monument should be erected at the city of Washington, under which with permission of his lady, the body of the General should be deposited.

2nd. That there should be a funeral procession from congress hall to the German Lutheran church, to hear an oration delivered by one of the members of congress.

3d. That the members of congress should wear full mourning during the session.

4th. That it should be recommended to the people of the United States to wear crape on the left arm, as mourning, for thirty days.

But, thank God, the people of the United States needed not the hint contained in the last resolution. Though they could not all very elegantly speak, yet their actions showed that they all very deeply felt what they owed to Washington. For, in every city, village, and hamlet, the people were so struck on hearing of his death, that long before they heard of the resolution of congress, they ran together to ease their troubled minds in talking and hearing talk of Washington, and to devise some public mode of testifying their sorrow for his death. Every where throughout the continent, churches and court houses were hung in black, mourning was put on, processions were made, and sermons preached, while the crowded houses listened with pleasure to the praises of Washington, or sighed and wept when they heard of his toils and battles for his country.

Ichabod Crane's classroom and students

WASHINGTON IRVING

The Legend of Sleepy Hollow

(1820)

When Thomas Jefferson attempted to answer European critics who complained that America had not produced "one man of genius in a single art or a single science," he could point to Washington in politics, to Franklin and Rittenhouse in science, but only to the future in the arts. Viewing this constant quest for a genuinely national culture with which to challenge European pretension, one can appreciate the importance of Washington Irving; his Sketch Book, published in 1820, was the first book by an American writer on an American theme that received critical recognition from major writers of Europe.

Irving was both a self-conscious American patriot – at about age six he had received George Washington's blessings – and a European man of letters. He depicted the world of his native city, New York, and the "glorious river," the Hudson, whose shores provided the setting for so many of his tales. He gently spoofed both provincial manners and urban pretensions, yet also wrote voluminously of Spanish history, the English countryside, and German folklore. He served his country in several diplomatic posts, which is also to say that he spent about half his adult life away from home, happily hobnobbing, in his phrase, "hand-in-glove with nobility and mobility." His great importance to the evolution of American literature and American nationalism required that he be in Europe, that he indicate to the world what the presumably backwoods republic could produce in the way of a gentleman and a writer. What Franklin did for the American reputation in politics and science, Irving – a lesser man – achieved in literature.

"The Legend of Sleepy Hollow" is Irving at his best. In this story Irving creates both a sense of place and of rich tradition, illustrating how the raw republic could nonetheless offer some of the same resources for literature as Europe, with its long past and romantic associations. Regional cultures in the varied American landscape were an alternative to the diversity of European history, one that has remained of continuing importance in American art and literature.

The Legend of Sleepy Hollow

Found among the papers of the late Diedrich Knickerbocker

A pleasing land of drowsy head it was,
Of dreams that wave before the half-shut eye;
And of gay castles in the clouds that pass,
For ever flushing round a summer sky.

CASTLE OF INDOLENCE

In the bosom of one of those spacious coves which indent the eastern shore of the Hudson, at that broad expansion of the river denominated by the ancient Dutch navigators the Tappan Zee, and where they always prudently shortened sail, and implored the protection of St. Nicholas when they crossed, there lies a small market-town or rural port, which by some is called Greensburgh, but which is more generally and properly known by the name of Tarry Town. This name was given, we are told, in former days, by the good housewives of the adjacent country, from the inveterate propensity of their husbands to linger about the village tavern on market days. Be that as it may, I do not vouch for the fact, but merely advert to it, for the sake of being precise and authentic. Not far from this village, perhaps about two miles, there is a little valley, or rather lap of land, among high hills, which is one of the quietest places in the whole world. A small brook glides through it, with just murmur enough to lull one to repose; and the occasional whistle of a quail, or tapping of a woodpecker, is almost the only sound that ever breaks in upon the uniform tranquillity.

I recollect that, when a stripling, my first exploit in squirrel-shooting was in a grove of tall walnut-trees that shades one side of the valley. I had wandered into it at noon time, when all nature is peculiarly quiet, and was startled by the roar of my own gun, as it broke the Sabbath stillness around, and was prolonged and reverberated by the angry echoes. If ever I should wish for a retreat, whither I might steal from the world and its distractions, and dream quietly away the remnant of a troubled life, I know of none more promising than this little valley.

From the listless repose of the place, and the peculiar character of its inhabitants, who are descendants from the original Dutch settlers, this sequestered glen has long been known by the name of SLEEPY HOLLOW, and its rustic lads are called the Sleepy Hollow Boys throughout all the neighboring country. A drowsy, dreamy influence seems to hang over the land, and to pervade the very atmosphere. Some say that the place was bewitched by a high German doctor, during the early days of the settlement; others, that an old Indian chief, the prophet or wizard of his tribe, held his powwows there before the country was discovered by Master Hendrick Hudson. Certain it is, the place still continues under the sway of some witching power, that holds a spell over the minds of the good people, causing them to walk in a continual reverie. They are given to all kinds of marvellous beliefs; are subject to trances and visions; and frequently see strange sights, and hear music and voices in the air. The whole neighborhood abounds with local tales, haunted spots, and twilight superstitions; stars shoot and meteors glare oftener across the valley than in any other part of the country, and the nightmare, with her whole nine fold, seems to make it the favorite scene of her gambols.

The dominant spirit, however, that haunts this enchanted region, and seems to be commander-in-chief of all the powers of the air, is the apparition of a figure on horseback without a head. It is said by some to be the ghost of a Hessian trooper, whose head had been carried away by a cannon-ball, in some nameless battle during the revolutionary war; and who is ever and anon seen by the country folk, hurrying along in the gloom of night, as if on the wings of the wind. His haunts are not confined to the valley, but extend at times to the adjacent roads, and especially to the vicinity of a church at no great distance. Indeed, certain of the most authentic historians of those parts, who have been careful in collecting and collating the floating facts concerning this spectre, allege that the body of the trooper, having been buried in the church-yard, the ghost rides forth to the scene of battle in nightly quest of his head; and that the rushing speed with which he sometimes passes along the Hollow, like a midnight blast, is owing to his being belated, and in a hurry to get back to the church-yard before daybreak.

Such is the general purport of this legendary superstition, which has furnished materials for many a wild story in that region of shadows; and the spectre is known, at all the country firesides, by the name of the Headless Horseman of Sleepy Hollow.

It is remarkable that the visionary propensity I have mentioned is not confined to the native inhabitants of the valley, but is unconsciously imbibed by every one who resides there for a time. However wide awake they may have been before they entered that sleepy region, they are sure, in a little time, to inhale the witching influence of the air, and begin to grow imaginative—to dream dreams, and see apparitions.

I mention this peaceful spot with all possible laud; for it is in such little retired Dutch valleys, found here and there embosomed in the great State of New-York, that population, manners, and customs, remain fixed; while the great torrent of migration and improvement, which is making such incessant changes in other parts of this restless country, sweeps by them unobserved. They are like those little nooks of still water which border a rapid stream; where we may see the straw and bubble riding quietly at anchor, or slowly revolving in their mimic harbor, undisturbed by the rush of the passing current.

Though many years have elapsed since I trod the drowsy shades of Sleepy Hollow, yet I question whether I should not still find the same trees and the same families vegetating in its sheltered bosom.

In this by-place of nature, there abode, in a remote period of American history, that is to say, some thirty years since, a worthy wight of the name of Ichabod Crane; who sojourned, or, as he expressed it, "tarried," in Sleepy Hollow, for the purpose of instructing the children of the vicinity. He was a native of Connecticut; a State which supplies the Union with pioneers for the mind as well as for the forest, and sends forth yearly its legions of frontier woodsmen and country schoolmasters. The cognomen of Crane was not inapplicable to his person. He was tall, but exceedingly lank, with narrow shoulders, long arms and legs, hands that dangled a mile out of his sleeves, feet that might have served for shovels, and his whole frame most loosely hung together. His head was small, and flat at top, with huge ears, large green glassy eyes, and a long snipe nose, so that it looked like a weather-cock, perched upon his spindle neck, to tell which way the wind blew. To see him striding along the profile of a hill on a windy day, with his clothes bagging and fluttering about him, one might have mistaken him for the genius of famine descending upon the earth, or some scarecrow eloped from a cornfield.

His school-house was a low building of one large room, rudely constructed of logs; the windows partly glazed, and partly patched with leaves of old copy-books. It was most ingeniously secured at vacant hours, by a withe twisted in the handle of the door, and stakes set against the window shutters; so that, though a thief might get in with perfect ease, he would find some embarrassment in getting out; an idea most probably borrowed by the architect, Yost Van Houten, from the mystery of an eel-pot. The school-house stood in a rather lonely but pleasant situation, just at the foot of a woody hill, with a brook running close by, and a formidable birch tree growing at one end of it. From hence the low murmur of his pupils' voices, conning over their lessons, might be heard in a drowsy summer's day, like the hum of a bee-hive; interrupted now and then by the authoritative voice of the master, in the tone of menace or command; or, peradventure, by the appalling sound of the birch, as he urged some tardy loiterer along the flowery path of knowledge. Truth to say, he was a conscientious man, and ever bore in mind the golden maxim, "Spare the rod and spoil the child."—Ichabod Crane's scholars certainly were not spoiled.

I would not have it imagined, however, that he was one of those cruel potentates of the school, who joy in the smart of their subjects; on the contrary, he administered justice with discrimination rather than severity; taking the burthen off the backs of the weak, and laying it on those of the strong. Your mere puny stripling, that winced at the least flourish of the rod, was passed by with indulgence; but the claims of justice were satisfied by inflicting a double portion on some little, tough, wrong-headed, broad-skirted Dutch urchin, who sulked and swelled and grew dogged and sullen beneath the birch. All this he called "doing his duty by their parents;" and he never inflicted a chastisement without following it by the assurance, so consolatory to the smarting urchin, that "he would remember it, and thank him for it the longest day he had to live."

When school hours were over, he was even the companion and playmate of the larger boys; and on holiday afternoons would convoy some of the smaller ones home, who happened to have pretty sisters, or good housewives for mothers, noted for the comforts of the cupboard. Indeed it behooved him to keep on good terms with his pupils. The revenue arising from his school was small, and would have been scarcely sufficient to furnish him with daily bread, for he was a huge feeder, and though lank, had the dilating powers of an anaconda; but to help out his maintenance, he was, according to country custom in those parts, boarded and lodged at the houses of the farmers, whose children he instructed. With these he lived successively a week at a time; thus going the rounds of the neighborhood, with all his worldly effects tied up in a cotton handkerchief.

That all this might not be too onerous on the purses of his rustic patrons, who are apt to consider the costs of schooling a grievous burden, and schoolmasters as mere drones, he had various ways of rendering himself both useful and agreeable. He assisted the farmers occasionally in the lighter labors of their farms; helped to make hay; mended the fences; took the horses to water; drove the cows from pasture; and cut wood for the winter fire. He laid aside, too, all the dominant dignity and absolute sway with which he lorded it in his little empire, the school, and became wonderfully gentle and ingratiating. He found favor in the eyes of the mothers, by petting the children, particularly the youngest; and like the lion bold, which whilom so magnanimously the lamb did hold, he would sit with a child on one knee, and rock a cradle with his foot for whole hours together.

In addition to his other vocations, he was the singing-master of the neighborhood, and picked up many bright shillings by instructing the young folks in psalmody. It was a matter of no little vanity to him, on Sundays, to take his station in front of the church gallery, with a band of chosen singers; where, in his own mind, he completely carried away the palm from the parson. Certain it is, his voice resounded far above all the rest of the congregation; and there are peculiar quavers still to be heard in that church, and which may even be heard half a mile off, quite to the opposite side of the mill-pond, on a still Sunday morning, which are said to be legitimately descended from the nose of Ichabod Crane. Thus, by divers little make-shifts in that ingenious way which is commonly denominated "by hook and by crook," the worthy pedagogue got on tolerably enough, and was thought, by all who understood nothing of the labor of headwork, to have a wonderfully easy life of it.

The schoolmaster is generally a man of some importance in the female circle of a rural neighborhood; being considered a kind of idle gentlemanlike personage, of vastly superior taste and accomplishments to the rough country swains, and, indeed, inferior in learning only to the parson. His appearance, therefore, is apt to occasion some little stir at the tea-table of a farmhouse, and the addition of a supernumerary dish of cakes or sweetmeats, or, peradventure, the parade of a silver tea-pot. Our man of letters, therefore, was peculiarly happy in the smiles of all the country damsels. How he would figure among them in the churchyard, between services on Sundays! gathering grapes for them from the wild vines that overrun the surrounding trees; reciting for their amusement all the epitaphs on the tombstones; or sauntering, with a whole bevy of them, along the banks of the adjacent millpond; while the more bashful country bumpkins hung sheepishly back, envying his superior elegance and address.

From his half itinerant life, also, he was a kind of travelling gazette, carrying the whole budget of local gossip from house to house; so that his appearance was always greeted with satisfaction. He was, moreover, esteemed by the women as a man of great erudition, for he had read several books quite through, and was a perfect master of Cotton Mather's history of New England Witchcraft, in which, by the way, he most firmly and potently believed.

He was, in fact, an odd mixture of small shrewdness and simple credulity. His appetite for the marvellous, and his powers of digesting it, were equally extraordinary; and both had been increased by his residence in this spellbound region. No tale was too gross or monstrous for his capacious swallow. It was often his delight, after his school was dismissed in the afternoon, to stretch himself on the rich bed of clover, bordering the little brook that whimpered by his school-house, and there con over old Mather's direful tales, until the gathering dusk of the evening made the printed page a mere mist before his eyes. Then, as he wended his way, by swamp and stream and awful woodland, to the farmhouse where he happened to be quartered, every sound of nature, at that witching hour, fluttered his excited imagination: the moan of the whip-poor-will from the hill-side; the boding cry of the tree-toad, that harbinger of storm; the dreary hooting of the screech-owl, or the sudden rustling in the thicket of birds frightened from their roost. The fire-flies, too, which sparkled most vividly in the darkest places, now and then startled him, as one of uncommon brightness would stream across his path; and if, by chance, a huge blockhead of a beetle came winging his blundering flight against him, the poor varlet was ready to give up the ghost, with the idea that he was struck with a witch's token. His only resource on such occasions, either to drown thought, or drive away evil spirits, was to sing psalm tunes;—and the good people of Sleepy Hollow, as they sat by their doors of an evening, were often filled with awe, at hearing his nasal melody, "in linked sweetness long drawn out," floating from the distant hill, or along the dusky road.

Another of his sources of fearful pleasure was to pass long winter evenings with the old Dutch wives, as they sat spinning by the fire, with a row of apples roasting and spluttering along the hearth, and listen to their marvellous tales of ghosts and goblins, and haunted fields, and haunted brooks, and haunted bridges, and haunted houses, and particularly of the headless horseman, or galloping Hessian of the Hollow, as they sometimes called him. He would delight them equally by his anecdotes of witchcraft, and of the direful omens and portentous sights and sounds in the air, which prevailed in the earlier times of Connecticut; and would frighten them wofully with speculations upon comets and shooting stars; and with the alarming fact that the world did absolutely turn round, and that they were half the time topsy-turvy!

But if there was a pleasure in all this, while snugly cuddling in the chimney corner of a chamber that was all of a ruddy glow from the crackling wood fire, and where, of course, no spectre dared to show his face, it was dearly purchased by the terrors of his subsequent walk homewards. What fearful shapes and shadows beset his path amidst the dim and ghastly glare of a snowy night!—With what wistful look did he eye every trembling ray of light streaming across the waste fields from some distant window!—How often was he appalled by some shrub covered with snow, which, like a sheeted spectre, beset his very path!—How often did he shrink with curdling awe at the sound of his own steps on the frosty crust beneath his feet; and dread to look over his shoulder, lest he should behold some uncouth being tramping close behind him!—and how often was he thrown into complete dismay by some rushing blast, howling among the trees, in the idea that it was the Galloping Hessian on one of his nightly scourings!

All these, however, were mere terrors of the night, phantoms of the mind that walk in darkness; and though he had seen many spectres in his time, and been more than once beset by Satan in divers shapes, in his lonely perambulations, yet daylight put an end to all these evils; and he would have passed a pleasant life of it, in despite of the devil and all his works, if his path had not been crossed by a being that causes more perplexity to mortal man than ghosts, goblins, and the whole race of witches put together, and that was—a woman.

Among the musical disciples who assembled, one evening in each week, to receive his instructions in psalmody, was Katrina Van Tassel, the daughter and only child of a substantial Dutch farmer. She was a blooming lass of fresh eighteen; plump as a partridge; ripe and melting and rosy cheeked as one of her father's peaches, and universally famed not merely for her beauty, but her vast expectations. She was withal a little of a coquette, as might be perceived even in her dress, which was a mixture of ancient and modern fashions, as most suited to set off her charms. She wore the ornaments of pure yellow gold, which her great-great-grandmother had brought over from Saardam; the tempting stomacher of the olden time; and withal a provokingly short petticoat, to display the prettiest foot and ankle in the country round.

Ichabod Crane had a soft and foolish heart towards the sex; and it is not to be wondered at, that so tempting a morsel soon found favor in his eyes; more especially after he had visited her in her paternal mansion. Old Baltus Van Tassel was a perfect picture of a thriving, contented, liberal-hearted farmer. He seldom, it is true, sent either his eyes or his thoughts beyond the boundaries of his own farm; but within those every thing was snug, happy, and well-conditioned. He was satisfied with his wealth, but not proud of it; and piqued himself upon the hearty abundance, rather than the style in which he lived. His stronghold was situated on the banks of the Hudson, in one of those green, sheltered, fertile nooks, in which the Dutch farmers are so fond of nestling. A great elm-tree spread its broad branches over it; at the foot of which bubbled up a spring of the softest and sweetest water, in a little well, formed of a barrel; and then stole sparkling away through the grass, to a neighboring brook, that bubbled along among alders and dwarf willows. Hard by the farmhouse was a vast barn, that might have served for a church; every window and crevice of which seemed bursting forth with the treasures of the farm; the flail was busily resounding within it from morning to night; swallows and martins skimmed twittering about the eaves; and rows of pigeons, some with one eye turned up, as if watching the weather, some with their heads under their wings, or buried in their bosoms, and others swelling, and cooing, and bowing about their dames, were enjoying the sunshine on the roof. Sleek unwieldy porkers were grunting in the repose and abundance of their pens; whence sallied forth, now and then, troops of sucking pigs, as if to snuff the air. A stately squadron of snowy geese were riding in an adjoining pond, convoying whole fleets of ducks; regiments of turkeys were gobbling through the farmyard, and guinea fowls fretting about it, like ill-tempered housewives, with their peevish discontented cry. Before the barn door strutted the gallant cock, that pattern of a husband, a warrior, and a fine gentleman, clapping his burnished wings, and crowing in the pride and gladness of his heart—sometimes tearing up the earth with his feet, and then generously calling his ever-hungry family of wives and children to enjoy the rich morsel which he had discovered.

The pedagogue's mouth watered, as he looked upon this sumptuous promise of luxurious winter fare. In his devouring mind's eye, he pictured to himself every roasting-pig running about with a pudding in his belly, and an apple in his mouth; the pigeons were snugly put to bed in a comfortable pie, and tucked in with a coverlet of crust; the geese were swimming in their own gravy; and the ducks pairing cosily in dishes, like snug married couples, with a decent competency of onion sauce. In the porkers he saw carved out the future sleek side of bacon, and juicy relishing ham; not a turkey but he beheld daintily trussed up, with its gizzard under its wing, and, peradventure, a necklace of savory sausages; and even bright chanticleer himself lay sprawling on his back, in a side-dish, with uplifted claws, as if craving that quarter which his chivalrous spirit disdained to ask while living.

As the enraptured Ichabod fancied all this, and as he rolled his great green eyes over the fat meadow-lands, the rich fields of wheat, of rye, of buckwheat, and Indian corn, and the orchards burthened with ruddy fruit, which surrounded the warm tenement of Van Tassel, his heart yearned after the damsel who was to inherit these domains, and his imagination expanded with the idea, how they might be readily turned into cash, and the money invested in immense tracts of wild land, and shingle palaces in the wilderness. Nay, his busy fancy already realized his hopes, and presented to him the blooming Katrina, with a whole family of children, mounted on the top of a wagon loaded with household trumpery, with pots and kettles dangling beneath; and he beheld himself bestriding a pacing mare, with a colt at her heels, setting out for Kentucky, Tennessee, or the Lord knows where.

When he entered the house the conquest of his heart was complete. It was one of those spacious farmhouses, with high-ridged, but lowly-sloping roofs, built in the style handed down from the first Dutch settlers; the low projecting eaves forming a piazza along the front, capable of being closed up in bad weather. Under this were hung flails, harness, various utensils of husbandry, and nets for fishing in the neighboring river. Benches were built along the sides for summer use; and a great spinning-wheel at one end, and a churn at the other, showed the various uses to which this important porch might be devoted. From this piazza the wondering Ichabod entered the hall, which formed the centre of the mansion and the place of usual residence. Here, rows of resplendent pewter, ranged on a long dresser, dazzled his eyes. In one corner stood a huge bag of wool ready to be spun; in another a quantity of linsey-woolsey just from the loom; ears of Indian corn, and strings of dried apples and peaches, hung in gay festoons along the walls, mingled with the gaud of red peppers; and a door left ajar gave him a peep into the best parlor, where the claw-footed chairs, and dark mahogany tables, shone like mirrors; and irons, with their accompanying shovel and tongs, glistened from their covert of asparagus tops; mock-oranges and conch-shells decorated the mantel piece; strings of various colored birds' eggs were suspended above it; a great ostrich egg was hung from the centre of the room, and a corner cupboard, knowingly left open, displayed immense treasures of old silver and well-mended china.

From the moment Ichabod laid his eyes upon these regions of delight, the peace of his mind was at an end, and his only study was how to gain the affections of the peerless daughter of Van Tassel. In this enterprise, however, he had more real difficulties than generally fell to the lot of a knight-errant of yore, who seldom had any thing but giants, enchanters, fiery dragons, and such like easily-conquered adversaries, to contend with; and had to make his way merely through gates of iron and brass, and walls of adamant, to the castle keep, where the lady of his heart was confined; all which he achieved as easily as a man would carve his way to the centre of a Christmas pie; and then the lady gave him her hand as a matter of course. Ichabod, on the contrary, had to win his way to the heart of a country coquette, beset with a labyrinth of whims and caprices, which were for ever presenting new difficulties and impediments; and he had to encounter a host of fearful adversaries of real flesh and blood, the numerous rustic admirers, who beset every portal to her heart; keeping a watchful and angry eye upon each other, but ready to fly out in the common cause against any new competitor.

Among these the most formidable was a burly, roaring, roystering blade, of the name of Abraham, or, according to the Dutch abbreviation, Brom Van Brunt, the hero of the country round, which rang with his feats of strength and hardihood. He was broad-shouldered and double-jointed, with short curly black hair, and a bluff, but not unpleasant countenance, having a mingled air of fun and arrogance. From his Herculean frame and great powers of limb, he had received the nickname of BROM BONES, by which he was universally known. He was famed for great knowledge and skill in horsemanship, being as dexterous on horseback as a Tartar. He was foremost at all races and cock-fights; and, with the ascendency which bodily strength acquires in rustic life, was the umpire in all disputes, setting his hat on one side, and giving his decisions with an air and tone admitting of no gainsay or appeal. He was always ready for either a fight or a frolic; but had more mischief than ill-will in his composition; and, with all his overbearing roughness, there was a strong dash of waggish good humor at bottom. He had three or four boon companions, who regarded him as their model, and at the head of whom he scoured the country, attending every scene of feud or merriment for miles round. In cold weather he was distinguished by a fur cap, surmounted with a flaunting fox's tail; and when the folks at a country gathering descried this well-known crest at a distance, whisking about among a squad of hard riders, they always stood by for a squall. Sometimes his crew would be heard dashing along past the farmhouses at midnight, with whoop and halloo, like a troop of Don Cossacks; and the old dames, startled out of their sleep, would listen for a moment till the hurry-scurry had clattered by, and then exclaim, "Ay, there goes Brom Bones and his gang!" The neighbors looked upon him with a mixture of awe, admiration, and good will; and when any madcap prank, or rustic brawl, occurred in the vicinity, always shook their heads, and warranted Brom Bones was at the bottom of it.

This rantipole hero had for some time singled out the blooming Katrina for the object of his uncouth gallantries, and though his amorous toyings were something like the gentle caresses and endearments of a bear, yet it was whispered that she did not altogether discourage his hopes. Certain it is, his advances were signals for rival candidates to retire, who felt no inclination to cross a lion in his amours; insomuch, that when his horse was seen tied to Van Tassel's paling, on a Sunday night, a sure sign that his master was courting, or, as it is termed, "sparking," within, all other suitors passed by in despair, and carried the war into other quarters.

Such was the formidable rival with whom Ichabod Crane had to contend, and, considering all things, a stouter man than he would have shrunk from the competition, and a wiser man would have despaired. He had, however, a happy mixture of pliability and perseverance in his nature; he was in form and spirit like a supple-jack—yielding, but tough; though he bent, he never broke; and though he bowed beneath the slightest pressure, yet, the moment it was away—jerk! he was as erect, and carried his head as high as ever.

To have taken the field openly against his rival would have been madness; for he was not a man to be thwarted in his amours, any more than that stormy lover, Achilles. Ichabod, therefore, made his advances in a quiet and gently-insinuating manner. Under cover of his character of singing-master, he made frequent visits at the farmhouse; not that he had any thing to apprehend from the meddlesome interference of parents, which is so often a stumbling-block in the path of lovers. Balt Van Tassel was an easy indulgent soul; he loved his daughter better even than his pipe, and, like a reasonable man and an excellent father, let her have her way in every thing. His notable little wife, too, had enough to do to attend to her housekeeping and manage her poultry; for, as she sagely observed, ducks and geese are foolish things, and must be looked after, but girls can take care of themselves. Thus while the busy dame bustled about the house, or plied her spinning-wheel at one end of the piazza, honest Balt would sit smoking his evening pipe at the other, watching the achievements of a little wooden warrior, who, armed with a sword in each hand, was most valiantly fighting the wind on the pinnacle of the barn. In the mean time, Ichabod would carry on his suit with the daughter by the side of the spring under the great elm, or sauntering along in the twilight, that hour so favorable to the lover's eloquence.

I profess not to know how women's hearts are wooed and won. To me they have always been matters of riddle and admiration. Some seem to have but one vulnerable point, or door of access; while others have a thousand avenues, and may be captured in a thousand different ways. It is a great triumph of skill to gain the former, but a still greater proof of generalship to maintain possession of the latter, for the man must battle for his fortress at every door and window. He who wins a thousand common hearts is therefore entitled to some renown; but he who keeps undisputed sway over the heart of a coquette, is indeed a hero. Certain it is, this was not the case with the redoubtable Brom Bones; and from the moment Ichabod Crane made his advances, the interests of the former evidently declined; his horse was no longer seen tied at the palings on Sunday nights, and a deadly feud gradually arose between him and the preceptor of Sleepy Hollow.

Brom, who had a degree of rough chivalry in his nature, would fain have carried matters to open warfare, and have settled their pretensions to the lady, according to the mode of those most concise and simple reasoners, the knights-errant of yore—by single combat; but Ichabod was too conscious of the superior might of his adversary to enter the lists against him: he had overheard a boast of Bones, that he would "double the schoolmaster up, and lay him on a shelf of his own school-house;" and he was too wary to give him an opportunity. There was something extremely provoking in this obstinately pacific system; it left Brom no alternative but to draw upon the funds of rustic waggery in his disposition, and to play off boorish practical jokes upon his rival. Ichabod became the object of whimsical persecution to Bones, and his gang of rough riders. They harried his hitherto peaceful domains; smoked out his singing school, by stopping up the chimney; broke into the school-house at night, in spite of its formidable fastenings of withe and window stakes, and turned every thing topsy-turvy: so that the poor schoolmaster began to think all the witches in the country held their meetings there. But what was still more annoying, Brom took all opportunities of turning him into ridicule in presence of his mistress, and had a scoundrel dog whom he taught to whine in the most ludicrous manner, and introduced as a rival of Ichabod's to instruct her in psalmody.

In this way matters went on for some time, without producing any material effect on the relative situation of the contending powers. On a fine autumnal afternoon, Ichabod, in pensive mood, sat enthroned on the lofty stool whence he usually watched all the concerns of his little literary realm. In his hand he swayed a ferule, that sceptre of despotic power; the birch of justice reposed on three nails, behind the throne, a constant terror to evil doers; while on the desk before him might be seen sundry contraband articles and prohibited weapons, detected upon the persons of idle urchins; such as half-munched apples, popguns, whirligigs, fly-cages, and whole legions of rampant little paper game-cocks. Apparently there had been some appalling act of justice recently inflicted, for his scholars were all busily intent upon their books, or slyly whispering behind them with one eye kept upon the master; and a kind of buzzing stillness reigned throughout the schoolroom. It was suddenly interrupted by the appearance of a negro, in tow-cloth jacket and trowsers, a round-crowned fragment of a hat, like the cap of Mercury, and mounted on the back of a ragged, wild, half-broken colt, which he managed with a rope by way of halter. He came clattering up to the school door with an invitation to Ichabod to attend a merry-making or "quilting frolic," to be held that evening at Mynheer Van Tassel's; and having delivered his message with that air of importance, and effort at fine language, which a negro is apt to display on petty embassies of the kind, he dashed over the brook, and was seen scampering away up the hollow, full of the importance and hurry of his mission.

All was now bustle and hubbub in the late quiet schoolroom. The scholars were hurried through their lessons, without stopping at trifles; those who were nimble skipped over half with impunity, and those who were tardy, had a smart application now and then in the rear, to quicken their speed, or help them over a tall word. Books were flung aside without being put away on the shelves, inkstands were overturned, benches thrown down, and the whole school was turned loose an hour before the usual time, bursting forth like a legion of young imps, yelping and racketing about the green, in joy at their early emancipation.

The gallant Ichabod now spent at least an extra half hour at his toilet, brushing and furbishing up his best, and indeed only suit of rusty black, and arranging his looks by a bit of broken looking-glass, that hung up in the school-house. That he might make his appearance before his mistress in the true style of a cavalier, he borrowed a horse from the farmer with whom he was domiciliated, a choleric old Dutchman, of the name of Hans Van Ripper, and, thus gallantly mounted, issued forth, like a knight-errant in quest of adventures. But it is meet I should, in the true spirit of romantic story, give some account of the looks and equipments of my hero and his steed. The animal he bestrode was a broken-down plough-horse, that had outlived almost every thing but his viciousness. He was gaunt and shagged, with a ewe neck and a head like a hammer; his rusty mane and tail were tangled and knotted with burrs; one eye had lost its pupil, and was glaring and spectral; but the other had the gleam of a genuine devil in it. Still he must have had fire and mettle in his day, if we may judge from the name he bore of Gunpowder. He had, in fact, been a favorite steed of his master's, the choleric Van Ripper, who was a furious rider, and had infused, very probably, some of his own spirit into the animal; for, old and broken-down as he looked, there was more of the lurking devil in him than in any young filly in the country.

Ichabod was a suitable figure for such a steed. He rode with short stirrups, which brought his knees nearly up to the pommel of the saddle; his sharp elbows stuck out like grasshoppers'; he carried his whip perpendicularly in his hand, like a sceptre, and, as his horse jogged on, the motion of his arms was not unlike the flapping of a pair of wings. A small wool hat rested on the top of his nose, for so his scanty strip of forehead might be called; and the skirts of his black coat fluttered out almost to the horse's tail. Such was the appearance of Ichabod and his steed, as they shambled out of the gate of Hans Van Ripper, and it was altogether such an apparition as is seldom to be met with in broad daylight.

It was, as I have said, a fine autumnal day, the sky was clear and serene, and nature wore that rich and golden livery which we always associate with the idea of abundance. The forests had put on their sober brown and yellow, while some trees of the tenderer kind had been nipped by the frosts into brilliant dyes of orange, purple, and scarlet. Streaming files of wild ducks began to make their appearance high in the air; the bark of the squirrel might be heard from the groves of beech and hickory nuts, and the pensive whistle of the quail at intervals from the neighboring stubble-field.

The small birds were taking their farewell banquets. In the fulness of their revelry, they fluttered, chirping and frolicking, from bush to bush, and tree to tree, capricious from the very profusion and variety around them. There was the honest cock-robin, the favorite game of stripling sportsmen, with its loud querulous note; and the twittering blackbirds flying in sable clouds; and the golden-winged woodpecker, with his crimson crest, his broad black gorget, and splendid plumage; and the cedar bird, with its red-tipt wings and yellow-tipt tail, and its little monteiro cap of feathers; and the blue jay, that noisy coxcomb, in his gay light-blue coat and white under-clothes; screaming and chattering, nodding and bobbing and bowing, and pretending to be on good terms with every songster of the grove.

As Ichabod jogged slowly on his way, his eye, ever open to every symptom of culinary abundance, ranged with delight over the treasures of jolly autumn. On all sides he beheld vast store of apples; some hanging in oppressive opulence on the trees; some gathered into baskets and barrels for the market; others heaped up in rich piles for the cider-press. Farther on he beheld great fields of Indian corn, with its golden ears peeping from their leafy coverts, and holding out the promise of cakes and hasty pudding; and the yellow pumpkins lying beneath them, turning up their fair round bellies to the sun, and giving ample prospects of the most luxurious of pies; and anon he passed the fragrant buckwheat fields, breathing the odor of the beehive, and as he beheld them, soft anticipations stole over his mind of dainty slapjacks, well buttered, and garnished with honey or treacle, by the delicate little dimpled hand of Katrina Van Tassel.

Thus feeding his mind with many sweet thoughts and "sugared suppositions," he journeyed along the sides of a range of hills which look out upon some of the goodliest scenes of the mighty Hudson.

The sun gradually wheeled his broad disk down into the west. The wide bosom of the Tappan Zee lay motionless and glassy, excepting that here and there a gentle undulation waved and prolonged the blue shadow of the distant mountain. A few amber clouds floated in the sky, without a breath of air to move them. The horizon was of a fine golden tint, changing gradually into a pure apple green, and from that into the deep blue of the mid-heaven. A slanting ray lingered on the woody crests of the precipices that overhung some parts of the river, giving greater depth to the dark-gray and purple of their rocky sides. A sloop was loitering in the distance, dropping slowly down with the tide, her sail hanging uselessly against the mast; and as the reflection of the sky gleamed along the still water, it seemed as if the vessel was suspended in the air.

It was toward evening that Ichabod arrived at the castle of the Heer Van Tassel, which he found thronged with the pride and flower of the adjacent country. Old farmers, a spare leathern-faced race, in homespun coats and breeches, blue stockings, huge shoes, and magnificent pewter buckles. Their brisk withered little dames, in close crimped caps, long-waisted shortgowns, homespun petticoats, with scissors and pincushions, and gay calico pockets hanging on the outside. Buxom lasses, almost as antiquated as their mothers, excepting where a straw hat, a fine ribbon, or perhaps a white frock, gave symptoms of city innovation. The sons, in short square-skirted coats with rows of stupendous brass buttons, and their hair generally queued in the fashion of the times, especially if they could procure an eel-skin for the purpose, it being esteemed, throughout the country, as a potent nourisher and strengthener of the hair.

Brom Bones, however, was the hero of the scene, having come to the gathering on his favorite steed Daredevil, a creature, like himself, full of mettle and mischief, and which no one but himself could manage. He was, in fact, noted for preferring vicious animals, given to all kinds of tricks, which kept the rider in constant risk of his neck, for he held a tractable well-broken horse as unworthy of a lad of spirit.

Fain would I pause to dwell upon the world of charms that burst upon the enraptured gaze of my hero, as he entered the state parlor of Van Tassel's mansion. Not those of the bevy of buxom lasses, with their luxurious display of red and white; but the ample charms of a geniune Dutch country tea-table, in the sumptuous time of autumn. Such heaped-up platters of cakes of various and almost indescribable kinds, known only to experienced Dutch housewives! There was the doughty dough-nut, the tenderer oly koek, and the crisp and crumbling cruller; sweet cakes and short cakes, ginger cakes and honey cakes, and the whole family of cakes. And then there were apple pies and peach pies and pumpkin pies; besides slices of ham and smoked beef; and moreover delectable dishes of preserved plums, and peaches, and pears, and quinces; not to mention broiled shad and roasted chickens; together with bowls of milk and cream, all mingled higgledy-piggledy, pretty much as I have enumerated them, with the motherly tea-pot sending up its clouds of vapor from the midst—Heaven bless the mark! I want breath and time to discuss this banquet as it deserves, and am too eager to get on with my story. Happily, Ichabod Crane was not in so great a hurry as his historian, but did ample justice to every dainty.

He was a kind and thankful creature, whose heart dilated in proportion as his skin was filled with good cheer; and whose spirits rose with eating as some men's do with drink. He could not help, too, rolling his large eyes round him as he ate, and chuckling with the possibility that he might one day be lord of all this scene of almost unimaginable luxury and splendor. Then, he thought, how soon he'd turn his back upon the old school-house; snap his fingers in the face of Hans Van Ripper, and every other niggardly patron, and kick any itinerant pedagogue out of doors that should dare to call him comrade!

Old Baltus Van Tassel moved about among his guests with a face dilated with content and good humor, round and jolly as the harvest moon. His hospitable attentions were brief, but expressive, being confined to a shake of the hand, a slap on the shoulder, a loud laugh, and a pressing invitation to "fall to, and help themselves."

And now the sound of the music from the common room, or hall, summoned to the dance. The musician was an old grayheaded negro, who had been the itinerant orchestra of the neighborhood for more than half a century. His instrument was as old and battered as himself. The greater part of the time he scraped on two or three strings, accompanying every movement of the bow with a motion of the head; bowing almost to the ground, and stamping with his foot whenever a fresh couple were to start.

Ichabod prided himself upon his dancing as much as upon his vocal powers. Not a limb, not a fibre about him was idle; and to have seen his loosely hung frame in full motion, and clattering about the room, you would have thought Saint Vitus himself, that blessed patron of the dance, was figuring before you in person. He was the admiration of all the negroes; who, having gathered, of all ages and sizes, from the farm and the neighborhood, stood forming a pyramid of shining black faces at every door and window, gazing with delight at the scene, rolling their white eye-balls, and showing grinning rows of ivory from ear to ear. How could the flogger of urchins be otherwise than animated and joyous? the lady of his heart was his partner in the dance, and smiling graciously in reply to all his amorous oglings; while Brom Bones, sorely smitten with love and jealousy, sat brooding by himself in one corner.

When the dance was at an end, Ichabod was attracted to a knot of the sager folks, who, with old Van Tassel, sat smoking at one end of the piazza, gossiping over former times, and drawing out long stories about the war.

This neighborhood, at the time of which I am speaking, was one of those highly-favored places which abound with chronicle and great men. The British and American line had run near it during the war; it had, therefore, been the scene of marauding, and infested with refugees, cow-boys, and all kinds of border chivalry. Just sufficient time had elapsed to enable each story-teller to dress up his tale with a little becoming fiction, and, in the indistinctness of his recollection, to make himself the hero of every exploit.

There was the story of Doffue Martling, a large blue-bearded Dutchman, who had nearly taken a British frigate with an old iron nine-pounder from a mud breastwork, only that his gun burst at the sixth discharge. And there was an old gentleman who shall be nameless, being too rich a mynheer to be lightly mentioned, who, in the battle of Whiteplains, being an excellent master of defence, parried a musket ball with a small sword, insomuch that he absolutely felt it whiz round the blade, and glance off at the hilt: in proof of which, he was ready at any time to show the sword, with the hilt a little bent. There were several more that had been equally great in the field, not one of whom but was persuaded that he had a considerable hand in bringing the war to a happy termination.

But all these were nothing to the tales of ghosts and apparitions that succeeded. The neighborhood is rich in legendary treasures of the kind. Local tales and superstitions thrive best in these sheltered long-settled retreats; but are trampled under foot by the shifting throng that forms the population of most of our country places. Besides, there is no encouragement for ghosts in most of our villages, for they have scarcely had time to finish their first nap, and turn themselves in their graves, before their surviving friends have travelled away from the neighborhood; so that when they turn out at night to walk their rounds, they have no acquaintance left to call upon. This is perhaps the reason why we so seldom hear of ghosts except in our long-established Dutch communities.

The immediate cause, however, of the prevalence of supernatural stories in these parts, was doubtless owing to the vicinity of Sleepy Hollow. There was a contagion in the very air that blew from that haunted region; it breathed forth an atmosphere of dreams and fancies infecting all the land. Several of the Sleepy Hollow people were present at Van Tassel's, and, as usual, were doling out their wild and wonderful legends. Many dismal tales were told about funeral trains, and mourning cries and wailings heard and seen about the great tree where the unfortunate Major André was taken, and which stood in the neighborhood. Some mention was made also of the woman in white, that haunted the dark glen at Raven Rock, and was often heard to shriek on winter nights before a storm, having perished there in the snow. The chief part of the stories, however, turned upon the favorite spectre of Sleepy Hollow, the headless horseman, who had been heard several times of late, patrolling the country; and, it was said, tethered his horse nightly among the graves in the churchyard.

The sequestered situation of this church seems always to have made it a favorite haunt of troubled spirits. It stands on a knoll, surrounded by locust-trees and lofty elms, from among which its decent whitewashed walls shine modestly forth, like Christian purity beaming through the shades of retirement. A gentle slope descends from it to a silver sheet of water, bordered by high trees, between which, peeps may be caught at the blue hills of the Hudson. To look upon its grass-grown yard, where the sunbeams seem to sleep so quietly, one would think that there at least the dead might rest in peace. On one side of the church extends a wide woody dell, along which raves a large brook among broken rocks and trunks of fallen trees. Over a deep black part of the stream, not far from the church, was formerly thrown a wooden bridge; the road that led to it, and the bridge itself, were thickly shaded by overhanging trees, which cast a gloom about it, even in the daytime; but occasioned a fearful darkness at night. This was one of the favorite haunts of the headless horseman; and the place where he was most frequently encountered. The tale was told of old Brouwer, a most heretical disbeliever in ghosts, how he met the horseman returning from his foray into Sleepy Hollow, and was obliged to get up behind him; how they galloped over bush and brake, over hill and swamp, until they reached the bridge; when the horseman suddenly turned into a skeleton, threw old Brouwer into the brook, and sprang away over the tree-tops with a clap of thunder.

This story was immediately matched by a thrice marvellous adventure of Brom Bones, who made light of the galloping Hessian as an arrant jockey. He affirmed that, on returning one night from the neighboring village of Sing Sing, he had been overtaken by this midnight trooper; that he had offered to race with him for a bowl of punch, and should have won it too, for Daredevil beat the goblin horse all hollow, but, just as they came to the church-bridge, the Hessian bolted, and vanished in a flash of fire.

All these tales, told in that drowsy undertone with which men talk in the dark, the countenances of the listeners only now and then receiving a casual gleam from the glare of a pipe, sank deep in the mind of Ichabod. He repaid them in kind with large extracts from his invaluable author, Cotton Mather, and added many marvellous events that had taken place in his native State of Connecticut, and fearful sights which he had seen in his nightly walks about Sleepy Hollow.

The revel now gradually broke up. The old farmers gathered together their families in their wagons, and were heard for some time rattling along the hollow roads, and over the distant hills. Some of the damsels mounted on pillions behind their favorite swains, and their light-hearted laughter, mingling with the clatter of hoofs, echoed along the silent woodlands, sounding fainter and fainter until they gradually died away—and the late scene of noise and frolic was all silent and deserted. Ichabod only lingered behind, according to the custom of country lovers, to have a tête-à-tête with the heiress, fully convinced that he was now on the high road to success. What passed at this interview I will not pretend to say, for in fact I do not know. Something, however, I fear me, must have gone wrong, for he certainly sallied forth, after no very great interval, with an air quite desolate and chop-fallen.—Oh these women! these women! Could that girl have been playing off any of her coquettish tricks?—Was her encouragement of the poor pedagogue all a mere sham to secure her conquest of his rival?—Heaven only knows, not I!—Let it suffice to say, Ichabod stole forth with the air of one who had been sacking a hen-roost, rather than a fair lady's heart. Without looking to the right or left to notice the scene of rural wealth, on which he had so often gloated, he went straight to the stable, and with several hearty cuffs and kicks, roused his steed most uncourteously from the comfortable quarters in which he was soundly sleeping, dreaming of mountains of corn and oats, and whole valleys of timothy and clover.

It was the very witching time of night that Ichabod, heavy-hearted and crest-fallen, pursued his travel homewards, along the sides of the lofty hills which rise above Tarry Town, and which he had traversed so cheerily in the afternoon. The hour was as dismal as himself. Far below him, the Tappan Zee spread its dusky and indistinct waste of waters, with here and there the tall mast of a sloop, riding quietly at anchor under the land. In the dead hush of midnight, he could even hear the barking of the watch dog from the opposite shore of the Hudson; but it was so vague and faint as only to give an idea of his distance from this faithful companion of man. Now and then, too, the long-drawn crowing of a cock, accidentally awakened, would sound far, far off, from some farmhouse away among the hills—but it was like a dreaming sound in his ear. No signs of life occurred near him, but occasionally the melancholy chirp of a cricket, or perhaps the guttural twang of a bull-frog, from a neighboring marsh, as if sleeping uncomfortably, and turning suddenly in his bed.

All the stories of ghosts and goblins that he had heard in the afternoon, now came crowding upon his recollection. The night grew darker and darker; the stars seemed to sink deeper in the sky, and driving clouds occasionally hid them from his sight. He had never felt so lonely and dismal. He was, moreover, approaching the very place where many of the scenes of the ghost stories had been laid. In the centre of the road stood an enormous tulip-tree, which towered like a giant above all the other trees of the neighborhood, and formed a kind of landmark. Its limbs were gnarled, and fantastic, large enough to form trunks for ordinary trees, twisting down almost to the earth, and rising again into the air. It was connected with the tragical story of the unfortunate André, who had been taken prisoner hard by; and was universally known by the name of Major André's tree. The common people regarded it with a mixture of respect and superstition, partly out of sympathy for the fate of its ill-starred namesake, and partly from the tales of strange sights and doleful lamentations told concerning it.

As Ichabod approached this fearful tree, he began to whistle: he thought his whistle was answered—it was but a blast sweeping sharply through the dry branches. As he approached a little nearer, he thought he saw something white, hanging in the midst of the tree—he paused and ceased whistling; but on looking more narrowly, perceived that it was a place where the tree had been scathed by lightning, and the white wood laid bare. Suddenly he heard a groan—his teeth chattered and his knees smote against the saddle: it was but the rubbing of one huge bough upon another, as they were swayed about by the breeze. He passed the tree in safety, but new perils lay before him.

About two hundred yards from the tree a small brook crossed the road, and ran into a marshy and thickly-wooded glen, known by the name of Wiley's swamp. A few rough logs, laid side by side, served for a bridge over this stream. On that side of the road where the brook entered the wood, a group of oaks and chestnuts, matted thick with wild grapevines, threw a cavernous gloom over it. To pass this bridge was the severest trial. It was at this identical spot that the unfortunate André was captured, and under the covert of those chestnuts and vines were the sturdy yoemen concealed who surprised him. This has ever since been considered a haunted stream, and fearful are the feelings of the schoolboy who has to pass it alone after dark.

As he approached the stream his heart began to thump; he summoned up, however, all his resolution, gave his horse half a score of kicks in the ribs, and attempted to dash briskly across the bridge; but instead of starting forward, the perverse old animal made a lateral movement, and ran broadside against the fence. Ichabod, whose fears increased with the delay, jerked the reins on the other side, and kicked lustily with the contrary foot: it was all in vain; his steed started, it is true, but it was only to plunge to the opposite side of the road into a thicket of brambles and alder bushes. The schoolmaster now bestowed both whip and heel upon the starveling ribs of old Gunpowder, who dashed forward, snuffling and snorting, but came to a stand just by the bridge, with a suddenness that had nearly sent his rider sprawling over his head. Just at this moment a plashy tramp by the side of the bridge caught the sensitive ear of Ichabod. In the dark shadow of the grove, on the margin of the brook, he beheld something huge, misshapen, black and towering. It stirred not, but seemed gathered up in the gloom, like some gigantic monster ready to spring upon the traveller.

The hair of the affrighted pedagogue rose upon his head with terror. What was to be done? To turn and fly was now too late; and besides, what chance was there of escaping ghost or goblin, if such it was, which could ride upon the wings of the wind? Summoning up, therefore, a show of courage, he demanded in stammering accents—"Who are you?" He received no reply. He repeated his demand in a still more agitated voice. Still there was no answer. Once more he cudgelled the sides of the inflexible Gunpowder, and, shutting his eyes, broke forth with involuntary fervor into a psalm tune. Just then the shadowy object of alarm put itself in motion, and, with a scramble and a bound, stood at once in the middle of the road. Though the night was dark and dismal, yet the form of the unknown might now in some degree be ascertained. He appeared to be a horseman of large dimensions, and mounted on a black horse of powerful frame. He made no offer of molestation or sociability, but kept aloof on one side of the road, jogging along on the blind side of old Gunpowder, who had now got over his fright and waywardness.

Ichabod, who had no relish for this strange midnight companion, and bethought himself of the adventure of Brom Bones with the Galloping Hessian, now quickened his steed, in hopes of leaving him behind. The stranger, however, quickened his horse to an equal pace. Ichabod pulled up, and fell into a walk, thinking to lag behind—the other did the same. His heart began to sink within him; he endeavored to resume his psalm tune, but his parched tongue clove to the roof of his mouth, and he could not utter a stave. There was something in the moody and dogged silence of this pertinacious companion, that was mysterious and appalling. It was soon fearfully accounted for. On mounting a rising ground, which brought the figure of his fellow-traveller in relief against the sky, gigantic in height, and muffled in a cloak, Ichabod was horror-struck, on perceiving that he was headless!—but his horror was still more increased, on observing that the head, which should have rested on his shoulders, was carried before him on the pommel of the saddle: his terror rose to desperation; he rained a shower of kicks and blows upon Gunpowder, hoping, by a sudden movement, to give his companion the slip—but the spectre started full jump with him. Away then they dashed, through thick and thin; stones flying, and sparks flashing at every bound. Ichabod's flimsy garments fluttered in the air, as he stretched his long lank body away over his horse's head, in the eagerness of his flight.

They had now reached the road which turns off to Sleepy Hollow; but Gunpowder, who seemed possessed with a demon, instead of keeping up it, made an opposite turn, and plunged headlong down hill to the left. This road leads through a sandy hollow, shaded by trees for about a quarter of a mile, where it crosses the bridge famous in goblin story, and just beyond swells the green knoll on which stands the whitewashed church.

As yet the panic of the steed had given his unskilful rider an apparent advantage in the chase; but just as he had got half way through the hollow, the girths of the saddle gave way, and he felt it slipping from under him. He seized it by the pommel, and endeavored to hold it firm, but in vain; and had just time to save himself by clasping old Gunpowder round the neck, when the saddle fell to the earth, and he heard it trampled under foot by his pursuer. For a moment the terror of Hans Van Ripper's wrath passed across his mind—for it was his Sunday saddle; but this was no time for petty fears; the goblin was hard on his haunches; and (unskilful rider that he was!) he had much ado to maintain his seat; sometimes slipping on one side, sometimes on another, and sometimes jolted on the high ridge of his horse's back-bone, with a violence that he verily feared would cleave him asunder.

An opening in the trees now cheered him with the hopes that the church bridge was at hand. The wavering reflection of a silver star in the bosom of the brook told him that he was not mistaken. He saw the walls of the church dimly glaring under the trees beyond. He recollected the place where Brom Bones's ghostly competitor had disappeared. "If I can but reach that bridge," thought Ichabod, "I am safe." Just then he heard the black steed panting and blowing close behind him; he even fancied that he felt his hot breath. Another convulsive kick in the ribs, and old Gunpowder sprang upon the bridge; he thundered over the resounding planks; he gained the opposite side; and now Ichabod cast a look behind to see if his pursuer should vanish, according to rule, in a flash of fire and brimstone. Just then he saw the goblin rising in his stirrups, and in the very act of hurling his head at him. Ichabod endeavored to dodge the horrible missile, but too late. It encountered his cranium with a tremendous crash—he was tumbled headlong into the dust, and Gunpowder, the black steed, and the goblin rider, passed by like a whirlwind.

The next morning the old horse was found without his saddle, and with the bridle under his feet, soberly cropping the grass at his master's gate. Ichabod did not make his appearance at breakfast—dinner-hour came, but no Ichabod. The boys assembled at the schoolhouse, and strolled idly about the banks of the brook; but no schoolmaster. Hans Van Ripper now began to feel some uneasiness about the fate of poor Ichabod, and his saddle. An inquiry was set on foot, and after diligent investigation they came upon his traces. In one part of the road leading to the church was found the saddle trampled in the dirt; the tracks of horses' hoofs deeply dented in the road, and evidently at furious speed, were traced to the bridge, beyond which, on the bank of a broad part of the brook, where the water ran deep and black, was found the hat of the unfortunate Ichabod, and close beside it a shattered pumpkin.

The brook was searched, but the body of the schoolmaster was not to be discovered. Hans Van Ripper, as executor of his estate, examined the bundle which contained all his worldly effects. They consisted of two shirts and a half; two stocks for the neck; a pair or two of worsted stockings; an old pair of corduroy small-clothes; a rusty razor; a book of psalm tunes, full of dogs' ears; and a broken pitchpipe. As to the books and furniture of the school-house, they belonged to the community, excepting Cotton Mather's History of Witchcraft, a New England Almanac, and a book of dreams and fortune-telling; in which last was a sheet of foolscap much scribbled and blotted in several fruitless attempts to make a copy of verses in honor of the heiress of Van Tassel. These magic books and the poetic scrawl were forthwith consigned to the flames by Hans Van Ripper; who from that time forward determined to send his children no more to school; observing, that he never knew any good come of this same reading and writing. Whatever money the schoolmaster possessed, and he had received his quarter's pay but a day or two before, he must have had about his person at the time of his disappearance.

The mysterious event caused much speculation at the church on the following Sunday. Knots of gazers and gossips were collected in the churchyard, at the bridge, and at the spot where the hat and pumpkin had been found. The stories of Brouwer, of Bones, and a whole budget of others, were called to mind; and when they had diligently considered them all, and compared them with the symptoms of the present case, they shook their heads, and came to the conclusion that Ichabod had been carried off by the galloping Hessian. As he was a bachelor, and in nobody's debt, nobody troubled his head any more about him. The school was removed to a different quarter of the hollow, and another pedagogue reigned in his stead.

It is true, an old farmer, who had been down to New York on a visit several years after, and from whom this account of the ghostly adventure was received, brought home the intelligence that Ichabod Crane was still alive; that he had left the neighborhood, partly through fear of the goblin and Hans Van Ripper, and partly in mortification at having been suddenly dismissed by the heiress; that he had changed his quarters to a distant part of the country; had kept school and studied law at the same time, had been admitted to the bar, turned politician, electioneered, written for the newspapers, and finally had been made a justice of the Ten Pound Court. Brom Bones too, who shortly after his rival's disappearance conducted the blooming Katrina in triumph to the altar, was observed to look exceedingly knowing whenever the story of Ichabod was related, and always burst into a hearty laugh at the mention of the pumpkin; which led some to suspect that he knew more about the matter than he chose to tell.

The old country wives, however, who are the best judges of these matters, maintain to this day that Ichabod was spirited away by supernatural means; and it is a favorite story often told about the neighborhood round the winter evening fire. The bridge became more than ever an object of superstitious awe, and that may be the reason why the road has been altered of late years, so as to approach the church by the border of the mill-pond. The school-house being deserted, soon fell to decay, and was reported to be haunted by the ghost of the unfortunate pedagogue; and the ploughboy, loitering homeward of a still summer evening, has often fancied his voice at a distance, chanting a melancholy psalm tune among the tranquil solitudes of Sleepy Hollow.

"The County Election" by George Caleb Bingham

ALEXIS de TOCQUEVILLE

Democracy in America

(1835, 1840)

Alexis Charles Henri Maurice Clérel de Tocqueville, a twenty-five-year-old French official, arrived in the United States in May 1831 with his friend Gustave de Beaumont. Both were magistrates supposedly come to examine the American prison system. Actually Tocqueville, son of an old family of the lesser nobility, had come on a far greater mission. In his native France, democracy—the ending of class distinctions and the rule of the majority—had come hand-in-hand with revolution, producing the violent overthrow of the ancien regime. **In America, Tocqueville hoped, he could see "the image of**

democracy itself, with its inclinations, its character, its prejudices, and its passions, in order to learn what we have to fear or to hope from its progress."

Tocqueville believed – contrary to what most members of the aristocracy believed about both the American and the French revolutions – that democracy and revolution were not fratricidal twins, rising and falling together. This bold new insight allowed him to analyze the American experience with fewer preconceptions about the ultimate fate of the democratic experiment than any other serious outside observer of the period. He took the most striking difference he observed between the new world and the old – the emphasis on equality of condition – and used it as the basis for perhaps the most influential analysis of the American character ever written.

Tocqueville saw that the drive toward democracy and equality would help to define what it was to be an American. Men raised among equals would voluntarily limit their ambitions lest they overstepped their neighbors' bounds. They would welcome change, but fear radical change – which, they felt, could only create inequalities. They would be pacifistic most of the time, but ferocious when aroused; they would favor toleration, but fear to hold opinions very different from their neighbors. Equality, in short, was a whole career in itself, the career upon which an entire nation had embarked.

Tocqueville continues to be read because he proved quite a good prophet, especially about the psychology of democracy. He recognized that democracy itself was not inherently unstable or revolutionary. He saw too that it was not radical; that despite various dangers, the United States was likely to be the most stable of nations. Tocqueville also detected most of what those future dangers might be: slavery, the rise of captains of industry, and the threat of an aggressive and restless army. To a large extent, when people talk about how the American character has changed under the impact of industrialism, modern communications, affluence, or the like, they are implicitly comparing their perception of Americans now to the remarkably persuasive "image of democracy itself" that Tocqueville drew over a century ago.

Why Great Revolutions Will Become More Rare

A people that has existed for centuries under a system of castes and classes can arrive at a democratic state of society only by passing through a long series of more or less critical transformations, accomplished by violent efforts, and after numerous vicissitudes, in the course of which property, opinions, and power are rapidly transferred from one to another. Even after this great revolution is consummated, the revolutionary habits produced by it may long be traced, and it will be followed by deep commotion. As all this takes place at the very time when social conditions are becoming more equal, it is inferred that some concealed relation and secret tie exists between the principle of equality itself and revolution, in so much that the one cannot exist without giving rise to the other.

On this point reasoning may seem to lead to the same result as experience. Among a people whose ranks are nearly equal, no ostensible bond connects men together or keeps them settled in their station. None of them have either a permanent right or power to command, none are forced by their condition to obey; but every man, finding himself possessed of some education and some resources, may choose his own path and proceed apart from all his fellow men. The same causes that make the members of the community independent of each other continually impel them to new and restless desires and constantly spur them onwards. It therefore seems natural that in a democratic community men, things, and opinions should be forever changing their form and place, and that democratic ages should be times of rapid and incessant transformation.

But is this really the case? Does the equality of social conditions habitually and permanently lead men to revolution? Does that state of society contain some perturbing principle which prevents the community from ever subsiding into calm and disposes the citizens to alter incessantly their laws, their principles, and their manners? I do not believe it; and as the subject is important, I beg for the reader's close attention.

Almost all the revolutions that have changed the aspect of nations have been made to consolidate or to destroy social inequality. Remove the secondary causes that have produced the great convulsions of the world and you will almost always find the principle of inequality at the bottom. Either the poor have attempted to plunder the rich, or the rich to enslave the poor. If, then, a state of society can ever be founded in which every man shall have something to keep and little to take from others, much will have been done for the peace of the world.

I am aware that among a great democratic people there will always be some members of the community in great poverty and others in great opulence; but the poor, instead of forming the immense majority of the nation, as is always the case in aristocratic communities, are comparatively few in number, and the laws do not bind them together by the ties of irremediable and hereditary penury.

The wealthy, on their side, are few and powerless; they have no privileges that attract public observation; even their wealth, as it is no longer incorporated and bound up with the soil, is impalpable and, as it were, invisible. As there is no longer a race of poor men, so there is no longer a race of rich men; the latter spring up daily from the multitude and relapse into it again. Hence they do not form a distinct class which may be easily marked out and plundered; and, moreover, as they are connected with the mass of their fellow citizens by a thousand secret ties, the people cannot assail them without inflicting an injury upon themselves.

Between these two extremes of democratic communities stands an innumerable multitude of men almost alike, who, without being exactly either rich or poor, possess sufficient property to desire the maintenance of order, yet not enough to excite envy. Such men are the natural enemies of violent commotions; their lack of agitation keeps all beneath them and above them still and secures the balance of the fabric of society.

Not, indeed, that even these men are contented with what they have got or that they feel a natural abhorrence for a revolution in which they might share the spoil without sharing the calamity; on the contrary, they desire, with unexampled ardor, to get rich, but the difficulty is to know from whom riches can be taken. The same state of society that constantly prompts desires, restrains these desires within necessary limits; it gives men more liberty of changing, and less interest in change.

Not only are the men of democracies not naturally desirous of revolutions, but they are afraid of them. All revolutions more or less threaten the tenure of property; but most of those who live in democratic countries are possessed of property; not only do they possess property, but they live in the condition where men set the greatest store upon their property.

If we attentively consider each of the classes of which society is composed, it is easy to see that the passions created by property are keenest and most tenacious among the middle classes. The poor often care but little for what they possess, because they suffer much more from the want of what they have not than they enjoy the little they have. The rich have many other passions besides that of riches to satisfy; and, besides, the long and arduous enjoyment of a great fortune sometimes makes them in the end insensible to its charms. But the men who have a competency, alike removed from opulence and from penury, attach an enormous value to their possessions. As they are still almost within the reach of poverty, they see its privations near at hand and dread them; between poverty and themselves there is nothing but a scanty fortune, upon which they immediately fix their apprehensions and their hopes. Every day increases the interest they take in it, by the constant cares which it occasions; and they are the more attached to it by their continual exertions to increase the amount. The notion of surrendering the smallest part of it is insupportable to them, and they consider its total loss as the worst of misfortunes.

Now, these eager and apprehensive men of small property constitute the class that is constantly increased by the equality of conditions. Hence in democratic communities the majority of the people do not clearly see what they have to gain by a revolution, but they continually and in a thousand ways feel that they might lose by one.

I have shown, in another part of this work, that the equality of conditions naturally urges men to embark on commercial and industrial pursuits, and that it tends to increase and to distribute real property; I have also pointed out the means by which it inspires every man with an eager and constant desire to increase his welfare. Nothing is more opposed to revolutionary passions than these things. It may happen that the final result of a revolution is favorable to commerce and manufactures; but its first consequence will almost always be the ruin of manufactures and mercantile men, because it must always change at once the general principles of consumption and temporarily upset the existing proportion between supply and demand.

I know of nothing more opposite to revolutionary attitudes than commercial ones. Commerce is naturally adverse to all the violent passions; it loves to temporize, takes delight in compromise, and studiously avoids irritation. It is patient, insinuating, flexible, and never has recourse to extreme measures until obliged by the most absolute necessity. Commerce renders men independent of one another, gives them a lofty notion of their personal importance, leads them to seek to conduct their own affairs, and teaches how to conduct them well; it therefore prepares men for freedom, but preserves them from revolutions.

In a revolution the owners of personal property have more to fear than all others; for, on the one hand, their property is often easy to seize, and, on the other, it may totally disappear at any moment—a subject of alarm to which the owners of real property are less exposed, since, although they may lose the income of their estates, they may hope to preserve the land itself through the greatest vicissitudes. Hence the former are much more alarmed at the symptoms of revolutionary commotion than the latter. Thus nations are less disposed to make revolutions in proportion as personal property is augmented and distributed among them and as the number of those possessing it is increased.

Moreover, whatever profession men may embrace and whatever species of property they may possess, one characteristic is common to them all. No one is fully contented with his present fortune; all are perpetually striving, in a thousand ways, to improve it. Consider any one of them at any period of his life and he will be found engaged with some new project for the purpose of increasing what he has. Do not talk to him of the interests and the rights of mankind; this small domestic concern absorbs for the time all his thoughts and inclines him to defer political agitations to some other season. This not only prevents men from making revolutions, but deters men from desiring them. Violent political passions have but little hold on those who have devoted all their faculties to the pursuit of their well-being. The ardor that they display in small matters calms their zeal for momentous undertakings.

From time to time, indeed, enterprising and ambitious men will arise in democratic communities whose unbounded aspirations cannot be contented by following the beaten track. Such men like revolutions and hail their approach; but they have great difficulty in bringing them about unless extraordinary events come to their assistance. No man can struggle with advantage against the spirit of his age and country; and however powerful he may be supposed to be, he will find it difficult to make his contemporaries share in feelings and opinions that are repugnant to all their feelings and desires.

It is a mistake to believe that, when once equality of condition has become the old and uncontested state of society and has imparted its characteristics to the manners of a nation, men will easily allow themselves to be thrust into perilous risks by an imprudent leader or a bold innovator. Not indeed that they will resist him openly, by well-contrived schemes, or even by a premeditated plan of resistance. They will not struggle energetically against him, sometimes they will even applaud him; but they do not follow him. To his vehemence they secretly oppose their inertia, to his revolutionary tendencies their conservative interests, their homely tastes to his adventurous passions, their good sense to the flights of his genius, to his poetry their prose. With immense exertion he raises them for an instant, but they speedily escape from him and fall back, as it were, by their own weight. He strains himself to rouse the indifferent and distracted multitude and finds at last that he is reduced to impotence, not because he is conquered, but because he is alone.

I do not assert that men living in democratic communities are naturally stationary; I think, on the contrary, that a perpetual stir prevails in the bosom of those societies, and that rest is unknown there; but I think that men bestir themselves within certain limits, beyond which they hardly ever go. They are forever varying, altering, and restoring secondary matters; but they carefully abstain from touching what is fundamental. They love change, but they dread revolutions.

Although the Americans are constantly modifying or abrogating some of their laws, they by no means display revolutionary passions. It may be easily seen from the promptitude with which they check and calm themselves when public excitement begins to grow alarming, and at the very moment when passions seem most roused, that they dread a revolution as the worst of misfortunes and that every one of them is inwardly resolved to make great sacrifices to avoid such a catastrophe. In no country in the world is the love of property more active and more anxious than in the United States; nowhere does the majority display less inclination for those principles which threaten to alter, in whatever manner, the laws of property.

I have often remarked, that theories which are of a revolutionary nature, since they cannot be put in practice without a complete and sometimes a sudden change in the state of property and persons, are much less favorably viewed in the United States than in the great monarchical countries of Europe; if some men profess them, the bulk of the people reject them with instinctive abhorrence. I do not hesitate to say that most of the maxims commonly called democratic in France would be proscribed by the democracy of the United States. This may easily be understood: in America men have the opinions and passions of democracy; in Europe we have still the passions and opinions of revolution.

If ever America undergoes great revolutions, they will be brought about by the presence of the black race on the soil of the United States; that is to say, they will owe their origin, not to the equality, but to the inequality of condition.

When social conditions are equal, every man is apt to live apart, centered in himself and forgetful of the public. If the rulers of democratic nations were either to neglect to correct this fatal tendency or to encourage it from a notion that it weans men from political passions and thus wards off revolutions, they might eventually produce the evil they seek to avoid, and a time might come when the inordinate passions of a few men, aided by the unintelligent selfishness or the pusillanimity of the greater number, would ultimately compel society to pass through strange vicissitudes. In democratic communities revolutions are seldom desired except by a minority, but a minority may sometimes effect them.

I do not assert that democratic nations are secure from revolutions; I merely say that the state of society in those nations does not lead to revolutions, but rather wards them off. A democratic people left to itself will not easily embark in great hazards; it is only led to revolutions unawares; it may sometimes undergo them, but it does not make them: and I will add that when such a people has been allowed to acquire sufficient knowledge and experience, it will not allow them to be made.

I am well aware that in this respect public institutions may themselves do much; they may encourage or repress the tendencies that originate in the state of society. I therefore do not maintain, I repeat, that a people is secure from revolutions simply because conditions are equal in the community; but I think that, whatever the institutions of such a people may be, great revolutions will always be far less violent and less frequent than is supposed, and I can easily discern a state of polity which, when combined with the principle of equality, would render society more stationary than it has ever been in our western part of the world.

The observations I have here made on events may also be applied in part to opinions. Two things are surprising in the United States: the mutability of the greater part of human actions, and the singular stability of certain principles. Men are in constant motion; the mind of man appears almost unmoved. When once an opinion has spread over the country and struck root there, it would seem that no power on earth is strong enough to eradicate it. In the United States general principles in religion, philosophy, morality, and even politics do not vary, or at least are only modified by a hidden and often an imperceptible process; even the grossest prejudices are obliterated with incredible slowness amid the continual friction of men and things.

I hear it said that it is in the nature and the habits of democracies to be constantly changing their opinions and feelings. This may be true of small democratic nations, like those of the ancient world, in which the whole community could be assembled in a public place and then excited at will by an orator. But I saw nothing of the kind among the great democratic people that dwells upon the opposite shores of the Atlantic Ocean. What struck me in the United States was the difficulty of shaking the majority in an opinion once conceived or of drawing it off from a leader once adopted. Neither speaking nor writing can accomplish it; nothing but experience will avail, and even experience must be repeated.

This is surprising at first sight, but a more attentive investigation explains the fact. I do not think that it is as easy as is supposed to uproot the prejudices of a democratic people, to change its belief, to supersede principles once established by new principles in religion, politics, and morals; in a word, to make great and frequent changes in men's minds. Not that the human mind is there at rest, it is in constant agitation; but it is engaged in infinitely varying the consequences of known principles and in seeking for new consequences rather than in seeking for new principles. Its motion is one of rapid circumvolution rather than of straightforward impulse by rapid and direct effort; it extends its orbit by small continual and hasty movements, but it does not suddenly alter its position.

Men who are equal in rights, in education, in fortune, or, to comprise all in one word, in their social condition, have necessarily wants, habits, and tastes that are hardly dissimilar. As they look at objects under the same aspect, their minds naturally tend to similar conclusions; and though each of them may deviate from his contemporaries and form opinions of his own, they will involuntarily and unconsciously concur in a certain number of received opinions. The more attentively I consider the effects of equality upon the mind, the more am I persuaded that the intellectual anarchy which we witness about us is not, as many men suppose, the natural state of democratic nations. I think it is rather to be regarded as an accident peculiar to their youth, and that it breaks out only at that period of transition when men have already snapped the former ties which bound them together, but are still amazingly different in origin, education, and manners; so that, having retained opinions, propensities, and tastes of great diversity, nothing any longer prevents men from avowing them openly. The leading opinions of men become similar in proportion as their conditions assimilate: such appears to me to be the general and permanent law; the rest is casual and transient.

I believe that it will rarely happen to any man in a democratic community suddenly to frame a system of notions very remote from that which his contemporaries have adopted; and if some such innovator appeared, I apprehend that he would have great difficulty in finding listeners, still more in finding believers. When the conditions of men are almost equal, they do not easily allow themselves to be persuaded by one another. As they all live in close intercourse, as they have learned the same things together, and as they lead the same life, they are not naturally disposed to take one of themselves for a guide and to follow him implicitly. Men seldom take the opinion of their equal or of a man like themselves upon trust.

Not only is confidence in the superior attainments of certain individuals weakened among democratic nations, as I have elsewhere remarked, but the general notion of the intellectual superiority which any man whatsoever may acquire in relation to the rest of the community is soon overshadowed. As men grow more like each other, the doctrine of the equality of the intellect gradually infuses itself into their opinions, and it becomes more difficult for any innovator to acquire or to exert much influence over the minds of a people. In such communities sudden intellectual revolutions will therefore be rare; for if we read aright the history of the world, we shall find that great and rapid changes in human opinions have been produced far less by the force of reasoning than by the authority of a name.

Observe, too, that as the men who live in democratic societies are not connected with one another by any tie, each of them must be convinced individually, while in aristocratic society it is enough to convince a few; the rest follow. If Luther had lived in an age of equality and had not had princes and potentates for his audience, he would perhaps have found it more difficult to change the aspect of Europe.

Not, indeed, that the men of democracies are naturally strongly persuaded of the certainty of their opinions or are unwavering in belief; they frequently entertain doubts that no one, in their eyes, can remove. It sometimes happens at such times that the human mind would willingly change its position, but as nothing urges or guides it forward, it oscillates to and fro without progressive motion.*

Even when the confidence of a democratic people has been won, it is still no easy matter to gain their attention. It is extremely difficult to obtain a hearing from men living in democracies, unless it is to speak to them of themselves. They do not attend to the things said to them, because they are always fully engrossed with the things they are doing. For, indeed, few men are idle in democratic nations; life is passed in the midst of noise and excitement, and men are so engaged in acting that little time remains to them for thinking. I would especially remark, not only that they are employed, but that they are passionately devoted to their employments. They are always in action, and each of their actions absorbs their faculties; the zeal which they display in business puts out the enthusiasm they might otherwise entertain for ideas.

I think that it is extremely difficult to excite the enthusiasm of a democratic people for any theory which has not a palpable, direct, and immediate connection with the daily occupations of life; therefore they will not easily forsake their old opinions, for it is enthusiasm that flings the minds of men out of the beaten track and effects the great revolutions of the intellect as well as the great revolutions of the political world.

Thus democratic nations have neither time nor taste to go in search of novel opinions. Even when those they possess become doubtful, they still retain them because it would take too much time and inquiry to change them; they retain them, not as certain, but as established.

There are yet other and more cogent reasons which prevent any great change from being easily effected in the principles of a democratic people. I have already adverted to them in the nineteenth chapter.

If the influence of individuals is weak and hardly perceptible among such a people, the power exercised by the mass upon the mind of each individual is extremely great; I have already shown for what reasons. I would now observe that it is wrong to suppose that this depends solely upon the form of government and that the majority would lose its intellectual supremacy if it were to lose its political power.

In aristocracies men often have much greatness and strength of their own; when they find themselves at variance with the greater

*If I inquire what state of society is most favorable to the great revolutions of the mind, I find that it occurs somewhere between the complete equality of the whole community and the absolute separation of ranks. Under a system of castes generations succeed one another without altering men's positions; some have nothing more, others nothing better, to hope for. The imagination slumbers amid this universal silence and stillness, and the very idea of change fades from the human mind.

When ranks have been abolished and social conditions are almost equalized, all men are in ceaseless excitement, but each of them stands alone, independent and weak. This latter state of things is excessively different from the former one; yet it has one point of analogy: great revolutions of the human mind seldom occur in it.

But between these two extremes of the history of nations is an intermediate period, a period of glory as well as of ferment, when the conditions of men are not sufficiently settled for the mind to be lulled in torpor, when they are sufficiently unequal for men to exercise a vast power on the minds of one another, and when some few may modify the convictions of all. It is at such times that great reformers arise and new ideas suddenly change the face of the world.

number of their fellow countrymen, they withdraw to their own circle, where they support and console themselves. Such is not the case in a democratic country; there public favor seems as necessary as the air we breathe, and to live at variance with the multitude is, as it were, not to live. The multitude require no laws to coerce those who do not think like themselves: public disapprobation is enough; a sense of their loneliness and impotence overtakes them and drives them to despair.

Whenever social conditions are equal, public opinion presses with enormous weight upon the minds of each individual; it surrounds, directs, and oppresses him; and this arises from the very constitution of society much more than from its political laws. As men grow more alike, each man feels himself weaker in regard to all the rest; as he discerns nothing by which he is considerably raised above them or distinguished from them, he mistrusts himself as soon as they assail him. Not only does he mistrust his strength, but he even doubts of his right; and he is very near acknowledging that he is in the wrong, when the greater number of his countrymen assert that he is so. The majority do not need to force him; they convince him. In whatever way the powers of a democratic community may be organized and balanced, then, it will always be extremely difficult to believe what the bulk of the people reject or to profess what they condemn.

This circumstance is extraordinarily favorable to the stability of opinions. When an opinion has taken root among a democratic people and established itself in the minds of the bulk of the community, it afterwards persists by itself and is maintained without effort, because no one attacks it. Those who at first rejected it as false ultimately receive it as the general impression, and those who still dispute it in their hearts conceal their dissent; they are careful not to engage in a dangerous and useless conflict.

It is true that when the majority of a democratic people change their opinions, they may suddenly and arbitrarily effect strange revolutions in men's minds; but their opinions do not change without much difficulty, and it is almost as difficult to show that they are changed.

Time, events, or the unaided individual action of the mind will sometimes undermine or destroy an opinion, without any outward sign of the change. It has not been openly assailed, no conspiracy has been formed to make war on it, but its followers one by one noiselessly secede; day by day a few of them abandon it, until at last it is only professed by a minority. In this state it will still continue to prevail. As its enemies remain mute or only interchange their thoughts by stealth, they are themselves unaware for a long period that a great revolution has actually been effected; and in this state of uncertainty they take no steps; they observe one another and are silent. The majority have ceased to believe what they believed before, but they still affect to believe, and this empty phantom of public opinion is strong enough to chill innovators and to keep them silent and at a respectful distance.

We live at a time that has witnessed the most rapid changes of opinion in the minds of men; nevertheless it may be that the leading opinions of society will before long be more settled than they have been for several centuries in our history; that time has not yet come, but it may perhaps be approaching. As I examine more closely the natural wants and tendencies of democratic nations, I grow persuaded that if ever social equality is generally and permanently established in the world, great intellectual and political revolutions will become more difficult and less frequent than is supposed. Because the men of democracies appear always excited, uncertain, eager, changeable in their wills and in their positions, it is imagined that they are suddenly to abrogate their laws, to adopt new opinions, and to assume new manners. But if the principle of equality predisposes men to change, it also suggests to them certain interests and tastes that cannot be satisfied without a settled order of things. Equality urges them on, but at the same time it holds them back; it spurs them, but fastens them to earth; it kindles their desires, but limits their powers.

This, however, is not perceived at first; the passions that tend to sever the citizens of a democracy are obvious enough, but the hidden force that restrains and unites them is not discernible at a glance.

Amid the ruins which surround me shall I dare to say that revolutions are not what I most fear for coming generations? If men continue to shut themselves more closely within the narrow circle of domestic interests and to live on that kind of excitement, it is to be apprehended that they may ultimately become inaccessible to those great and powerful public emotions which perturb nations, but which develop them and recruit them. When property becomes so fluctuating and the love of property so restless and so ardent, I cannot but fear that men may arrive at such a state as to regard every new theory as a peril, every innovation as an irksome toil, every social improvement as a stepping-stone to revolution, and so refuse to move altogether for fear of being moved too far. I dread, and I confess it, lest they should at last so entirely give way to a cowardly love of present enjoyment as to lose sight of the interests of their future selves and those of their descendants and prefer to glide along the easy current of life rather than to make, when it is necessary, a strong and sudden effort to a higher purpose.

It is believed by some that modern society will be always changing its aspect; for myself, I fear that it will ultimately be too invariably fixed in the same institutions, the same prejudices, the same manners, so that mankind will be stopped and circumscribed; that the mind will swing backwards and forwards forever without begetting fresh ideas; that man will waste his strength in bootless and solitary trifling, and, though in continual motion, that humanity will cease to advance.

Why Democratic Nations Naturally Desire Peace, and Democratic Armies, War

The same interests, the same fears, the same passions that deter democratic nations from revolutions deter them also from war; the spirit of military glory and the spirit of revolution are weakened at the same time and by the same causes. The ever increasing numbers of men of property who are lovers of peace, the growth of personal wealth which war so rapidly consumes, the mildness of manners, the gentleness of heart, those tendencies to pity which are produced by the equality of conditions, that coolness of understanding which renders men comparatively insensible to the violent and poetical excitement of arms, all these causes concur to quench the military spirit. I think it may be admitted as a general and constant rule that among civilized nations the warlike passions will become more rare and less intense in proportion as social conditions are more equal.

War is nevertheless an occurrence to which all nations are subject, democratic nations as well as others. Whatever taste they may have for peace, they must hold themselves in readiness to repel aggression, or, in other words, they must have an army. Fortune, which has conferred so many peculiar benefits upon the inhabitants of the United States, has placed them in the midst of a wilderness, where they have, so to speak, no neighbors; a few thousand soldiers are sufficient for their wants. But this is peculiar to America, not to democracy.

The equality of conditions and the manners as well as the institutions resulting from it do not exempt a democratic people from the necessity of standing armies, and their armies always exercise a powerful influence over their fate. It is therefore of singular importance to inquire what are the natural propensities of the men of whom these armies are composed.

Among aristocratic nations, especially among those in which birth is the only source of rank, the same inequality exists in the army as in the nation; the officer is noble, the soldier is a serf; the one is naturally called upon to command, the other to obey. In aristocratic armies the private soldier's ambition is therefore circumscribed within very narrow limits. Nor has the ambition of the officer an unlimited range. An aristocratic body not only forms a part of the scale of ranks in the nation, but contains a scale of ranks within itself; the members of whom it is composed are placed one above another in a particular and unvarying manner. Thus one man is born to the command of a regiment, another to that of a company. When once they have reached the utmost object of their hopes, they stop of their own accord and remain contented with their lot.

There is, besides, a strong cause that in aristocracies weakens the officer's desire of promotion. Among aristocratic nations an officer, independently of his rank in the army, also occupies an elevated rank in society; the former is almost always, in his eyes, only an appendage to the latter. A nobleman who embraces the profession of arms follows it less from motives of ambition than from a sense of the duties imposed on him by his birth. He enters the army in order to find an honorable employment for the idle years of his youth and to be able to bring back to his home and his peers some honorable recollections of military life; but his principal object is not to obtain by that profession either property, distinction, or power, for he possesses these advantages in his own right and enjoys them without leaving his home.

In democratic armies all the soldiers may become officers, which makes the desire of promotion general and immeasurably extends the bounds of military ambition. The officer, on his part, sees nothing that naturally and necessarily stops him at one grade more than at another; and each grade has immense importance in his eyes because his rank in society almost always depends on his rank in the army. Among democratic nations it often happens that an officer has no property but his pay and no distinction but that of military honors; consequently, as often as his duties change, his fortune changes and he becomes, as it were, a new man. What was only an appendage to his position in aristocratic armies has thus become the main point, the basis of his whole condition.

Under the old French monarchy officers were always called by their titles of nobility; they are now always called by the title of their military rank. This little change in the forms of language suffices to show that a great revolution has taken place in the constitution of society and in that of the army.

In democratic armies the desire of advancement is almost universal: it is ardent, tenacious, perpetual; it is strengthened by all other desires and extinguished only with life itself. But it is easy to see that, of all armies in the world, those in which advancement must be slowest in time of peace are the armies of democratic countries. As the number of commissions is naturally limited while the number of competitors is almost unlimited, and as the strict law of equality is over all alike, none can make rapid progress; many can make no progress at all. Thus the desire of advancement is greater and the opportunities of advancement fewer there than elsewhere. All the ambitious spirits of a democratic army are consequently ardently desirous of war, because war makes vacancies and warrants the violation of that law of seniority which is the sole privilege natural to democracy.

We thus arrive at this singular consequence, that, of all armies, those most ardently desirous of war are democratic armies, and of all nations, those most fond of peace are democratic nations; and what makes these facts still more extraordinary is that these contrary effects are produced at the same time by the principle of equality.

All the members of the community, being alike, constantly harbor the wish and discover the possibility of changing their condition and improving their welfare; this makes them fond of peace, which is favorable to industry and allows every man to pursue his own little undertakings to their completion. On the other hand, this same equality makes soldiers dream of fields of battle, by increasing the value of military honors in the eyes of those who follow the profession of arms and by rendering those honors accessible to all. In either case the restlessness of the heart is the same, the taste for enjoyment is insatiable, the ambition of success as great; the means of gratifying it alone are different.

These opposite tendencies of the nation and the army expose democratic communities to great dangers. When a military spirit forsakes a people, the profession of arms immediately ceases to be held in honor and military men fall to the lowest rank of the public servants; they are little esteemed and no longer understood. The reverse of what takes place in aristocratic ages then occurs; the men who enter the army are no longer those of the highest, but of the lowest class. Military ambition is indulged only when no other is possible. Hence arises a circle of cause and consequence from which it is difficult to escape: the best part of the nation shuns the military profession because that profession is not honored, and the profession is not honored because the best part of the nation has ceased to follow it.

It is then no matter of surprise that democratic armies are often restless, ill-tempered, and dissatisfied with their lot, although their physical condition is commonly far better and their discipline less strict than in other countries. The soldier feels that he occupies an inferior position, and his wounded pride either stimulates his taste for hostilities that would render his services necessary or gives him a desire for revolution, during which he may hope to win by force of arms the political influence and personal importance now denied him.

The composition of democratic armies makes this last-mentioned danger much to be feared. In democratic communities almost every man has some property to preserve; but democratic armies are generally led by men without property, most of whom have little to lose in civil broils. The bulk of the nation is naturally much more afraid of revolutions than in the ages of aristocracy, but the leaders of the army much less so.

Moreover, as among democratic nations (to repeat what I have just remarked) the wealthiest, best-educated, and ablest men seldom adopt the military profession, the army, taken collectively, eventually forms a small nation by itself, where the mind is less enlarged and habits are more rude than in the nation at large. Now, this small uncivilized nation has arms in its possession and alone knows how to use them; for, indeed, the pacific temper of the community increases the danger to which a democratic people is exposed from the military and turbulent spirit of the army. Nothing is so dangerous as an army in the midst of an unwarlike nation; the excessive love of the whole community for quiet continually puts the constitution at the mercy of the soldiery.

It may therefore be asserted, generally speaking, that if democratic nations are naturally prone to peace from their interests and their propensities, they are constantly drawn to war and revolutions by their armies. Military revolutions, which are scarcely ever to be apprehended in aristocracies, are always to be dreaded among democratic nations. These perils must be reckoned among the most formidable that beset their future fate, and the attention of statesmen should be sedulously applied to find a remedy for the evil.

When a nation perceives that it is inwardly affected by the restless ambition of its army, the first thought which occurs is to give this inconvenient ambition an object by going to war. I do not wish to speak ill of war: war almost always enlarges the mind of a people and raises their character. In some cases it is the only check to the excessive growth of certain propensities that naturally spring out of the equality of conditions, and it must be considered as a necessary corrective to certain inveterate diseases to which democratic communities are liable.

War has great advantages, but we must not flatter ourselves that it can diminish the danger I have just pointed out. That peril is only suspended by it, to return more fiercely when the war is over; for armies are much more impatient of peace after having tasted military exploits. War could be a remedy only for a people who were always athirst for military glory.

I foresee that all the military rulers who may rise up in great democratic nations will find it easier to conquer with their armies than to make their armies live at peace after conquest. There are two things that a democratic people will always find very difficult, to begin a war and to end it.

Again, if war has some peculiar advantages for democratic nations, on the other hand it exposes them to certain dangers which aristocracies have no cause to dread to an equal extent. I shall point out only two of these.

Although war gratifies the army, it embarrasses and often exasperates that countless multitude of men whose minor passions every day require peace in order to be satisfied. Thus there is some risk of its causing, under another form, the very disturbance it is intended to prevent.

No protracted war can fail to endanger the freedom of a democratic country. Not indeed that after every victory it is to be apprehended that the victorious generals will possess themselves by force of the supreme power, after the manner of Sulla and Cæsar; the danger is of another kind. War does not always give over democratic communities to military government, but it must invariably and immeasurably increase the powers of civil government; it must almost compulsorily concentrate the direction of all men and the management of all things in the hands of the administration. If it does not lead to despotism by sudden violence, it prepares men for it more gently by their habits. All those who seek to destroy the liberties of a democratic nation ought to know that war is the surest and the shortest means to accomplish it. This is the first axiom of the science.

One remedy, which appears to be obvious when the ambition of soldiers and officers becomes the subject of alarm, is to augment the number of commissions to be distributed by increasing the army. This affords temporary relief, but it plunges the country into deeper difficulties at some future period. To increase the army may produce a lasting effect in an aristocratic community, because military ambition is there confined to one class of men, and the ambition of each individual stops, as it were, at a certain limit, so that it may be possible to satisfy all who feel its influence. But nothing is gained by increasing the army among a democratic people, because the number of aspirants always rises in exactly the same ratio as the army itself. Those whose claims have been satisfied by the creation of new commissions are instantly succeeded by a fresh multitude beyond all power of satisfaction; and even those who were but now satisfied soon begin to crave more advancement, for the same excitement prevails in the ranks of the army as in the civil classes of democratic society, and what men want is, not to reach a certain grade, but to have constant promotion. Though these wants may not be very vast, they are perpetually recurring. Thus a democratic nation, by augmenting its army, allays only for a time the ambition of the military profession, which soon becomes even more formidable because the number of those who feel it is increased.

I am of the opinion that a restless and turbulent spirit is an evil inherent in the very constitution of democratic armies and beyond hope of cure. The legislators of democracies must not expect to devise any military organization capable by its influence of calming and restraining the military profession; their efforts would exhaust their powers before the object could be attained.

The remedy for the vices of the army is not to be found in the army itself, but in the country. Democratic nations are naturally afraid of disturbance and of despotism; the object is to turn these natural instincts into intelligent, deliberate, and lasting tastes. When men have at last learned to make a peaceful and profitable use of freedom and have felt its blessings, when they have conceived a manly love of order and have freely submitted themselves to discipline, these same men, if they follow the profession of arms, bring into it, unconsciously and almost against their will, these same habits and manners. The general spirit of the nation, being infused into the spirit peculiar to the army, tempers the opinions and desires engendered by military life, or represses them by the mighty force of public opinion. Teach the citizens to be educated, orderly, firm, and free and the soldiers will be disciplined and obedient.

Any law that, in repressing the turbulent spirit of the army, should tend to diminish the spirit of freedom in the nation and to overshadow the notion of law and right would defeat its object; it would do much more to favor than to defeat the establishment of military tyranny.

After all, and in spite of all precautions, a large army in the midst of a democratic people will always be a source of great danger. The most effectual means of diminishing that danger would be to reduce the army, but this is a remedy that all nations are not able to apply.

George Catlin's portrait of Red Jacket

RED JACKET

Reply to Missionary Cram at Buffalo, New York, 1805

GEORGE CATLIN

Letters and Notes on the North American Indians

(1841)

When most Americans envision an Indian, they are in effect looking at George Catlin's paintings and drawings. Much of our image of the Indian, and certainly most of what went into the stage Indian of nineteenth-century melodrama and twentieth-century western movies came from Catlin's art, which he exhibited in many American cities between 1837 and 1852, and which graces many of our museums today. In this sense, Catlin succeeded in his life's work of enabling the "doomed" Indian civilization to "phoenix-like, . . . rise from the 'stain on a painter's palette,' and live again upon canvass, and stand forth for centuries yet to come, the living monuments of a noble race."

For many years Catlin traveled each summer through the West, living with different Indian tribes who allowed him to paint them, their villages, their artifacts, and scenes of their activities. His hard-won insights into Indian life and values are as apparent in his Letters as in his art. His sensitivity to the effects of their contact with white civilizations, and his acute perceptions of the conflicting image of the Indian in the mind of his compatriots, make Catlin one of the most important commentators on the North American Indian.

When Catlin met the Seneca chief, Red Jacket, the famous Indian orator was at the end of his long life. Ravaged by the effects of the "strong liquors" which, as he had long before told missionary Cram, had "slain thousands," Red Jacket was a pathetic exemplar of the fate of the Indian civilizations. Glimpsing Red Jacket in his full majesty answering Cram in 1805, and then viewing him through Catlin's eyes a quarter of a century later, offers a poignant instance of Catlin's vision of the two Indian cultures: those "yet unroused and unenticed from their wild haunts," and the "miserable living victims and dupes of white man's cupidity." Not long after Catlin visited him, Red Jacket—who had spent most of his life in a vain attempt to drive the white men, including the missionaries, off the Seneca reservation—was buried, contrary to all his wishes, with a Christian funeral in a Christian cemetery, mourned by his heirs in the Christian manner the missionaries had taught them.

Red Jacket's Reply to Missionary Cram at Buffalo, New York, 1805

Friend and brother, it was the will of the Great Spirit that we should meet together this day. He orders all things, and He has given us a fine day for our council. He has taken His garment from before the sun, and caused it to shine with brightness upon us; our eyes are opened, that we see clearly; our ears are unstopped, that we have been able to hear distinctly the words that you have spoken; for all these favours we thank the Great Spirit, and Him only.

Brother, this council fire was kindled by you; it was at your request that we came together at this time; we have listened with attention to what you have said; you requested us to speak our minds freely; this gives us great joy, for we now consider that we stand upright before you, and can speak what we think; all have heard your voice, and all speak to you as one man; our minds are agreed.

Brother, you say you want an answer to your talk, before you leave this place. It is right you should have one, as you are a great distance from home, and we do not wish to detain you; but we will first look back a little, and tell you what our fathers have told us, and what we have heard from the White people.

Brother, listen to what we say. There was a time when our forefathers owned this great land. Their seats extended from the rising to the setting sun. The Great Spirit had made it for the use of Indians. He had created the buffalo, the deer, and other animals for food. He made the bear and the beaver, and their skins served us for clothing. He had scattered them over the country, and taught us how to take them. He had caused the earth to produce corn for bread.

All this He had done for His Red children because he loved them. If we had any disputes about hunting grounds, they were generally settled without the shedding of much blood.

But an evil day came upon us; your forefathers crossed the great waters, and landed on this island. Their numbers were small; they found friends, and not enemies; they told us they had fled from their own country for fear of wicked men, and come here to enjoy their religion. They asked for a small seat; we took pity on them, granted their request, and they sat down amongst us; we gave them corn and meat; they gave us poison in return. The White people had now found our country, tidings were carried back, and more came amongst us; yet we did not fear them, we took them to be friends; they called us brothers; we believed them, and gave them a larger seat. At length their numbers had greatly increased; they wanted more land; they wanted our country. Our eyes were opened; and our minds became uneasy. Wars took place; Indians were hired to fight against Indians, and many of our people were destroyed. They also brought strong liquors among us; it was strong and powerful, and has slain thousands.

Brother, our seats were once large, and yours were very small; you have now become a great people, and we have scarcely a place left to spread our blankets; you have got our country, but are not satisfied; you want to force your religion upon us.

Brother, continue to listen. You say that you are sent to instruct us how to worship the Great Spirit agreeably to His mind, and if we do not take hold of the religion which you White people teach, we shall be unhappy hereafter; you say that you are right, and we are lost; how do we know this to be true? We understand that your religion is written in a book; if it was intended for us as well as you, why has not the Great Spirit given it to us, and not only to us, but why did He not give to our forefathers the knowledge of that book, with the means of understanding it rightly? We only know what you tell us about it; how shall we know when to believe, being so often deceived by the White people?

Brother, you say there is but one way to worship and serve the Great Spirit; if there is but one religion, why do you White people differ so much about it? Why not all agree, as you can all read the book?

Brother, we do not understand these things; we are told that your religion was given to your forefathers, and has been handed down from father to son. We also have a religion which was given to our forefathers, and has been handed down to us, their children. We worship that way. It teaches us to be thankful for all the favours we receive; to love each other, and to be united; we never quarrel about religion.

Brother, the Great Spirit has made us all; but He has made a great difference between His White and Red children; He has given us a different complexion and different customs; to you He has given the arts; to these He has not opened our eyes; we know these things to be true. Since He has made so great a difference between us in other things, why may we not conclude that He has given us a different religion according to our understanding? The Great Spirit does right; He knows what is best for his children; we are satisfied.

Brother, we do not wish to destroy your religion, or take it from you. We want only to enjoy our own.

Brother, you say you have not come to get our land or our money, but to enlighten our minds. I will now tell you that I have been at your meetings, and saw you collecting money from the meeting. I cannot tell what this money was intended for, but suppose it was for your minister, and if we should conform to your way of thinking, perhaps you may want some from us.

Brother, we are told that you have been preaching to White people in this place; these people are our neighbors, we are acquainted with them; we will wait a little while and see what effect your preaching has upon them. If we find it does them good, makes them honest, and less disposed to cheat Indians, we will then consider again what you have said.

Brother, you have now heard our answer to your talk, and this is all we have to say at present. As we are going to part, we will come and take you by the hand, and hope the Great Spirit will protect you on your journey, and return you safe to your friends.

Letters and Notes on the North American Indians

Letter—No. 1.

As the following pages have been hastily compiled, at the urgent request of a number of my friends, from a series of Letters and Notes written by myself during several years' residence and travel amongst a number of the wildest and most remote tribes of the North American Indians, I have thought it best to make this page the beginning of my book; dispensing with Preface, and even with Dedication, other than that which I hereby make of it, with all my heart, to those who will take the pains to read it.

If it be necessary to render any apology for beginning thus unceremoniously, my readers will understand that I had no space in these, my first volumes, to throw away; nor much time at my disposal, which I could, in justice, use for introducing myself and my works to the world.

Having commenced thus abruptly then, I will venture to take upon myself the sin of calling this one of the series of Letters of which I have spoken; although I am writing it several years later, and placing it at the beginning of my book; by which means I will be enabled briefly to introduce myself to my readers (who, as yet, know little or nothing of me), and also the subjects of the following epistles, with such explanations of the customs described in them, as will serve for a key or glossary to the same, and prepare the reader's mind for the information they contain.

Amidst the multiplicity of books which are, in this enlightened age, flooding the world, I feel it my duty, as early as possible, to beg pardon for making a book at all; and in the next (if my readers should become so much interested in my narrations, as to censure me for the brevity of the work) to take some considerable credit for not having trespassed too long upon their time and patience.

Leaving my readers, therefore, to find out what is in the book, without promising them anything, I proceed to say—of *myself,* that I was born in Wyöming, in North America, some thirty or forty years since, of parents who entered that beautiful and famed valley soon after the close of the revolutionary war, and the disastrous event of the "Indian massacre."

The early part of my life was whiled away, apparently, somewhat in vain, with books reluctantly held in one hand, and a rifle or fishing-pole firmly and affectionately grasped in the other.

At the urgent request of my father, who was a practising lawyer, I was prevailed upon to abandon these favourite themes, and also my occasional dabblings with the brush, which had secured already a corner in my affections; and I commenced reading the law for a profession, under the direction of Reeve and Gould, of Connecticut. I attended the lectures of these learned judges for two years—was admitted to the bar—and practised the law, as a sort of *Nimrodical* lawyer, in my native land, for the term of two or three years; when I very deliberately sold my law library and all (save my rifle and fishing-tackle), and converting their proceeds into brushes and paint pots; I commenced the art of painting in Philadelphia, without teacher or adviser.

I there closely applied my hand to the labours of the art for several years; during which time my mind was continually reaching for some branch or enterprise of the art, on which to devote a whole lifetime of enthusiasm; when a delegation of some ten or fifteen noble and dignified-looking Indians, from the wilds of the "Far West," suddenly arrived in the city, arrayed and equipped in all their classic beauty,—with shield and helmet,—with tunic and manteau,—tinted and tasselled off, exactly for the painter's palette!

In silent and stoic dignity, these lords of the forest strutted about the city for a few days, wrapped in their pictured robes, with their brows plumed with the quills of the war-eagle, attracting the gaze and admiration of all who beheld them. After this they took their leave for Washington City, and I was left to reflect and regret, which I did long and deeply, until I came to the following deductions and conclusions.

Black and blue cloth and civilization are destined, not only to veil, but to obliterate the grace and beauty of Nature. Man, in the simplicity and loftiness of his nature, unrestrained and unfettered by the disguises of art, is surely the most beautiful model for the painter,—and the country from which he hails is unquestionably the best study or school of the arts in the world: such I am sure, from the models I have seen, is the wilderness of North America. And the history and customs of such a people, preserved by pictorial illustrations, are themes worthy the lifetime of one man, and nothing short of the loss of my life, shall prevent me from visiting their country, and of becoming their historian.

There was something inexpressibly delightful in the above resolve, which was to bring me amidst such living models for my brush; and at the same time to place in my hands again, for my living and protection, the objects of my heart above-named; which had long been laid by to rust and decay in the city, without the remotest prospect of again contributing to my amusement.

I had fully resolved—I opened my views to my friends and relations, but got not one advocate or abettor. I tried fairly and faithfully, but it was in vain to reason with those whose anxieties were ready to fabricate every difficulty and danger that could be imagined, without being able to understand or appreciate the extent or importance of my designs, and I broke from them all,—from my wife and my aged parents,—myself my only adviser and protector.

With these views firmly fixed—armed, equipped, and supplied, I started out in the year 1832, and penetrated the vast and pathless wilds which are familiarly denominated the great "Far West" of the North American Continent, with a light heart, inspired with an enthusiastic hope and reliance that I could meet and overcome all the hazards and privations of a life devoted to the production of a literal and graphic delineation of the living manners, customs, and character of an interesting race of people, who are rapidly passing away from the face of the earth—lending a hand to a dying nation, who have no historians or biographers of their own to pourtray with fidelity their native looks and history; thus snatching from a hasty oblivion what could be saved for the benefit of posterity, and perpetuating it, as a fair and just monument, to the memory of a truly lofty and noble race.

I have spent about eight years already in the pursuit above-named, having been for the most of that time immersed in the Indian country, mingling with red men, and identifying myself with them as much as possible, in their games and amusements; in order the better to familiarize myself with their superstitions and mysteries, which are the keys to Indian life and character.

It was during the several years of my life just mentioned, and whilst I was in familiar participation with them in their sports and amusements, that I penned the following series of epistles, describing only such glowing or curious scenes and events as passed under my immediate observation; leaving their early history, and many of their traditions, language, &c. for a subsequent and much more elaborate work, for which I have procured the materials, and which I may eventually publish.

I set out on my arduous and perilous undertaking with the determination of reaching, ultimately, every tribe of Indians on the Continent of North America, and of bringing home faithful portraits of their principal personages, both men and women, from each tribe, views of their villages, games, &c. and full notes on their character and history. I designed, also, to procure their costumes, and a complete collection of their manufactures and weapons, and to perpetuate them in a *Gallery unique,* for the use and instruction of future ages.

I claim whatever merit there may have been in the originality of such a design, as I was undoubtedly the first artist who ever set out upon such a work, designing to carry his canvass to the Rocky Mountains; and a considerable part of the following Letters were written and published in the New York Papers, as early as the years 1832 and 1833; long before the Tours of Washington Irving, and several others, whose interesting narratives are before the world.

I have, as yet, by no means visited *all* the tribes; but I have progressed a very great way with the enterprise, and with far greater and more complete success than I expected.

I have visited forty-eight different tribes, the greater part of which I found speaking different languages, and containing in all 400,000 souls. I have brought home safe, and in good order, 310 portraits in oil, all painted in their native dress, and in their own wigwams; and also 200 other paintings in oil, containing views of their villages—their wigwams—their games and religious ceremonies—their dances—their ball plays—their buffalo hunting, and other amusements (containing in all, over 3000 full-length figures); and the landscapes of the country they live in, as well as a very extensive and curious collection of their costumes, and all their other manufactures, from the size of a wigwam down to the size of a quill or a rattle.

A considerable part of the above-named paintings, and Indian manufactures, will be found amongst the very numerous illustrations in the following pages; having been, in every instance, faithfully copied and reduced by my own hand, for the engraver, from my original paintings; and the reader of this book who will take the pains to step in to "CATLIN'S NORTH AMERICAN INDIAN GALLERY," will find nearly every scene and custom which is described in this work, as well as many others, carefully and correctly delineated, and displayed upon the walls, and every weapon (and every "Sachem" and every "Sagamore" who has wielded them) according to the tenor of the tales herein recited.

So much of *myself* and of my *works,* which is all that I wish to say at present.

Of the Indians, I have much more to say, and to the following delineations of them, and their character and customs, I shall make no further apology for requesting the attention of my readers.

The Indians (as I shall call them), the savages or red men of the forests and prairies of North America, are at this time a subject of great interest and some importance to the civilized world; rendered more particularly so in this age, from their relative position to, and their rapid declension from, the civilized nations of the earth. A numerous nation of human beings, whose origin is beyond the reach of human investigation,—whose early history is lost—whose term of national existence is nearly expired—three-fourths of whose country has fallen into the possession of civilized man within the short space of 250 years—twelve millions of whose bodies have fattened the soil in the mean time; who have fallen victims to whiskey, the small-pox and the bayonet; leaving at this time but a meagre proportion to live a short time longer, in the certain apprehension of soon sharing a similar fate.

The writer who would undertake to embody the whole history of such a people, with all their misfortunes and calamities, must needs have much more space than I have allotted to this epitome; and he must needs begin also (as I am doing) with those who are *living*, or he would be very apt to dwell upon the preamble of his work, until the present living remnants of the race should have passed away; and their existence and customs, like those of ages gone bye, become subjects of doubt and incredulity to the world for whom his book was preparing. Such an historian also, to do them justice, must needs correct many theories and opinions which have, either ignorantly or maliciously, gone forth to the world in indelible characters; and gather and arrange a vast deal which has been but imperfectly recorded, or placed to the credit of a people who have not had the means of recording it themselves; but have entrusted it, from necessity, to the honesty and punctuality of their enemies.

In such an history should be embodied, also, a correct account of their treatment, and the causes which have led to their rapid destruction; and a plain and systematical prophecy as to the time and manner of their final extinction, based upon the causes and the ratio of their former and present declension.

So Herculean a task may fall to my lot at a future period, or it may not; but I send forth these volumes at this time, fresh and full of their living deeds and customs, as a familiar and unstudied introduction (at least) to them and their native character; which I confidently hope will repay the readers who read for information and historical facts, as well as those who read but for amusement.

The world know generally, that the Indians of North America are copper-coloured, that their eyes and their hair are black, &c.; that they are mostly uncivilized, and consequently unchristianized; that they are nevertheless human beings, with features, thoughts, reason, and sympathies like our own; but few yet know how they *live,* how they *dress,* how they *worship,* what are their actions, their customs, their religion, their amusements, &c. as they practise them in the uncivilized regions of their uninvaded country, which it is the main object of this work, clearly and distinctly to set forth.

It would be impossible at the same time, in a book of these dimensions, to explain *all* the manners and customs of these people; but as far as they are narrated, they have been described by my pen, upon the spot, as I have seen them transacted; and if some few of my narrations should seem a *little too highly coloured,* I trust the world will be ready to extend to me that pardon which it is customary to yield to all artists whose main faults exist in the vividness of their colouring, rather than in the drawing of their pictures; but there is nothing else in them, I think, that I should ask pardon for, even though some of them should stagger credulity, and incur for me the censure of those critics, who sometimes, unthinkingly, or unmercifully, sit at home at their desks, enjoying the luxury of wine and a good cigar, over the simple narration of the honest and weather-worn traveller (who shortens his half-starved life in catering for the world), to condemn him and his work to oblivion, and his wife and his little children to poverty and starvation; merely because he describes scenes which they have not beheld, and which, consequently, they are unable to believe.

The Indians of North America, as I have before said, are copper-coloured, with long black hair, black eyes, tall, straight, and elastic forms—are less than two millions in number—were originally the undisputed owners of the soil, and got their title to their lands from the Great Spirit who created them on it,—were once a happy and flourishing people, enjoying all the comforts and luxuries of life which they knew of, and consequently cared for;—were sixteen millions in numbers, and sent that number of daily prayers to the Almighty, and thanks for his goodness and protection. Their country was entered by white men, but a few hundred years since; and thirty millions of these are now scuffling for the goods and luxuries of life, over the bones and ashes of twelve millions of red men; six millions of whom have fallen victims to the small-pox, and the remainder to the sword, the bayonet, and whiskey; all of which means of their death and destruction have been introduced and visited upon them by acquisitive white men; and by white men, also, whose forefathers were welcomed and embraced in the land where the poor Indian met and fed them with "ears of green corn and with pemican." Of the two millions remaining alive at this time, about 1,400,000, are already the miserable living victims and dupes of white man's cupidity, degraded, discouraged, and lost in the bewildering maze that is produced by the use of whiskey and its concomitant vices; and the remaining number are yet unroused and unenticed from their wild haunts or their primitive modes, by the dread or love of white man and his allurements.

It has been with these, mostly, that I have spent my time, and of these, chiefly, and their customs, that the following Letters treat. Their habits (and theirs alone) as we can see them transacted, are native, and such as I have wished to fix and preserve for future ages.

Of the dead, and of those who are dying, of those who have suffered death, and of those who are now trodden and kicked through it, I may speak more fully in some deductions at the close of this book; or at some future time, when I may find more leisure, and may be able to speak of these scenes without giving offence to the world, or to any body in it.

Such a portrait then as I have set forth in the following pages (taken by myself from the free and vivid realities of life, instead of the vague and uncertain imagery of recollection, or from the haggard deformities and distortions of disease and death), I offer to the world for their amusement, as well as for their information; and I trust they will pardon me, if it should be thought that I have over-estimated the Indian character, or at other times descended too much into the details and minutiæ of Indian mysteries and absurdities.

The reader, then, to understand me rightly, and draw from these Letters the information which they are intended to give, must follow me a vast way from the civilized world; he must needs wend his way from the city of New York, over the Alleghany, and far beyond the mighty Missouri, and even to the base and summit of the Rocky Mountains, some two or three thousand miles from the Atlantic coast. He should forget many theories he has read in the books of Indian barbarities, of wanton butcheries and murders; and divest himself, as far as possible, of the deadly prejudices which he has carried from his childhood, against this most unfortunate and most abused part of the race of his fellow-man.

He should consider, that if he has seen the savages of North America without making such a tour, he has fixed his eyes upon and drawn his conclusions (in all probability) only from those who inhabit the frontier; whose habits have been changed—whose pride has been cut down—whose country has been ransacked—whose wives and daughters have been shamefully abused—whose lands have been wrested from them—whose limbs have become enervated and naked by the excessive use of whiskey—whose friends and relations have been prematurely thrown into their graves—whose native pride and dignity have at last given way to the unnatural vices which civilized cupidity has engrafted upon them, to be silently nurtured and magnified by a burning sense of injury and injustice, and ready for that cruel vengeance which often falls from the hand that is palsied by refined abuses, and yet unrestrained by the glorious influences of refined and moral cultivation.—That if he has laid up, what he considers well-founded knowledge of these people, from books which he has read, and from newspapers only, he should pause at least, and withhold his sentence before he passes it upon the character of a people, who are dying at the hands of their enemies, without the means of recording their own annals—struggling in their nakedness with their simple weapons, against guns and gunpowder—against whiskey and steel, and disease, and mailed warriors who are continually trampling them to the earth, and at last exultingly promulgating from the very soil which they have wrested from the poor savage, the history of his cruelties and barbarities, whilst his bones are quietly resting under the very furrows which their ploughs are turning.

So great and unfortunate are the disparities between savage and civil, in numbers—in weapons and defences—in enterprise, in craft, and in education, that the former is almost universally the sufferer either in peace or in war; and not less so after his pipe and his tomahawk have retired to the grave with him, and his character is left to be entered upon the pages of history, and that justice done to his memory which, from necessity, he has intrusted to his enemy.

Amongst the numerous historians, however, of these strange people, they have had some friends who have done them justice; yet as a part of all systems of justice, whenever it is meted to the poor Indian, it comes invariably too late, or is administered at an ineffectual distance; and that too when his enemies are continually about him, and effectually applying the means of his destruction.

Some writers, I have been grieved to see, have written down the character of the North American Indian, as dark, relentless, cruel and murderous in the last degree; with scarce a quality to stamp his existence of a higher order than that of the brutes:—whilst others have given them a high rank, as I feel myself authorised to do, as honourable and highly-intellectual beings; and others, both friends and foes to the red man, have spoken of them as an "anomaly in nature!"

In this place I have no time or inclination to reply to so unaccountable an assertion as this; contenting myself with the belief, that the term would be far more correctly applied to that part of the human family who have strayed farthest from nature, than it could be to those who are simply moving in, and filling the sphere for which they were designed by the Great Spirit who made them.

From what I have seen of these people I feel authorised to say, that there is nothing very strange or unaccountable in their character; but that it is a simple one, and easy to be learned and understood, if the right means be taken to familiarize ourselves with it. Although it has its dark spots; yet there is much in it to be applauded, and much to recommend it to the admiration of the enlightened world. And I trust that the reader, who looks through these volumes with care, will be disposed to join me in the conclusion: that the North American Indian in his native state is an honest, hospitable, faithful, brave, warlike, cruel, revengeful, relentless,—yet honourable, contemplative and religious being.

If such be the case, I am sure there is enough in it to recommend it to the fair perusal of the world, and charity enough in all civilized countries, in this enlightened age, to extend a helping hand to a dying race; provided that prejudice and fear can be removed, which have heretofore constantly held the civilized portions in dread of the savage—and away from that familiar and friendly embrace, in which alone his true native character can be justly appreciated.

I am fully convinced, from a long familiarity with these people, that the Indian's misfortune has consisted chiefly in our ignorance of their true native character and disposition, which has always held us at a distrustful distance from them; inducing us to look upon them in no other light than that of a hostile foe, and worthy only of that system of continued warfare and abuse that has been for ever waged against them.

There is no difficulty in approaching the Indian and getting acquainted with him in his wild and unsophisticated state, and finding him an honest and honourable man; with feelings to meet feelings, if the above prejudice and dread can be laid aside, and any one will take the pains, as I have done, to go and see him in the simplicity of his native state, smoking his pipe under his own humble roof, with his wife and children around him, and his faithful dogs and horses hanging about his hospitable tenement.—So the world *may* see him and smoke his friendly pipe, which is invariably extended to them; and share, with a hearty welcome, the best that his wigwam affords for the appetite, which is always set out to a stranger the next moment after he enters.

But so the mass of the world, most assuredly will *not* see these people; for they are too far off, and approachable to those only whose avarice or cupidity alone lead them to those remote regions, and whose shame prevents them from publishing to the world the virtues which they have thrown down and trampled under foot.

The very use of the word savage, as it is applied in its general sense, I am inclined to believe is an abuse of the word, and the people to whom it is applied. The word, in its true definition, means no more than *wild,* or *wild man*; and a wild man may have been endowed by his Maker with all the humane and noble traits that inhabit the heart of a tame man. Our ignorance and dread or fear of these people, therefore, have given a new definition to the adjective; and nearly the whole civilized world apply the word *savage,* as expressive of the most ferocious, cruel, and murderous character that can be described.

The grisly bear is called savage, because he is blood-thirsty, ravenous and cruel; and so is the tiger, and they, like the poor red man, have been feared and dreaded (from the distance at which ignorance and prejudice have kept us from them, or from resented abuses which we have practised when we have come in close contact with them), until Van Amburgh shewed the world, that even these ferocious and unreasoning animals wanted only the friendship and close embrace of their master, to respect and to love him.

As evidence of the hospitality of these ignorant and benighted people, and also of their honesty and honour, there will be found recorded many striking instances in the following pages. And also, as an offset to these, many evidences of the dark and cruel, as well as ignorant and disgusting excesses of passions, unrestrained by the salutary influences of laws and Christianity.

I have roamed about from time to time during seven or eight years, visiting and associating with some three or four hundred thousand of these people, under an almost infinite variety of circumstances; and from the very many and decided voluntary acts of their hospitality and kindness, I feel bound to pronounce them, by nature, a kind and hospitable people. I have been welcomed generally in their country, and treated to the best that they could give me, without any charges made for my board; they have often escorted me through their enemies' country at some hazard to their own lives, and aided me in passing mountains and rivers with my awkward baggage; and under all of these circumstances of exposure, no Indian ever betrayed me, struck me a blow, or stole from me a shilling's worth of my property that I am aware of.

This is saying a great deal (and proving it too, if the reader will believe me) in favour of the virtues of these people; when it is borne in mind, as it should be, that there is no law in their land to punish a man for theft—that the commandments have never been divulged amongst them; nor can any human retribution fall upon the head of a thief, save the disgrace which attaches as a stigma to his character, in the eyes of his people about him.

And thus in these little communities, strange as it may seem, in the absence of all systems of jurisprudence, I have often beheld peace and happiness, and quiet, reigning supreme, for which even kings and emperors might envy them. I have seen rights and virtue protected, and wrongs redressed; and I have seen conjugal, filial and paternal affection in the simplicity and contentedness of nature. I have, unavoidably, formed warm and enduring attachments to some of these men which I do not wish to forget—who have brought me near to their hearts, and in our final separation have embraced me in their arms, and commended me and my affairs to the keeping of the Great Spirit.

For the above reasons, the reader will be disposed to forgive me for dwelling so long and so strong on the justness of the claims of these people; and for my occasional expressions of sadness, when my heart bleeds for the fate that awaits the remainder of their unlucky race; which is long to be outlived by the rocks, by the beasts, and even birds and reptiles of the country they live in;—set upon by their fellow-man, whose cupidity, it is feared, will fix no bounds to the Indian's earthly calamity, short of the grave.

I cannot help but repeat, before I close this Letter, that the tribes of the red men of North America, as a nation of human beings, are on their wane; that (to use their own very beautiful figure) "they are fast travelling to the shades of their fathers, towards the setting sun;" and that the traveller, who would see these people in their native simplicity and beauty, must needs be hastily on his way to the prairies and Rocky Mountains, or he will see them only as they are now seen on the frontiers, as a basket of *dead game,*—harassed, chased, bleeding and dead; with their plumage and colours despoiled, to be gazed amongst in vain for some system or moral, or for some scale by which to estimate their true native character, other than that which has too often recorded them; but a dark and unintelligible mass of cruelty and barbarity.

Without further comments I close this Letter, introducing my readers at once to the heart of the Indian country, only asking their forgiveness for having made it so long, and their patience whilst travelling through the following pages (as I journeyed through those remote realms) in search of information and rational amusement; in tracing out the true character of that *"strange anomaly"* of man in the simple elements of his nature, undissolved or compounded into the mysteries of enlightened and fashionable life.

* * *

Letter—No. 2.

Mouth of Yellow Stone, Upper Missouri, **1832.**

I arrived at this place yesterday in the steamer "Yellow Stone," after a voyage of nearly three months from St. Louis, a distance of two thousand miles, the greater part of which has never before been navigated by steam; and the almost insurmountable difficulties which continually oppose the *voyageur* on this turbid stream, have been by degrees overcome by the indefatigable zeal of Mr. Chouteau, a gentleman of great perseverance, and part proprietor of the boat. To the politeness of this gentleman I am indebted for my passage from St. Louis to this place, and I had also the pleasure of his *company,* with that of Major Sanford, the government agent for the Missouri Indians.

The American Fur Company have erected here, for their protection against the savages, a very substantial Fort, 300 feet square, with bastions armed with ordnance; and our approach to it under the continued roar of cannon for half an hour, and the shrill yells of the half-affrighted savages who lined the shores, presented a scene of the most thrilling and picturesque appearance. A voyage so full of incident, and furnishing so many novel scenes of the picturesque and romantic, as we have passed the numerous villages of the "astonished natives," saluting them with the puffing of steam and the thunder of artillery, would afford subject for many epistles; and I cannot deny myself the pleasure of occasionally giving you some little sketches of scenes that I have witnessed, and *am witnessing;* and of the singular feelings that are excited in the breast of the stranger travelling through this interesting country. Interesting (as I have said) and *luxurious,* for this is truly the land of Epicures; we are invited by the savages to feasts of *dog's meat,* as the most honourable food that can be presented to a stranger, and glutted with the more delicious food of beavers' tails, and buffaloes' tongues. You will, no doubt, be somewhat surprised on the receipt of a Letter from me, so far strayed into the Western World; and still more startled, when I tell you that I am here in the full enthusiasm and practice of my art. That enthusiasm alone has brought me into this remote region, 3500 miles from my native soil; the last 2000 of which have furnished me with almost unlimited models, both in landscape and the human figure, exactly suited to my feelings. I am now in the full possession and enjoyments of those conditions, on which alone I was induced to pursue the art as a profession; and in anticipation of which alone, my admiration for the art could ever have been kindled into a pure flame. I mean the free use of nature's undisguised models, with the privilege of selecting for myself. If I am here losing the benefit of the fleeting fashions of the day, and neglecting that elegant polish, which the world say an artist should draw from a continual intercourse with the polite world; yet have I this consolation, that in this country, I am entirely divested of those dangerous steps and allurements which beset an artist in fashionable life; and have little to steal my thoughts away from the contemplation of the beautiful models that are about me. If, also, I have not here the benefit of that feeling of emulation, which is the life and spur to the arts, where artists are associates together; yet am I surrounded by living models of such elegance and beauty, that I feel an unceasing excitement of a much higher order—the certainty that I am drawing knowledge from the true source. My enthusiastic admiration of man in the honest and elegant simplicity of nature, has always fed the warmest feelings of my bosom, and shut half the avenues to my heart against the specious refinements of the accomplished world. This feeling, together with the desire to study my art, independently of the embarrassments which the ridiculous fashions of civilized society have thrown in its way, has led me to the wilderness for a while, as the true school of the arts.

I have for a long time been of opinion, that the wilderness of our country afforded models equal to those from which the Grecian sculptors transferred to the marble such inimitable grace and beauty; and I am now more confirmed in this opinion, since I have immersed myself in the midst of thousands and tens of thousands of these knights of the forest; whose whole lives are lives of chivalry, and whose daily feats, with their naked limbs, might vie with those of the Grecian youths in the beautiful rivalry of the Olympian games.

No man's imagination, with all the aids of description that can be given to it, can ever picture the beauty and wildness of scenes that may be daily witnessed in this romantic country; of hundreds of these graceful youths, without a care to wrinkle, or a fear to disturb the full expression of pleasure and enjoyment that beams upon their faces—their long black hair mingling with their horses' tails, floating in the wind, while they are flying over the carpeted prairie, and dealing death with their spears and arrows to a band of infuriated buffaloes; or their splendid procession in a war parade, arrayed in all their gorgeous colours and trappings, moving with most exquisite grace and manly beauty, added to that bold defiance which man carries on his front, who acknowledges no superior on earth, and who is amenable to no laws except the laws of God and honour.

In addition to the knowledge of human nature and of my art, which I hope to acquire by this toilsome and expensive undertaking, I have another in view, which, if it should not be of equal service to me, will be of no less interest and value to posterity. I have, for many years past, contemplated the noble races of red men, who are now spread over these trackless forests and boundless prairies, melting away at the approach of civilization. Their rights invaded, their morals corrupted, their lands wrested from them, their customs changed, and therefore lost to the world; and they at last sunk into the earth, and the ploughshare turning the sod over their graves, and I have flown to their rescue—not of their lives or of their race (for they are "*doomed*" and must perish), but to the rescue of their looks and their modes, at which the acquisitive world may hurl their poison and every besom of destruction, and trample them down and crush them to death; yet, phœnix-like, they may rise from the "stain on a painter's palette," and live again upon canvass, and stand forth for centuries yet to come, the living monuments of a noble race. For this purpose, I have designed to visit every tribe of Indians on the Continent, if my life should be spared; for the purpose of procuring portraits of distinguished Indians, of both sexes in each tribe, painted in their native costume; accompanied with pictures of their villages, domestic habits, games, mysteries, religious ceremonies, &c. with anecdotes, traditions, and history of their respective nations.

If I should live to accomplish my design, the result of my labours will doubtless be interesting to future ages; who will have little else left from which to judge of the original inhabitants of this noble race of beings, who require but a few years more of the march of civilization and death, to deprive them of all their native customs and character. I have been kindly supplied by the Commander-in-Chief of the Army and the Secretary of War, with letters to the commander of every military post, and every Indian agent on the Western Frontier, with instructions to render me all the facilities in their power, which will be of great service to me in so arduous an undertaking. The opportunity afforded me by familiarity with so many tribes of human beings in the simplicity of nature, devoid of the deformities of art, of drawing fair conclusions in the interesting sciences of physiognomy and phrenology, of their manners and customs, rites, ceremonies, &c.; and the opportunity of examining the geology and mineralogy of this western, and yet unexplored country, will enable me occasionally to entertain you with much new and interesting information, which I shall take equal pleasure in communicating by an occasional Letter in my clumsy way.

* * *

Letter — No. 47

Sen-e-ca's

One thousand two hundred in numbers at present, living on their reserve, near Buffalo, and within a few miles of Niagara Falls, in the state of New York. This tribe formerly lived on the banks of the

Seneca and Cayuga lakes; but, like all the other tribes who have stood in the way of the "march of civilization," have repeatedly bargained away their country, and removed to the West; which easily accounts for the origin of the familiar phrase that is used amongst them, that "they are going to the setting sun."

This tribe, when first known to the civilized world, contained some eight or ten thousand; and from their position in the centre of the state of New York, held an important place in its history. The Senecas were one of the most numerous and effective tribes, constituting the compact called the "Six Nations;" which was a confederacy formed by six tribes, who joined in a league as an effective mode of gaining strength, and preserving themselves by combined efforts which would be sufficiently strong to withstand the assaults of neighbouring tribes, or to resist the incursions of white people in their country. This confederacy consisted of the Senecas, Oneidas, Onondagas, Cayugas, Mohawks, and Tuskaroras; and until the innovations of white people, with their destructive engines of war—with whiskey and small-pox, they held their sway in the country, carrying victory, and consequently terror and dismay, wherever they warred. Their war-parties were fearlessly sent into Connecticut and Massachusetts, to Virginia, and even to the Carolinas, and victory everywhere crowned their efforts. Their combined strength, however, in all its might, poor fellows, was not enough to withstand the siege of their insidious foes—a destroying flood that has risen and advanced, like a flood-tide upon them, and covered their country; has broken up their strongholds, has driven them from land to land; and in their retreat, has drowned the most of them in its waves.

The Senecas are the most numerous remnant of this compact; and have at their head an aged and very distinguished chief, familiarly known throughout the United States, by the name of *Red Jacket*. I painted this portrait from the life, in the costume in which he is represented; and indulged him also, in the wish he expressed, "that he might be seen standing on the Table Rock, at the Falls of Niagara; about which place he thought his spirit would linger after he was dead.". . .

The Senecas have had no battles to fight lately, and very little game to kill, except squirrels and pheasants; and their hands are turned to the plough, having become, most of them, tolerable farmers; raising the necessaries, and many of the luxuries of life, from the soil.

Of this interesting tribe, the visitors to my Gallery will find several other portraits and paintings of their customs; and in books that have been written, and are being compiled, a much more able and faithful account than I can give in an epistle of this kind.

The fame as well as the face of Red Jacket, is generally familiar to the citizens of the United States and the Canadas; and for the information of those who have not known him, I will briefly say, that he has been for many years the head chief of the scattered remnants of that once powerful compact, the Six Nations; a part of whom reside on their reservations in the vicinity of the Senecas, amounting perhaps in all, to about four thousand, and owning some two hundred thousand acres of fine lands. Of this Confederacy, the Mohawks and Cayugas, chiefly emigrated to Canada, some fifty years ago, leaving the Senecas, the Tuskaroras, Oneidas, and Onondagas in the state of New York, on fine tracts of land, completely surrounded with white population; who by industry and enterprize, are making the Indian lands too valuable to be long in their possession, who will no doubt be induced to sell out to the Government, or, in other words, to exchange them for lands West of the Mississippi, where it is the avowed intention of the Government to remove all the border tribes.*

Red Jacket has been reputed one of the greatest orators of his day; and, no doubt, more distinguished for his eloquence and his influence in council, than as a warrior, in which character I think history has not said much of him. This may be owing, in a great measure, to the fact that the wars of his nation were chiefly fought before his fighting days; and that the greater part of his life and his talents have been spent with his tribe, during its downfall; where, instead of the horrors of Indian wars, they have had a more fatal and destructive enemy to encounter, in the insidious encroachments of pale faces, which he has been for many years exerting his eloquence and all his talents to resist. Poor old chief—not all the eloquence of Cicero and Demosthenes would be able to avert the calamity, that awaits his declining nation—to resist the despoiling hand of mercenary white man, that opens and spreads liberally, but to entrap the unwary and ignorant within its withering grasp.

This talented old man has for many years past, strenuously remonstrated both to the Governor of New York, and the President of the United States, against the continual encroachments of white people; whom he represented as using every endeavour to wrest from them their lands—to destroy their game, introducing vices of a horrible character, and unknown to his people by nature! and most vehemently of all, has he continually remonstrated against the preaching of missionaries in his tribe; alleging, that the "black coats" (as he calls the clergymen), did more mischief than good in his tribe, by creating doubts and dissensions amongst his people! which are destructive of his peace, and dangerous to the success, and even *existence* of his tribe. Like many other great men who endeavour to soothe broken and painful feelings, by the kindness of the bottle, he has long since taken up whiskey-drinking to excess; and much of his time, lies drunk in his cabin, or under the corner of a fence, or wherever else its *kindness* urges the necessity of his dropping his helpless

*Since the above was written, the Senecas and all the other remnants of the Six Nations residing in the state of New York, have agreed in Treaties with the United States to remove to tracts of country assigned them, West of the Mississippi, twelve hundred miles from their reservations in the state of New York.

body and limbs, to indulge in the delightful *spell.* He is as great a drunkard as some of our most distinguished law-givers and lawmakers; and yet *ten times more culpable,* as he has little to do in life, and wields the destinies of a nation in his hands!

There are no better people to be found, than the Seneca Indians—none that I know of that are by Nature more talented and ingenious; nor any that would be found to be better neighbours, if the arts and abuses of white men and whiskey, could be kept away from them. They have mostly laid down their hunting habits, and become efficient farmers, raising fine crops of corn, and a great abundance of hogs, cattle and horses, and other necessaries and luxuries of life.

Emerson delivering one of his famous lectures

RALPH WALDO EMERSON

The American Scholar

(1837)

"The American Scholar" was Emerson's oration before the Phi Beta Kappa society of Harvard University on August 31, 1837. Given the occasion, it was a subversive address. His warning against "bibliomaniacs," his suggestion that "books are for the scholar's idle time," implicitly criticized the institution sponsoring his address. More basic still, his declaration of literary independence from Europe questioned the value of transmitting European culture, a goal to which Harvard was dedicated. Emerson's positive message demanded a new social role for American intellectuals: they should become democratic men of letters, learning from nature and action as well as books—"man seeing" rather than just "man thinking." Speaking to this particular audience, he gave his greatest attention to the scholar's tendency to avoid the ongoing world in favor of the past.

Emerson touched on one other issue that explains much of his contemporary importance: what he called "the gradual domestication of the idea of Culture." Emerson believed that Americans were not hostile to culture, only too preoccupied for it, and he always sought means of leading their attention to the cultural ideals implicit in everyday life. This became the function of Emerson the lecturer, a familiar figure in mid-nineteenth century America. Emerson led an army of speakers who brought, via the Lyceum, the "idea of Culture" to workaday America. More than any other single figure, he created the model of the man of letters in a democracy. This role, although having lost much ground to the alternative role of the intellectual as technical expert, continues to exist amid the same threats and contradictions that Emerson analyzed more than a century ago.

Mr. President and Gentlemen:

I greet you on the recommencement of our literary year. Our anniversary is one of hope, and, perhaps, not enough of labor. We do not meet for games of strength or skill, for the recitation of histories, tragedies, and odes, like the ancient Greeks; for parliaments of love and poesy, like the Troubadours; nor for the advancement of science, like our contemporaries in the British and European capitals. Thus far, our holiday has been simply a friendly sign of the survival of the love of letters amongst a people too busy to give to letters any more. As such it is precious as the sign of an indestructible instinct. Perhaps the time is already come when it ought to be, and will be, something else; when the sluggard intellect of this continent will look from under its iron lids and fill the postponed expectation of the world with something better than the exertions of mechanical skill. Our day of dependence, our long apprenticeship to the learning of other lands, draws to a close. The millions that around us are rushing into life, cannot always be fed on the sere remains of foreign harvests. Events, actions arise, that must be sung, that will sing themselves. Who can doubt that poetry will revive and lead in a new age, as the star in the constellation Harp, which now flames in our Zenith, astronomers announce, shall one day be the polestar for a thousand years?

In this hope I accept the topic which not only usage but the nature of our association seem to prescribe to this day—the American Scholar. Year by year we come up hither to read one more chapter of his biography. Let us inquire what light new days and events have thrown on his character and his hopes.

It is one of those fables which out of an unknown antiquity convey an unlooked-for wisdom, that the gods, in the beginning, divided Man into men, that he might be more helpful to himself; just as the hand was divided into fingers, the better to answer its end.

The old fable covers a doctrine ever new and sublime; that there is One Man—present to all particular man only partially, or through one faculty; and that you must take the whole society to find the whole man. Man is not a farmer, or a professor, or an engineer, but he is all. Man is priest, and scholar, and statesman, and producer, and soldier. In the *divided* or social state these functions are parceled out to individuals, each of whom aims to do his stint of the joint work, whilst each other performs his. The fable implies that the individual, to possess himself, must sometimes return from his own labor to embrace all the other laborers. But, unfortunately, this original unit, this fountain of power, has been so distributed to multitudes, has been so minutely subdivided and peddled out, that it is spilled into drops, and cannot be gathered. The state of society is one in which the members have suffered amputation from the trunk, and strut about so many walking monsters—a good finger, a neck, a stomach, an elbow, but never a man.

Man is thus metamorphosed into a thing, into many things. The planter, who is Man sent out into the field to gather food, is seldom cheered by any idea of the true dignity of his ministry. He sees his bushel and his cart, and nothing beyond, and sinks into the farmer, instead of Man on the farm. The tradesman scarcely ever gives an ideal worth to his work, but is ridden by the routine of his craft, and the soul is subject to dollars. The priest becomes a form; the attorney a statute-book; the mechanic a machine; the sailor a rope of the ship.

In this distribution of functions the scholar is the delegated intellect. In the right state he is *Man Thinking*. In the degenerate state, when the victim of society, he tends to become a mere thinker, or still worse, the parrot of other men's thinking.

In this view of him, as Man Thinking, the theory of his office is contained. Him Nature solicits with all her placid, all her monitory pictures; him the past instructs; him the future invites. Is not indeed every man a student, and do not all things exist for the student's behoof? And, finally, is not the true scholar the only true master? But the old oracle said, "All things have two handles: beware of the wrong one." In life, too often, the scholar errs with mankind and forfeits his privilege. Let us see him in his school, and consider him in reference to the main influences he receives.

I. The first in time and the first in importance of the influences upon the mind is that of nature. Every day, the sun; and, after sunset, Night and her stars. Ever the winds blow; ever the grass grows. Every day, men and women, conversing, beholding and beholden. The scholar is he of all men whom this spectacle most engages. He must settle its value in his mind. What is nature to him? There is never a beginning, there is never an end, to the inexplicable continuity of this web of God, but always circular power returning into itself. Therein it resembles his own spirit, whose beginning, whose ending, he never can find—so entire, so boundless. Far too as her splendors shine, system on system shooting like rays, upward, downward, without center, without circumference—in the mass and in the particle, Nature hastens to render account of herself to the mind. Classification begins. To the young mind every thing is individual, stands by itself. By and by, it finds how to join two things and see in them one nature; then three, then three thousand; and so, tyrannized over by its own unifying instinct, it goes on tying things together, diminishing anomalies, discovering roots running under ground whereby contrary and remote things cohere and flower out from one stem. It presently learns that since the dawn of history there has been a constant accumulation and classifying of facts. But what is classification but the perceiving that these objects are not chaotic, and are not foreign, but have a law which is also a law of the human mind? The astronomer discovers that geometry, a pure abstraction of the human mind, is the measure of planetary motion. The chemist finds proportions and intelligible method throughout matter; and science is nothing but the finding of analogy, identity, in the most remote parts. The ambitious soul sits down before each refractory fact; one after another reduces all strange constitutions, all new powers, to their class and their law, and goes on forever to animate the last fiber of organization, the outskirts of nature, by insight.

Thus to him, to this schoolboy under the bending dome of day, is suggested that he and it proceed from one root; one is leaf and one is flower; relation, sympathy, stirring in every vein. And what is that root? Is not that the soul of his soul? A thought too bold; a dream too wild. Yet when this spiritual light shall have revealed the law of more earthly natures—when he has learned to worship the soul, and to see that the natural philosophy that now is, is only the first gropings of its gigantic hand, he shall look forward to an ever expanding knowledge as to a becoming creator. He shall see that nature is the opposite of the soul, answering to it part for part. One is seal and one is print. Its beauty is the beauty of his own mind. Its laws are the laws of his own mind. Nature then becomes to him the measure of his attainments. So much of nature as he is ignorant of, so much of his own mind does he not yet possess. And, in fine, the ancient precept, "Know thyself," and the modern precept, "Study nature," become at last one maxim.

II. The next great influence into the spirit of the scholar is the mind of the Past—in whatever form, whether of literature, of art, of institutions, that mind is inscribed. Books are the best type of the influence of the past, and perhaps we shall get at the truth—learn the amount of this influence more conveniently—by considering their value alone.

The theory of books is noble. The scholar of the first age received into him the world around; brooded thereon; gave it the new arrangement of his own mind, and uttered it again. It came into his life; it went out from him truth. It came to him short-lived actions; it went out from him immortal thoughts. It came to him business; it went from him poetry. It was dead fact; now, it is quick thought. It can stand, it can go. It now endures, it now flies, it now inspires. Precisely in proportion to the depth of mind from which it issued, so high does it soar, so long does it sing.

Or, I might say, it depends on how far the process had gone, of transmuting life into truth. In proportion to the completeness of the distillation, so will the purity and imperishableness of the product be. But none is quite perfect. As no air-pump can by any means make a perfect vacuum, so neither can any artist entirely exclude the conventional, the local, the perishable from his book, or write a book of pure thought, that shall be as efficient, in all respects, to a remote posterity, as to contemporaries, or rather to the second age. Each age, it is found, must write its own books; or rather, each generation for the next succeeding. The books of an older period will not fit this.

Yet hence arises a grave mischief. The sacredness which attaches to the act of creation, the act of thought, is transferred to the record. The poet chanting was felt to be a divine man: henceforth the chant is divine also. The writer was a just and wise spirit: henceforward it is settled the book is perfect; as love of the hero corrupts into worship of his statue. Instantly the book becomes noxious: the guide is a tyrant. The sluggish and perverted mind of the multitude, slow to open to the incursions of Reason, having once so opened, having once received this book, stands upon it, and makes an outcry if it is disparaged. Colleges are built on it. Books are written on it by thinkers, not by Man Thinking; by men of talent, that is, who start wrong, who set out from accepted dogmas, not from their own sight of principles. Meek young men grow up in libraries, believing it their duty to accept the views which Cicero, which Locke, which Bacon, have given; forgetful that Cicero, Locke, and Bacon were only young men in libraries when they wrote these books.

Hence, instead of Man Thinking, we have the bookworm. Hence the book-learned class, who value books, as such; not as related to nature and the human constitution, but as making a sort of Third Estate with the world and the soul. Hence the restorers of readings, the emendators, the bibliomaniacs of all degrees.

Books are the best of things, well used; abused, among the worst. What is the right use? What is the one end which all means go to effect? They are for nothing but to inspire. I had better never see a book than to be warped by its attraction clean out of my own orbit, and made a satellite instead of a system. The one thing in the world, of value, is the active soul. This every man is entitled to; this every man contains within him, although in almost all men obstructed and as yet unborn. The soul active sees absolute truth and utters truth, or creates. In this action it is genius; not the privilege of here and there a favorite, but the sound estate of every man. In its essence it is progressive. The books, the college, the school of art, the institution of any kind, stop with some past utterance of genius. This is good, say they—let us hold by this. They pin me down. They look backward and not forward. But genius looks forward: the eyes of man are set in his forehead, not in his hindhead: man hopes: genius creates. Whatever talents may be, if the man create not, the pure efflux of the Deity is not his;—cinders and smoke there may be, but not yet flame. There are creative manners, there are creative actions, and creative words; manners, actions, words, that is, indicative of no custom or authority, but springing spontaneous from the mind's own sense of good and fair.

On the other part, instead of being its own seer, let it receive from another mind its truth, though it was in torrents of light, without periods of solitude, inquest, and self-recovery, and a fatal disservice is done. Genius is always sufficiently the enemy of genius by over-influence. The literature of every nation bears me witness. The English dramatic poets have Shakespearized now for two hundred years.

Undoubtedly there is a right way of reading, so it be sternly subordinated. Man Thinking must be subdued by his instruments. Books are for the scholar's idle time. When he can read God directly, the hour is too precious to be wasted in other men's transcripts of their readings. But when the intervals of darkness come, as come they must—when the sun is hid and the stars withdraw their shining—we repair to the lamps which were kindled by their ray, to guide our steps to the East again, where the dawn is. We hear, that we may speak. The Arabian proverb says, "A fig tree, looking on a fig tree, becometh fruitful."

It is remarkable, the character of the pleasure we derive from the best books. They impress us with the conviction that one nature wrote and the same reads. We read the verses of one of the great English poets, of Chaucer, of Marvell, of Dryden, with the most modern joy—with a pleasure, I mean, which is in great part caused by the abstraction of all *time* from their verses. There is some awe mixed with the joy of our surprise, when this poet, who lived in some past world, two or three hundred years ago, says that which lies close to my own soul, that which I had also had well-nigh thought and said. But for the evidence thence afforded to the philosophical doctrine of the identity of all minds, we should suppose some preestablished harmony, some foresight of souls that were to be, and some preparation of stores for their future wants, like the fact observed in insects, who lay up food before death for the young grub they shall never see.

I would not be hurried by any love of system, by any exaggeration of instincts, to underrate the Book. We all know, that as the human body can be nourished on any food, though it were boiled grass and the broth of shoes, so the human mind can be fed by any knowledge. And great and heroic men have existed who had almost no other information than by the printed page. I only would say that it needs a strong head to bear that diet. One must be an inventor to read well. As the proverb says, "He that would bring home the wealth of the Indies, must carry out the wealth of the Indies." There is then creative reading as well as creative writing. When the mind is braced by labor and invention, the page of whatever book we read becomes luminous with manifold allusion. Every sentence is doubly significant, and the sense of our author is as broad as the world. We then see, what is always true, that as the seer's hour of vision is short and rare among heavy days and months, so is its record, perchance, the least part of his volume. The discerning will read, in his Plato or Shakespeare, only that least part—only the authentic utterances of the oracle;—all the rest he rejects, were it never so many times Plato's and Shakespeare's.

Of course there is a portion of reading quite indispensable to a wise man. History and exact science he must learn by laborious reading. Colleges, in like manner, have their indispensable office—to teach elements. But they can only highly serve us when they aim not to drill, but to create; when they gather from far every ray of various genius to their hospitable halls and by the concentrated fires, set the hearts of their youth on flame. Thought and knowledge are natures in which apparatus and pretension avail nothing. Gowns and pecuniary foundations, though of towns of gold, can never countervail the least sentence or syllable of wit. Forget this, and our American colleges will recede in their public importance, whilst they grow richer every year.

III. There goes in the world a notion that the scholar should be a recluse, a valetudinarian—as unfit for any handiwork or public labor as a penknife for an axe. The so-called "practical men" sneer at speculative men, as if, becuase they speculate or *see*, they could do nothing. I have heard it said that the clergy—who are always, more universally than any other class, the scholars of their day—are addressed as women; that the rough, spontaneous conversation of men they do not hear, but only a mincing and diluted speech. They are often virtually disfranchised; and indeed there are advocates for their celibacy. As far as this is true of the studious classes, it is not just and wise. Action is with the scholar subordinate, but it is essential. Without it he is not yet man. Without it thought can never ripen into truth. Whilst the world hangs before the eye as a cloud of beauty, we cannot even see its beauty. Inaction is cowardice, but there can be no scholar without the heroic mind. The preamble of thought, the transition through which it passes from the unconscious to the conscious is action. Only so much do I know, as I have lived. Instantly we know whose words are loaded with life, and whose not.

The world—this shadow of the soul, or *other me*—lies wide around. Its attractions are the keys which unlock my thoughts and make me acquainted with myself. I run eagerly into this resounding tumult. I grasp the hands of those next me, and take my place in the ring to suffer and to work, taught by an instinct that so shall the dumb abyss be vocal with speech. I pierce its order; I dissipate its fear; I dispose of it within the circuit of my expanding life. So much only of life as I know by experience, so much of the wilderness have I vanquished and planted, or so far have I extended my being, my dominion. I do not see how any man can afford, for the sake of his nerves and his nap, to spare any action in which he can partake. It is pearls and rubies to his discourse. Drudgery, calamity, exasperation, want, are instructors in eloquence and wisdom. The true scholar grudges every opportunity of action past by, as a loss of power. It is the raw material out of which the intellect molds her splendid products. A strange process, too, this by which experience is converted into thought, as a mulberry leaf is converted into satin. The manufacture goes forward at all hours.

The actions and events of our childhood and youth are now matters of calmest observation. They lie like fair pictures in the air. Not so with our recent actions—with the business which we now have in hand. On this we are quite unable to speculate. Our affections as yet circulate through it. We no more feel or know it than we feel the feet, or the hand, or the brain of our body. The new deed is yet a part of life—remains for a time immersed in our unconscious life. In some contemplative hour it detaches itself from the life like a ripe fruit, to become a thought of the mind. Instantly it is raised, transfigured; the corruptible has put on incorruption. Henceforth it is an object of beauty, however base its origin and neighborhood. Observe too the impossibility of antedating this act. In its grub state, it cannot fly, it cannot shine, it is a dull grub. But suddenly, without observation, the selfsame thing unfurls beautiful wings, and is an angel of wisdom. So is there no fact, no event, in our private history, which shall not, sooner or later, lose its adhesive, inert form, and astonish us by soaring from our body into the empyrean. Cradle and infancy, school and playground, the fear of boys, and dogs, and ferules, the love of little maids and berries, and many another fact that once filled the whole sky, are gone already; friend and relative, profession and party, town and country, nation and world, must also soar and sing.

Of course, he who has put forth his total strength in fit action has the richest return of wisdom. I will not shut myself out of this globe of action, and transplant an oak into a flowerpot, there to hunger and pine; nor trust the revenue of some single faculty, and exhaust one vein of thought, much like those Savoyards, who, getting their livelihood by carving shepherds, shepherdesses, and smoking Dutchmen, for all Europe, went out one day to the mountain to find stock, and discovered that they had whittled up the last of their pine trees. Authors we have, in numbers, who have written out their vein, and who, moved by a commendable prudence, sail for Greece or Palestine, follow the trapper into the prairie, or ramble round Algiers, to replenish their merchantable stock.

If it were only for a vocabulary, the scholar would be covetous of action. Life is our dictionary. Years are well spent in country labors; in town; in the insight into trades and manufactures; in frank intercourse with many men and women; in science; in art; to the one end of mastering in all their facts a language by which to illustrate and embody our perceptions. I learn immediately from any speaker how much he has already lived, through the poverty or the splendor of his speech. Life lies behind us as the quarry from whence we get tiles and copestones for the masonry of today. This is the way to learn grammar. Colleges and books only copy the language which the field and the work yard made.

But the final value of action, like that of books, and better than books, is that it is a resource. That great principle of Undulation in nature, that shows itself in the inspiring and expiring of the breath; in desire and satiety; in the ebb and flow of the sea; in day and night; in heat and cold; and, as yet more deeply ingrained in every atom and every fluid, is known to us under the name of Polarity—these "fits of easy transmission and reflection," as Newton called them, are the law of nature because they are the law of spirit.

The mind now thinks, now acts, and each fit reproduces the other. When the artist has exhausted his materials, when the fancy no longer paints, when thoughts are no longer apprehended and books are a weariness—he has always the resource *to live.* Character is higher than intellect. Thinking is the function. Living is the functionary. The stream retreats to its source. A great soul will be strong to live, as well as strong to think. Does he lack organ or medium to impart his truths? He can still fall back on this elemental force of living them. This is a total act. Thinking is a partial act. Let the grandeur of justice shine in his affairs. Let the beauty of affection cheer his lowly roof. Those "far from fame," who dwell and act with him, will feel the force of his constitution in the doings and passages of the day better than it can be measured by any public and designed display. Time shall teach him that the scholar loses no hour which the man lives. Herein he unfolds the sacred germ of his instinct, screened from influence. What is lost in seemliness is gained in strength. Not out of those on whom systems of education have exhausted their culture, comes the helpful giant to destroy the old or to build the new, but out of unhandseled savage nature; out of terrible Druids and Berserkers come at last Alfred and Shakespeare.

I hear therefore with joy whatever is beginning to be said of the dignity and necessity of labor to every citizen. There is virtue yet in the hoe and the spade, for learned as well as for unlearned hands. And labor is everywhere welcome; always we are invited to work; only be this limitation observed, that a man shall not for the sake of wider activity sacrifice any opinion to the popular judgments and modes of action.

I have now spoken of the education of the scholar by nature, by books, and by action. It remains to say somewhat of his duties.

They are such as become Man Thinking. They may all be comprised in self-trust. The office of the scholar is to cheer, to raise, and to guide men by showing them facts amidst appearances. He plies the slow, unhonored, and unpaid task of observation. Flamsteed and Herschel, in their glazed observatories, may catalogue the stars with the praise of all men, and the results being splendid and useful, honor is sure. But he, in his private observatory, cataloguing obscure and nebulous stars of the human mind, which as yet no man has thought of as such—watching days and months sometimes for a few facts; correcting still his old records;—must relinquish display and immediate fame. In the long period of his preparation he must betray often an ignorance and shiftlessness in popular arts, incurring the disdain of the able who shoulder him aside. Long he must stammer in his speech; often forgo the living for the dead. Worse yet, he must accept—how often!—poverty and solitude. For the ease and pleasure of treading the old road, accepting the fashions, the education, the religion of society, he takes the cross of making his own, and, of course, the self-accusation, the faint heart, the frequent uncertainty and loss of time, which are the nettles and tangling vines in the way of the self-relying and self-directed; and the state of virtual hostility in which he seems to stand to society, and especially to educated society. For all this loss and scorn, what offset? He is to find consolation in exercising the highest function of human nature. He is one who raises himself from private considerations and breathes and lives on public and illustrious thoughts. He is the world's eye. He is the world's heart. He is to resist the vulgar prosperity that retrogrades ever to barbarism, by preserving and communicating heroic sentiments, noble biographies, melodious verse, and the conclusions of history. Whatsoever oracles the human heart, in all emergencies, in all solemn hours, has uttered as its commentary on the world of actions—these he shall receive and impart. And whatsoever new verdict Reason from her inviolable seat pronounces on the passing men and events of today—this he shall hear and promulgate.

These being his functions, it becomes him to feel all confidence in himself, and to defer never to the popular cry. He and he only knows the world. The world of any moment is the merest appearance. Some great decorum, some fetish of a government, some ephemeral trade, or war, or man, is cried up by half mankind and cried down by the other half, as if all depended on this particular up or down. The odds are that the whole question is not worth the poorest thought which the scholar has lost in listening to the controversy. Let him not quit his belief that a popgun is a popgun, though the ancient and honorable of the earth affirm it to be the crack of doom. In silence, in steadiness, in severe abstraction, let him hold by himself; add observation to observation, patient of neglect, patient of reproach, and bide his own time—happy enough if he can satisfy himself alone that this day he has seen something truly. Success treads on every right step. For the instinct is sure, that prompts him to tell his brother what he thinks. He then learns that in going down into the secrets of his own mind he has descended into the secrets of all minds. He learns that he who has mastered any law in his private thoughts, is master to that extent of all men whose language he speaks, and of all into whose language his own can be translated. The poet, in utter solitude remembering his spontaneous thoughts and recording them, is found to have recorded that which men in crowded cities find true for them also. The orator distrusts at first the fitness of his frank confessions, his want of knowledge of the persons he addresses, until he finds that he is the complement of his hearers—that they drink his words because he fulfills for them their own nature; the deeper he dives into his privatest, secretest presentiment, to his wonder he finds this is the most acceptable, most public, and universally true. The people delight in it; the better part of every man feels, This is my music; this is myself.

In self-trust all the virtues are comprehended. Free should the scholar be—free and brave. Free even to the definition of freedom, "without any hindrance that does not arise out of his own constitution." Brave; for fear is a thing which a scholar by his very function puts behind him. Fear always springs from ignorance. It is a shame to him if his tranquillity, amid dangerous times, arise from the presumption that like children and women, his is a protected class; or if he seek a temporary peace by the diversion of his thoughts from politics or vexed questions, hiding his head like an ostrich in the flowering bushes, peeping into microscopes, and turning rhymes, as a boy whistles to keep his courage up. So is the danger a danger still; so is the fear worse. Manlike let him turn and face it. Let him look into its eye and search its nature, inspect its origin—see the whelping of this lion—which lies no great way back; he will then find in himself a perfect comprehension of its nature and extent; he will have made his hands meet on the other side, and can henceforth defy it and pass on superior. The world is his who can see through its pretension. What deafness, what stone-blind custom, what overgrown error you behold is there only by sufferance—by your sufferance. See it to be a lie, and you have already dealt it its mortal blow.

Yes, we are the cowed—we the trustless. It is a mischievous notion that we are come late into nature; that the world was finished a long time ago. As the world was plastic and fluid in the hands of God, so it is ever to so much of his attributes as we bring to it. To ignorance and sin, it is flint. They adapt themselves to it as they may; but in proportion as a man has any thing in him divine, the firmament flows before him and takes his signet and form. Not he is great who can alter matter, but he who can alter my state of mind. They are the kings of the world who give the color of their present thought to all nature and all art, and persuade men by the cheerful serenity of their carrying the matter, that this thing which they do is the apple which the ages have desired to pluck, now at last ripe, and inviting nations to the harvest. The great man makes the great thing. Wherever Macdonald sits, there is the head of the table. Linnaeus makes botany the most alluring of studies, and wins it from the farmer and the herbwoman; Davy, chemistry; and Cuvier, fossils. The day is always his who works in it with serenity and great aims. The unstable estimates of men crowd to him whose mind is filled with a truth, as the heaped waves of the Atlantic follow the moon.

For this self-trust, the reason is deeper than can be fathomed—darker than can be enlightened. I might not carry with me the feeling of my audience in stating my own belief. But I have already shown the ground of my hope, in adverting to the doctrine that man is one. I believe man has been wronged; he has wronged himself. He has almost lost the light that can lead him back to his prerogatives. Men are become of no account. Men in history, men in the world of today, are bugs, are spawn, and are called "the mass" and "the herd." In a century, in a millennium, one or two men; that is to say, one or two approximations to the right state of every man. All the rest behold in the hero or the poet their own green and crude being—ripened; yes, and are content to be less, so *that* may attain to its full stature. What a testimony, full of grandeur, full of pity, is borne to the demands of his own nature, by the poor clansman, the poor partisan, who rejoices in the glory of his chief. The poor and the low find some amends to their immense moral capacity, for their acquiescence in a political and social inferiority. They are content to be brushed like flies from the path of a great person, so that justice shall be done by him to that common nature which it is the dearest desire of all to see enlarged and glorified. They sun themselves in the great man's light, and feel it to be their own element. They cast the dignity of man from their downtrod selves upon the shoulders of a hero, and will perish to add one drop of blood to make that great heart beat, those giant sinews combat and conquer. He lives for us, and we live in him.

Men, such as they are, very naturally seek money or power; and power because it is as good as money—the "spoils," so called, "of office." And why not? for they aspire to the highest, and this, in their sleepwalking, they dream is highest. Wake them and they shall quit the false good and leap to the true, and leave governments to clerks and desks. This revolution is to be wrought by the gradual domestication of the idea of Culture. The main enterprise of the world for splendor, for extent, is the upbuilding of a man. Here are the materials strewn along the ground. The private life of one man shall be a more illustrious monarchy, more formidable to its enemy, more sweet and serene in its influence to its friend, than any kingdom in history. For a man, rightly viewed, comprehendeth the particular natures of all men. Each philosopher, each bard, each actor has only done for me, as by a delegate, what one day I can do for myself. The books which once we valued more than the apple of the eye, we have quite exhausted. What is that but saying that we have come up with the point of view which the universal mind took through the eyes of one scribe; we have been that man, and have passed on. First, one, then another, we drain all cisterns, and waxing greater by all these supplies, we crave a better and more abundant food. The man has never lived that can feed us ever. The human mind cannot be enshrined in a person who shall set a barrier on any one side of this unbounded, unboundable empire. It is one central fire, which, flaming now out of the lips of Etna, lightens the capes of Sicily, and now out of the throat of Vesuvius, illuminates the towers and vineyards of Naples. It is one light which beams out of a thousand stars. It is one soul which animates all men.

But I have dwelt perhaps tediously upon this abstraction of the Scholar. I ought not to delay longer to add what I have to say of nearer reference to the time and to this country.

Historically, there is thought to be a difference in the ideas which predominate over successive epochs, and there are data for marking the genius of the Classic, of the Romantic, and now of the Reflective or Philosophical age. With the views I have intimated of the oneness or the identity of the mind through all individuals, I do not much dwell on these differences. In fact, I believe each individual passes through all three. The boy is a Greek; the youth, romantic; the adult reflective. I deny not, however, that a revolution in the leading idea may be distinctly enough traced.

Our age is bewailed as the age of Introversion. Must that needs be evil? We, it seems, are critical; we are embarrassed with second thoughts; we cannot enjoy any thing for hankering to know whereof the pleasure consists; we are lined with eyes; we see with our feet; the time is infected with Hamlet's unhappiness—

"Sicklied o'er with the pale cast of thought."

It is so bad then? Sight is the last thing to be pitied. Would we be blind? Do we fear lest we should outsee nature and God, and drink truth dry? I look upon the discontent of the literary class as a mere announcement of the fact that they find themselves not in the state of mind of their fathers, and regret the coming state as untried; as a boy dreads the water before he has learned that he can swim. If there is any period one would desire to be born in, is it not the age of Revolution; when the old and the new stand side by side and admit of being compared; when the energies of all men are searched by fear and by hope; when the historic glories of the old can be compensated by the rich possibilities of the new era? This time, like all times, is a very good one, if we but know what to do with it.

I read with some joy of the auspicious signs of the coming days, as they glimmer already through poetry and art, through philosophy and science, through church and state.

One of these signs is the fact that the same movement which effected the elevation of what was called the lowest class in the state, assumed in literature a very marked and as benign an aspect. Instead of the sublime and beautiful, the near, the low, the common, was explored and poetized. That which had been negligently trodden under foot by those who were harnessing and provisioning themselves for long journeys into far countries, is suddenly found to be richer than all foreign parts. The literature of the poor, the feelings of the child, the philosophy of the street, the meaning of household life, are the topics of the time. It is a great stride. It is a sign—is it not?—of new vigor when the extremities are made active, when currents of warm life run into the hands and the feet. I ask not for the great, the remote, the romantic; what is doing in Italy or Arabia; what is Greek art, or Provençal minstrelsy; I embrace the common, I explore and sit at the feet of the familiar. . . . Give me insight into today, and you may have the antique and future worlds. What would we really know the meaning of? The meal in the firkin; the milk in the pan; the ballad in the street; the news of the boat; the glance of the eye; the form and the gait of the body;—show me the ultimate reason of these matters; show me the sublime presence of the highest spiritual cause lurking, as always it does lurk, in these suburbs and extremities of nature; let me see every trifle bristling with the polarity that ranges it instantly on an eternal law; and the shop, the plow, and the ledger referred to the like cause by which light undulates and poets sing;—and the world lies no longer a dull miscellany and lumber room, but has form and order; there is no trifle, there is no puzzle, but one design unites and animates the farthest pinnacle and the lowest trench.

This idea has inspired the genius of Goldsmith, Burns, Cowper, and, in a newer time, of Goethe, Wordsworth, and Carlyle. This idea they have differently followed and with various success. In contrast with their writing, the style of Pope, of Johnson, of Gibbon, looks cold and pedantic. This writing is blood-warm. Man is surprised to find that things near are not less beautiful and wondrous than things remote. The near explains the far. The drop is a small ocean. A man is related to all nature. This perception of the worth of the vulgar is fruitful in discoveries. Goethe, in this very thing the most modern of the moderns, has shown us as none ever did, the genius of the ancients.

There is one man of genius who has done much for this philosophy of life, whose literary value has never yet been rightly estimated;—I mean Emanuel Swedenborg. The most imaginative of men, yet writing with the precision of a mathematician, he endeavored to engraft a purely philosophical Ethics on the popular Christianity of his time. Such an attempt of course must have difficulty which no genius could surmount. But he saw and showed the connection between nature and the affections of the soul. He pierced the emblematic or spiritual character of the visible, audible, tangible world. Especially did his shade-loving muse hover over and interpret the lower parts of nature; he showed the mysterious bond that allies moral evil to the foul material forms, and has given in epical parables a theory of insanity, of beasts, of unclean and fearful things.

Another sign of our times, also marked by an analogous political movement, is the new importance given to the single person. Every thing that tends to insulate the individual—to surround him with barriers of natural respect, so that each man shall feel the world is his, and man shall treat with man as a sovereign state with a sovereign state—tends to true union as well as greatness. "I learned," said the melancholy Pestalozzi, "that no man in God's wide earth is either willing or able to help any other man." Help must come from the bosom alone. The scholar is that man who must take up into himself all the ability of the time, all the contributions of the past, all the hopes of the future. He must be an university of knowledges. If there be one lesson more than another which should pierce his ear, it is, The world is nothing, the man is all; in yourself is the law of all nature, and you know not yet how a globule of sap ascends; in yourself slumbers the whole of Reason; it is for you to know all; it is for you to dare all. Mr. President and Gentlemen, this confidence in the unsearched might of man belongs by all motives, by all prophecy, by all preparation, to the American Scholar. We have listened too long to the courtly muses of Europe. The spirit of the American freeman is already suspected to be timid, imitative, tame. Public and private avarice make the air we breathe thick and fat. The scholar is decent, indolent, complaisant. See already the tragic consequence. The mind of this country, taught to aim at low objects, eats upon itself. There is no work for any but the decorous and the complaisant. Young men of the fairest promise, who begin life upon our shores, inflated by the mountain winds, shined upon by all the stars of God, find the earth below not in unison with these, but are hindered from action by the disgust which the principles on which business is managed inspire, and turn drudges, or die of disgust, some of them suicides. What is the remedy? They did not yet see, and thousands of young men as hopeful now crowding to the barriers for the career do not yet see, that if the single man plant himself indomitably on his instincts, and there abide, the huge world will come round to him. Patience—patience; with the shades of all the good and great for company; and for solace and perspective of your own infinite life; and for work the study and the communication of principles, the making those instincts prevalent, the conversion of the world. Is it not the chief disgrace in the world, not to be an unit;—not to be reckoned one character;—not to yield that peculiar fruit which each man was created to bear, but to be reckoned in the gross, in the hundred, or the thousand, of the party, the section, to which we belong; and our opinion predicted geographically as the north, or the south? Not so, brothers and friends—please God, ours shall not be so. We will walk on our own feet; we will work with our own hands; we will speak our own minds. The study of letters shall be no longer a name for pity, for doubt, and for sensual indulgence. The dread of man and the love of man shall be a wall of defense and a wreath of joy around all. A nation of men will for the first time exist, because each believes himself inspired by the Divine Soul which also inspires all men.

Strike of women shoemakers in Massachusetts, 1860

MARGARET FULLER

Woman in the Nineteenth Century

(1845)

For every generation of writers, it has been said, there is a "dark lady of literature," a figure of romance and intellectuality, whose friendships flower in literary masterpieces, whose life becomes the subject of poetry and romantic novels, whose ideas, life, and personality strike chords through the writings of an entire culture. Such figures become the darlings of critics seeking to reach beneath the surface of a novel or a poem. Their own works, however, tend to be left unread. Margaret Fuller could easily serve as the model for this stereotypical concept of artistic inspiration. A dashing heroic figure, a confidante of the major intellectual lights of mid-nineteenth century Boston — men like Ralph Waldo Emerson, William Henry Channing, Henry David Thoreau — a model for the heroine of a major novel (Nathaniel Hawthorne's The Blithedale Romance), a woman whose life breathed romance and historic adventure, she was in fact a major theorist of the women's movement, a major critic, and an important writer.

Woman in the Nineteenth Century, Margaret Fuller's most important book, grew from the "conversations" she held between 1839 and 1844 in a well-known bookshop in Boston. These "conversations" were in fact a course which she ran for "well-educated and thinking women" (a critic acidly described them as "gorgeous pedants") in which the group discussed art, literature, and other cultural topics as well as the role of women. Somewhere between continuing education and consciousness raising, their content can be measured by Fuller's book. Obviously the conversation was erudite, ranging through all of western history and literature. More striking, the perspective is thoroughly modern: Woman in the Nineteenth Century can serve as an unabridged text for the twentieth-century women's movement. It calls for — and explores the many meanings of — full cultural and intellectual equality between the sexes rather than confining its plea to the specific issues which the nineteenth-century women's movement emphasized. In fact, the eclipse of Fuller's reputation must in part result from the long era after the Civil War during which the movement focused so narrowly on winning the vote. Today, in a new era in which men and women struggle to rise to the heights she surveyed, her message has at last become more important than her fascinating life.

Of all its banners, none has been more steadily upheld, and under none have more valor and willingness for real sacrifices been shown, than that of the champions of the enslaved African. And this band it is which, partly from a natural following out of principles, partly because many women have been prominent in that cause, makes just now the warmest appeal in behalf of Woman.

Though there has been a growing liberality on this subject, yet society at large is not so prepared for the demands of this party, but that its members are and will be for some time coldly regarded as the Jacobins of their day.

"Is it not enough," cries the irritated trader, "that you have done all you could to break up the national union and thus destroy the prosperity of our country, but now you must be trying to break up family union, to take my wife away from the cradle and the kitchen-hearth to vote at polls and preach from a pulpit? Of course, if she does such things, she cannot attend to those of her own sphere. She is happy enough as she is. She has more leisure than I have—every means of improvement, every indulgence."

"Have you asked her whether she was satisfied with these *indulgences?*"

"No, but I know she is. She is too amiable to desire what would make me unhappy, and too judicious to wish to step beyond the sphere of her sex. I will never consent to have our peace disturbed by any such discussions."

"'Consent—you?' It is not consent from you that is in question—it is assent from your wife."

"Am not I the head of my house?"

"You are not the head of your wife. God has given her a mind of her own."

"I am the head, and she the heart."

"God grant you play true to one another, then! I suppose I am to be grateful that you did not say she was only the hand. If the head represses no natural pulse of the heart, there can be no question as to your giving your consent. Both will be of one accord, and there needs but to present any question to get a full and true answer. There is no need of precaution, of indulgence, or consent. But our doubt is whether the heart *does* consent with the head, or only obeys its decrees with a passiveness that precludes the exercise of its natural powers, or a repugnance that turns sweet qualities to bitter, or a doubt that lays waste the fair occasions of life. It is to ascertain the truth that we propose some liberating measures."

Thus vaguely are these questions proposed and discussed at present. But their being proposed at all implies much thought and suggests more. Many women are considering within themselves what they need that they have not, and what they can have if they find they need it. Many men are considering whether women are capable of being and having more than they are and have, *and* whether, if so, it will be best to consent to improvement in their condition.

This morning, I open the Boston *Daily Mail,* and find in its "poet's corner" a translation of Schiller's "Dignity of Woman." In the advertisement of a book on America, I see in the table of contents this sequence, "Republican Institutions. American Slavery. American Ladies."

I open the *Deutsche Schnellpost,* published in New York, and find at the head of a column, *Juden- und Frauen-emanzipation in Ungarn* ("Emancipation of Jews and Women in Hungary").

The past year has seen action in the Rhode Island legislature to secure married women rights over their own property, where men showed that a very little examination of the subject could teach them much; an article in the *Democratic Review* on the same subject more largely considered, written by a woman impelled, it is said, by glaring wrong to a distinguished friend, having shown the defects in the existing laws and the state of opinion from which they spring; and an answer from the revered old man, J. Q. Adams, in some respects the Phocion of his time, to an address made him by some ladies. To this last I shall again advert in another place.

These symptoms of the times have come under my view quite accidentally: one who seeks may each month or week collect more.

The numerous party, whose opinions are already labeled and adjusted too much to their mind to admit of any new light, strive by lectures on some model woman of bridelike beauty and gentleness, by writing and lending little treatises intended to mark out with precision the limits of Woman's sphere and Woman's mission, to prevent other than the rightful shepherd from climbing the wall, or the flock from using any chance to go astray.

Without enrolling ourselves at once on either side, let us look upon the subject from the best point of view which today offers; no better, it is to be feared, than a high house-top. A high hilltop or at least a cathedral-spire would be desirable.

It may well be an Anti-Slavery party that pleads for Woman, if we consider merely that she does not hold property on equal terms with men; so that if a husband dies without making a will, the wife, instead of taking at once his place as head of the family, inherits only a part of his fortune, often brought him by herself, as if she were a child or ward only, not an equal partner.

We will not speak of the innumerable instances in which profligate and idle men live upon the earnings of industrious wives; or if the wives leave them and take with them the children to perform the double duty of mother and father, follow from place to place and threaten to rob them of the children, if deprived of the rights of a husband as they call them, planting themselves in their poor lodgings, frightening them into paying tribute by taking from them the children, running into debt at the expense of these otherwise so overtasked helots. Such instances count up by scores within my own memory. I have seen the husband who had stained himself by a long course of low vice, till his wife was wearied from her heroic forgiveness by finding that his treachery made it useless, and that if she would provide bread for herself and her children, she must be separate from his ill fame—I have known this man come to install himself in the chamber of a woman who loathed him, and say she should never take food without his company. I have known these men steal their children, whom they knew they had no means to maintain, take them into dissolute company, expose them to bodily danger, to frighten the poor woman to whom, it seems, the fact that she alone had borne the pangs of their birth and nourished their infancy does not give an equal right to them. I do believe that this mode of kidnaping—and it is frequent enough in all classes of society—will be by the next age viewed as it is by Heaven now, and that the man who avails himself of the shelter of men's laws to steal from a mother her own children, or arrogate any superior right in them, save that of superior virtue, will bear the stigma he deserves in common with him who steals grown men from their motherland, their hopes, and their homes.

I said we will not speak of this now; yet I *have* spoken, for the subject makes me feel too much. I could give instances that would startle the most vulgar and callous; but I will not, for the public opinion of their own sex is already against such men, and where cases of extreme tyranny are made known, there is private action in the wife's favor. But she ought not to need this, nor, I think, can she long. Men must soon see that as on their own ground Woman is the weaker party, she ought to have legal protection which would make such oppression impossible. But I would not deal with "atrocious instances" except in the way of illustration, neither demand from men a partial redress in some one matter, but go to the root of the whole. If principles could be established, particulars would adjust themselves aright. Ascertain the true destiny of Woman; give her legitimate hopes, and a standard within herself; marriage and all other relations would by degrees be harmonized with these.

But to return to the historical progress of this matter. Knowing that there exists in the minds of men a tone of feeling toward women as toward slaves, such as is expressed in the common phrase, "Tell that to women and children"; that the infinite soul can only work through them in already ascertained limits; that the gift of reason, Man's highest prerogative, is allotted to them in much lower degree; that they must be kept from mischief and melancholy by being constantly engaged in active labor, which is to be furnished and directed by those better able to think, &c., &c.—we need not multiply instances, for who can review the experience of last week without recalling words which imply, whether in jest or earnest, these views or views like these—knowing this, can we wonder that many reformers think that measures are not likely to be taken in behalf of women, unless their wishes could be publicly represented by women?

"That can never be necessary," cry the other side. "All men are privately influenced by women; each has his wife, sister, or female friends, and is too much biased by these relations to fail of representing their interests; and if this is not enough, let them propose and enforce their wishes with the pen. The beauty of home would be destroyed, the delicacy of the sex be violated, the dignity of halls of legislation degraded by an attempt to introduce them there. Such duties are inconsistent with those of a mother"; and then we have ludicrous pictures of ladies in hysterics at the polls, and senate chambers filled with cradles.

But if in reply we admit as truth that Woman seems destined by nature rather for the inner circle, we must add that the arrangements of civilized life have not been as yet such as to secure it to her. Her circle, if the duller, is not the quieter. If kept from "excitement," she is not from drudgery. Not only the Indian squaw carries the burdens of the camp, but the favorites of Louis XIV accompany him in his journeys, and the washerwoman stands at her tub and carries home her work at all seasons and in all states of health. Those who think the physical circumstances of Woman would make a part in the affairs of national government unsuitable are by no means those who think it impossible for Negresses to endure field work even during pregnancy, or for seamstresses to go through their killing labors.

As to the use of the pen, there was quite as much opposition to Woman's possessing herself of that help to free agency as there is now to her seizing on the rostrum or the desk; and she is likely to draw, from a permission to plead her cause that way, opposite inferences to what might be wished by those who now grant it.

As to the possibility of her filling with grace and dignity any such position, we should think those who had seen the great actresses and heard the Quaker preachers of modern times would not doubt that Woman can express publicly the fullness of thought and creation without losing any of the peculiar beauty of her sex. What can pollute and tarnish is to act thus from any motive except that something needs to be said or done. Woman could take part in the processions, the songs, the dances of old religion; no one fancied her delicacy was impaired by appearing in public for such a cause.

As to her home, she is not likely to leave it more than she now does for balls, theaters, meetings for promoting missions, revival meetings, and others to which she flies in hope of an animation for her existence commensurate with what she sees enjoyed by men. Governors of ladies' fairs are no less engrossed by such a charge than the governor of a state by his; presidents of Washingtonian societies no less away from home than presidents of conventions. If men look straitly to it, they will find that unless their lives are domestic, those of the women will not be. A house is no home unless it contain food and fire for the mind as well as for the body. The female Greek of our day is as much in the street as the male to cry, "What news?" We doubt not it was the same in Athens of old. The women, shut out from the market-place, made up for it at the religious festivals. For human beings are not so constituted that they can live without expansion. If they do not get it in one way, they must in another or perish.

As to men's representing women fairly at present, while we hear from men who owe to their wives not only all that is comfortable or graceful but all that is wise in the arrangement of their lives the frequent remark, "You cannot reason with a woman"—when from those of delicacy, nobleness, and poetic culture falls the contemptuous phrase "women and children," and that in no light sally of the hour, but in works intended to give a permanent statement of the best experiences—when not one man in the million, shall I say? no, not in the hundred million, can rise above the belief that Woman was made *for Man*—when such traits as these are daily forced upon the attention, can we feel that Man will always do justice to the interests of Woman? Can we think that he takes a sufficiently discerning and religious view of her office and destiny *ever* to do her justice, except when prompted by sentiment—accidentally or transiently, that is, for the sentiment will vary according to the relations in which he is placed? The lover, the poet, the artist are likely to view her nobly. The father and the philosopher have some chance of liberality; the man of the world, the legislator for expediency none.

Under these circumstances, without attaching importance in themselves to the changes demanded by the champions of Woman, we hail them as signs of the times. We would have every arbitrary barrier thrown down. We would have every path laid open to Woman as freely as to Man. Were this done and a slight temporary fermentation allowed to subside, we should see crystallizations more pure and of more various beauty. We believe the divine energy would pervade nature to a degree unknown in the history of former ages, and that no discordant collision but a ravishing harmony of the spheres would ensue.

Yet then and only then will mankind be ripe for this, when inward and outward freedom for Woman as much as for Man shall be acknowledged as a *right*, not yielded as a concession. As the friend of the Negro assumes that one man cannot by right hold another in bondage, so should the friend of Woman assume that Man cannot by right lay even well-meant restrictions on Woman. If the Negro be a soul, if the woman be a soul, appareled in flesh, to one Master only are they accountable. There is but one law for souls, and if there is to be an interpreter of it, he must come not as man or son of man, but as son of God.

Were thought and feeling once so far elevated that Man should esteem himself the brother and friend, but nowise the lord and tutor, of Woman—were he really bound with her in equal worship—arrangements as to function and employment would be of no consequence. What Woman needs is not as a woman to act or rule, but as a nature to grow, as an intellect to discern, as a soul to live freely and unimpeded to unfold such powers as were given her when we left our common home. If fewer talents were given her, yet if allowed the free and full employment of these, so that she may render back to the giver his own with usury, she will not complain; nay, I dare to say she will bless and rejoice in her earthly birthplace, her earthly lot. Let us consider what obstructions impede this good era, and what signs give reason to hope that it draws near.

I was talking on this subject with Miranda, a woman, who, if any in the world could, might speak without heat and bitterness of the position of her sex. Her father was a man who cherished no sentimental reverence for Woman, but a firm belief in the equality of the sexes. She was his eldest child, and came to him at an age when he needed a companion. From the time she could speak and go alone, he addressed her not as a plaything but as a living mind. Among the few verses he ever wrote was a copy addressed to this child, when the first locks were cut from her head; and the reverence expressed on this occasion for that cherished head, he never belied. It was to him the temple of immortal intellect. He respected his child, however, too much to be an indulgent parent. He called on her for clear judgment, for courage, for honor and fidelity; in short, for such virtues as he knew. In so far as he possessed the keys to the wonders of this universe, he allowed free use of them to her, and by the incentive of a high expectation he forbade, so far as possible, that she should let the privilege lie idle.

Thus this child was early led to feel herself a child of the spirit. She took her place easily not only in the world of organized being, but in the world of mind. A dignified sense of self-dependence was given as all her portion, and she found it a sure anchor. Herself securely anchored, her relations with others were established with equal security. She was fortunate in a total absence of those charms which might have drawn to her bewildering flatteries, and in a strong electric nature which repelled those who did not belong to her and attracted those who did. With men and women her relations were noble—affectionate without passion, intellectual without coldness. The world was free to her, and she lived freely in it. Outward adversity came and inward conflict, but that faith and self-respect had early been awakened which must always lead at last to an outward serenity and an inward peace.

Of Miranda I had always thought as an example, that the restraints upon the sex were insuperable only to those who think them so, or who noisily strive to break them. She had taken a course of her own, and no man stood in her way. Many of her acts had been unusual, but excited no uproar. Few helped but none checked her; and the many men who knew her mind and her life showed to her confidence as to a brother, gentleness as to a sister. And not only refined, but very coarse men approved and aided one in whom they saw resolution and clearness of design. Her mind was often the leading one, always effective.

When I talked with her upon these matters and had said very much what I have written, she smilingly replied: "And yet we must admit that I have been fortunate, and this should not be. My good father's early trust gave the first bias, and the rest followed of course. It is true that I have had less outward aid in after years than most women; but that is of little consequence. Religion was early awakened in my soul—a sense that what the soul is capable to ask it must attain, and that though I might be aided and instructed by others, I must depend on myself as the only constant friend. This self-dependence, which was honored in me, is deprecated as a fault in most women. They are taught to learn their rule from without, not to unfold it from within.

"This is the fault of Man, who is still vain, and wishes to be more important to Woman than by right he should be."

"Men have not shown this disposition toward you," I said.

"No, because the position I early was enabled to take was one of self-reliance. And were all women as sure of their wants as I was, the result would be the same. But they are so overloaded with precepts by guardians who think that nothing is so much to be dreaded for a woman as originality of thought or character, that their minds are impeded by doubts till they lose their chance of fair, free proportions. The difficulty is to get them to the point from which they shall naturally develop self-respect and learn self-help.

"Once I thought that men would help to forward this state of things more than I do now. I saw so many of them wretched in the connections they had formed in weakness and vanity. They seemed so glad to esteem women whenever they could.

"'The soft arms of affection,' said one of the most discerning spirits, 'will not suffice for me, unless on them I see the steel bracelets of strength.'

"But early I perceived that men never in any extreme of despair wished to be women. On the contrary, they were ever ready to taunt one another at any sign of weakness with,

Art thou not like the women, who–

The passage ends various ways, according to the occasion and rhetoric of the speaker. When they admired any woman, they were inclined to speak of her as 'above her sex.' Silently I observed this, and feared it argued a rooted skepticism which for ages had been fastening on the heart and which only an age of miracles could eradicate. Ever I have been treated with great sincerity; and I look upon it as a signal instance of this, that an intimate friend of the other sex said in a fervent moment that I 'deserved in some star to be a man.' He was much surprised when I disclosed my view of my position and hopes, when I declared my faith that the feminine side, the side of love, of beauty, of holiness, was now to have its full chance, and that if either were better, it was better now to be a woman; for even the slightest achievement of good was furthering an especial work of our time. He smiled incredulously. 'She makes the best she can of it,' thought he. 'Let Jews believe the pride of Jewry, but I am of the better sort, and know better.'

"Another used as highest praise in speaking of a character in literature, the words 'a manly woman.'

"So in the noble passage of Ben Jonson:

I meant the day-star should not brighter ride,
Nor shed like influence from its lucent seat;
I meant she should be courteous, facile, sweet,
Free from that solemn vice of greatness, pride;
I meant each softest virtue there should meet,
Fit in that softer bosom to abide,
Only a learned and a manly *soul*
I purposed her, that should with even powers
The rock, the spindle, and the shears control
Of destiny, and spin her own free hours.

"Methinks," said I, "you are too fastidious in objecting to this. Jonson in using the word 'manly' only meant to heighten the picture of this, the true, the intelligent fate with one of the deeper colors."

"And yet," said she, "so invariable is the use of this word when a heroic quality is to be described, and I feel so sure that persistence and courage are the most womanly no less than the most manly qualities, that I would exchange these words for others of a larger sense, at the risk of marring the fine tissue of the verse. Read, 'A heavenward and instructed soul,' and I should be satisfied. Let it not be said, wherever there is energy or creative genius, 'She has a masculine mind.'"

This by no means argues a willing want of generosity toward Woman. Man is as generous toward her as he knows how to be.

Wherever she has herself arisen in national or private history and nobly shone forth in any form of excellence, men have received her not only willingly, but with triumph. Their encomiums, indeed, are always in some sense mortifying; they show too much surprise. "Can this be you?" he cries to the transfigured Cinderella; "well, I should never have thought it, but I am very glad. We will tell everyone that you have *'surpassed your sex.'*"

In everyday life, the feelings of the many are stained with vanity. Each wishes to be lord in a little world, to be superior at least over one; and he does not feel strong enough to retain a lifelong ascendancy over a strong nature. Only a Theseus could conquer before he wed the Amazonian queen. Hercules wished rather to rest with Dejanira, and received the poisoned robe as a fit guerdon. The tale should be interpreted to all those who seek repose with the weak.

But not only is Man vain and fond of power, but the same want of development, which thus affects him morally, prevents his intellectually discerning the destiny of Woman. The boy wants no woman, but only a girl to play ball with him and mark his pocket handkerchief.

Thus, in Schiller's "Dignity of Woman," beautiful as the poem is, there is no "grave and perfect man," but only a great boy to be softened and restrained by the influence of girls. Poets—the elder brothers of their race—have usually seen further; but what can you expect of everyday men, if Schiller was not more prophetic as to what women must be? Even with Richter, one foremost thought about a wife was that she would "cook him something good." But as this is a delicate subject, and we are in constant danger of being accused of slighting what are called "the functions," let me say in behalf of Miranda and myself that we have high respect for those who "cook something good," who create and preserve fair order in houses and prepare therein the shining raiment for worthy inmates, worthy guests. Only these "functions" must not be a drudgery or enforced necessity, but a part of life. Let Ulysses drive the beeves home, while Penelope there piles up the fragrant loaves; they are both well employed if these be done in thought and love, willingly. But Penelope is no more meant for a baker or weaver solely, than Ulysses for a cattle-herd.

The sexes should not only correspond to and appreciate, but prophesy to one another. In individual instances this happens. Two persons love in one another the future good which they aid one another to unfold. This is imperfectly or rarely done in the general life. Man has gone but little way; now he is waiting to see whether Woman can keep step with him, but instead of calling out like a good brother, "You can do it, if you only think so," or impersonally, "Anyone can do what he tries to do"; he often discourages with schoolboy brag: "Girls can't do that; girls can't play ball." But let anyone defy their taunts, break through and be brave and secure, they rend the air with shouts.

* * *

Civilized Europe is still in a transition state about marriage; not only in practice but in thought. It is idle to speak with contempt of the nations where polygamy is an institution or seraglios a custom, while practices far more debasing haunt, well-nigh fill, every city and every town, and so far as union of one with one is believed to be the only pure form of marriage, a great majority of societies and individuals are still doubtful whether the earthly bond must be a meeting of souls, or only supposes a contract of convenience and utility. Were Woman established in the rights of an immortal being, this could not be. She would not in some countries be given away by her father, with scarcely more respect for her feelings than is shown by the

Indian chief who sells his daughter for a horse, and beats her if she runs away from her new home. Nor in societies where her choice is left free, would she be perverted by the current of opinion that seizes her, into the belief that she must marry, if it be only to find a protector and a home of her own. Neither would Man, if he thought the connection of permanent importance, form it so lightly. He would not deem it a trifle that he was to enter into the closest relations with another soul, which, if not eternal in themselves, must eternally affect his growth. Neither did he believe Woman capable of friendship, would he by rash haste lose the chance of finding a friend in the person who might probably live half a century by his side. Did love to his mind stretch forth into infinity, he would not miss his chance of its revelations, that he might the sooner rest from his weariness by a bright fireside, and secure a sweet and graceful attendant "devoted to him alone." Were he a step higher, he would not carelessly enter into a relation where he might not be able to do the duty of a friend, as well as a protector from external ill, to the other party, and have a being in his power pining for sympathy, intelligence, and aid that he could not give.

What deep communion, what real intercourse is implied in sharing the joys and cares of parentage, when any degree of equality is admitted between the parties! It is true that in a majority of instances the man looks upon his wife as an adopted child, and places her to the other children in the relation of nurse or governess rather than that of parent. Her influence with them is sure; but she misses the education which should enlighten that influence, by being thus treated. It is the order of nature that children should complete the education, moral and mental, of parents by making them think what is needed for the best culture of human beings, and conquer all faults and impulses that interfere with their giving this to these dear objects who represent the world to them. Father and mother should assist one another to learn what is required for this sublime priesthood of Nature. But for this a religious recognition of equality is required.

Where this thought of equality begins to diffuse itself, it is shown in four ways.

First: The household partnership. In our country the woman looks for a "smart but kind" husband; the man for a "capable, sweet-tempered" wife. The man furnishes the house; the woman regulates it. Their relation is one of mutual esteem, mutual dependence. Their talk is of business; their affection shows itself by practical kindness. They know that life goes more smoothly and cheerfully to each for the other's aid; they are grateful and content. The wife praises her husband as a "good provider"; the husband, in return, compliments her as a "capital housekeeper." This relation is good so far as it goes.

Next comes a closer tie, which takes the form either of mutual idolatry or of intellectual companionship. The first, we suppose, is to no one a pleasing subject of contemplation. The parties weaken and narrow one another; they lock the gate against all the glories of the universe that they may live in a cell together. To themselves they seem the only wise; to all others steeped in infatuation; the gods smile as they look forward to the crisis of cure; to men, the woman seems an unlovely siren; to women, the man an effeminate boy.

The other form, of intellectual companionship, has become more and more frequent. Men engaged in public life, literary men, and artists have often found in their wives companions and confidantes in thought no less than in feeling. And as the intellectual development of Woman has spread wider and risen higher, they have not unfrequently shared the same employment; as in the case of Roland and his wife, who were friends in the household and in the nation's councils, read, regulated home affairs, or prepared public documents together indifferently. It is very pleasant, in letters begun by Roland and finished by his wife, to see the harmony of mind and the difference of nature; one thought but various ways of treating it.

This is one of the best instances of a marriage of friendship. It was only friendship, whose basis was esteem; probably neither party knew love except by name. Roland was a good man, worthy to esteem and be esteemed; his wife as deserving of admiration as able to do without it.

Madame Roland is the fairest specimen we yet have of her class; as clear to discern her aim, as valiant to pursue it as Spenser's Britomart; austerely set apart from all that did not belong to her whether as Woman or as mind. She is an antetype of a class to which the coming time will afford a field—the Spartan matron brought by the culture of the age of books to intellectual consciousness and expansion. Self-sufficingness, strength, and clear-sightedness were in her combined with a power of deep and calm affection. She, too, would have given a son or husband the device for his shield: "Return with it or upon it"; and this not because she loved little, but much. The page of her life is one of unsullied dignity. Her appeal to posterity is one against the injustice of those who committed such crimes in the name of Liberty. She makes it in behalf of herself and her husband. I would put beside it on the shelf a little volume, containing a similar appeal from the verdict of contemporaries to that of mankind made by Godwin in behalf of his wife, the celebrated, the by most men detested Mary Wollstonecraft. In his view it was an appeal from the injustice of those who did such wrong in the name of virtue. Were this little book interesting for no other cause, it would be so for the generous affection evinced under the peculiar circumstances. This man had courage to love and honor this woman in the face of the world's sentence and of all that was repulsive in her own past history. He believed he saw of what soul she was, and that the impulses she had struggled to act out were noble, though the opinions to which they had led might not be thoroughly weighed. He loved her, and he defended her for the meaning and tendency of her inner life. It was a good fact.

Mary Wollstonecraft, like Madame Dudevant (commonly known as George Sand) in our day, was a woman whose existence better proved the need of some new interpretation of Woman's Rights than anything she wrote. Such beings as these, rich in genius, of most tender sympathies, capable of high virtue and a chastened harmony, ought not to find themselves by birth in a place so narrow that in breaking bonds they become outlaws. Were there as much room in the world for such as in Spenser's poem for Britomart, they would not run their heads so wildly against the walls, but prize their shelter rather. They find their way at last to light and air, but the world will not take off the brand it has set upon them. The champion of the Rights of Woman found in Godwin one who would plead that cause like a brother. He who delineated with such purity of traits the form of Woman in the Marguerite of whom the weak St. Leon could never learn to be worthy—a pearl indeed whose price was above rubies—was not false in life to the faith by which he had hallowed his romance. He acted as he wrote, like a brother. This form of appeal rarely fails to touch the basest man: "Are you acting toward other women in the way you would have men act toward your sister?" George Sand smokes, wears male attire, wishes to be addressed as *"Mon frère"*—perhaps if she found those who were as brothers indeed, she would not care whether she were brother or sister. We rejoice to see that she, who expresses such a painful contempt for men in most of her works as shows she must have known great wrong from them, depicts in *La Roche Mauprat* a man raised by the workings of love from the depths of savage sensualism to a moral and intellectual life. It was love for a pure object, for a steadfast woman, one of those who the Italian said could make the "stair to heaven."

This author, beginning like the many in assault upon bad institutions, and external ills, yet deepening the experience through comparative freedom, sees at last that the only efficient remedy must come from individual character. These bad institutions indeed, it may always be replied, prevent individuals from forming good character, therefore we must remove them. Agreed; yet keep steadily the higher aim in view. Could you clear away all the bad forms of society, it is vain unless the individual begin to be ready for better. There must be a parallel movement in these two branches of life. And all the rules left by Moses availed less to further the best life than the living example of one Messiah.

Still the mind of the age struggles confusedly with these problems, better discerning as yet the ill it can no longer bear than the good by which it may supersede it. But women like Sand will speak now and cannot be silenced; their characters and their eloquence alike foretell an era when such as they shall easier learn to lead true lives. But though such forebode, not such shall be parents of it. Those who would reform the world must show that they do not speak in the heat of wild impulse; their lives must be unstained by passionate error; they must be severe lawgivers to themselves. They must be religious students of the divine purpose with regard to man, if they would not confound the fancies of a day with the requisitions of eternal good. Their liberty must be the liberty of law and knowledge. But as to the transgressions against custom which have caused such outcry against those of noble intention, it may be observed that the resolve of Héloïse to be only the mistress of Abélard, was that of one who saw in practice around her the contract of marriage made the seal of degradation. Shelley feared not to be fettered unless so to be was to be false. Wherever abuses are seen, the timid will suffer; the bold will protest. But society has a right to outlaw them till she has revised her law; and this she must be taught to do by one who speaks with authority, not in anger or haste.

If Godwin's choice of the calumniated authoress of the *Rights of Woman* for his honored wife be a sign of a new era, no less so is an article to which I have alluded some pages back, published five or six years ago in one of the English reviews, where the writer in doing full justice to Héloïse, shows his bitter regret that she lives not now to love him, who might have known better how to prize her love than did the egotistical Abélard.

These marriages, these characters, with all their imperfections express an onward tendency. They speak of aspiration of soul, of energy of mind, seeking clearness and freedom. Of a like promise are the tracts lately published by Goodwyn Barmby (the European pariah, as he calls himself) and his wife Catharine. Whatever we may think of their measures, we see in them wedlock; the two minds are wed by the only contract that can permanently avail, that of a common faith and a common purpose.

We might mention instances nearer home of minds, partners in work and in life, sharing together on equal terms public and private interests, and which wear not on any side the aspect of offense shown by those last-named: persons who steer straight onward, yet in our comparatively free life have not been obliged to run their heads against any wall. But the principles which guide them might under petrified and oppressive institutions have made them warlike, paradoxical, and in some sense pariahs. The phenomena are different, the law is the same in all these cases. Men and women have been obliged to build up their house anew from the very foundation. If they found stone ready in the quarry, they took it peaceably; otherwise they alarmed the country by pulling down old towers to get materials.

These are all instances of marriage as intellectual companionship. The parties meet mind to mind, and a mutual trust is produced which can buckler them against a million. They work together for a common purpose, and in all these instances with the same implement—the pen. The pen and the writing-desk furnish forth as naturally the retirement of Woman as of Man.

* * *

The fourth and highest grade of marriage union is the religious, which may be expressed as pilgrimage toward a common shrine. This includes the others: home sympathies and household wisdom, for these pilgrims must know how to assist each other along the dusty way; intellectual communion, for how sad it would be on such a journey to have a companion to whom you could not communicate your thoughts and aspirations as they sprang to life; who would have no feeling for the prospects that open more and more glorious as we advance; who would never see the flowers that may be gathered by the most industrious traveler! It must include all these.

Such a fellow-pilgrim Count Zinzendorf seems to have found in his countess, of whom he thus writes:

"Twenty-five years' experience has shown me that just the helpmeet whom I have is the only one that could suit my vocation. Who else could have so carried through my family affairs? Who lived so spotlessly before the world? Who so wisely aided me in my rejection of a dry morality? Who so clearly set aside the Pharisaism which as years passed threatened to creep in among us? Who so deeply discerned as to the spirits of delusion which sought to bewilder us? Who would have governed my whole economy so wisely, richly, and hospitably when circumstances commanded? Who have taken indifferently the part of servant or mistress, without on the one side affecting an especial spirituality; on the other, being sullied by any worldly pride? Who, in a community where all ranks are eager to be on a level, would from wise and real causes have known how to maintain inward and outward distinctions? Who without a murmur have seen her husband encounter such dangers by land and sea? Who undertaken with him and *sustained* such astonishing pilgrimages? Who amid such difficulties would have always held up her head and supported me? Who found such vast sums of money, and acquitted them on her own credit? And finally, who of all human beings could so well understand and interpret to others my inner and outer being as this one of such nobleness in her way of thinking, such great intellectual capacity, and so free from the theological perplexities that enveloped me!"

Let anyone peruse with all intentness the lineaments of this portrait, and see if the husband had not reason with this air of solemn rapture and conviction to challenge comparison? We are reminded of the majestic cadence of the line whose feet step in the just proportion of Humanity,

Daughter of God and Man, accomplished Eve!

An observer* adds this testimony:

*Spangenberg.

"We may in many marriages regard it as the best arrangement, if the man has so much advantage over his wife that she can, without much thought of her own, be led and directed by him as by a father. But it was not so with the count and his consort. She was not made to be a copy; she was an original; and while she loved and honored him, she thought for herself on all subjects, with so much intelligence that he could and did look on her as a sister and friend also."

Compare with this refined specimen of a religiously civilized life the following imperfect sketch of a North American Indian, and we shall see that the same causes will always produce the same results. The Flying Pigeon (Ratchewaine) was the wife of a barbarous chief, who had six others; but she was his only true wife because the only one of a strong and pure character, and having this, inspired a veneration as like as the mind of the man permitted to that inspired by the Countess Zinzendorf. She died when her son was only four years old, yet left on his mind a feeling of reverent love worthy the thought of Christian chivalry. Grown to manhood, he shed tears on seeing her portrait.

The Flying Pigeon

"Ratchewaine was chaste, mild, gentle in her disposition, kind, generous, and devoted to her husband. A harsh word was never known to proceed from her mouth; nor was she ever known to be in a passion. Mahaskah used to say of her after her death that her hand was shut when those who did not want came into her presence; but when the really poor came in it was like a strainer full of holes, letting all she held in it pass through. In the exercise of generous feeling she was uniform. It was not indebted for its exercise to whim nor caprice nor partiality. No matter of what nation the applicant for her bounty was, or whether at war or peace with her nation; if he were hungry, she fed him; if naked, she clothed him; and if houseless, she gave him shelter. The continued exercise of this generous feeling kept her poor. And she has been known to give away her last blanket—all the honey that was in the lodge, the last bladder of bear's oil, and the last piece of dried meat.

"She was scrupulously exact in the observance of all the religious rites which her faith imposed upon her. Her conscience is represented to have been extremely tender. She often feared that her acts were displeasing to the Great Spirit, when she would blacken her face and retire to some lone place and fast and pray."

To these traits should be added, but for want of room, anecdotes which show the quick decision and vivacity of her mind. Her face was in harmony with this combination. Her brow is as ideal and the eyes and lids as devout and modest as the Italian picture of the Madonna, while the lower part of the face has the simplicity and childish strength of the Indian race. Her picture presents the finest specimen of Indian beauty we have ever seen. Such a Woman is the sister and friend of all beings, as the worthy Man is their brother and helper.

With like pleasure we survey the pairs wedded on the eve of missionary effort. They, indeed, are fellow-pilgrims on the well-made road, and whether or no they accomplish all they hope for the sad Hindu or the nearer savage, we feel that in the burning waste their love is like to be a healing dew, in the forlorn jungle a tent of solace to one another. They meet as children of one Father to read together one book of instruction.

* * *

But to return to the thread of my subject.

Another sign of the times is furnished by the triumphs of Female Authorship. These have been great and are constantly increasing. Women have taken possession of so many provinces for which men had pronounced them unfit, that though these still declare there are some inaccessible to them, it is difficult to say just *where* they must stop.

The shining names of famous women have cast light upon the path of the sex, and many obstructions have been removed. When a Montagu could learn better than her brother and use her lore afterward to such purpose as an observer, it seemed amiss to hinder women from preparing themselves to see, or from seeing all they could when prepared. Since Somerville has achieved so much, will any young girl be prevented from seeking a knowledge of the physical sciences if she wishes it? De Staël's name was not so clear of offense; she could not forget the Woman in the thought; while she was instructing you as a mind, she wished to be admired as a Woman; sentimental tears often dimmed the eagle glance. Her intellect, too, with all its splendor, trained in a drawing-room, fed on flattery, was tainted and flawed; yet its beams make the obscurest schoolhouse in New England warmer and lighter to the little rugged girls who are gathered together on its wooden bench. They may never through life hear her name, but she is not the less their benefactress.

The influence has been such that the aim certainly is now, in arranging school instruction for girls, to give them as fair a field as boys. As yet, indeed, these arrangements are made with little judgment or reflection; just as the tutors of Lady Jane Grey and other distinguished women of her time taught them Latin and Greek, because they knew nothing else themselves, so now the improvement in the education of girls is to be made by giving them young men as teachers, who only teach what has been taught themselves at college, while methods and topics need revision for these new subjects, which could better be made by those who had experienced the same wants. Women are often at the head of these institutions; but they have as yet seldom been thinking women, capable of organizing a new whole for the wants of the time, and choosing persons to officiate in the departments. And when some portion of instruction of a good sort is got from the school, the far greater proportion which is infused from the general atmosphere of society contradicts its purport. Yet books and a little elementary instruction are not furnished in vain. Women are better aware how great and rich the universe is, not so easily blinded by narrowness or partial views of a home circle. "Her mother did so before her" is no longer a sufficient excuse. Indeed it was never received as an excuse to mitigate the severity of censure, but was adduced as a reason, rather, why there should be no effort made for reformation.

Whether much or little has been done, or will be done—whether women will add to the talent of narration the power of systematizing—whether they will carve marble as well as draw and paint—is not important. But that it should be acknowledged that they have intellect which needs developing—that they should not be considered complete if beings of affection and habit alone—is important.

Yet even this acknowledgment, rather conquered by Woman than proffered by Man, has been sullied by the usual selfishness. Too much is said of women being better educated that they may become better companions and mothers *for men*. They should be fit for such companionship, and we have mentioned with satisfaction instances where it has been established. Earth knows no fairer, holier relation than that of a mother. It is one which rightly understood must both promote and require the highest attainments. But a being of infinite scope must not be treated with an exclusive view to any one relation. Give the soul free course, let the organization both of body and mind be freely developed, and the being will be fit for any and every relation to which it may be called. The intellect, no more than the sense of hearing, is to be cultivated merely that Woman may be a more valuable companion to Man, but because the Power who gave a power by its mere existence signifies that it must be brought out toward perfection.

In this regard of self-dependence, and a greater simplicity and fullness of being, we must hail as a preliminary the increase of the class contemptuously designated as "old maids."

We cannot wonder at the aversion with which old bachelors and old maids have been regarded. Marriage is the natural means of forming a sphere, of taking root in the earth; it requires more strength to do this without such an opening; very many have failed, and their imperfections have been in everyone's way. They have been more partial, more harsh, more officious and impertinent than those compelled by severer friction to render themselves endurable. Those who have a more full experience of the instincts have a distrust as to whether the unmarried can be thoroughly human and humane, such as is hinted in the saying, "Old maids' and bachelors' children are well cared for," which derides at once their ignorance and their presumption.

Yet the business of society has become so complex that it could now scarcely be carried on without the presence of these despised auxiliaries; and detachments from the army of aunts and uncles are wanted to stop gaps in every hedge. They rove about, mental and moral Ishmaelites, pitching their tents amid the fixed and ornamented homes of men.

In a striking variety of forms, genius of late, both at home and abroad, has paid its tribute to the character of the aunt and the uncle, recognizing in these personages the spiritual parents who have supplied defects in the treatment of the busy or careless actual parents.

They also gain a wider, if not so deep experience. Those who are not intimately and permanently linked with others are thrown upon themselves; and if they do not there find peace and incessant life, there is none to flatter them that they are not very poor and very mean.

A position which so constantly admonishes may be of inestimable benefit. The person may gain, undistracted by other relationships, a closer communion with the one. Such a use is made of it by saints and sibyls. Or she may be one of the lay sisters of charity, a canoness bound by an inward vow—or the useful drudge of all men, the Martha, much sought, little prized—or the intellectual interpreter of the varied life she sees; the Urania of a half-formed world's twilight.

Or she may combine all these. Not "needing to care that she may please a husband," a frail and limited being, her thoughts may turn to the center, and she may, by steadfast contemplation entering into the secret of truth and love, use it for the good of all men instead of a chosen few, and interpret through it all the forms of life. It is possible, perhaps, to be at once a priestly servant and a loving muse.

Saints and geniuses have often chosen a lonely position, in the faith that if, undisturbed by the pressure of near ties, they would give themselves up to the inspiring spirit, it would enable them to understand and reproduce life better than actual experience could.

How many "old maids" take this high stand we cannot say: it is an unhappy fact that too many who have come before the eye are gossips rather, and not always good-natured gossips. But if these abuse, and none make the best of their vocation, yet it has not failed to produce some good results. It has been seen by others, if not by themselves, that beings, likely to be left alone, need to be fortified and furnished within themselves; and education and thought have tended more and more to regard these beings as related to absolute Being, as well as to others. It has been seen that as the breaking of no bond ought to destroy a man, so ought the missing of none to hinder him from growing. And thus a circumstance of the time which springs rather from its luxury than its purity, has helped to place women on the true platform.

Perhaps the next generation, looking deeper into this matter, will find that contempt is put upon old maids or old women at all, merely because they do not use the elixir which would keep them always young. Under its influence, a gem brightens yearly which is only seen to more advantage through the fissures Time makes in the casket. No one thinks of Michelangelo's "Persican Sibyl" or St. Theresa or Tasso's Leonora or the Greek Electra as an old maid, more than of Michelangelo or Canova as old bachelors, though all had reached the period in life's course appointed to take that degree.

See a common woman at forty; scarcely has she the remains of beauty, of any soft poetic grace which gave her attraction as Woman, which kindled the hearts of those who looked on her to sparkling thoughts, or diffused round her a roseate air of gentle love. See her who was indeed a lovely girl in the coarse, full-blown dahlia flower of what is commonly matron-beauty, "fat, fair, and forty," showily dressed, and with manners as broad and full as her frill or satin cloak. People observe, "How well she is preserved!" "She is a fine woman still," they say. This woman, whether as a duchess in diamonds or one of our city dames in mosaics, charms the poet's heart no more, and would look much out of place kneeling before the Madonna. She "does well the honors of her house"—"leads society"—is in short always spoken and thought of upholstery-wise.

Or see that careworn face from which every soft line is blotted—those faded eyes from which lonely tears have driven the flashes of fancy, the mild white beam of a tender enthusiasm. This woman is not so ornamental to a tea party; yet she would please better in picture. Yet surely she, no more than the other, looks as a human being should at the end of forty years. Forty years! Have they bound those brows with no garland? Shed in the lamp no drop of ambrosial oil?

Not so looked the Iphigenia in Aulis. Her forty years had seen her in anguish, in sacrifice, in utter loneliness. But those pains were borne for her father and her country; the sacrifice she had made pure for herself and those around her. Wandering alone at night in the vestal solitude of her imprisoning grove, she has looked up through its "living summits" to the stars, which shed down into her aspect their own lofty melody. At forty she would not misbecome the marble.

Not so looks the Persica. She is withered; she is faded; the drapery that enfolds her has in its dignity an angularity, too, that tells of age, of sorrow, of a stern resignation to the *must*. But her eye, that torch of the soul, is untamed, and in the intensity of her reading we see a soul invincibly young in faith and hope. Her age is her charm, for it is the night of the past that gives this beacon-fire leave to shine. Wither more and more, black Chrysalid, thou dost but give the winged beauty time to mature its splendors!

Not so looked Vittoria Colonna after her life of a great hope and of true conjugal fidelity. She had been not merely a bride but a wife, and each hour had helped to plume the noble bird. A coronet of pearls will not shame her brow; it is white and ample, a worthy altar for love and thought.

Even among the North American Indians, a race of men as completely engaged in mere instinctive life as almost any in the world, and where each chief, keeping many wives as useful servants, of course looks with no kind eye on celibacy in Woman, it was excused in the following instance mentioned by Mrs. Jameson. A woman dreamt in youth that she was betrothed to the Sun. She built her a wigwam apart, filled it with emblems of her alliance and means of an independent life. There she passed her days, sustained by her own exertions and true to her supposed engagement.

In any tribe, we believe, a woman who lived as if she was betrothed to the Sun would be tolerated, and the rays which made her youth blossom sweetly would crown her with a halo in age.

There is on this subject a nobler view than heretofore, if not the noblest, and improvement here must coincide with that in the view taken of marriage. "We must have units before we can have union," says one of the ripe thinkers of the times.

* * *

The especial genius of Woman I believe to be electrical in movement, intuitive in function, spiritual in tendency. She excels not so easily in classification or recreation, as in an instinctive seizure of causes, and a simple breathing out of what she receives that has the singleness of life, rather than the selecting and energizing of art.

More native is it to her to be the living model of the artist than to set apart from herself any one form in objective reality; more native to inspire and receive the poem than to create it. In so far as soul is in her completely developed, all soul is the same; but in so far as it is modified in her as Woman, it flows, it breathes, it sings, rather than deposits soil or finishes work; and that which is especially feminine flushes in blossom the face of earth, and pervades like air and water all this seeming solid globe, daily renewing and purifying its life. Such may be the especially feminine element spoken of as Femality. But it is no more the order of nature that it should be incarnated pure in any form, than that the masculine energy should exist unmingled with it in any form.

Male and female represent the two sides of the great radical dualism. But in fact they are perpetually passing into one another. Fluid hardens to solid, solid rushes to fluid. There is no wholly masculine man, no purely feminine woman.

History jeers at the attempts of physiologists to bind great original laws by the forms which flow from them. They make a rule; they say from observation what can and cannot be. In vain! Nature provides exceptions to every rule. She sends women to battle, and sets Hercules spinning; she enables women to bear immense burdens, cold, and frost; she enables the man who feels maternal love to nourish his infant like a mother. Of late she plays still gayer pranks. Not only she deprives organizations but organs of a necessary end. She enables people to read with the top of the head and see with the pit of the stomach. Presently she will make a female Newton and a male siren.

Man partakes of the feminine in the Apollo; Woman of the masculine as Minerva.

What I mean by the Muse is that unimpeded clearness of the intuitive powers, which a perfectly truthful adherence to every admonition of the higher instincts would bring to a finely organized human being. It may appear as prophecy or as poesy. It enabled Cassandra to foresee the results of actions passing round her; the Seeress to behold the true character of the person through the mask of his customary life. (Sometimes she saw a feminine form behind the man, sometimes the reverse.) It enabled the daughter of Linnaeus to see the soul of the flower exhaling from the flower.* It gave a man, but a poet-man, the power of which he thus speaks: "Often in my contemplation of nature, radiant intimations and as it were sheaves of light appear before me as to the facts of cosmogony, in which my mind has perhaps taken especial part." He wisely adds, "But it is necessary with earnestness to verify the knowledge we gain by these flashes of light." And none should forget this. Sight must be verified by light before it can deserve the honors of piety and genius. Yet sight comes first, and of this sight of the world of causes, this approximation to the region of primitive motions, women I hold to be especially capable. Even without equal freedom with the other sex, they have already shown themselves so; and should these faculties have free play, I believe they will open new, deeper, and purer sources of joyous inspiration than have as yet refreshed the earth.

Let us be wise, and not impede the soul. Let her work as she will. Let us have one creative energy, one incessant revelation. Let it take what form it will, and let us not bind it by the past to man or woman, black or white. Jove sprang from Rhea, Pallas from Jove. So let it be.

If it has been the tendency of these remarks to call Woman rather to the Minerva side—if I, unlike the more generous writer, have spoken from society no less than the soul—let it be pardoned! It is love that has caused this—love for many incarcerated souls that might be freed could the idea of religious self-dependence be established in them, could the weakening habit of dependence on others be broken up.

* * *

It is therefore that I would have Woman lay aside all thought, such as she habitually cherishes, of being taught and led by men. I would have her, like the Indian girl, dedicate herself to the Sun, the Sun of Truth, and go nowhere if his beams did not make clear the path. I would have her free from compromise, from complaisance, from

*The daughter of Linnaeus states that while looking steadfastly at the red lily, she saw its spirit hovering above it as a red flame. It is true this, like many fair spirit-stories, may be explained away as an optical illusion, but its poetic beauty and meaning would even then make it valuable as an illustration of the spiritual fact.

helplessness, because I would have her good enough and strong enough to love one and all beings, from the fullness, not the poverty of being.

Men as at present instructed will not help this work, because they also are under the slavery of habit. I have seen with delight their poetic impulses. A sister is the fairest ideal, and how nobly Wordsworth and even Byron have written of a sister!

There is no sweeter sight than to see a father with his little daughter. Very vulgar men become refined to the eye when leading a little girl by the hand. At that moment, the right relation between the sexes seems established, and you feel as if the man would aid in the noblest purpose, if you ask him in behalf of his little daughter. Once, two fine figures stood before me thus. The father of very intellectual aspect, his falcon eye softened by affection as he looked down on his fair child; she the image of himself, only more graceful and brilliant in expression. I was reminded of Southey's Kehama; when, lo, the dream was rudely broken! They were talking of education, and he said:

"I shall not have Maria brought too forward. If she knows too much, she will never find a husband; superior women hardly ever can."

"Surely," said his wife with a blush, "you wish Maria to be as good and wise as she can, whether it will help her to marriage or not."

"No," he persisted, "I want her to have a sphere and a home, and someone to protect her when I am gone."

It was a trifling incident, but made a deep impression. I felt that the holiest relations fail to instruct the unprepared and perverted mind. If this man indeed could have looked at it on the other side, he was the last that would have been willing to have been taken himself for the home and protection he could give, but would have been much more likely to repeat the tale of Alcibiades with his phials.

But men do *not* look at both sides, and women must leave off asking them and being influenced by them, but retire within themselves, and explore the groundwork of life till they find their peculiar secret. Then, when they come forth again, renovated and baptized, they will know how to turn all dross to gold, and will be rich and free though they live in a hut, tranquil if in a crowd. Then their sweet singing shall not be from passionate impulse, but the lyrical overflow of a divine rapture, and a new music shall be evolved from this many-chorded world.

Grant her, then, for a while the armor and the javelin. Let her put from her the press of other minds, and meditate in virgin loneliness. The same idea shall reappear in due time as Muse, or Ceres, the all-kindly, patient Earth Spirit.

* * *

I believe that at present women are the best helpers of one another.

Let them think, let them act, till they know what they need.

We only ask of men to remove arbitrary barriers. Some would like to do more. But I believe it needs that Woman show herself in her native dignity to teach them how to aid her; their minds are so encumbered by tradition.

When Lord Edward Fitzgerald traveled with the Indians, his manly heart obliged him at once to take the packs from the squaws and carry them. But we do not read that the red men followed his example, though they are ready enough to carry the pack of the white woman, because she seems to them a superior being.

Let Woman appear in the mild majesty of Ceres, and rudest churls will be willing to learn from her.

You ask: what use will she make of liberty, when she has so long been sustained and restrained?

I answer: in the first place this will not be suddenly given. I read yesterday a debate of this year on the subject of enlarging women's rights over property. It was a leaf from the classbook that is preparing for the needed instruction. The men learned visibly as they spoke. The champions of Woman saw the fallacy of arguments on the opposite side, and were startled by their own convictions. With their wives at home, and the readers of the paper, it was the same. And so the stream flows on; thought urging action, and action leading to the evolution of still better thought.

But were this freedom to come suddenly, I have no fear of the consequences. Individuals might commit excesses, but there is not only in the sex a reverence for decorums and limits inherited and enhanced from generation to generation, which many years of other life could not efface, but a native love in Woman, as Woman, of proportion, of "the simple art of not too much"—a Greek moderation which would create immediately a restraining party, the natural legislators and instructors of the rest, and would gradually establish such rules as are needed to guard without impeding life.

The Graces would lead the choral dance, and teach the rest to regulate their steps to the measure of beauty.

But if you ask me what offices they may fill, I reply—any. I do not care what case you put; let them be sea-captains, if you will. I do not doubt there are women well fitted for such an office, and if so, I should be as glad to see them in it as to welcome the maid of Saragossa or the maid of Missolonghi or the Suliote heroine or Emily Plater.

I think women need especially at this juncture a much greater range of occupation than they have, to rouse their latent powers. A party of travelers lately visited a lonely hut on a mountain. There they found an old woman, who told them she and her husband had lived their forty years. "Why," they said, "did you choose so barren a spot?" She did not know; *"it was the man's notion."*

And during forty years she had been content to act, without knowing why, upon the "man's notion." I would not have it so.

In families that I know, some little girls like to saw wood, others to use carpenters' tools. Where these tastes are indulged, cheerfulness and good-humor are promoted. Where they are forbidden, because "such things are not proper for girls," they grow sullen and mischievous.

Fourier had observed these wants of women, as no one can fail to do who watches the desires of little girls or knows the ennui that haunts grown women, except where they make to themselves a serene little world by art of some kind. He therefore, in proposing a great variety of employments in manufactures or the care of plants and animals, allows for one third of women as likely to have a taste for masculine pursuits, one third of men for feminine.

Who does not observe the immediate glow and serenity that is diffused over the life of women before restless or fretful by engaging in gardening, building, or the lowest department of art? Here is something that is not routine, something that draws forth life towards the infinite.

I have no doubt, however, that a large proportion of women would give themselves to the same employments as now, because there are circumstances that must lead them. Mothers will delight to make the nest soft and warm. Nature would take care of that; no need to clip the wings of any bird that wants to soar and sing, or finds in itself the strength of pinion for a migratory flight unusual to its kind. The difference would be that *all* need not be constrained to employments for which *some* are unfit.

I have urged upon the sex self-subsistence in its two forms of self-reliance and self-impulse, because I believe them to be the needed means of the present juncture.

I have urged on Woman independence of Man, not that I do not think the sexes mutually needed by one another, but because in Woman this fact has led to an excessive devotion which has cooled love, degraded marriage, and prevented either sex from being what it should be to itself or the other.

I wish Woman to live *first* for God's sake. Then she will not make an imperfect man her god, and thus sink to idolatry. Then she will not take what is not fit for her from a sense of weakness and poverty. Then if she finds what she needs in Man embodied, she will know how to love and be worthy of being loved.

By being more a soul she will not be less Woman, for nature is perfected through spirit.

Now there is no woman, only an overgrown child.

That her hand may be given with dignity, she must be able to stand alone. I wish to see men and women capable of such relations as are depicted by Landor in his *Pericles and Aspasia,* where grace is the natural garb of strength, and the affections are calm, because deep. The softness is that of a firm tissue, as when

The gods approve
The depth, but not the tumult of the soul,
A fervent, not ungovernable love.

A profound thinker has said, "No married woman can represent the female world, for she belongs to her husband. The idea of Woman must be represented by a virgin."

But that is the very fault of marriage and of the present relation between the sexes, that the woman *does* belong to the man instead of forming a whole with him. Were it otherwise, there would be no such limitation to the thought.

Woman, self-centered, would never be absorbed by any relation; it would be only an experience to her as to man. It is a vulgar error that love, *a* love, to Woman is her whole existence; she also is born for Truth and Love in their universal energy. Would she but assume her inheritance, Mary would not be the only virgin mother. Not Manzoni alone would celebrate in his wife the virgin mind with the maternal wisdom and conjugal affections. The soul is ever young, ever virgin.

And will not she soon appear? The woman who shall vindicate their birthright for all women; who shall teach them what to claim, and how to use what they obtain? Shall not her name be for her era Victoria, for her country and life Virginia? Yet predictions are rash; she herself must teach us to give her the fitting name.

An idea not unknown to ancient times has of late been revived, that in the metamorphoses of life the soul assumes the form first of Man, then of Woman, and takes the chances and reaps the benefits of either lot. Why then, say some, lay such emphasis on the rights or needs of Woman? What she wins not as Woman will come to her as Man.

That makes no difference. It is not Woman, but the law of right, the law of growth that speaks in us and demands the perfection of each being in its kind—apple as apple, Woman as Woman. Without adopting your theory, I know that I, a daughter, live through the life of Man; but what concerns me now is that my life be a beautiful, powerful, in a word, a complete life in its kind. Had I but one more moment to live I must wish the same.

Suppose at the end of your cycle, your great world-year, all will be completed whether I exert myself or not (and the supposition is *false*—but suppose it true), am I to be indifferent about it? Not so! I must beat my own pulse true in the heart of the world; for *that* is virtue, excellence, health.

Thou, Lord of Day, didst leave us tonight so calmly glorious, not dismayed that cold winter is coming, not postponing thy beneficence to the fruitful summer! Thou didst smile on thy day's work when it was done, and adorn thy down-going as thy up-rising, for thou art loyal, and it is thy nature to give life, if thou canst, and shine at all events!

I stand in the sunny noon of life. Objects no longer glitter in the dews of morning, neither are yet softened by the shadows of evening. Every spot is seen, every chasm revealed. Climbing the dusty hill, some fair effigies that once stood for symbols of human destiny have been broken; those I still have with me show defects in this broad light. Yet enough is left, even by experience, to point distinctly to the glories of that destiny; faint but not to be mistaken streaks of the future day. I can say with the bard,

Though many have suffered shipwreck, still beat noble hearts.

Always the soul says to us all, cherish your best hopes as a faith, and abide by them in action. Such shall be the effectual fervent means to their fulfillment:

For the Power to whom we bow
Has given its pledge that, if not now,
They of pure and steadfast mind,
By faith exalted, truth refined,
Shall *hear all music loud and clear,*
Whose first notes they ventured here.
Then fear not thou to wind the horn,
Though elf and gnome thy courage scorn;
Ask for the castle's King and Queen;
Though rabble rout may rush between,
Beat thee senseless to the ground,
In the dark beset thee round;
Persist to ask, and it will come;
Seek not for rest in humbler home;
So shalt thou see, what few have seen,
The palace home of King and Queen.

November 15, 1844

THE FUGITIVE'S SONG,
NEW ENGLAND
LITH. OF E. W. BOUVE BOSTON
WORDS
composed and respectfully dedicated, in token of confident esteem to
FREDERICK DOUGLASS
A Graduate from the
"PECULIAR INSTITUTION"
For his fearless advocacy, signal ability and wonderful success in behalf of
HIS BROTHERS IN BONDS.
(and to the FUGITIVES FROM SLAVERY in the)
FREE STATES & CANADAS.
by their friend
JESSE HUTCHINSON JUNR.
BOSTON, Published by HENRY PRENTISS 33 Court St.
Entered according to act of congress in the year 1845 by Henry Prentiss in the clerks office of the district court of Massachusetts

FREDERICK DOUGLASS

Life as a Slave

(1855)

Frederick Douglass, who began his life as a slave in eastern Maryland, wrote the most memorable and impressive of the many "slave narratives," the first important literary genre of black Americans. Unlike so many of them, however, Douglass' was wholly the product of his own pen, with no white abolitionist to guide his hand. A runaway slave who became a distinguished abolitionist—by far the most prominent black abolitionist—Douglass remained an important figure in the post-Civil War Republican party, and continued to be a symbol of leadership for blacks throughout and beyond his long life.

Slave narratives offered the best single source for the

abolitionist view of slavery. Abolition was overwhelmingly a moral movement, and Douglass' account presented slavery as the opposite of what nineteenth-century Americans saw as the font of all morality—the family. Douglass' mother, he explains, "had many children, but NO FAMILY! The domestic hearth, with its holy lessons and precious endearments, is abolished in the case of a slave-mother and her children." His father is "shrouded in a mystery . . . . Slavery has no use for either fathers or families, and its laws do not recognize their existence in the social arrangements of the plantation." Slavery destroys the family structure and actively militates against sexual morality. Douglass, in fact, plays artfully with the rumor that he may be the son of the plantation master, transforming the plantation into a monstrous, perverted family. No other image of slavery cut so deeply into the national psyche. And when this view of slavery as the perversion of family finally dominated popular art in the best-selling novel Uncle Tom's Cabin, the war had—morally speaking—already begun.

I

In Talbot county, Eastern Shore, Maryland, near Easton, the county town of that county, there is a small district of country, thinly populated, and remarkable for nothing that I know of more than for the worn-out, sandy, desert-like appearance of its soil, the general dilapidation of its farms and fences, the indigent and spiritless character of its inhabitants, and the prevalence of ague and fever.

The name of this singularly unpromising and truly famine stricken district is Tuckahoe, a name well known to all Marylanders, black and white. It was given to this section of country probably, at the first, merely in derision; or it may possibly have been applied to it, as I have heard, because some one of its earlier inhabitants had been guilty of the petty meanness of stealing a hoe—or taking a hoe—that did not belong to him. Eastern Shore men usually pronounce the word *took,* as *tuck; Took-a-hoe,* therefore, is, in Maryland parlance, *Tuckahoe.* But, whatever may have been its origin—and about this I will not be positive—that name has stuck to the district in question; and it is seldom mentioned but with contempt and derision, on account of the barrenness of its soil, and the ignorance, indolence, and poverty of its people. Decay and ruin are everywhere visible, and the thin population of the place would have quitted it long ago, but for the Choptank river, which runs through it, from which they take abundance of shad and herring, and plenty of ague and fever.

It was in this dull, flat, and unthrifty district, or neighborhood, surrounded by a white population of the lowest order, indolent and drunken to a proverb, and among slaves, who seemed to ask, *"Oh! what's the use?"* every time they lifted a hoe, that I—without any fault of mine—was born, and spent the first years of my childhood.

The reader will pardon so much about the place of my birth, on the score that it is always a fact of some importance to know where a man is born, if, indeed, it be important to know anything about him. In regard to the *time* of my birth, I cannot be as definite as I have been respecting the *place.* Nor, indeed, can I impart much knowledge concerning my parents. Genealogical trees do not flourish among slaves. A person of some consequence here in the north, sometimes designated *father,* is literally abolished in slave law and slave practice. It is only once in a while that an exception is found to this statement. I never met with a slave who could tell me how old he was. Few slave-mothers know anything of the months of the year, nor of the days of the month. They keep no family records, with marriages, births, and deaths. They measure the ages of their children by spring time, winter time, harvest time, planting time, and the like; but these soon become undistinguishable and forgotten. Like other slaves, I cannot tell how old I am. This destitution was among my earliest troubles. I learned when I grew up, that my master—and this is the case with masters generally—allowed no questions to be put to him, by which a slave might learn his age. Such questions are deemed evidence of impatience, and even of impudent curiosity. From certain events, however, the dates of which I have since learned, I suppose myself to have been born about the year 1817.

* * *

Living here, with my dear old grandmother and grandfather, it was a long time before I knew myself to be *a slave.* I knew many other things before I knew that. Grandmother and grandfather were the greatest people in the world to me; and being with them so snugly in their own little cabin—I supposed it be their own—knowing no higher authority over me or the other children than the authority of grandmamma, for a time there was nothing to disturb me; but, as I grew larger and older, I learned by degrees the sad fact, that the "little hut," and the lot on which it stood, belonged not to my dear old grandparents, but to some person who lived a great distance off, and who was called, by grandmother, "Old Master." I further learned the sadder fact, that not only the house and lot, but that grandmother herself, (grandfather was free,) and all the little children around her, belonged to this mysterious personage, called by grandmother, with every mark of reverence, "Old Master." Thus early did clouds and shadows begin to fall upon my path. Once on the track—troubles never come singly—I was not long in finding out another fact, still more grievous to my childish heart. I was told that this "old master," whose name seemed ever to be mentioned with fear and shuddering, only allowed the children to live with grandmother for a limited time, and that in fact as soon as they were big enough, they were promptly taken away, to live with the said "old master." These were distressing revelations indeed; and though I was quite too young to comprehend the full import of the intelligence, and mostly spent my childhood days in gleesome sports with the other children, a shade of disquiet rested upon me.

The absolute power of this distant "old master" had touched my young spirit with but the point of its cold, cruel iron, and left me something to brood over after the play and in moments of repose. Grandmammy was, indeed, at that time, all the world to me; and the thought of being separated from her, in any considerable time, was more than an unwelcome intruder. It was intolerable.

* * *

I was a slave—born a slave—and though the fact was incomprehensible to me, it conveyed to my mind a sense of my entire dependence on the will of *somebody* I had never seen; and, from some cause or other, I had been made to fear this somebody above all else on earth. Born for another's benefit, as the *firstling* of the cabin flock I was soon to be selected as a meet offering to the fearful and inexorable *demigod,* whose huge image on so many occasions haunted my childhood's imagination. When the time of my departure was decided upon, my grandmother, knowing my fears, and in pity for them, kindly kept me ignorant of the dreaded event about to transpire. Up to the morning (a beautiful summer morning) when we were to start, and, indeed, during the whole journey—a journey which, child as I was, I remember as well as if it were yesterday—she kept the sad fact hidden from me. This reserve was necessary; for, could I have known all, I should have given grandmother some trouble in getting me started. As it was, I was helpless, and she—dear woman!—led me along by the hand, resisting, with the reserve and solemnity of a priestess, all my inquiring looks to the last.

The distance from Tuckahoe to Wye river—where my old master lived—was full twelve miles, and the walk was quite a severe test of the endurance of my young legs. The journey would have proved too severe for me, but that my dear old grandmother—blessings on her memory!—afforded occasional relief by "toting" me (as Marylanders have it) on her shoulder. My grandmother, though advanced in years—as was evident from more than one gray hair, which peeped from between the ample and graceful folds of her newly-ironed bandana turban—was yet a woman of power and spirit. She was marvelously straight in figure, elastic, and muscular. I seemed hardly to be a burden to her. She would have "toted" me farther, but that I felt myself too much of a man to allow it, and insisted on walking. Releasing dear grandmamma from carrying me, did not make me altogether independent of her, when we happened to pass through portions of the somber woods which lay between Tuckahoe and Wye river. She often found me increasing the energy of my grip, and holding her clothing, lest something should come out of the woods and eat me up. Several old logs and stumps imposed upon me, and got themselves taken for wild beasts. I could see their legs, eyes, and ears, or I could see something like eyes, legs, and ears, till I got close enough to them to see that the eyes were knots, washed white with rain, and the legs were broken limbs, and the ears, only ears owing to the point from which they were seen. Thus early I learned that the point from which a thing is viewed is of some importance.

As the day advanced the heat increased; and it was not until the afternoon that we reached the much dreaded end of the journey. I found myself in the midst of a group of children of many colors; black, brown, copper colored, and nearly white. I had not seen so many children before. Great houses loomed up in different directions, and a great many men and women were at work in the fields. All this hurry, noise, and singing was very different from the stillness of Tuckahoe. As a new comer, I was an object of special interest; and, after laughing and yelling around me, and playing all sorts of wild tricks, they (the children) asked me to go out and play with them. This I refused to do, preferring to stay with grandmamma. I could not help feeling that our being there boded no good to me. Grandmamma looked sad. She was soon to lose another object of affection, as she had lost many before. I knew she was unhappy, and the shadow fell from her brow on me, though I knew not the cause.

All suspense, however, must have an end; and the end of mine, in this instance, was at hand. Affectionately patting me on the head, and exhorting me to be a good boy, grandmamma told me to go and play with the little children. "They are kin to you," said she; "go and play with them." Among a number of cousins were Phil, Tom, Steve, and Jerry, Nance and Betty.

Grandmother pointed out my brother Perry, my sister Sarah, and my sister Eliza, who stood in the group. I had never seen my brother nor my sisters before; and, though I had sometimes heard of them, and felt a curious interest in them, I really did not understand what they were to me, or I to them. We were brothers and sisters, but what of that? Why should they be attached to me, or I to them? Brothers and sisters we were by blood; but *slavery* had made us strangers. I heard the words brother and sisters, and knew they must mean something; but slavery had robbed these terms of their true meaning. The experience through which I was passing, they had passed through before. They had already been initiated into the mysteries of old master's domicile, and they seemed to look upon me with a certain degree of compassion; but my heart clave to my grandmother. Think it not strange, dear reader, that so little sympathy of feeling existed between us. The conditions of brotherly and sisterly feeling were wanting—we had never nestled and played together. My poor mother, like many other slave-women, had *many children*, but NO FAMILY! The domestic hearth, with its holy lessons and precious endearments, is abolished in the case of a slave-mother and her children. "Little children, love one another," are words seldom heard in a slave cabin.

I really wanted to play with my brother and sisters, but they were strangers to me, and I was full of fear that grandmother might leave without taking me with her. Entreated to do so, however, and that, too, by my dear grandmother, I went to the back part of the house, to play with them and the other children. *Play*, however, I did not, but stood with my back against the wall, witnessing the playing of the others. At last, while standing there, one of the children, who had been in the kitchen, ran up to me, in a sort of roguish glee, exclaiming, "Fed, Fed! grandmammy gone! grandmammy gone!" I could not believe it; yet, fearing the worst, I ran into the kitchen, to see for myself, and found it even so. Grandmammy had indeed gone, and was now far away, "clean" out of sight. I need not tell all that happened now. Almost heart-broken at the discovery, I fell upon the ground, and wept a boy's bitter tears, refusing to be comforted. My brother and sisters came around me, and said, "Don't cry," and gave me peaches and pears, but I flung them away, and refused all their kindly advances. I had never been deceived before; and I felt not only grieved at parting—as I supposed forever—with my grandmother, but indignant that a trick had been played upon me in a matter so serious.

It was now late in the afternoon. The day had been an exciting and wearisome one, and I knew not how or where, but I suppose I sobbed myself to sleep. There is a healing in the angel wing of sleep, even for the slave-boy; and its balm was never more welcome to any wounded soul than it was to mine, the first night I spent at the domicile of old master. The reader may be surprised that I narrate so minutely an incident apparently so trivial, and which must have occurred when I was not more than seven years old; but as I wish to give a faithful history of my experience in slavery, I cannot withhold a circumstance which, at the time, affected me so deeply. Besides, this was, in fact, my first introduction to the realities of slavery.

II

If the reader will now be kind enough to allow me time to grow bigger, and afford me an opportunity for my experience to become greater, I will tell him something, by-and-by, of slave life, as I saw, felt, and heard it, on Col. Edward Lloyd's plantation, and at the house of old master, where I had now, despite of myself, most suddenly, but not unexpectedly, been dropped. Meanwhile, I will redeem my promise to say something more of my dear mother.

I say nothing of *father,* for he is shrouded in a mystery I have never been able to penetrate. Slavery does away with fathers, as it does away with families. Slavery has no use for either fathers or families, and its laws do not recognize their existence in the social arrangements of the plantation. When they *do* exist, they are not the outgrowths of slavery, but are antagonistic to that system. The order of civilization is reversed here. The name of the child is not expected to be that of its father, and his condition does not necessarily affect that of the child. He may be the slave of Mr. Tilgman; and his child, when born, may be the slave of Mr. Gross. He may be a *freeman;* and yet his child may be a *chattel.* He may be white, glorying in the purity of his Anglo-Saxon blood; and his child may be ranked with the blackest slaves. Indeed, he *may* be, and often *is,* master and father to the same child. He can be father without being a husband, and may sell his child without incurring reproach, if the child be by a woman in whose veins courses one thirty-second part of African blood. My father was a white man, or nearly white. It was sometimes whispered that my master was my father.

But to return, or rather, to begin. My knowledge of my mother is very scanty, but very distinct. Her personal appearance and bearing are ineffaceably stamped upon my memory. She was tall, and finely proportioned; of deep black, glossy complexion; had regular features, and, among the other slaves, was remarkably sedate in her manners. There is in *"Prichard's Natural History of Man,"* the head of a figure—on page 157—the features of which so resemble those of my mother, that I often recur to it with something of the feeling which I suppose others experience when looking upon the pictures of dear departed ones.

Yet I cannot say that I was very deeply attached to my mother; certainly not so deeply as I should have been had our relations in childhood been different. We were separated, according to the common custom, when I was but an infant, and, of course, before I knew my mother from any one else.

* * *

Summoned away to her account, with the impassable gulf of slavery between us during her entire illness, my mother died without leaving me a single intimation of *who* my father was. There was a whisper, that my master was my father; yet it was only a whisper, and I cannot say that I ever gave it credence. Indeed, I now have reason to think he was not; nevertheless, the fact remains, in all its glaring odiousness, that, by the laws of slavery, children, in all cases, are reduced to the condition of their mothers. This arrangement admits of the greatest license to brutal slaveholders, and their profligate sons, brothers, relations and friends, and gives to the pleasure of sin, the additional attraction of profit. A whole volume might be written on this single feature of slavery, as I have observed it.

One might imagine, that the children of such connections, would fare better, in the hands of their masters, than other slaves. The rule is quite the other way; and a very little reflection will satisfy the reader that such is the case. A man who will enslave his own blood, may not be safely relied on for magnanimity. Men do not love those who remind them of their sins—unless they have a mind to repent—and the mulatto child's face is a standing accusation against him who is master and father to the child. What is still worse, perhaps, such a child is a constant offense to the wife. She hates its very presence, and when a slaveholding woman hates, she wants not means to give that hate telling effect. Women—white women, I mean—are IDOLS at the south, not WIVES, for the slave women are preferred in many instances; and if these *idols* but nod, or lift a finger, woe to the poor victim: kicks, cuffs and stripes are sure to follow. Masters are frequently compelled to sell this class of their slaves, out of deference to the feelings of their white wives; and shocking and scandalous as it may seem for a man to sell his own blood to the traffickers in human flesh, it is often an act of humanity toward the slave-child to be thus removed from his merciless tormentors.

* * *

After what I have now said of the circumstances of my mother, and my relations to her, the reader will not be surprised, nor be disposed to censure me, when I tell but the simple truth, viz: that I received the tidings of her death with no strong emotions of sorrow for her, and with very little regret for myself on account of her loss. I had to learn the value of my mother long after her death, and by witnessing the devotion of other mothers to their children.

There is not, beneath the sky, an enemy to filial affection so destructive as slavery. It had made my brothers and sisters strangers to me; it converted the mother that bore me, into a myth; it shrouded my father in mystery, and left me without an intelligible beginning in the world.

My mother died when I could not have been more than eight or nine years old, on one of old master's farms in Tuckahoe, in the neighborhood of Hillsborough. Her grave is, as the grave of the dead at sea, unmarked, and without stone or stake.

* * *

III

Although my old master—Capt. Anthony—gave me at first . . . very little attention, and although that little was of a remarkably mild and gentle description, a few months only were sufficient to convince me that mildness and gentleness were not the prevailing or governing traits of his character. These excellent qualities were displayed only occasionally. He could, when it suited him, appear to be literally insensible to the claims of humanity, when appealed to by the helpless against an aggressor, and he could himself commit outrages, deep, dark and nameless. Yet he was not by nature worse than other men. Had he been brought up in a free state, surrounded by the just restraints of free society—restraints which are necessary to the freedom of all its members, alike and equally—Capt. Anthony might have been as humane a man, and every way as respectable, as many who now oppose the slave system; certainly as humane and respectable as are members of society generally. The slaveholder, as well as the slave, is the victim of the slave system. A man's character greatly takes its hue and shape from the form and color of things about him. Under the whole heavens there is no relation more unfavorable to the development of honorable character, than that sustained by the slaveholder to the slave. Reason is imprisoned here, and passions run wild. Like the fires of the prairie, once lighted, they are at the mercy of every wind, and must burn, till they have consumed all that is combustible within their remorseless grasp. Capt. Anthony could be kind, and, at times, he even showed an affectionate disposition. Could the reader have seen him gently leading me by the hand—as he sometimes did—patting me on the head, speaking to me in soft, caressing tones and calling me his "little Indian boy," he would have deemed him a kind old man, and, really, almost fatherly. But the pleasant moods of a slaveholder are remarkably brittle; they are easily snapped; they neither come often, nor remain long. His temper is subjected to perpetual trials; but, since these trials are never borne patiently, they add nothing to his natural stock of patience.

* * *

Howsoever the slaveholder may allow himself to act toward his slave, and, whatever cruelty he may deem it wise, for example's sake, or for the gratification of his humor, to inflict, he cannot, in the absence of all provocation, look with pleasure upon the bleeding wounds of a defenseless slave-woman. When he drives her from his presence without redress, or the hope of redress, he acts, generally, from motives of policy, rather than from a hardened nature, or from innate brutality. Yet, let but his own temper be stirred, his own passions get loose, and the slave-owner will go *far beyond* the overseer in cruelty. He will convince the slave that his wrath is far more terrible and boundless, and vastly more to be dreaded, than that of the underling overseer. What may have been mechanically and heartlessly done by the overseer, is now done with a will. The man who now wields the lash is irresponsible. He may, if he pleases, cripple or kill, without fear of consequences; except in so far as it may concern profit or loss. To a man of violent temper—as my old master was—this was but a very slender and inefficient restraint. I have seen him in a tempest of passion, such as I have just described—a passion into which entered all the bitter ingredients of pride, hatred, envy, jealousy, and the thirst for revenge.

The circumstances which I am about to narrate, and which gave rise to this fearful tempest of passion, are not singular nor isolated in slave life, but are common in every slaveholding community in which I have lived. They are incidental to the relation of master and slave, and exist in all sections of slaveholding countries.

The reader will have noticed that, in enumerating the names of the slaves who lived with my old master, *Esther* is mentioned. This was a young woman who possessed that which is ever a curse to the slave-girl; namely,—personal beauty. She was tall, well formed, and made a fine appearance. The daughters of Col. Lloyd could scarcely surpass her in personal charms. Esther was courted by Ned Roberts, and he was as fine looking a young man, as she was a woman. He was the son of a favorite slave of Col. Lloyd. Some slaveholders would have been glad to promote the marriage of two such persons; but, for some reason or other, my old master took it upon him to break up the growing intimacy between Esther and Edward. He strictly ordered her to quit the company of said Roberts, telling her that he would punish her severely if he ever found her again in Edward's company. This unnatural and heartless order was, of course, broken. A woman's love is not to be annihilated by the peremptory command of any one, whose breath is in his nostrils. It was impossible to keep Edward and Esther apart. Meet they would, and meet they did. Had old master been a man of honor and purity, his motives, in this matter, might have been viewed more favorably. As it was, his motives were as abhorrent, as his methods were foolish and contemptible. It was too evident that he was not concerned for the girl's welfare. It is one of the damning characteristics of the slave system, that it robs its victims of every earthly incentive to a holy life. The fear of God, and the hope of heaven, are found sufficient to sustain many slave-women, amidst the snares and dangers of their strange lot; but, this side of God and heaven, a slave-woman is at the mercy of the power, caprice and passion of her owner. Slavery provides no means for the honorable continuance of the race. Marriage—as imposing obligations on the parties to it—has no existence here, except in such hearts as are purer and higher than the standard morality around them. It is one of the consolations of my life, that I know of many honorable instances of persons who maintained their honor, where all around was corrupt.

Esther was evidently much attached to Edward, and abhorred—as she had reason to do—the tyrannical and base behavior of old master. Edward was young, and fine looking, and he loved and courted her. He might have been her husband, in the high sense just alluded to; but WHO and *what* was this old master? His attentions were plainly brutal and selfish, and it was as natural that Esther should loathe him, as that she should love Edward. Abhorred and circumvented as he was, old master, having the power, very easily took revenge. I happened to see this exhibition of his rage and cruelty toward Esther. The time selected was singular. It was early in the morning, when all besides was still, and before any of the family, in the house or kitchen, had left their beds. I saw but few of the shocking preliminaries, for the cruel work had begun before I awoke. I was probably awakened by the shrieks and piteous cries of poor Esther. My sleeping place was on the floor of a little, rough closet, which opened into the kitchen; and through the cracks of its unplaned boards, I could distinctly see and hear what was going on, without being seen by old master. Esther's wrists were firmly tied, and the twisted rope was fastened to a strong staple in a heavy wooden joist above, near the fireplace. Here she stood, on a bench, her arms tightly drawn over her breast. Her back and shoulders were bare to the waist. Behind her stood old master, with cowskin in hand, preparing his barbarous work with all manner of harsh, coarse, and tantalizing epithets. The screams of his victim were most piercing. He was cruelly deliberate, and protracted the torture, as one who was delighted with the scene. Again and again he drew the hateful whip through his hand, adjusting it with a view of dealing the most pain-giving blow. Poor Esther had never yet been severely whipped, and her shoulders were plump and tender. Each blow, vigorously laid on, brought screams as well as blood. *"Have mercy; Oh! have mercy"* she cried; *"I won't do so no more;"* but her piercing cries seemed only to increase his fury. His answers to them are too coarse and blasphemous to be produced here. The whole scene, with all its attendants, was revolting and shocking, to the last degree; and when the motives of this brutal castigation are considered, language has no power to convey a just sense of its awful criminality. After laying on some thirty or forty stripes, old master untied his suffering victim, and let her get down. She could scarcely stand, when untied. From my heart I pitied her, and—child though I was—the outrage kindled in me a feeling far from peaceful; but I was hushed, terrified, stunned, and could do nothing, and the fate of Esther might be mine next. The scene here described was often repeated in the case of poor Esther, and her life, as I knew it, was one of wretchedness.

* * *

IV

[These incidents led me] to inquire into the nature and history of slavery. *Why am I a slave? Why are some people slaves, and others masters? Was there ever a time when this was not so? How did the relation commence?* These were the perplexing questions which began now to claim my thoughts, and to exercise the weak powers of my mind, for I was still but a child, and knew less than children of the same age in the free states. As my questions concerning these things were only put to children a little older, and little better informed than myself, I was not rapid in reaching a solid footing. By some means I learned from these inquiries, that *"God, up in the sky,"* made every body; and that he made *white* people to be masters and mistresses, and *black* people to be slaves. This did not satisfy me, nor lessen my interest in the subject. I was told, too, that God was good, and that He knew what was best for me, and best for everybody. This was less satisfactory than the first statement; because it came, point blank, against all my notions of goodness. It was not good to let old master cut the flesh off Esther, and make her cry so. Besides, how did people know that God made black people to be slaves? Did they go up in the sky and learn it? or, did He come down and tell them so? All was dark here. It was some relief to my hard notions of the goodness of God, that, although he made white men to be slaveholders, he did not make them to be *bad* slaveholders, and that, in due time, he would punish the bad slaveholders; that he would, when they died, send them to the bad place, where they would be "burnt up." Nevertheless, I could not reconcile the relation of slavery with my crude notions of goodness.

Then, too, I found that there were puzzling exceptions to this theory of slavery on both sides, and in the middle. I knew of blacks who were *not* slaves; I knew of whites who were *not* slaveholders; and I knew of persons who were *nearly* white, who were slaves. *Color,* therefore, was a very unsatisfactory basis for slavery.

Once, however, engaged in the inquiry, I was not very long in finding out the true solution of the matter. It was not *color,* but *crime,* not *God,* but *man,* that afforded the true explanation of the existence of slavery; nor was I long in finding out another important truth, viz: what man can make, man can unmake. The appalling darkness faded away, and I was master of the subject. There were slaves here, direct from Guinea; and there were many who could say that their fathers and mothers were stolen from Africa—forced from their homes, and compelled to serve as slaves. This, to me, was knowledge; but it was a kind of knowledge which filled me with a burning hatred of slavery, increased my suffering, and left me without the means of breaking away from my bondage. Yet it was knowledge quite worth possessing. I could not have been more than seven or eight years old, when I began to make this subject my study. It was with me in the woods and fields; along the shore of the river, and wherever my boyish wanderings led me; and though I was, at that time, quite ignorant of the existence of the free states, I distinctly remember being, *even then,* most strongly impressed with the idea of being a freeman some day. This cheering assurance was an inborn dream of my human nature—a constant menace to slavery—and one which all the powers of slavery were unable to silence or extinguish.

* * *

The remark is not unfrequently made, that slaves are the most contented and happy laborers in the world. They dance and sing, and make all manner of joyful noises—so they do; but it is a great mistake to suppose them happy because they sing. The songs of the slave represent the sorrows, rather than the joys, of his heart; and he is relieved by them, only as an aching heart is relieved by its tears. Such is the constitution of the human mind, that, when pressed to extremes, it often avails itself of the most opposite methods. Extremes meet in mind as in matter. When the slaves on board of the "Pearl" were overtaken, arrested, and carried to prison—their hopes for freedom blasted—as they marched in chains they sang, and found (as Emily Edmunson tells us) a melancholy relief in singing. The singing of a man cast away on a desolate island, might be as appropriately considered an evidence of his contentment and happiness, as the singing of a slave. Sorrow and desolation have their songs, as well as joy and peace. Slaves sing more to *make* themselves happy, than to express their happiness.

It is the boast of slaveholders, that their slaves enjoy more of the physical comforts of life than the peasantry of any country in the world. My experience contradicts this. The men and the women slaves on Col. Lloyd's farm, received, as their monthly allowance of food, eight pounds of pickled pork, or their equivalent in fish. The pork was often tainted, and the fish was of the poorest quality—herrings, which would bring very little if offered for sale in any northern market. With their pork or fish, they had one bushel of Indian meal—unbolted—of which quite fifteen per cent. was fit only to feed pigs. With this, one pint of salt was given; and this was the entire monthly allowance of a full grown slave, working constantly in the open field, from morning until night, every day in the month except Sunday, and living on a fraction more than a quarter of a pound of meat per day, and less than a peck of corn-meal per week. There is no kind of work that a man can do which requires a better supply of food to prevent physical exhaustion, than the field-work of a slave. So much for the slave's allowance of food; now for his raiment. The yearly allowance of clothing for the slaves on this plantation, consisted of two tow-linen shirts—such linen as the coarsest crash towels are made of; one pair of trowsers of the same material, for summer, and a pair of trowsers and a jacket of woolen, most slazily put together, for winter; one pair of yarn stockings, and one pair of shoes of the coarsest description. The slave's entire apparel could not have cost more than eight dollars per year. The allowance of food and clothing for the little children, was committed to their mothers, or to the older slave-women having the care of them. Children who were unable to work in the field, had neither shoes, stockings, jackets nor trowsers given them. Their clothing consisted of two coarse tow-linen shirts . . . per year; and when these failed them, as they often did, they went naked until the next allowance day. Flocks of little children from five to ten years old, might be seen on Col. Lloyd's plantation, as destitute of clothing as any little heathen on the west coast of Africa; and this, not merely during the summer months, but during the frosty weather of March. The little girls were no better off than the boys; all were nearly in a state of nudity.

As to beds to sleep on, they were known to none of the field hands; nothing but a coarse blanket—not so good as those used in the north to cover horses—was given them, and this only to the men and women. The children stuck themselves in holes and corners, about the quarters; often in the corner of the huge chimneys, with their feet in the ashes to keep them warm. The want of beds, however, was not considered a very great privation. Time to sleep was of far greater importance, for, when the day's work is done, most of the slaves have their washing, mending and cooking to do; and, having few or none of the ordinary facilities for doing such things, very many of their sleeping hours are consumed in necessary preparations for the duties of the coming day.

The sleeping apartments—if they may be called such—have little regard to comfort or decency. Old and young, male and female, married and single, drop down upon the common clay floor, each covering up with his or her blanket,—the only protection they have from cold or exposure. The night, however, is shortened at both ends. The slaves work often as long as they can see, and are late in cooking and mending for the coming day; and, at the first gray streak of morning, they are summoned to the field by the driver's horn.

More slaves are whipped for oversleeping than for any other fault. Neither age nor sex finds any favor. The overseer stands at the quarter door, armed with stick and cowskin, ready to whip any who may be a few minutes behind time. When the horn is blown, there is a rush for the door, and the hindermost one is sure to get a blow from the overseer. Young mothers who worked in the field, were allowed an hour, about ten o'clock in the morning, to go home to nurse their children. Sometimes they were compelled to take their children with them, and to leave them in the corner of the fences, to prevent loss of time in nursing them. The overseer generally rides about the field on horseback. A cowskin and a hickory stick are his constant companions. The cowskin is a kind of whip seldom seen in the northern states. It is made entirely of untanned, but dried, ox hide, and is about as hard as a piece of well-seasoned live oak. It is made of various sizes, but the usual length is about three feet. The part held in the hand is nearly an inch in thickness; and, from the extreme end of the butt or handle, the cowskin tapers its whole length to a point. This makes it quite elastic and springy. A blow with it, on the hardest back, will gash the flesh, and make the blood start. Cowskins are painted red, blue and green, and are the favorite slave whip. I think this whip worse than the "cat-o'-nine-tails." It condenses the whole strength of the arm to a single point, and comes with a spring that makes the air whistle. It is a terrible instrument, and is so handy, that the overseer can always have it on his person, and ready for use. The temptation to use it is ever strong; and an overseer can, if disposed, always have cause for using it. With him, it is literally a word and a blow, and, in most cases, the blow comes first.

As a general rule, slaves do not come to the quarters for either breakfast or dinner, but take their "ash cake" with them, and eat it in the field. This was so on the home plantation; probably, because the distance from the quarter to the field, was sometimes two, and even three miles.

The dinner of the slaves consisted of a huge piece of ash cake, and a small piece of pork, or two salt herrings. Not having ovens, nor any suitable cooking utensils, the slaves mixed their meal with a little water, to such thickness that a spoon would stand erect in it; and, after the wood had burned away to coals and ashes, they would place the dough between oak leaves and lay it carefully in the ashes, completely covering it; hence, the bread is called ash cake. The surface of this peculiar bread is covered with ashes, to the depth of a sixteenth part of an inch, and the ashes, certainly, do not make it very grateful to the teeth, nor render it very palatable. The bran, or coarse part of the meal, is baked with the fine, and bright scales run through the bread. This bread, with its ashes and bran, would disgust and choke a northern man, but it is quite liked by the slaves. They eat it with avidity, and are more concerned about the quantity than about the quality. They are far too scantily provided for, and are worked too steadily, to be much concerned for the quality of their food. The few minutes allowed them at dinner time, after partaking of their coarse repast, are variously spent. Some lie down on the "turning row," and go to sleep; others draw together, and talk; and others are at work with needle and thread, mending their tattered garments. Sometimes you may hear a wild, hoarse laugh arise from a circle, and often a song. Soon, however, the overseer comes dashing through the field. "*Tumble up! Tumble up,* and to *work, work,*" is the cry; and, now, from twelve o'clock (mid-day) till dark, the human cattle are in motion, wielding their clumsy hoes; hurried on by no hope of reward, no sense of gratitude, no love of children, no prospect of bettering their condition; nothing, save the dread and terror of the slave-driver's lash. So goes one day, and so comes and goes another.

Huck Finn and his father

MARK TWAIN

Huckleberry Finn

(1884)

Huckleberry Finn is one of the great epics of American literature. It tells about the encounters of young Huck with the Mississippi River and the "civilized" life that lines its shores. The two are sufficiently opposed to sharpen Huck's own sense of right and wrong; like most young people, he expects life to be fair and is always "in a sweat" over someone else's predicament. When fate puts him and "Nigger Jim" together on a raft floating down the great river, a bond of love grows between them that makes the evils of slavery increasingly plain to Huck.

This novel was once banned from many public schools and libraries for its subversive nature: its questioning of moral and religious codes as well as its bad language and grammar. Yet

in this picturesque story, as Lionel Trilling observes, there is the virtue of American colloquial speech, an ease and freedom, a simplicity and gracefulness of expression. Ernest Hemingway in fact remarked that "all modern American literature comes from one book by Mark Twain called Huckleberry Finn."

'How do you come to be here, Jim, and how'd you get here?'

He looked pretty uneasy, and didn't say nothing for a minute. Then he says:

'Maybe I better not tell.'

'Why, Jim?'

'Well, dey's reasons. But you wouldn't tell on me ef I 'uz to tell you, would you, Huck?'

'Blamed if I would, Jim.'

'Well, I b'lieve you, Huck. I—I *run off*.'

'Jim!'

'But mind, you said you wouldn't tell—you know you said you wouldn't tell, Huck.'

'Well, I did. I said I wouldn't, and I'll stick to it. Honest *injun* I will. People would call me a low-down Ablitionist and despise me for keeping mum—but that don't make no difference. I ain't agoing to tell, and I ain't agoing back there anyways. So now, le's know all about it.'

'Well, you see, it 'uz dis way. Ole Missus—dat's Miss Watson—she pecks on me all de time, en treats me pooty rough, but she awluz said she wouldn' sell me down to Orleans. But I noticed dey wuz a nigger trader roun' de place considable, lately, en I begin to git oneasy. Well, one night I creeps to de do', pooty late, en de do' warn't quite shet, en I hear ole missus tell the widder she gwyne to sell me down to Orleans, but she didn' want to, but she could git eight hund'd dollars for me, en it 'uz sich a big stack o' money she couldn' resis'. De widder she try to git her to say she wouldn' do it, but I never waited to hear de res'. I lit out mighty quick, I tell you.

'I tuck out en shin down de hill en 'spec to steal a skift 'long de sho' som'ers 'bove de town, but dey wuz people a-stirrin' yit, so I hid in de old tumble-down copper shop on de bank to wait for everybody to go 'way. Well, I wuz dah all night. Dey wuz somebody roun' all de time. 'Long 'bout six in the mawnin', skifts begin to go by, en 'bout eight er nine every skift dat went 'long wuz talkin' 'bout how yo' pap come over to de town en say you's killed. Dese las' skifts wuz full o' ladies en genlmen agoin' over for to see de place. Sometimes dey'd pull up at de sho' en takes a res' b'fo' dey started acrost, so by de talk I got to know all 'bout de killin'. I 'uz powerful sorry you's killed, Huck, but I ain't no mo', now.

'I laid dah under de shavins all day. I 'uz hungry, but I warn't afeared; bekase I knowed ole missus en de widder wuz goin' to start to de camp-meetn' right arter breadfas' en be gone all day, en dey knows I goes off wid de cattle 'bout daylight, so dey wouldn' 'spec to see me roun' de place, en so dey wouldn' miss me tell arter dark in de evenin'. De yuther servants wouldn' miss me, kase dey'd shin out en take holiday, soon as de ole folks 'uz' out'n de way.

'Well, when it come dark I tuck out up de river road, en went 'bout two mile er more to whah dey warn't no houses. I'd made up my mine 'bout what i's agwyne to do. You see ef I kep' on tryin' to git away afoot, de dogs 'ud track me; ef I stole a skift to cross over, dey'd miss dat skift, you see, en dey'd know 'bout whah I'd lan' on de yuther side en whah to pick up my track. So I says, a raff is what I's arter; it doan' *make* no track.

'I see a light a-comin' roun' de p'int, bymeby, so I wade' in en shove' a log ahead o' me, en swum more'n half-way acrost de river, en got in 'mongst de drift-wood, en kep' my head down low, en kinder swum agin de current tell the raff come along. Den I swum to de stern uv it, en tuck aholt. It clouded up en 'uz pooty dark for a little while. So I clumb up en laid down on de planks. De men 'uz all 'way yonder in de middle, whah de lantern wuz. De river wuz arisin' en dey wuz a good current; so I reck'n'd 'at by fo' in de mawnin' I'd be twenty-five mile down de river, en den I'd slip in, jis' b'fo daylight, en swim asho' en take to de woods on de Illinoi side.

'But I didn' have no luck. When we 'uz mos' down to de head er de islan', a man begin to come aft wid de lantern. I see it warn't no use fer to wait, so I slid overboard, en struck out fer de islan'. Well, I had a notion I could lan' mos' anywhers, but I couldn't—bank too bluff. I 'uz mos' to de foot er de islan' b'fo' I foun' a good place. I went into de woods en jedged I wouldn' fool wid raffs no mo', long as dey move de lantern roun' so. I had my pipe en a plug er dog-leg, en some matches in my cap, en dey warn't wet, so I 'uz all right.'

'And so you ain't had no meat nor breat to eat all this time? Why didn't you get mud-turkles?'

'How you gwyne to git'm? You can't slip up on um en grab um; en how's a body gwyne to hit um wid a rock? How could a body do it in de night? en I warn't gwyne to show myself on de bank in de day-time.'

'Well, that's so. You've had to keep in the woods all the time, of course. Did you hear 'em shooting the cannon?'

'Oh, yes. I knowed dey was arter you. I see um go by heah; watched um thoo de bushes.'

* * *

I wanted to go and look at a place right about the middle of the island, that I'd found when I was exploring; so we started, and soon got to it, because the island was only three miles long and a quarter of mile wide.

This place was a tolerable long steep hill or ridge, about forty foot high. We had a rough time getting to the top, the sides was so steep and the bushes so thick. We tramped and clumb around all over it, and by-and-by found a good big cavern in the rock, most up to the top on the side towards Illinois. The cavern was as big as two or three rooms bunched together, and Jim could stand up straight in it. It was cool in there. Jim was for putting our traps in there, right away, but I said we didn't want to be climbing up and down there all the time.

Jim said if we had the canoe hid in a good place, and had all the traps in the cavern, we could rush there if anybody was to come to the island, and they would never find us without dogs. And besides, he said them little birds had said it was going to rain, and did I want the things to get wet?

So we went back and got the canoe and paddled up abreast the cavern, and lugged all the traps up there. Then we hunted up a place close by to hide the canoe in, amongst the thick willows. We took some fish off of the lines and set them again, and begun to get ready for dinner.

The door of the cavern was big enough to roll a hogshead in, and on one side of the door the floor stuck out a little bit and was flat and a good place to build a fire on. So we built it there and cooked dinner.

We spread the blankets inside for a carpet, and eat our dinner in there. We put all the other things handy at the back of the cavern. Pretty soon it darkened up and begun to thunder and lighten; so the birds was right about it. Directly it begun to rain, and it rained like all fury, too, and I never see the wind blow so. It was one of these regular summer storms. It would get so dark that it looked all blue-black outside, and lovely; and the rain would thrash along by so thick that the trees off a little way looked dim and spider-webby; and here would come a blast of wind that would bend the trees down and turn up the pale underside of the leaves; and then a perfect ripper of a gust would follow along and set the branches to tossing their arms as if they was just wild; and next, when it was just about the bluest and blackest—*fst!* it was as bright as glory and you'd have a little glimpse of tree-tops a-plunging about, away off yonder in the storm, hundreds of yards further than you could see before; dark as sin again in a second, and now you'd hear the thunder let go with an awful crash and then go rumbling, grumbling, tumbling down the sky towards the underside of the world, like rolling empty barrels downstairs, where it's long stairs and they bounce a good deal, you know.

'Jim, this is nice,' I says. 'I wouldn't want to be no-where else but here. Pass me along another hunk of fish and some hot corn-bread.'

'Well, you wouldn't a ben here, 'f it hadn't ben for Jim. You'd a ben down dah in de woods widout any dinner, en gittin' mos' drownded, too, dat you would, honey. Chickens knows when it's gwyne to rain, en so do de birds, chile.'

The river went on raising and raising for ten or twelve days, till at last it was over the banks. The water was three or four foot deep on the island in the low places and on the Illinois bottom. On that side it was a good many miles wide; but on the Missouri side it was the same old distance across—a half a mile—because the Missouri shore was just a wall of high bluffs.

Daytimes we paddled all over the island in the canoe. It was mighty cool and shady in the deep woods even if the sun was blazing outside. We went winding in and out amongst the trees; and sometimes the vines hung so thick we had to back away and go some other way. Well, on every old broken-down tree you could see rabbits, and snakes, and such things; and when the island had been overflowed a day or two, they got so tame, on account of being hungry, that you could paddle right up and put your hand on them if you wanted to; but not the snakes and turtles—they would slide off in the water. The ridge our cavern was in was full of them. We could a had pets enough if we'd wanted them.

One night we catched a little section of a lumber raft—nice pine planks. It was twelve foot wide and about fifteen or sixteen foot long, and the top stood above-water six or seven inches, a solid level floor. We could see saw-logs go by in the daylight, sometimes, but we let them go; we didn't show ourselves in daylight.

Another night, when we was up at the head of the island, just before daylight, here comes a frame house down, on the west side. She was a two-storey, and tilted over, considerable. We paddled out and got aboard—clumb in at an upstairs window. But it was too dark to see yet, so we made the canoe fast and set in her to wait for daylight.

The light begun to come before we got to the foot of the island. Then we looked in at the window. We could make out a bed, and a table, and two old chairs, and lots of things around on the floor; and there was clothes hanging against the wall. There was something laying on the floor in the far corner that looked like a man. So Jim says:

'Hello, you!'

But it didn't budge. So I hollered again, and then Jim says:

'De man ain't asleep—he's dead. You hold still—I'll go en see.'

He went and bent down and looked, and says:

'It's a dead man. Yes, indeedy; naked, too. He's ben shot in de back. I reck'n he's ben dead two er three days. Come in, Huck, but doan' look at his face—it's too gashly.'

I didn't look at him at all. Jim throwed some old rags over him, but he needn't done it; I didn't want to see him. There was heaps of old greasy cards scattered around over the floor, and old whisky bottles, and a couple of masks made out of black cloth; and all over the walls was the ignorantest kind of words and pictures, made with charcoal. There was two old dirty calico dresses, and a sun-bonnet, and some women's under-clothes, hanging against the wall, and some men's clothing, too. We put the lot into the canoe; it might come good. There was a boy's old speckled straw hat on the floor; I took that too. And there was a bottle that had had milk in it; and it had a rag stopper for a baby to suck. We would a took the bottle, but it was broke. There was a seedy old chest, and an old hair trunk with the hinges broke. They stood open, but there warn't nothing left in them that was any account. The way things was scattered about, we reckoned the people left in a hurry and warn't fixed so as to carry off most of their stuff.

We got an old tin lantern, and a butcher knife without any handle, and a bran-new Barlow knife worth two bits in any store, and a lot of tallow candles, and a tin candlestick, and a gourd, and a tin cup, and a ratty old bed-quilt off the bed, and a reticule with needles and pins and beeswax and buttons and thread and all such truck in it, and a hatchet and some nails, and a fish-line as thick as my little finger, with some monstrous hooks on it, and a roll of buckskin, and a leather dog-collar, and a horse-shoe, and some vials of medicine that didn't have no label on them; and just as we was leaving I found a tolerable good curry-comb, and Jim he found a ratty old fiddle-bow, and a wooden leg. The straps was broke off of it, but barring that, it was a good enough leg, though it was too long for me and not long enough for Jim, and we couldn't find the other one, though we hunted all around.

And so, take it all around, we made a good haul. When we was ready to shove off, we was a quarter of a mile below the island, and it was pretty broad day; so I made Jim lay down in the canoe and cover up with the quilt, because if he set up, people could tell he was a nigger a good ways off. I paddled over to the Illinois shore, and drifted down most a half a mile doing it. I crept up the dead water under the bank, and hadn't no accidents and didn't see nobody. We got home all safe.

* * *

Next morning I said it was getting slow and dull, and I wanted to get a stirring up, some way. I said I reckoned I would slip over the river and find out what was going on. Jim liked that notion; but he said I must go in the dark and look sharp. Then he studied it over and said, Couldn't I put on some of them old things and dress up like a girl? That was a good notion, too. So we shortened up one of the calico gowns and I turned up my trowser-legs to my knees and got into it. Jim hitched it behind with the hooks, and it was a fair fit. I put on the sun-bonnet and tied it under my chin, and then for a body to look in and see my face was like looking down a joint of stove-pipe. Jim said nobody would know me, even in the daytime, hardly. I practised around all day to get the hang of the things, and by-and-by I could do pretty well in them, only Jim said I didn't walk like a girl; and he said I must quit pulling up my gown to get at my britches pocket. I took notice, and done better.

I started up the Illinois shore in the canoe just after dark.

I started across to the town from a little below the ferry landing, and the drift of the current fetched me in at the bottom of the town. I tied up and started along the bank. There was a light burning in a little shanty that hadn't been lived in for a long time, and I wondered who had took up quarters there. I slipped up and peeped in at the window. There was a woman about forty years old in there, knitting by a candle that was on a pine table. I didn't know her face; she was a stranger, for you couldn't start a face in that town that I didn't know.

Now this was lucky, because I was weakening; I was getting afraid I had come; people might know my voice and find me out. But if this woman had been in such a little town two days she could tell me all I wanted to know; so I knocked at the door, and made up my mind I wouldn't forget I was a girl.

'Come in,' says the woman, and I did. She says: 'Take a cheer.'

I done it. She looked me all over with her little shiny eyes, and says:

'What might your name be?'

'Sarah Williams.'

'Where 'bouts do you live? In this neighbourhood?'

'No'm. In Hookerville, seven mile below. I've walked all the way, and I'm all tired out.'

'Hungry, too, I reckon. I'll find you something.'

'No'm, I ain't hungry. I was so hungry I had to stop two mile below here at a farm; so I ain't hungry no more. It's what makes me so late. My mother's down sick, and out of money and everything, and I come to tell my uncle, Abner Moore. He lives at the upper end of the town, she says. I hain't ever been here before. Do you know him?'

'No; but I don't know everybody yet. I haven't lived here quite two weeks. It's a considerable ways to the upper end of the town. You better stay here all night. Take off you bonnet.'

'No,' I says, 'I'll rest awhile, I reckon, and go on. I ain't afeard of the dark.'

She said she wouldn't let me go by myself, but her husband would be in by-and-by, maybe in a hour and a half, and she'd send him along with me. Then she got to talking about her husband, and about her relations up the river, and her relations down the river, and about how much better off they used to was, and how they didn't know but they'd made a mistake coming to our town, instead of letting well alone—and so on and so on, till I was afeared *I* had made a mistake coming to her to find out what was going on in the town; but by-and-by she dropped on to pap and the murder, and then I was pretty willing to let her clatter right along. She told about me and Tom Sawyer finding the six thousand dollars (only she got it ten) and all about pap and what a hard lot he was, and what a hard lot I was, and at last she got down to where I was murdered. I says:

'Who done it? We've heard considerable about these goings on, down in Hookerville, but we don't know who 'twas that killed Huck Finn.'

'Well, I reckon there's a right smart chance of people *here* that'd like to know who killed him. Some thinks old Finn done it himself.'

'No—is that so?'

'Most everybody thought it at first. He'll never know how nigh he come to getting lynched. But before night they changed around and judged it was done by a runaway nigger named Jim.'

'Why *he*—'

I stopped. I reckoned I better keep still. She run on, and never noticed I had put in at all.

'The nigger run off the very night Huck Finn was killed. So there's a reward out for him—three hundred dollars. And there's a reward out for old Finn too—two hundred dollars. You see, he come to town the morning after the murder, and told about it, and was out with 'em on the ferry-boat hunt, and right away after he up and left. Before night they wanted to lynch him, but he was gone, you see. Well, next day they found out the nigger was gone; they found out he hadn't ben seen sence ten o'clock the night the murder was done. So then they put it on him, you see, and while they was full of it, next day back comes old Finn and went boo-hooing to Judge Thatcher to get money to hunt for the nigger all over Illinois with. The judge give him some, and that evening he got drunk and was around till after midnight with a couple of mighty hard-looking strangers, and then went off with them. Well, he hain't come back sence, and they ain't looking for him back till this thing blows over a little, for people thinks now that he killed his boy and fixed things so folks would think robbers done it, and then he'd get Huck's money without having to bother a long time with a lawsuit. People do say he warn't any good to do it. Oh, he's sly, I reckon. If he don't come back for a year, he'll be all right. You can't prove anything on him, you know; everything will be quieted down then, and he'll walk into Huck's money as easy as nothing.'

'Yes, I reckon so, 'm. I don't see nothing in the way of it. Has everybody quit thinking the nigger done it?'

'Oh, no, not everybody. A good many thinks he done it. But they'll get the nigger pretty soon, now, and maybe they can scare it out of him.'

'Why, are they after him yet?'

'Well, you're innocent, ain't you! Does three hundred dollars lay round every day for people to pick up? Some folks thinks the nigger ain't far from here. I'm one of them—but I hain't talked it around. A few days ago I was talking with an old couple that lives next door in the log shanty, and they happened to say hardly anybody ever goes to that island over yonder that they call Jackson's Island. Don't anybody live there? says I. No, nobody, says they. I didn't say any more, but I done some thinking. I was pretty near certain I'd seen smoke over there, about the head of the island, a day or two before that, so I says to myself, like as not that nigger's hiding over there; anyway, says I, it's worth the touble to give the place a hunt. I hain't seen any smoke sence, so I reckon maybe he's gone, if it was him; but husband's going over to see—him and another man. He was gone up the river; but he got back to-day and I told him as soon as he got here two hours ago.'

I had got so uneasy I couldn't set still. I had to do something with my hands; so I took up a needle off of the table and went to threading it. My hands shook, and I was making a bad job of it. When the woman stopped talking, I looked up, and she was looking at me pretty curious, and smiling a little. I put down the needle and thread and let on to be interested—and I was, too—and says:

"Three hundred dollars is a power of money. I wish my mother could get it. Is your husband going over there tonight?'

'Oh, yes. He went up-town with the man I was telling you of, to get a boat and see if they could borrow another gun. They'll go over after midnight.'

'Couldn't they see better if they was to wait till daytime?'

'Yes. And couldn't the nigger see better, too? After midnight he'll likely be asleep, and they can slip around through the woods and hunt up his camp-fire all the better for the dark, if he's got one.'

'I didn't think of that.'

The woman kept looking at me pretty curious, and I didn't feel a bit comfortable. Pretty soon she says:

'What did you say your name was, honey?'

'M—Mary Williams.'

Somehow it didn't seem to me that I said it was Mary before, so I didn't look up; seemed to me I said it was Sarah; so I felt sort of cornered, and was afeard maybe I was looking it too. I wished the woman would say something more; the longer she set still, the uneasier I was. But now she says:

'Honey, I thought you said it was Sarah when you first come in?'

'Oh, yes'm, I did. Sarah Mary Williams. Sarah's my first name. Some calls me Sarah, some calls me Mary.'

'Oh, that's the way of it?'

'Yes'm.'

I was feeling better, then, but I wished I was out of there, anyway. I couldn't look up yet.

Well, the woman fell to talking about how hard times was, and how poor they had to live, and how the rats was as free as if they owned the place, and so forth, and so on, and then I got easy again. She was right about the rats. You'd see one stick his nose out of a hole in the corner every little while. She said she had to have things handy to throw at them when she was alone, or they wouldn't give her no peace. She showed me a bar of lead, twisted up into a knot, and said she was a good shot with it generly, but she'd wrenched her arm a day or two ago, and didn't know whether she could throw true, now. But she watched for a chance, and directly she banged away at a rat, but she missed him wide, and said 'Ouch!' it hurt her arm so. Then she told me to try for the next one. I wanted to be getting away before the old man got back, but of course I didn't let on. I got the thing, and the first rat that showed his nose I let drive, and if he'd a stayed where he was he'd a been a tolerable sick rat. She said that that was first-rate, and she reckoned I would hive the next one. She went and got the lump of lead and fetched it back and brought along a hank of yarn, which she wanted me to help her with. I help up my two hands and she put the hank over them and went on talking about her and her husband's matters. But she broke off to say:

'Keep your eye on the rats. You better have the lead in your lap, handy.'

So she dropped the lump into my lap, just at that moment, and I clapped my legs together on it and she went on talking. But only about a minute. Then she took off the hank and looked me straight in the face, but very pleasant, and says:

'Come, now—what's your real name?'

'Wh-what, mum?'

'What's your real name? Is it Bill, or Tom, or Bob?—or what is it?'

I reckon I shook like a leaf, and I didn't know hardly what to do. But I says:

'Please to don't poke fun at a poor girl like me, mum. If I'm in the way, here, I'll—''

'No, you won't. Set down and stay where you are. I ain't going to hurt you, and I ain't going to tell on you, nuther. You just tell me your secret, and trust me. I'll keep it; and what's more, I'll help you. So'll my old man, if you want him to. You see, you're a runaway 'prentice—that's all. It ain't anything. There ain't any harm in it. You've been treated bad, and you made up your mind to cut. Bless you, child, I wouldn't tell on you. Tell me all about it, now—that's a good boy.'

So I said it wouldn't be no use to try to play it any longer, and I would just make a clean breast and tell her everything, but she mustn't go back on her promise. Then I told her my father and mother was dead, and the law had bound me out to a mean old farmer in the country thirty mile back from the river, and he treated me so bad I couldn't stand it no longer; he went away to be gone a couple of days, and so I took my chance and stole some of his daughter's old clothes, and cleared out, and I had been three nights coming the thirty miles; I travelled nights, and hid daytimes and slept, and the bag of bread and meat I carried from home lasted me all the way and I had a plenty. I said I believed my uncle, Abner Moore, would take care of me, and so that was why I struck out for this town of Goshen.

'Goshen, child? This ain't Goshen. This is St Petersburg. Goshen's ten mile further up the river. Who told you this was Goshen?'

'Why, a man I met at daybreak this morning, just as I was going to turn into the woods for my regular sleep. He told me when the roads forked I must take the right hand, and five mile would fetch me to Goshen.'

'He was drunk, I reckon. He told you exactly wrong.'

'Well, he did act like he was drunk, but it ain't no matter now. I got to be moving along. I'll fetch Goshen before daylight.'

'Hold on a minute. I'll put you up a snack to eat. You might want it.'

So she put me up a snack, and says:

'Say—when a cow's laying down, which end of her get up first? Answer up prompt, now—don't stop to study over it. Which end gets up first?'

'The hind end, mum.'

'Well, then, a horse?'

'The for'rard end, mum.'

'Which side of a tree does the most moss grow on?'

'North side.'

'If fifteen cows is browsing on a hill-side, how many of them eats with their heads pointed the same direction?'

'The whole fifteen, mum.'

'Well, I reckon you *have* lived in the country. I thought maybe you was trying to hocus me again. What's your real name, now?'

'George Peters, mum.'

'Well, try to remember it, George. Don't forget and tell me it's Elexander before you go, and then get out by saying it's George-Elexander when I catch you. And don't go about women in that old calico. You do a girl tolerable poor, but you might fool men, maybe. Bless you, child, when you set out to thread a needle, don't hold the thread still and fetch the needle up to it; hold the needle still and poke the thread at it—that's the way a woman most always does; but a man always does t'other way. And when you throw at a rat or anything, hitch yourself up a tip-toe, and fetch your hand up over your head as awkward as you can, and miss your rat about six or seven foot. Throw stiff-armed from the shoulder, like there was a pivot there for it to turn on—like a girl; not from the wrist and elbow, with your arm out to one side, like a boy. And mind you, when a girl tries to catch anything in her lap, she throws her knees apart; she don't clap them together, the way you did when you catched the lump of lead. Why, I spotted you for a boy when you was threading the needle; and I contrived the other things just to make certain. Now trot along to your uncle, Sarah Mary Williams George Elexander Peters, and if you get into trouble you send word to Mrs Judith Loftus, which is me, and I'll do what I can to get you out of it. Keep the river road, all the way, and next time you tramp, take shoes and socks with you. The river road's a rocky one, and your feet'll be in a condition when you get to Goshen, I reckon.'

I went up the bank about fifty yards, and then I doubled on my tracks and slipped back to where my canoe was, a good piece below the house. I jumped in and was off in a hurry. I went up-stream far enough to make the head of the island, and then started across. I took off the sun-bonnet, for I didn't want no blinders on, then. When I was about the middle, I hear the clock begin to strike; so I stops and listens; the sound come faint over the water, but clear—eleven. When

I struck the head of the island I never waited to blow, though I was most winded, but I shoved right into the timber where my old camp used to be, and started a good fire there on a high-and-dry spot.

Then I jumped in the canoe and dug out for our place a mile and a half below, as hard as I could go. I landed, and slopped through the timber and up the ridge and into the cavern. There Jim laid, sound asleep on the ground. I roused him out and says:

'Git up and hump yourself, Jim! There ain't a minute to lose. They're after us!'

Jim never asked no questions, he never said a word; but the way he worked for the next half an hour showed about how he was scared. By that time everything we had in the world was on our raft and she was ready to be shoved out from the willow cove where she was hid. We put out the camp-fire at the cavern the first thing, and didn't show a candle outside after that.

I took the canoe out from shore a little piece and took a look, but if there was a boat around I couldn't see it, for stars and shadows ain't good to see by. Then we got out the raft and slipped along down in the shade, past the foot of the island, dead still, never saying a word.

It must a been close on to one o'clock when we got below the island at last, and the raft did seem to go mighty slow. If a boat was to come along, we was going to take to the canoe and break for the Illinois shore; and it was well a boat didn't come, for we hadn't ever thought to put the gun into the canoe, or a fishing-line or anything to eat. We was in ruther too much of a sweat to think of so many things. It warn't good judgement to put *everything* on the raft.

If the men went to the island, I just expect they found the camp-fire I built, and watched it all night for Jim to come. Anyways, they stayed away from us, and if my building the fire never fooled them it warn't no fault of mine. I played it as low-down on them as I could.

When the first streak of day begun to show, we tied up to a tow-head in a big bend on the Illinois side, and hacked off cotton-wood branches with the hatchet and covered up the raft with them so she looked like there had been a cave-in in the bank there. A tow-head is a sand-bar that has cotton-woods on it as thick as harrow-teeth.

We had mountains on the Missouri shore and heavy timber on the Illinois side, and the channel was down the Missouri shore at that place, so we warn't afraid of anybody running across us. We laid there all day and watched the rafts and steamboats spin down the Missouri shore, and up-bound steamboats fight the big river in the middle. I told Jim all about the time I had jabbering with that woman; and Jim said she was a smart one, and if she was to start after us herself *she* wouldn't set down and watch a camp-fire—no, sir, she'd fetch a dog. Well, then, I said, why couldn't she tell her husband to fetch a dog? Jim said he bet she did think of it by the time the men was ready to start, and he believed they must a gone uptown to get a dog, and so they lost all that time, or else we wouldn't be here on a tow-head sixteen or seventeen mile below the village—no, indeedy, we would be in that same old town again. So I said I didn't care what was the reason they didn't get us, as long as they didn't.

When it was beginning to come on dark, we poked our heads out of the cotton-wood thicket and looked up, and down, and across; nothing in sight; so Jim took up some of the top planks of the raft and built a snug wigwam to get under in blazing weather and rainy, and to keep the things dry. Jim made a floor for the wigwam, and raised it a foot or more above the level of the raft, so now the blankets and all the traps was out of the reach of steamboat waves. Right in the middle of the wigwam we made a layer of dirt about five or six inches deep with a frame around it for to hold it to its place; this was to build a fire on in sloppy weather or chilly; the wigwam would keep it from being seen. We made an extra steering oar, too, because one of the others might get broke, on a snag or something. We fixed up a short forked stick to hang the old lantern on; because we must always light the lantern whenever we see a steamboat coming down-stream, to keep from getting run over; but we wouldn't have to light it for up-stream boats unless we see we was in what they call a 'crossing'; for the river was pretty high yet, very low banks being still a little under-water; so up-bound boats didn't always run the channel, but hunted easy water.

This second night we run between seven and eight hours, with a current that was making over four mile an hour. We catched fish, and talked, and we took a swim now and then to keep off sleepiness. It was kind of solemn, drifting down the big still river, laying on our backs looking up at the stars, and we didn't ever feel like talking loud, and it warn't often that we laughed, only a little kind of a low chuckle. We had mighty good weather, as a general thing, and nothing ever happened to us at all, that night, nor the next, nor the next.

Every night we passed towns, some of them away up on black hill-sides, nothing but just a shiny bed of lights, not a house could you see. The fifth night we passed St Louis, and it was like the whole world lit up. In St Petersburg they used to say there was twenty or thirty thousand people in St Louis, but I never believed it till I see that wonderful spread of lights at two o'clock that still night. There warn't a sound there; everybody was asleep.

Every night, now, I used to slip ashore, towards ten o'clock, at some little village, and buy ten or fifteen cents' worth of meal or bacon or other stuff to eat; and sometimes I lifted a chicken that warn't roosting comfortable, and took him along. Pap always said, take a chicken when you get a chance, because if you don't want him yourself you can easy find somebody that does, and a good deed ain't ever forgot. I never see pap when he didn't want the chicken himself, but that is what he used to say, anyway.

Mornings, before daylight, I slipped into corn-fields and borrowed a watermelon, or a mushmelon, or a punkin, or some new corn, or things of that kind. Pap always said it warn't no harm to borrow things, if you was meaning to pay them back, sometime; but the widow said it warn't anything but a soft name for stealing, and no decent body would do it. Jim said he reckoned the widow was partly right and pap was partly right; so the best way would be for us to pick out two or three things from the list and say we wouldn't borrow them any more—then he reckoned it wouldn't be no harm to borrow the others. So we talked it over all one night, drifting along down the river, trying to make up our minds whether to drop the watermelons, or the cantelopes, or the mushmelons, or what. But towards daylight we got it all settled satisfactory, and concluded to drop crab-apples and p'simmons. We warn't feeling just right before that, but it was all comfortable now. I was glad the way it came out, too, because crab-apples ain't ever good, and the p'simmons wouldn't be ripe for two or three months yet.

We shot a water-fowl, now and then, that got up too early in the morning or didn't go to bed early enough in the evening. Take it all around, we lived pretty high.

* * *

We judged that three nights more would fetch us to Cairo, at the bottom of Illinois, where the Ohio River comes in, and that was what we was after. We would sell the raft and get on a steamboat and go way up the Ohio amongst the free States, and then be out of trouble.

Well, the second night a fog begun to come on, and we made for a tow-head to tie to, for it wouldn't do to try to run in fog; but when I paddled ahead in the canoe, with the line, to make fast, there warn't anything but little saplings to tie to. I passed the line around one of them right on the edge of the cut bank, but there was a stiff current, and the raft come bomming down so lively she tore it out by the roots and away she went. I see the fog closing down, and it made me so sick and scared I couldn't budge for most a half a minute it seemed to me—and then there warn't no raft in sight; you couldn't see twenty yards. I jumped into the canoe and run back to the stern and grabbed the paddle and set her back a stroke. But she didn't come. I was in such a hurry I hadn't untied her. I got up and tried to untie her, but I was so excited my hands shook so I couldn't hardly do anything with them.

As soon as I got started I took out after the raft, hot and heavy, right down the tow-head. That was all right as far as it went, but the tow-head warn't sixty yards long, and the minute I flew by the foot of it I shot out into the solid white fog, and hadn't no more idea which way I was going than a dead man.

Thinks I, it won't do to paddle; first I know I'll run into the bank or a tow-head or somehting; I got to set still and float, and yet it's mighty fidgety business to have to hold your hands still at such a time. I whooped and listened. Away down there, somewheres, I hears a small whoop, and up comes my spirits. I went tearing after it, listening sharp it hear it again. The next time it come, I see I warn't heading for it but heading away to the right of it. And the next time, I was heading away to the left of it—and not gaining on it much, either, for I was flying around, this way and that and t'other, but it was going straight ahead all the time.

I did wish the fool would think to beat a tin pan, and beat it all the time, but he never did, and it was the still places between the whoops that was making the trouble for me. Well, I fought along, and directly I hears the whoop *behind* me. I was tangled good, now. That was somebody else's whoop, or else I was turned around.

I throwed the paddle down. I heard the whoop again; it was behind me yet, but in a different place; it kept coming, and kept changing its place, and I kept answering, till by-and-by it was in front of me again and I knowed the current had swung the canoe's head down-stream and I was all right, if that was Jim and not some other raftsman hollering. I couldn't tell nothing about voices in a fog, for nothing don't look natural nor sound natural in a fog.

The whooping went on, and in about a minute I come a booming down on a cut bank with smoky ghosts of big trees on it, and the current throwed me off to the left and shot by, amongst a lot of snags that fairly roared, the current was tearing by them so swift.

In another second or two it was solid white and still again. I set perfectly still, then, listening to my heart thump, and I reckon I didn't draw a breath while it thumped a hundred.

I just give up, then. I knowed what the matter was. That cut bank was an island, and Jim had gone down t'other side of it. It warn't no tow-head, that you could float by in ten minutes. It had the big timber of a regular island; it might be five or six mile long and more than a half a mile wide.

I kept quiet, with my ears cocked, about fifteen minutes, I reckon. I was floating along, of course, four or five mile an hour; but you don't ever think of that. No, you *feel* like you are laying dead still on the water; and if a little glimpse of a snag slips by, you don't think to yourself how fast *you're* going, but you catch your breath and think, my! how that snag's tearing along. If you think it ain't dismal and lonesome out in a fog that way, by yourself, in the night, you try it once—you'll see.

Next, for about a half an hour, I whoops now and then: at last I hears the answer a long ways off, and tries to follow it, but I couldn't do it, and directly I judged I'd got into a nest of tow-heads, for I had little dim glimpses of them on both sides of me, sometimes just a narrow channel between; and some that I couldn't see, I knowed was there, because I'd hear the wash of the current against the old dead brush and trash that hung over the banks. Well, I warn't long losing the whoops, down amongst the tow-heads; and I only tried to chase them a little while, anyway, because it was worse than chasing a

Jack-o-lantern. You never knowed a sound dodge around so, and swap places so quick and so much.

I had to claw away from the bank pretty lively, four or five times, to keep from knocking the islands out of the river; and so I judged the raft must be butting into the bank every now and then, or else it would get further ahead and clear out of hearing—it was floating a little faster than what I was.

Well, I seemed to be in the open river again, by-and-by, but I couldn't hear no sign of a whoop nowheres. I reckoned Jim had fetched up on a snag, maybe, and it was all up with him. I was good and tired, so I laid down in the canoe and said I wouldn't bother no more. I didn't want to go to sleep, of course; but I was so sleepy I couldn't help it; so I thought I would take just one little cat-nap.

But I reckon it was more than a cat-nap, for when I waked up the stars was shining bright, the fog was all gone, and I was spinning down a big bend stern first. First I didn't know where I was; I thought I was dreaming; and when things begun to come back to me, they seemed to come up dim out of last week.

It was a monstrous big river here, with the tallest and the thickest kind of timber on both banks; just a solid wall, as well as I could see, by the stars. I looked away down-stream, and seen a black speck on the water. I took out after it; but when I got to it it warn't nothing but a couple of saw-logs made fast together. Then I see another speck, and chased that; then another, and this time I was right. It was the raft.

When I got to it Jim was sitting with his head down between his knees, asleep, with his right arm hanging over the steering-oar. The other oar was smashed off, and the raft was littered up with leaves and branches and dirt. So she'd had a rough time.

I made fast and laid down under Jim's nose on the raft, and begun to gap, and stretch my fists out against Jim, and says:

'Hello, Jim, have I been asleep? Why didn't you stir me up?'

'Goodness gracious, is dat you, Huck? En you ain' dead—you ain' drownded—you's back agin? It's too good for true, honey, it's too good for true. Lemme look at you, chile, lemme feel o' you. No, you ain' dead! you's back agin, 'live en soun', jis de same ole Huck—de same ole Huck, thanks to goodness!'

'What's the matter with you, Jim? You been a-drinking?'

'Drinkin'? Has I ben a-drinkin'? Has I had a chance to be a-drinkin'?'

'Well, then, what makes you talk so wild?'

'How does I talk wild?'

'*How?* Why, hain't you been talking about my coming back, and all that stuff, as if I'd been gone away?'

'Huck—Huck Finn, you look me in de eye, look me in de eye. *Hain't* you ben gone away?'

'Gone away? Why, what in the nation do you mean? I hain't been gone anywheres. Where would I go to?'

'Well, looky here, boss, dey's sumf'n wrong, dey is. Is I *me,* or who *is* I? Is I heah, or whah *is* I? Now dat's what I wants to know?'

'Well, I think you're here, plain enough, but I think you're a tangle-headed old fool, Jim.'

'I is, is I? Well you answer me dis. Didn't you tote out de line in de canoe, fer to make fas' to de tow-head?'

'No, I didn't. What tow-head? I hain't seen no tow-head.'

'You hain't seen no tow-head? Looky here—didn't de line pull loose en de raf' go a-hummin' down de river, en leave you en de canoe behine in de fog?'

'What fog?'

'Why *de* fog. De fog dat's ben aroun' all night. En didn't you whoop, en didn't I whoop, tell we got mix' up in de islands en one un us got los' en t'other one was jis' as good as los', 'kase he didn' know whah he wuz? En didn't I bust up agin a lot er dem islands en have a turrible time en mos' git drownded? Now ain' dat so, boss—ain't it so? You answer me dat.'

'Well, this is too many for me, Jim. I hain't seen no fog, nor no islands, nor no troubles, nor nothing. I been setting here talking with you all night till you went to sleep about ten minutes ago, and I reckon I done the same. You couldn't a got drunk in that time, so of course you've been dreaming.'

'Dad fetch it, how is I gwyne to dream all dat in ten minutes?'

'Well, hang it all, you did dream it, because there didn't any of it happen.'

'But Huck, it's all jis' as plain to me as—'

'It don't make no difference how plain it is, there ain't nothing in it. I know, because I've been here all the time.'

Jim didn't say nothing for about five minutes, but set there studying over it. Then he says:

'Well, den, I reck'n I did dream it, Huck; but dog my cats ef it ain't de powerfullest dream I ever see. En I hain't ever had no dream b'fo' dat's tired me like dis one.'

'Oh, well, that's all right, because a dream does tire a body like everything, sometimes. But this one was a staving dream—tell me all about it, Jim.'

So Jim went to work and told me the whole thing right through, just as it happened, only he painted it up considerable. Then he said he must start in and ''terpret' it, because it was sent for a warning. He said the first tow-head stood for a man that would try to do us some good, but the current was another man that would get us away from him. The whoops was warnings that would come to us every now and then, and if we didn't try hard to make out to understand them they'd just take us into bad luck, 'stead of keeping us out of it. The lot of tow-heads was troubles we was going to get into with quarrelsome people and all kinds of mean folks, but if we minded our business and didn't talk back and aggravate them, we would pull through and get out of the fog and into the big clear river, which was the free States, and wouldn't have no more trouble.

It had clouded up pretty dark just after I got on to the raft, but it was clearing up again, now.

'Oh, well, that's all interpreted well enough, as far as it goes, Jim,' I says; 'but what does *these* things stand for?'

It was the leaves and rubbish on the raft, and the smashed oar. You could see them first-rate, now.

Jim looked at the trash, and then looked at me, and back at the trash again. He had got the dream fixed so strong in his head that he couldn't seem to shake it loose and get the facts back into its place again, right away. But when he did get the thing straightened around, he looked at me steady, without ever smiling, and says:

'What do dey stan' for? I's gwyne to tell you. When I got all wore out wid work, en wid de callin' for you, en went to sleep, my heart wuz mos' broke bekase you wuz los', en I didn' k'yer no mo' what become er me en de raf'. En when I wake up en fine you back agin, all safe en soun', de tears come en I could a got down on my knees en kiss' yo' foot I's so thankful. En all you wuz thinkin' 'bout wuz how you could make a fool uv ole Jim wid a lie. Dat truck dah is *trash;* en trash is what people is dat puts dirt on de head er dey fren's en makes 'em ashamed.'

Then he got up slow, and walked to the wigwam, and went in there, without saying anything but that. But that was enough. It made me feel so mean I could almost kiss *his* foot to get him to take it back.

It was fifteen minutes before I could work myself up to go and humble myself to a nigger—but I done it, and I warn't ever sorry for it afterwards, neither. I didn't do him no more mean tricks, and I wouldn't done that one if I'd a knowed it would make him feel that way.

We slept most all day, and started out at night, a little ways behind a monstrous long raft that was as long going by as a procession. She had four long sweeps at each end, so we judged she carried as many as thirty men, likely. She had five big wigwams aboard, wide apart, and an open camp-fire in the middle, and a tall flag-pole at each end. There was a power of style about her. It *amounted* to something being a raftsman on such a craft as that.

We went drifting down into a big bend, and the night clouded up and got hot. The river was very wide, and was walled with solid timber on both sides; you couldn't see a break in it hardly ever, or a light. We talked about Cairo, and wondered whether we would know it when we got to it. I said likely we wouldn't, because I had heard say there warn't but about a dozen houses there, and if they didn't happen to have them lit up, how was we going to know we was passing a town? Jim said if the two big rivers joined together there, that would show. But I said maybe we might think we was passing the foot of an island and coming into the same old river again. That disturbed Jim—and me too. So the question was, what to do? I said, paddle ashore the first time a light showed, and tell them pap was behind, coming along with a trading-scow, and was a green hand at the business, and wanted to know how far it was to Cairo. Jim thought it was a good idea, so we took a smoke on it and waited.

There warn't nothing to do, now, but to look out sharp for the town, and not pass it without seeing it. He said he'd be mighty sure to see it, because he'd be a free man the minute he seen it, but if he missed it he'd be in the slave country again and no more show for freedom. Every little while he jumps up and says:

'Dah she is!'

But it warn't. It was Jack-o-lanterns, or lightning-bugs; so he set down again, and went to watching, same as before. Jim said it made him all over trembly and feverish to be so close to freedom. Well, I can tell you it made me all over trembly and feverish, too, to hear him, because I begun to get it through my head that he *was* most free—and who was to blame for it? Why, *me.* I couldn't get that out of my conscience, no how nor no way. It got to troubling me so I couldn't rest; I couldn't stay still in one place. It hadn't ever come home to me before, what this thing was that I was doing. But now it did; and it staid with me, and scorched me more and more. I tried to make out to myself that *I* warn't to blame, because *I* didn't run Jim off from his rightful owner; but it warn't no use, conscience up and says, every time, 'But you knowed he was running for his freedom, and you could a paddled ashore and told somebody.' That was so—I couldn't get around that, no way. That was where it pinched. Conscience says to me, 'What had poor Miss Watson done to you, that you could see her nigger go off right under your eyes and never say one single word? What did that poor old woman do to you, that you could treat her so mean? Why, she tried to learn you your book, she tried to learn you your manners, she tried to be good to you every way she knowed how. *That's* what she done.'

I got to feeling so mean and so miserable I most wished I was dead. I fidgeted up and down the raft, abusing myself to myself, and Jim was fidgeting up and down past me. We neither of us could keep still. Every time he danced around and says, 'Dah's Cairo!' it went through me like a shot, and I thought if it *was* Cairo I reckoned I would die of miserableness.

Jim talked out loud all the time while I was talking to myself. He was saying how the first thing he would do when he got to a free State he would go to saving up money and never spend a single cent, and when he got enough he would buy his wife, which was owned on a farm close to where Miss Watson lived; and then they would both work to buy the two children, and if their master wouldn't sell them, they'd get an Ab'litionist to go and steal them.

It most froze me to hear such talk. He wouldn't ever dared to talk such talk in his life before. Just see what a difference it made in him the minute he judged he was about free. It was according to the old saying, 'Give a nigger an inch and he'll take an ell.' Thinks I, this is what comes of my not thinking. Here was this nigger which I had as good as helped to run away, coming right out flat-footed and saying he would steal his children—children that belonged to a man I didn't even know; a man that hadn't ever done me no harm.

I was sorry to hear Jim say that, it was such a lowering of him. My conscience got to stirring me up hotter than ever; until at last I says to it, 'Let up on me—it ain't too late, yet—I'll paddle ashore at the first light, and tell.' I felt easy, and happy, and light as a feather, right off. All my troubles was gone. I went to looking out sharp for a light, and sort of singing to myself. By-and-by one showed. Jim sings out:

'We's safe, Huck, we's safe! Jump up and crack yo' heels, dat's de good ole Cairo at las', I jis knows it!'

I says:

'I'll take the canoe and go see, Jim. It mightn't be, you know.'

He jumped and got the canoe ready, and put his old coat in the bottom for me to set on, and give me the paddle; and as I shoved off, he says:

'Pooty soon I'll be a-shout'n for joy, en I'll say, it's all on accounts o' Huck; I's a free man, en I couldn't ever ben free ef it hadn' been for Huck; Huck done it. Jim won't ever forgit you, Huck; you's de bes' fren' Jim's ever had; en you'd de *only* fren' ole Jim's got now.'

I was paddling off, all in a sweat to tell him; but when he says this, it seemed to kind of take the tuck all out of me. I went along slow then, and I warn't right down certain whether I was glad I started or whether I warn't. When I was fifty yards off, Jim says:

'Dah you goes, de ole true Huck; de on'y white genlman dat ever kep' his promise to ole Jim.'

Well, I just felt sick. But I says, I *got* to do it—I can't get *out* of it. Right then, along comes a skiff with two men in it, with guns, and they stopped and I stopped. One of them says:

'What's that, yonder?'

'A piece of a raft,' I says.

'Do you belong on it?'

'Yes, sir.'

'Any men on it?'

'Only one, sir.'

'Well, there's five niggers run off to-night, up yonder above the head of the bend. Is your man white or black?'

I didn't answer up prompt. I tried to, but the words wouldn't come. I tried, for a second or two, to brace up and out with it, but I warn't man enough—hadn't the spunk of a rabbit. I see I was weakening; so I just give up trying, and up and says:

'He's white.'

'I reckon we'll go and see for ourselves.'

'I wish you would,' says I, 'because it's pap that's there, and maybe you'd help me tow the raft ashore where the light is. He's sick—and so is mam and Mary Ann.'

'Oh, the devil! we're in a hurry, boy. But I s'pose we've go to. Come—buckle to your paddle, and let's get along.'

I buckled to my paddle and they laid to their oars. When we had made a stroke or two, I says:

'Pap'll be mighty much obleeged to you, I can tell you. Everybody goes away when I want them to help me tow the raft ashore, and I can't do it by myself.'

'Well, that's infernal mean. Odd, too. Say, boy, what's the matter with your father?'

'It's the—a—the—well, it ain't anything much.'

They stopped pulling. It warn't but a mighty ways to the raft, now. One says:

'Boy, that's a lie. What *is* the matter with your pap? Answer up square, now, and it'll be the better for you.'

'I will, sir, I will, honest—but don't leave us, please. It's the—the—gentlemen, if you'll only pull ahead, and let me heave you the head-line, you won't have to come a-near the raft—please do.'

'Set her back, John, set her back!' says one. They backed water. 'Keep away, boy—keep to looard. Confound it, I just expect the wind has blowed it to us. Your pap's got the smallpox, and you know it precious well. Why didn't you come out and say so? Do you want to spread it all over?'

'Well,' says I, a-blubbering, 'I've told everybody before, and then they just went away and left us.'

'Poor devil, there's something in that. We are right down sorry for you, but we—well, hang it, we don't want the smallpox, you see. Look here, I'll tell you what to do. Don't you try to land by yourself, or you'll smash everything to pieces. You float along down about twenty miles and you'll come to a town on the left-hand side of the river. It will be long after sun-up, then, and when you ask for help, you tell them your folks are all down with chills and fever. Don't be a fool again, and let people guess what is the matter. Now we're trying to do you a kindness; so you just put twenty miles between us, that's a good boy. It wouldn't do any good to land yonder where the light is—it's only a woodyard. Say—I reckon your father's poor, and I'm bound to say he's in pretty hard luck. Here—I'll put a twenty-dollar gold piece on this board, and you get it when it floats by. I feel mighty mean to leave you, but my kingdom! it won't do to fool with smallpox, don't you see?'

'Hold on, Parker,' says the other man, 'here's a twenty to put on the board for me. Good-bye, boy, you do as Mr Parker told you, and you'll be all right.'

'That's so, my boy—good-bye, good-bye. If you see any runaway niggers, you get help and nab them, and you can make some money by it.'

'Good-bye, sir,' says I, 'I won't let no runaway niggers get by me if I can help it.'

They went off and I got aboard the raft, feeling bad and low, because I knowed very well I had done wrong, and I see it warn't no use for me to try to learn to do right; a body that don't get *started* right when he's little, ain't got no show—when the pinch comes there ain't nothing to back him up and keep him to his work, and so he gets beat. Then I thought a minute, and says to myself, hold on,—s'pose you'd a done right and give Jim up; would you felt better than what you do now? No, says I, I'd feel bad—I'd feel just the same way I do now. Well, then, says I, what's the use you learning to do right, when it's troublesome to do right and ain't no trouble to do wrong, and the wages is just the same? I was stuck. I couldn't answer that. So I reckoned I wouldn't bother no more about it, but after this always do whichever comes handiest at the time.

I went into the wigwam; Jim warn't there. I looked all around; he warn't anywhere. I says:

'Jim!'

'Here I is, Huck. Is dey out o' sight yit? Don't talk loud.'

He was in the river, under the stern oar, with just his nose out. I told him they was out of sight, so he come aboard. He says:

'I was a-listenin' to all de talk, en I slips into de river en was gwyne to shove for sho' if dey come aboard. Den I was gwyne to swim to de raf' agin when dey was gone. But lawsy, how you did fool 'em, Huck! Dat *wuz* de smartes' dodge! I tell you, chile, I 'speck it save' old Jim—ole Jim ain't gwyne to forgit you for dat, honey.'

Then we talked about the money. It was a pretty good raise, twenty dollars apiece. Jim said we could take deck passage on a steamboat now, and the money would last us as far as we wanted to go in the free States. He said twenty mile more warn't far for the raft to go, but he wished we was already there.

135,000 SETS, 270,000 VOLUMES SOLD.

UNCLE TOM'S CABIN

FOR SALE HERE.

AN EDITION FOR THE MILLION, COMPLETE IN 1 Vol., PRICE 37 1-2 CENTS.
" " IN GERMAN, IN 1 Vol., PRICE 50 CENTS.
" " IN 2 Vols,. CLOTH, 6 PLATES, PRICE $1.50.
SUPERB ILLUSTRATED EDITION, IN 1 Vol., WITH 153 ENGRAVINGS,
PRICES FROM $2.50 TO $5.00.

The Greatest Book of the Age.

HARRIET BEECHER STOWE

Uncle Tom's Cabin

(1852)

The modern reader can easily misunderstand Uncle Tom's Cabin. But to Mrs. Stowe's nineteenth-century audience—the largest audience for any previous work of American fiction—she was not pursuing slavery with a bludgeon. Her instrument was at least as delicate as a surgeon's knife, and she operated on the national psyche, not just the system of slavery.

The slave was commercial property, and the business of slavery passed through northern as well as southern hands. This trade in human beings tore against the fabric of a society whose warp was the family and whose woof was Christianity and the morality it supports. Wendell Phillips, the famous abolitionist, once complained that Mrs. Stowe had scant awareness of the slavery movement's "real obstacles and difficulties." What she did possess, however, was a firm sense of the uneasiness that many Americans felt over the disrupting tendencies of commerce and a mobile society. Instead of making slavery a direct contrast with the "free" society of the North, she made it a grotesque extension and intensification of that world. Men "alive to nothing but trade and profit – cool, and unhesitating, and unrelenting as death and the grave roamed the American earth, building things and disrupting and destroying lives." Under slavery, men of commerce could take their avarice to its final extension: trade in human flesh. Mrs. Stowe originally subtitled her book The Man That Was a Thing, and correctly noted – despite the paternal ideals of some slaveholders – the entrepreneurial bent of the system of slavery. Northerners understood her picture of slavery because it reached the uneasiness they felt about their own society. Southerners knew this too: their many replies to Uncle Tom's Cabin aimed ineffectual blows at northern commercial society. No wonder southerners were so unrelievedly furious at the little lady whose book helped make the great war.

I

Late in the afternoon of a chilly day in February, two gentlemen were sitting alone over their wine, in a well-furnished dining parlor, in the town of P——, in Kentucky. There were no servants present, and the gentlemen, with chairs closely approaching, seemed to be discussing some subject with great earnestness.

For convenience' sake, we have said, hitherto, two *gentlemen*. One of the parties, however, when critically examined, did not seem, strictly speaking, to come under the species. He was a short thick-set man, with coarse commonplace features, and that swaggering air of pretension which marks a low man who is trying to elbow his way upward in the world. He was much overdressed, in a gaudy vest of many colors, a blue neckerchief, bedropped gayly with yellow spots, and arranged with a flaunting tie, quite in keeping with the general air of the man. His hands, large and coarse, were plentifully bedecked with rings; and he wore a heavy gold watch-chain, with a bundle of seals of portentous size, and a great variety of colors, attached to it,—which, in the ardor of conversation, he was in the habit of flourishing and jingling with evident satisfaction. His conversation was in free and easy defiance of Murray's Grammar, and was garnished at convenient intervals with various profane expressions, which not even the desire to be graphic in our account shall induce us to transcribe.

His companion, Mr. Shelby, had the appearance of a gentleman; and the arrangements of the house, and the general air of the housekeeping, indicated easy, and even opulent circumstances. As we before stated, the two were in the midst of an earnest conversation.

"That is the way I should arrange the matter," said Mr. Shelby.

"I can't make trade that way,—I positively can't, Mr. Shelby," said the other, holding up a glass of wine between his eye and the light.

"Why, the fact is, Haley, Tom is an uncommon fellow; he is certainly worth that sum anywhere,—steady, honest, capable, manages my whole farm like a clock."

"You mean honest, as niggers go," said Haley, helping himself to a glass of brandy.

"No; I mean, really, Tom is a good, steady, sensible, pious fellow. He got religion at a camp-meeting, four years ago; and I believe he really *did* get it. I've trusted him, since then, with everything I have,—money, house, horses,—and let him come and go round the country; and I always found him true and square in everything."

"Some folks don't believe there is pious niggers, Shelby," said Haley, with a candid flourish of his hand, "but *I do*. I had a fellow, now, in this yer last lot I took to Orleans,—'twas as good as a meetin', now, really, to hear that critter pray; and he was quite gentle and quiet like. He fetched me a good sum, too, for I bought him cheap of a man that was 'bliged to sell out; so I realized six hundred on him. Yes, I consider religion a valeyable thing in a nigger, when it's the genuine article, and no mistake."

"Well, Tom's got the real article, if ever a fellow had," rejoined the other. "Why, last fall, I let him go to Cincinnati alone, to do business for me, and bring home five hundred dollars. 'Tom,' says I to him, 'I trust you, because I think you're a Christian,—I know you wouldn't cheat.' Tom comes back, sure enough; I knew he would. Some low fellows, they say, said to him, 'Tom, why don't you make tracks for Canada?' 'Ah, master trusted me, and I couldn't,'—they told me about it. I am sorry to part with Tom, I must say. You ought to let him cover the whole balance of the debt; and you would, Haley, if you had any conscience."

"Well, I've got just as much conscience as any man in business can afford to keep,—just a little, you know, to swear by, as 'twere," said the trader, jocularly; "and, then, I'm ready to do anything in reason to 'blige friends; but this yer, you see, is a leetle too hard on a fellow,—a leetle too hard." The trader sighed contemplatively, and poured out some more brandy.

"Well then, Haley, how will you trade?" said Mr. Shelby, after an uneasy interval of silence.

"Well, haven't you a boy or gal that you could throw in with Tom?"

"Hum!—none that I could well spare; to tell you the truth, it's only hard necessity makes me willing to sell at all. I don't like parting with any of my hands, that's a fact."

Here the door opened, and a small quadroon boy, between four and five years of age, entered the room. There was something in his appearance remarkably beautiful and engaging. His black hair, fine as floss silk, hung in glossy curls about his round dimpled face, while a pair of large dark eyes, full of fire and softness, looked out from beneath the rich, long lashes, as he peered curiously into the apartment. A gay robe of scarlet and yellow plaid, carefully made and neatly fitted, set off to advantage the dark and rich style of his beauty; and a certain comic air of assurance, blended with bashfulness, showed that he had been not unused to being petted and noticed by his master.

"Hulloa, Jim Crow!" said Mr. Shelby, whistling, and snapping a bunch of raisins towards him, "pick that up, now!"

The child scampered, with all his little strength, after the prize, while his master laughed.

"Come here, Jim Crow," said he. The child came up, and the master patted the curly head, and chucked him under the chin.

"Now, Jim, show this gentleman how you can dance and sing." The boy commenced one of those wild, grotesque songs common among the negroes, in a rich, clear voice, accompanying his singing with many comic evolutions of the hands, feet, and whole body, all in perfect time to the music.

"Bravo!" said Haley, throwing him a quarter of an orange.

"Now, Jim, walk like old Uncle Cudjoe when he has the rheumatism," said his master.

Instantly the flexible limbs of the child assumed the appearance of deformity and distortion, as, with his back humped up, and his master's stick in his hand, he hobbled about the room, his childish face drawn into a doleful pucker, and spitting from right to left, in imitation of an old man.

Both gentlemen laughed uproariously.

"Now, Jim," said his master, "show us how old Elder Robbins leads the psalm." The boy drew his chubby face down to a formidable length, and commenced toning a psalm tune through his nose with imperturbable gravity.

"Hurrah! bravo! what a young 'un!" said Haley; "that chap's a case, I'll promise. Tell you what," said he, suddenly clapping his hand on Mr. Shelby's shoulder, "fling in that chap and I'll settle the business,—I will. Come, now, if that an't doing the thing up about the rightest!"

At this moment, the door was pushed gently open, and a young quadroon woman, apparently about twenty-five, entered the room.

There needed only a glance from the child to her, to identify her as its mother. There was the same rich, full, dark eye, with its long lashes; the same ripples of silky black hair. The brown of her complexion gave way on the cheek to a perceptible flush, which deepened as she saw the gaze of the strange man fixed upon her in bold and undisguised admiration. Her dress was of the neatest possible fit, and set off to advantage her finely moulded shape; a delicately formed hand and a trim foot and ankle were items of appearance that did not escape the quick eye of the trader, well used to run up at a glance the points of a fine female article.

"Well, Eliza?" said her master, as she stopped and looked hesitatingly at him.

"I was looking for Harry, please, sir"; and the boy bounded toward her, showing his spoils, which he had gathered in the skirt of his robe.

"Well, take him away, then," said Mr. Shelby; and hastily she withdrew, carrying the child on her arm.

"By Jupiter," said the trader, turning to him in admiration, "there's an article, now! You might make your fortune on that ar gal in Orleans, any day. I've seen over a thousand, in my day, paid down for gals not a bit handsomer."

"I don't want to make my fortune on her," said Mr. Shelby, dryly; and, seeking to turn the conversation, he uncorked a bottle of fresh wine, and asked his companion's opinion of it.

"Capital, sir—first chop!" said the trader; then turning, and slapping his hand familiarly on Shelby's shoulder, he added,—

"Come, how will you trade about the gal?—what shall I say for her,—what'll you take?"

"Mr. Haley, she is not to be sold," said Shelby. "My wife would not part with her for her weight in gold."

"Ay, ay! women always say such things, cause they han't no sort of calculation. Just show 'em how many watches, feathers, and trinkets one's weight in gold would buy, and that alters the case. *I* reckon."

"I tell you, Haley, this must not be spoken of; I say no, and I mean no," said Shelby, decidedly.

"Well, you'll let me have the boy, though," said the trader; "you must own I've come down pretty handsomely for him."

"What on earth can you want with the child?" said Shelby.

"Why, I've got a friend that's going into this yer branch of the business,—wants to buy up handsome boys to raise for the market. Fancy articles entirely,—sell for waiters, and so on, to rich 'uns, that can pay for handsome 'uns. It sets off one of yer great places,—a real handsome boy to open door, wait and tend. They fetch a good sum; and this little devil is such a comical, musical concern, he's just the article."

"I would rather not sell him," said Mr. Shelby, thoughtfully; "the fact is, sir, I'm a humane man, and I hate to take the boy from his mother, sir."

"O, you do?—La! yes,—something of that ar natur. I understand, perfectly. It is mighty onpleasant getting on with women, sometimes. I al'ays hates these yer screechin', screamin' times. They are *mighty* onpleasant; but, as I manages business, I generally avoids 'em, sir. Now, what if you get the girl off for a day, or a week, or so; then the thing's done quietly,—all over before she comes home. Your wife might get her some ear-rings, or a new gown, or some such truck, to make up with her."

"I'm afraid not."

"Lor bless ye, yes! These critters an't like white folks, you know; they gets over things, only manage right. Now, they say," said Haley, assuming a candid and confidential air, "that this kind o'trade is hardening to the feelings; but I never found it so. Fact is, I never could do things up the way some fellers manage the business. I've seen 'em as would pull a woman's child out of her arms, and set him up to sell, and she screechin' like mad all the time; very bad policy,—damages the article,—makes 'em quite unfit for service sometimes. I knew a real handsome gal once, in Orleans, as was entirely ruined by this sort o' handling. The fellow that was trading for her didn't want her baby; and she was one of your real high sort, when her blood was up. I tell you, she squeezed up her child in her arms, and talked, and went on real awful. It kinder makes my blood run cold to think on 't; and when they carried off the child, and locked her up, she jest went ravin' mad, and died in a week. Clear waste, sir, of a thousand dollars, just for want of management,—there's where 'tis. It's always best to do the humane thing, sir; that's been *my* experience." And the trader leaned back in his chair, and folded his arm, with an air of virtuous decision, apparently considering himself a second Wilberforce.

The subject appeared to interest the gentleman deeply; for while Mr. Shelby was thoughtfully peeling an orange, Haley broke out afresh, with becoming diffidence, but as if actually driven by the force of truth to say a few words more.

"It don't look well, now, for a feller to be praisin' himself; but I say it jest because it's the truth. I believe I'm reckoned to bring in about the finest droves of niggers that is brought in,—at least, I've been told so; if I have once, I reckon I have a hundred times,—all in good case,—fat and likely, and I lose as few as any man in the business. And I lays it all to my management, sir; and humanity, sir, I may say, is the great pillar of *my* management."

Mr. Shelby did not know what to say, and so he said, "Indeed!"

"Now, I've been laughed at for my notions, sir, and I've been talked to. They an't pop'lar, and they an't common; but I stuck to 'em, sir; I've stuck to 'em, and realized well on 'em; yes, sir, they have paid their passage, I may say," and the trader laughed at his joke.

There was something so piquant and original in these elucidations of humanity, that Mr. Shelby could not help laughing in company. Perhaps you laugh too, dear reader; but you know humanity comes out in a variety of strange forms nowadays, and there is no end to the odd things that humane people will say and do.

Mr. Shelby's laugh encouraged the trader to proceed.

"It's strange now, but I never could beat this into people's heads. Now, there was Tom Loker, my old partner, down in Natchez; he was a clever fellow, Tom was, only the very devil with niggers,—on principle 'twas, you see, for a better-hearted feller never broke bread; 'twas his *system,* sir. I used to talk to Tom. 'Why, Tom,' I used to say, 'when your gals takes on and cry, what's the use o' crackin' on 'em over the head, and knockin' on 'em round? It's ridiculous,' says I, 'and don't do no sort o' good. Why, I don't see no harm in their cryin',' says I; 'it's natur,' says I, 'and if natur can't blow off one way, it will another. Besides, Tom,' says I, 'it jest spiles your gals; they get sickly, and down in the mouth; and sometimes they gets ugly,—particularly yallow gals do,—and it's the devil and all gettin' on 'em broke in. Now,' says I, 'why can't you kinder coax 'em up, and speak 'em fair? Depend on it, Tom, a little humanity, thrown in along, goes a heap further than all your jawin' and crackin'; and it pays better,' says I, 'depend on't.' But Tom couldn't get the hang on't; and he spiled so many for me, that I had to break off with him, though he was a good-hearted fellow, and as fair a business hand as is goin'."

"And do you find your ways o' managing do the business better than Tom's?" said Mr. Shelby.

"Why, yes, sir, I may say so. You see, when I any ways can, I takes a leetle care about the onpleasant parts, like selling young uns and that,—get the gals out of the way,—out of sight, out of mind, you know,—and when it's clean done, and can't be helped, they naturally gets used to it. 'Tan't, you know, as if it was white folks, that's brought up in the way of 'spectin' to keep their children and wives, and all that. Niggers, you know, that's fetched up properly han't no kind of 'spectations of no kind; so all these things comes easier."

"I'm afraid mine are not properly brought up, then," said Mr. Shelby.

"S'pose not; you Kentucky folks spile your niggers. You mean well by 'em, but 'tan't no real kindness, arter all. Now, a nigger, you see, what's got to be hacked and tumbled round the world, and sold to Tom, and Dick, and the Lord knows who, 'tan't no kindness to be givin' on him notions and expectations, and bringin' on him up too well, for the rough and tumble comes all the harder on him arter. Now, I venture to say, your niggers would be quite chop-fallen in a place where some of your plantation niggers would be singing and whooping like all possessed. Every man, you know, Mr. Shelby, naturally thinks well of his own ways; and I think I treat niggers just about as well as it's ever worth while to treat 'em."

"It's a happy thing to be satisfied," said Mr. Shelby, with a slight shrug, and some perceptible feelings of a disagreeable nature.

"Well," said Haley, after they had both silently picked their nuts for a season, "what do you say?"

"I'll think the matter over, and talk with my wife," said Mr. Shelby. "Meantime, Haley, if you want the matter carried on in the quiet way you speak of, you'd best not let your business in this neighborhood be known. It will get out among my boys, and it will not be a particularly quiet business getting away any of my fellows, if they know it, I'll promise you."

"O, certainly, by all means, mum! of course. But I'll tell you, I'm in a devil of a hurry, and shall want to know, as soon as possible, what I may depend on," said he, rising and putting on his overcoat.

"Well, call up this evening, between six and seven, and you shall have my answer," said Mr. Shelby, and the trader bowed himself out of the apartment.

"I'd like to have been able to kick the fellow down the steps," said he to himself, as he saw the door fairly closed, "with his impudent assurance; but he knows how much he has me at advantage. If anybody had ever said to me that I should sell Tom down south to one of those rascally traders, I should have said, 'Is thy servant a dog, that he should do this thing?' And now it must come, for aught I see. And Eliza's child, too! I know that I shall have some fuss with wife about that; and, for that matter, about Tom, too. So much for being in debt,—heigh-ho. The fellow sees his advantage, and means to push it."

Perhaps the mildest form of the system of slavery is to be seen in the State of Kentucky. The general prevalence of agricultural pursuits of a quiet and gradual nature, not requiring those periodic seasons of hurry and pressure that are called for in the business of more southern districts, makes the task of the negro a more healthful and reasonable one; while the master, content with a more gradual style of acquisition, has not those temptations to hard-heartedness which always overcome frail human nature when the prospect of sudden and rapid gain is weighed in the balance, with no heavier counterpoise than the interests of the helpless and unprotected.

Whoever visits some estates there, and witnesses the good-humored indulgence of some masters and mistresses and the affectionate loyalty of some slaves, might be tempted to dream the oft-fabled poetic legend of a patriarchal institution, and all that; but over and above the scene there broods a portentous shadow,—the shadow of *law*. So long as the law considers all these human beings, with beating hearts and living affections, only as so many *things* belonging to a master,—so long as the failure, or misfortune, or imprudence, or death of the kindest owner may cause them any day to exchange a life of kind protection and indulgence for one of hopeless misery and toil,—so long it is impossible to make anything beautiful or desirable in the best-regulated administration of slavery.

Mr. Shelby was a fair average kind of man, good-natured and kindly, and disposed to easy indulgence of those around him, and there had never been a lack of anything which might contribute to the physical comfort of the negroes on his estate. He had, however, speculated largely and quite loosely; had involved himself deeply, and his notes to a large amount had come into the hands of Haley; and this small piece of information is the key to the preceding conversation.

Now, it had so happened that, in approaching the door, Eliza had caught enough of the conversation to know that a trader was making offers to her master for somebody.

She would gladly have stopped at the door to listen, as she came out; but her mistress just then calling, she was obliged to hasten away.

Still she thought she heard the trader make an offer for her boy;—could she be mistaken? Her heart swelled and throbbed, and she involuntarily strained him so tight that the little fellow looked up into her face in astonishment.

"Eliza, girl, what ails you to-day?" said her mistress, when Eliza had upset the wash-pitcher, knocked down the workstand, and finally was abstractedly offering her mistress a long nightgown in place of the silk dress she had ordered her to bring from the wardrobe.

Eliza started. "O, missis!" she said, raising her eyes; then, bursting into tears, she sat down in a chair, and began sobbing.

"Why, Eliza, child! what ails you?" said her mistress.

"O, missis, missis," said Eliza, "there's been a trader talking with master in the parlor! I heard him."

"Well, silly child, suppose there has."

"O, missis, *do* you suppose mas'r would sell my Harry?" And the poor creature threw herself into a chair, and sobbed convulsively.

"Sell him! No, you foolish girl! You know your master never deals with those southern traders, and never means to sell any of his servants, as long as they behave well. Why, you silly child, who do you think would want to buy your Harry? Do you think all the world are set on him as you are, you goosie? Come, cheer up, and hook my dress. There now, put my back hair up in that pretty braid you learnt the other day, and don't go listening at doors any more."

"Well, but, missis, *you* never would give your consent—to—to—"

"Nonsense, child! to be sure I shouldn't. What do you talk so for? I would as soon have one of my own children sold. But really, Eliza, you are getting altogether too proud of that little fellow. A man can't put his nose into the door, but you think he must be coming to buy him."

Reassured by her mistress's confident tone, Eliza proceeded nimbly and adroitly with her toilet, laughing at her own fears as she proceeded.

Mrs. Shelby was a woman of a high class, both intellectually and morally. To that natural magnanimity and generosity of mind which one often marks as characteristic of the women of Kentucky, she added high moral and religious sensibility and principle, carried out with great energy and ability into practical results. Her husband, who made no professions to any particular religious character, nevertheless reverenced and respected the consistency of hers, and stood, perhaps, a little in awe of her opinion. Certain it was that he gave her unlimited scope in all her benevolent efforts for the comfort, instruction, and improvement of her servants, though he never took any decided part in them himself. In fact, if not exactly a believer in the doctrine of the efficiency of the extra good works of saints, he really seemed somehow or other to fancy that his wife had piety and benevolence enough for two,—to indulge a shadowy expectation of getting into heaven through her superabundance of qualities to which he made no particular pretension.

The heaviest load on his mind, after his conversation with the trader, lay in the foreseen necessity of breaking to his wife the arrangement contemplated,—meeting the importunities and opposition which he knew he should have reason to encounter.

Mrs. Shelby, being entirely ignorant of her husband's embarrassments, and knowing only the general kindliness of his temper, had been quite sincere in the entire incredulity with which she had met Eliza's suspicions. In fact, she dismissed the matter from her mind, without a second thought; and being occupied in preparations for an evening visit, it passed out of her thoughts entirely.

II

Eliza had been brought up by her mistress, from girlhood, as a petted and indulged favorite.

The traveller in the south must often have remarked that peculiar air of refinement, that softness of voice and manner, which seems in many cases to be a particular gift to the quadroon and mulatto women. These natural graces in the quadroon are often united with beauty of the most dazzling kind, and in almost every case with a personal appearance prepossessing and agreeable. Eliza, such as we have described her, is not a fancy sketch, but taken from remembrance, as we saw her, years ago, in Kentucky. Safe under the protecting care of her mistress, Eliza had reached maturity without those temptations which make beauty so fatal an inheritance to a slave. She had been married to a bright and talented young mulatto man, who was a slave on a neighboring estate, and bore the name of George Harris.

This young man had been hired out by his master to work in a bagging factory, where his adroitness and ingenuity caused him to be considered the first hand in the place. He had invented a machine for the cleaning of the hemp, which, considering the education and circumstances of the inventor, displayed quite as much mechanical genius as Whitney's cotton-gin.*

He was possessed of a handsome person and pleasing manners, and was a general favorite in the factory. Nevertheless, as this young man was in the eye of the law not a man, but a thing, all these superior qualifications were subject to the control of a vulgar, narrow-minded, tyrannical master. This same gentleman, having heard of the fame of George's invention, took a ride over to the factory, to see what this intelligent chattel had been about. He was received with great enthusiasm by the employer, who congratulated him on possessing so valuable a slave.

He was waited upon over the factory, shown the machinery by George, who, in high spirits, talked so fluently, held himself so erect, looked so handsome and manly, that his master began to feel an uneasy consciousness of inferiority. What business had his slave to be marching round the country, inventing machines, and holding up his head among gentlemen? He'd soon put a stop to it. He'd take him back, and put him to hoeing and digging, and "see if he'd step about so smart." Accordingly, the manufacturer and all hands concerned were astounded when he suddenly demanded George's wages, and announced his intention of taking him home.

"But, Mr. Harris," remonstrated the manufacturer, "isn't this rather sudden?"

"What if it is?—isn't the man *mine?*"

"We would be willing, sir, to increase the rate of compensation."

"No object at all, sir. I don't need to hire any of my hands out, unless I've a mind to."

"But, sir, he seems peculiarly adapted to this business."

"Dare say he may be; never was much adapted to anything that I set him about, I'll be bound."

*A machine of this description was really the invention of a young colored man in Kentucky.

"But only think of his inventing this machine," interposed one of the workmen, rather unluckily.

"O yes!—a machine for saving work, is it? He'd invent that, I'll be bound; let a nigger alone for that, any time. They are all labor-saving machines themselves, every one of 'em. No, he shall tramp!"

George had stood like one transfixed, at hearing his doom thus suddenly pronounced by a power that he knew was irresistible. He folded his arms, tightly pressed in his lips, but a whole volcano of bitter feelings burned in his bosom, and sent streams of fire through his veins. He breathed short, and his large dark eyes flashed like live coals; and he might have broken out into some dangerous ebullition, had not the kindly manufacturer touched him on the arm, and said, in a low tone,—

"Give way, George; go with him for the present. We'll try to help you, yet."

The tyrant observed the whisper, and conjectured its import, though he could not hear what was said; and he inwardly strengthened himself in his determination to keep the power he possessed over his victim.

George was taken home, and put to the meanest drudgery of the farm. He had been able to repress every disrespectful word; but the flashing eye, the gloomy and troubled brow, were part of a natural language that could not be repressed,—indubitable signs, which showed too plainly that the man could not become a thing.

It was during the happy period of his employment in the factory that George had seen and married his wife. During that period,—being much trusted and favored by his employer,—he had free liberty to come and go at discretion. The marriage was highly approved of by Mrs. Shelby, who, with a little womanly complacency in match-making, felt pleased to unite her handsome favorite with one of her own class who seemed in every way suited to her; and so they were married in her mistress's great parlor, and her mistress herself adorned the bride's beautiful hair with orange-blossoms, and threw over it the bridal veil, which certainly could scarce have rested on a fairer head; and there was no lack of white gloves, and cake and wine,—of admiring guests to praise the bride's beauty, and her mistress's indulgence and liberality. For a year or two Eliza saw her husband frequently, and there was nothing to interrupt their happiness, except the loss of two infant children, to whom she was passionately attached, and whom she mourned with a grief so intense as to call for gentle remonstrance from her mistress, who sought, with maternal anxiety, to direct her naturally passionate feelings within the bounds of reason and religion.

After the birth of little Harry, however, she had gradually become tranquillized and settled; and every bleeding tie and throbbing nerve, once more entwined with that little life, seemed to become sound and healthful, and Eliza was a happy woman up to the time that her husband was rudely torn from his kind employer, and brought under the iron sway of his legal owner.

The manufacturer, true to his word, visited Mr. Harris a week or two after George had been taken away, when, as he hoped, the heat of the occasion had passed away, and tried every possible inducement to lead him to restore him to his former employment.

"You needn't trouble to talk any longer," said he doggedly; "I know my own business, sir."

"I did not presume to interfere with it, sir. I only thought that you might think it for your interest to let your man to us on the terms proposed."

"O, I understand the matter well enough. I saw your winking and whispering, the day I took him out of the factory; but you don't come it over me that way. It's a free country, sir; the man's *mine*, and I do what I please with him,—that's it!"

And so fell George's last hope;—nothing before him but a life of toil and drudgery, rendered more bitter by every little smarting vexation and indignity which tyrannical ingenuity could devise.

A very humane jurist once said, The worst use you can put a man to is to hang him. No; there is another use that a man can be put to that is worse!

III

Mrs. Shelby had gone on her visit, and Eliza stood in the veranda, rather dejectedly looking after the retreating carriage, when a hand was laid on her shoulder. She turned, and a bright smile lighted up her fine eyes.

"George, is it you? How you frightened me! Well; I am so glad you's come! Missis is gone to spend the afternoon; so come into my little room, and we'll have the time all to ourselves."

Saying this, she drew him into a neat little apartment opening on the veranda, where she generally sat at her sewing, within call of her mistress.

"How glad I am!—why don't you smile?—and look at Harry,—how he grows." The boy stood shyly regarding his father through his curls, holding close to the skirts of his mother's dress. "Isn't he beautiful?" said Eliza, lifting his long curls and kissing him.

"I wish he'd never been born!" said George, bitterly. "I wish I'd never been born myself!"

Surprised and frightened, Eliza sat down, leaned her head on her husband's shoulder, and burst into tears.

"There now, Eliza, it's too bad for me to make you feel so, poor girl!" said he, fondly; "it's too bad. O, how I wish you never had seen me,—you might have been happy!"

"George! George! how can you talk so? What dreadful thing has happened, or is going to happen? I'm sure we've been very happy, till lately."

"So we have, dear," said George. Then drawing his child on his knee, he gazed intently on his glorious dark eyes, and passed his hands through his long curls.

"Just like you, Eliza; and you are the handsomest woman I ever saw, and the best one I ever wish to see; but, O, I wish I'd never seen you, nor you me!"

"O, George, how can you!"

"Yes, Eliza, it's all misery, misery, misery! My life is bitter as wormwood; the very life is burning out of me. I'm a poor, miserable, forlorn drudge; I shall only drag you down with me, that's all. What's the use of our trying to do anything, trying to know anything, trying to be anything? What's the use of living? I wish I was dead!"

"O, now, dear George, that is really wicked! I know how you feel about losing your place in the factory, and you have a hard master; but pray be patient, and perhaps something—"

"Patient!" said he, interrupting her; "haven't I been patient? Did I say a word when he came and took me away for no earthly reason, from the place where everybody was kind to me? I'd paid him truly every cent of my earnings,—and they all say I worked well."

"Well, it *is* dreadful," said Eliza; "but, after all, he is your master, you know."

"My master! and who made him my master? That's what I think of,—what right has he to me? I'm a man as much as he is. I'm a better man than he is. I know more about business than he does; I am a better manager than he is; I can read better than he can; I can write a better hand,—and I've learned it all myself, and no thanks to him.—I've learned it in spite of him; and now what right has he to make a dray-horse of me?—to take me from things I can do, and do better than he can, and put me to work that any horse can do? He tries to do it; he says he'll bring me down and humble me, and he puts me to just the hardest, meanest, and dirtiest work, on purpose!"

"O, George! George! you frighten me! Why, I never heard you talk so; I'm afraid you'll do something dreadful. I don't wonder at your feelings, at all; but O, do be careful—do, do—for my sake,—for Harry's!"

"I have been careful, and I have been patient, but it's growing worse and worse: flesh and blood can't bear it any longer;—every chance he can get to insult and torment me, he takes. I thought I could do my work well, and keep on quiet, and have some time to read and learn out of work hours; but the more he sees I can do, the more he loads on. He says that though I don't say anything, he sees I've got the devil in me, and he means to bring it out; and one of these days it will come out in a way that he won't like, or I'm mistaken!"

"O dear! what shall we do?" said Eliza, mournfully.

"It was only yesterday," said George, "as I was busy loading stones into a cart, that young Mas'r Tom stood there, slashing his whip so near the horse that the creature was frightened. I asked him to stop, as pleasant as I could,—he just kept right on. I begged him again, and then he turned on me, and began striking me. I held his hand, and then he screamed and kicked and ran to his father, and told him that I was fighting him. He came in a rage, and said he'd teach me who was my master; and he tied me to a tree, and cut switches for young master, and told him that he might whip me till he was tired;—and he did do it! If I don't make him remember it, some time!" and the brow of the young man grew dark, and his eyes burned with an expression that made his young wife tremble. "Who made this man my master? That's what I want to know!" he said.

"Well," said Eliza, mournfully, "I always thought that I must obey my master and mistress, or I couldn't be a Christian."

"There is some sense in it, in your case; they have brought you up like a child, fed you, clothed you, indulged you, and taught you, so that you have a good education; that is some reason why they should claim you. But I have been kicked and cuffed and sworn at, and at the best only let alone; and what do I owe? I've paid for all my keeping a hundred times over. I *won't* bear it. No, I *won't!*" he said, clenching his hand with a fierce frown.

Eliza trembled, and was silent. She had never seen her husband in this mood before; and her gentle system of ethics seemed to bend like a reed in the surges of such passions.

"You know poor little Carlo, that you gave me," added George; "the creature has been about all the comfort that I've had. He has slept with me nights, and followed me around days, and kind o' looked at me as if he understood how I felt. Well, the other day I was just feeding him with a few old scraps I picked up by the kitchen door, and Mas'r came along, and said I was feeding him up at his expense, and that he couldn't afford to have every nigger keeping his dog, and ordered me to tie a stone to his neck and throw him in the pond."

"O, George, you didn't do it!"

"Do it? not I!—but he did. Mas'r and Tom pelted the poor drowning creature with stones. Poor thing! he looked at me so mournful, as if he wondered why I didn't save him. I had to take a flogging because I wouldn't do it myself. I don't care. Mas'r will find out that I'm one that whipping won't tame. My day will come yet, if he don't look out."

"What are you going to do? O, George, don't do anything wicked; if you only trust in God, and try to do right, he'll deliver you."

"I an't a Christian like you, Eliza; my heart's full of bitterness; I can't trust in God. Why does he let things be so?"

"O, George, we must have faith. Mistress says that when all things go wrong to us, we must believe that God is doing the very best."

"That's easy to say for people that are sitting on their sofas and riding in their carriages; but let 'em be where I am, I guess it would come some harder. I wish I could be good; but my heart burns, and can't be reconciled, anyhow. You couldn't, in my place,—you can't now, if I tell you all I've got to say. You don't know the whole yet."

"What can be coming now?"

"Well, lately Mas'r has been saying that he was a fool to let me marry off the place; that he hates Mr. Shelby and all his tribe, because they are proud, and hold their heads up above him, and that I've got proud notions from you; and he says he won't let me come here any more, and that I shall take a wife and settle down on his place. At first he only scolded and grumbled these things; but yesterday he told me that I should take Mina for a wife, and settle down in a cabin with her, or he would sell me down river."

"Why—but you were married to *me,* by the minister, as much as if you'd been a white man!" said Eliza, simply.

"Don't you know a slave can't be married? There is no law in this country for that; I can't hold you for my wife if he chooses to part us. That's why I wish I'd never seen you,—why I wish I'd never been born; it would have been better for us both,—it would have been better for this poor child if he had never been born. All this may happen to him yet!"

"O, but master is so kind!"

"Yes, but who knows?—he may die,—and then he may be sold to nobody knows who. What pleasure is it that he is handsome, and smart, and bright? I tell you, Eliza, that a sword will pierce through your soul for every good and pleasant thing your child is or has; it will make him worth too much for you to keep!"

The words smote heavily on Eliza's heart; the vision of the trader came before her eyes, and, as if some one had struck her a deadly blow, she turned pale and gasped for breath. She looked nervously out on the veranda, where the boy, tired of the grave conversation, had retired, and where he was riding triumphantly up and down on Mr. Shelby's walking-stick. She would have spoken to tell her husband her fears, but checked herself.

"No, no,—he has enough to bear, poor fellow!" she thought. "No, I won't tell him; besides, it an't true. Missis never deceives us."

"So, Eliza, my girl," said the husband, mournfully, "bear up, now; and good by, for I'm going."

"Going, George! Going where?"

"To Canada," said he, straightening himself up; "and when I'm there, I'll buy you; that's all the hope that's left us. You have a kind master, that won't refuse to sell you. I'll buy you and the boy;—God helping me, I will!"

"O, dreadful! if you should be taken?"

"I won't be taken, Eliza; I'll *die* first! I'll be free, or I'll die!"

"You won't kill yourself!"

"No need of that. They will kill me, fast enough; they never will get me down the river alive!"

"O, George, for my sake, do be careful! Don't do anything wicked; don't lay hands on yourself, or anybody else. You are tempted too much—too much; but don't—go you must—but go carefully, prudently; pray God to help you."

"Well, then, Eliza, hear my plan. Mas'r took it into his head to send me right by here, with a note to Mr. Symmes, that lives a mile past. I believe he expected I should come here to tell you what I have. It would please him if he thought it would aggravate 'Shelby's folks,' as he calls 'em. I'm going home quite resigned, you understand, as if all was over. I've got some preparations made,—and there are those that will help me; and, in the course of a week or so, I shall be among the missing, some day. Pray for me, Eliza; perhaps the good Lord will hear *you*."

"O, pray yourself, George, and go trusting in him; then you won't do anything wicked."

"Well, now, *good by*," said George, holding Eliza's hands, and gazing into her eyes, without moving. They stood silent; then there were last words, and sobs, and bitter weeping,—such parting as those may make whose hope to meet again is as the spider's web,—and the husband and wife were parted.

* * *

IV

Mr. and Mrs. Shelby had retired to their apartment for the night. He was lounging in a large easy chair, looking over some letters that had come in the afternoon mail, and she was standing before her mirror, brushing out the complicated braids and curls in which Eliza had arranged her hair; for, noticing her pale cheeks and haggard eyes, she had excused her attendance that night, and ordered her to bed. The employment, naturally enough, suggested her conversation with the girl in the morning; and, turning to her husband, she said, carelessly,—

"By the by, Arthur, who was that low-bred fellow that you lugged in to our dinner-table to-day?"

"Haley is his name," said Shelby, turning himself rather uneasily in his chair, and continuing with his eyes fixed on a letter.

"Haley! Who is he, and what may be his business here, pray?"

"Well, he's a man that I transacted some business with, last time I was at Natchez," said Shelby.

"And he presumed on it to make himself quite at home, and call and dine here, ay?"

"Why, I invited him; I had some accounts with him," said Shelby.

"Is he a negro-trader?" said Mrs. Shelby, noticing a certain embarrassment in her husband's manner.

"Why, my dear, what put that into your head?" said Shelby, looking up.

"Nothing,—only Eliza came in here, after dinner, in a great worry, crying and taking on, and said you were talking with a trader, and that she heard him make an offer for her boy,—the ridiculous little goose!"

"She did, hey?" said Mr. Shelby, returning to his paper, which he seemed for a few moments quite intent upon, not perceiving that he was holding it bottom upwards.

"It will have to come out," said he, mentally; "as well now as ever."

"I told Eliza," said Mrs. Shelby, as she continued brushing her hair, "that she was a little fool for her pains, and that you never had anything to do with that sort of persons. Of course, I knew you never meant to sell any of our people,—least of all, to such a fellow."

"Well, Emily," said her husband, "so I have always felt and said; but the fact is that my business lies so that I cannot get on without. I shall have to sell some of my hands."

"To that creature? Impossible! Mr. Shelby, you cannot be serious."

"I'm sorry to say that I am," said Mr. Shelby. "I've agreed to sell Tom."

"What! our Tom?—that good, faithful creature!—been your faithful servant from a boy! O, Mr. Shelby!—and you have promised him his freedom, too,—you and I have spoken to him a hundred times of it. Well, I can believe anything now,—I can believe *now* that you could sell little Harry, poor Eliza's only child!" said Mrs. Shelby, in a tone between grief and indignation.

"Well, since you must know all, it is so. I have agreed to sell Tom and Harry both; and I don't know why I am to be rated, as if I were a monster, for doing what every one does every day."

"But why, of all others, choose these?" said Mrs. Shelby. "Why sell them, of all on the place, if you must sell at all?"

"Because they will bring the highest sum of any,—that's why. I could choose another, if you say so. The fellow made me a high bid on Eliza, if that would suit you any better," said Mr. Shelby.

"The wretch!" said Mrs. Shelby, vehemently.

"Well, I didn't listen to it, a moment,—out of regard to your feelings, I wouldn't—so give me some credit."

"My dear," said Mrs. Shelby, recollecting herself, "forgive me. I have been hasty. I was surprised, and entirely unprepared for this;—but surely you will allow me to intercede for these poor creatures. Tom is a noble-hearted, faithful fellow, if he is black. I do believe, Mr. Shelby, that if he were put to it, he would lay down his life for you."

"I know it,—I dare say;—but what's the use of all this?—I can't help myself."

"Why not make a pecuniary sacrifice? I'm willing to bear my part of the inconvenience. O, Mr. Shelby, I have tried—tried most faithfully, as a Christian woman should—to do my duty to these poor, simple, dependent creatures. I have cared for them, instructed them, watched over them, and known all their little cares and joys, for years; and how can I ever hold up my head again among them, if, for the sake of a little paltry gain, we sell such a faithful, excellent, confiding creature as poor Tom, and tear from him in a moment all we have taught him to love and value? I have taught them the duties of the family, of parent and child, and husband and wife; and how can I bear to have this open acknowledgment that we care for no tie, no duty, no relation, however sacred, compared with money? I have talked with Eliza about her boy,—her duty to him as a Christian mother, to watch over him, pray for him, and bring him up in a Christian way; and now what can I say, if you tear him away, and sell him, soul and body, to a profane, unprincipled man, just to save a little money? I have told her that one soul is worth more than all the money in the world; and how will she believe me when she sees us turn round and sell her child?—sell him, perhaps, to certain ruin of body and soul!"

"I'm sorry you feel so about it, Emily,—indeed I am," said Mr. Shelby; "and I respect your feelings, too, though I don't pretend to share them to their full extent; but I tell you now, solemnly, it's of no use,—I can't help myself. I didn't mean to tell you this, Emily; but, in plain words, there is no choice between selling these two and selling everything. Either they must go, or *all* must. Haley has come into possession of a mortgage, which, if I don't clear off with him directly, will take everything before it. I've raked, and scraped, and borrowed, and all but begged,—and the price of these two was needed to make up the balance, and I had to give them up. Haley fancied the child; he agreed to settle the matter that way, and no other. I was in his power, and *had* to do it. If you feel so to have them sold, would it be any better to have *all* sold?"

Mrs. Shelby stood like one stricken. Finally, turning to her toilet, she rested her face in her hands, and gave a sort of groan.

"This is God's curse on slavery!—a bitter, bitter, most accursed thing!—a curse to the master and a curse to the slave! I was a fool to think I could make anything good out of such a deadly evil. It is a sin to hold a slave under laws like ours,—I always felt it was,—I always thought so when I was a girl,—I thought so still more after I joined the church; but I thought I could gild it over,—I thought, by kindness, and care, and instruction, I could make the condition of mine better than freedom,—fool that I was!"

"Why, wife, you are getting to be an abolitionist, quite."

"Abolitionist; if they knew all I know about slavery they *might* talk! We don't need them to tell us; you know I never thought that slavery was right,—never felt willing to own slaves."

"Well, therein you differ from many wise and pious men," said Mr. Shelby. "You remember Mr. B.'s sermon, the other Sunday?"

"I don't want to hear such sermons; I never wish to hear Mr. B. in our church again. Ministers can't help the evil, perhaps,—can't cure it, any more than we can,—but defend it!—it always went against my common sense. And I think you didn't think much of that sermon, either."

"Well," said Shelby, "I must say these ministers sometimes carry matters further than we poor sinners would exactly dare to do. We men of the world must wink pretty hard at various things, and get used to a deal that isn't the exact thing. But we don't quite fancy, when women and ministers come out broad and square, and go beyond us in matters of either modesty or morals, that's a fact. But now, my dear, I trust you see the necessity of the thing, and you see that I have done the very best that circumstances would allow."

"O yes, yes!" said Mrs. Shelby, hurriedly and abstractedly fingering her gold watch,—"I haven't any jewelry of any amount," she added, thoughtfully; "but would not this watch do something?—it was an expensive one when it was bought. If I could only at least save Eliza's child, I would sacrifice anything I have."

"I'm sorry, very sorry, Emily," said Mr. Shelby. "I'm sorry this takes hold of you so; but it will do no good. The fact is, Emily, the thing's done; the bills of sale are already signed, and in Haley's hands; and you must be thankful it is no worse. That man has had it in his power to ruin us all,—and now he is fairly off. If you knew the man as I do, you'd think that we had had a narrow escape."

"Is he so hard, then?"

"Why, not a cruel man, exactly, but a man of leather,—a man alive to nothing but trade and profit,—cool, and unhesitating, and unrelenting, as death and the grave. He'd sell his own mother at a good percentage,—not wishing the old woman any harm, either."

"And this wretch owns that good, faithful Tom, and Eliza's child!"

"Well, my dear, the fact is that this goes rather hard with me; it's a thing I hate to think of. Haley wants to drive matters, and take possession to-morrow. I'm going to get out my horse bright and early, and be off. I can't see Tom, that's a fact; and you had better arrange a drive somewhere, and carry Eliza off. Let the thing be done when she is out of sight."

"No, no," said Mrs. Shelby; "I'll be in no sense accomplice or help in this cruel business. I'll go and see poor old Tom, God help him, in his distress! They shall see, at any rate, that their mistress can feel for and with them. As to Eliza, I dare not think about it. The Lord forgive us! What have we done, that this cruel necessity should come on us?"

There was one listener to this conversation whom Mr. and Mrs. Shelby little suspected.

Communicating with their apartment was a large closet, opening by a door into the outer passage. When Mrs. Shelby had dismissed Eliza for the night, her feverish and excited mind had suggested the idea of this closet; and she had hidden herself there, and, with her ear pressed close against the crack of the door, had lost not a word of the conversation.

When the voices died into silence, she rose and crept stealthily away. Pale, shivering, with rigid features and compressed lips, she looked an entirely altered being from the soft and timid creature she had been hitherto. She moved cautiously along the entry, paused one moment at her mistress's door, and raised her hands in mute appeal to Heaven, and then turned and glided into her own room. It was a quiet, neat apartment, on the same floor with her mistress. There was the pleasant sunny window, where she had often sat singing at her sewing; there a little case of books, and various little fancy articles, ranged by them, the gifts of Christmas holidays; there was her simple wardrobe in the closet and in the drawers:—here was, in short, her home; and, on the whole, a happy one it had been to her. But there, on the bed, lay her slumbering boy, his long curls falling negligently around his unconscious face, his rosy mouth half open, his little fat hands thrown out over the bedclothes, and a smile spread like a sunbeam over his whole face.

"Poor boy! poor fellow!" said Eliza; "they have sold you! but your mother will save you yet!"

No tear dropped over that pillow; in such straits as these the heart has no tears to give,—it drops only blood, bleeding itself away in silence. She took a piece of paper and a pencil, and wrote hastily,—

"O, Missis dear Missis! don't think me ungrateful,—don't think hard of me, any way,—I heard all you and master said to-night. I am going to try to save my boy,—you will not blame me! God bless and reward you for all your kindness!"

Hastily folding and directing this, she went to a drawer and made up a little package of clothing for her boy, which she tied with a handkerchief firmly round her waist; and, so fond is a mother's remembrance, that, even in the terrors of that hour, she did not forget to put in the little package one or two of his favorite toys, reserving a gayly painted parrot to amuse him, when she should be called on to awaken him. It was some trouble to arouse the little sleeper; but, after some effort, he sat up, and was playing with his bird, while his mother was putting on her bonnet and shawl.

"Where are you going, mother?" said he, as she drew near the bed, with his little coat and cap.

His mother drew near, and looked so earnestly into his eyes, that he at once divined that something unusual was the matter.

"Hush, Harry," she said; "mustn't speak loud, or they will hear us. A wicked man was coming to take little Harry away from his mother, and carry him 'way off in the dark; but mother won't let him,—she's going to put on her little boy's cap and coat, and run off with him, so the ugly man can't catch him."

Saying these words, she had tied and buttoned on the child's simple outfit, and, taking him in her arms, she whispered to him to be very still; and, opening a door in her room which led into the outer veranda, she glided noiselessly out.

It was a sparkling, frosty, starlight night, and the mother wrapped the shawl close round her child, as, perfectly quiet with vague terror, he clung round her neck.

Old Bruno, a great Newfoundland, who slept at the end of the porch, rose, with a low growl, as she came near. She gently spoke his name, and the animal, an old pet and playmate of hers, instantly, wagging his tail, prepared to follow her, though apparently revolving much, in his simple dog's head, what such an indiscreet midnight promenade might mean. Some dim idea of imprudence or impropriety in the measure seemed to embarrass him considerably; for he often stopped, as Eliza glided forward, and looked wistfully, first at her and then at the house, and then, as if reassured by reflection, he pattered along after her again. A few minutes brought them to the window of Uncle Tom's cottage, and Eliza, stopping, tapped lightly on the window-pane.

The prayer-meeting at Uncle Tom's had, in the order of hymn-singing, been protracted to a very late hour; and, as Uncle Tom had indulged himself in a few lengthy solos afterwards, the consequence was, that, although it was now between twelve and one o'clock, he and his worthy helpmeet were not yet asleep.

"Good Lord! what's that?" said Aunt Chloe, starting up and hastily drawing the curtain. "My sakes alive, if it an't Lizy! Get on your clothes, old man, quick!—there's old Bruno, too, a pawin' round; what on airth! I'm gwine to open the door."

And, suiting the action to the word, the door flew open, and the light of the tallow candle, which Tom had hastily lighted, fell on the haggard face and dark, wild eyes of the fugitive.

"Lord bless you!—I'm skeered to look at ye, Lizy! Are ye tuck sick, or what's come over ye?"

"I'm running away,—Uncle Tom and Aunt Chloe,—carrying off my child,—Master sold him!"

"Sold him?" echoed both, lifting up their hands in dismay.

"Yes, sold him!" said Eliza, firmly; "I crept into the closet by Mistress's door to-night, and I heard Master tell Missis that he had sold my Harry, and you, Uncle Tom, both, to a trader; and that he was going off this morning on his horse, and that the man was to take possession to-day."

Tom had stood, during this speech, with his hands raised, and his eyes dilated, like a man in a dream. Slowly and gradually, as its meaning came over him, he collapsed, rather than seated himself, on his old chair, and sunk his head down upon his knees.

"The good Lord have pity on us!" said Aunt Chloe. "O, it don't seem as if it was true! What has he done, that Mas'r should sell *him?*"

"He hasn't done anything,—it isn't for that. Master don't want to sell; and Missis,—she's always good. I heard her plead and beg for us; but he told her 'twas no use; that he was in this man's debt, and that this man had got the power over him; and that if he didn't pay him off clear, it would end in his having to sell the place and all the people, and move off. Yes, I heard him say there was no choice between selling these two and selling all, the man was driving him so hard. Master said he was sorry; but O, Missis,—you ought to have heard her talk! If she an't a Christian and an angel, there never was one. I'm a wicked girl to leave her so; but, then, I can't help it. She said, herself, one soul was worth more than the world; and this boy has a soul, and if I let him be carried off, who knows what'll become of it? It must be right; but, if it an't right, the Lord forgive me, for I can't help doing it!"

"Well, old man!" said Aunt Chloe, "why don't you go, too? Will you wait to be toted down river, where they kill niggers with hard work and starving? I'd a heap rather die than go there, any day! There's time for ye,—be off with Lizy,—you've got a pass to come and go any time. Come, bustle up, and I'll get your things together."

Tom slowly raised his head, and looked sorrowfully but quietly around, and said,—

"No, no,—I an't going. Let Eliza go,—it's her right! I wouldn't be the one to say no,—tan't in *natur* for her to stay; but you heard what she said! If I must be sold, or all the people on the place, and every-thing go to rack, why, let me be sold. I s'pose I can b'ar it as well as any on 'em," he added, while something like a sob and a sigh shook his broad, rough chest convulsively. "Mas'r always found me on the spot,—he always will. I never have broke trust, nor used my pass no ways contrary to my word, and I never will. It's better for me alone to go, than to break up the place and sell all. Mas'r an't to blame, Chloe, and he'll take care of you and the poor—"

Here he turned to the rough trundle-bed full of little woolly heads, and broke fairly down. He leaned over the back of the chair, and covered his face with his large hands. Sobs, heavy, hoarse, and loud, shook the chair, and great tears fell through his fingers on the floor; just such tears, sir, as you dropped into the coffin where lay your first-born son; such tears, woman, as you shed when you heard the cries of your dying babe. For, sir, he was a man,—and you are but another man. And, woman, though dressed in silk and jewels, you are but a woman, and, in life's great straits and mighty griefs, ye feel but one sorrow!

"And now," said Eliza, as she stood in the door, "I saw my husband only this afternoon, and I little knew then what was to come. They have pushed him to the very last standing-place, and he told me, to-day, that he was going to run away. Do try, if you can, to get word to him. Tell him how I went, and why I went; and tell him I'm going to try and find Canada. You must give my love to him, and tell him, if I never see him again,"—she turned away, and stood with her back to them for a moment, and then added, in a husky voice, "tell him to be as good as he can, and try and meet me in the kingdom of heaven."

"Call Bruno in there," she added. "Shut the door on him, poor beast! He mustn't go with me!"

A few last words and tears, a few simple adieus and blessings, and, clasping her wondering and afrighted child in her arms, she glided noiselessly away.

John Brown mural in Kansas state capitol

HENRY DAVID THOREAU

A Plea for Captain John Brown

(1859)

John Brown, that lank, hard-eyed, and bearded fanatic, appeared to Henry David Thoreau as the pre-ordained occupant of a waiting pedestal: the American as Old Testament Prophet, direct representative of a God of Wrath and Righteousness. Thoreau was not entirely wrong. While Brown's soul was marching on, his body—or likenesses of it—promptly did mount to an appointed place in the national pantheon of heroes. There John Brown remains, the joy of enthusiasts and myth-makers, the bane of historians and pragmatists.

For most of his life, John Brown was a total failure. The historian James C. Malin has found that Brown had a minimal role in the struggles to make a "bleeding Kansas" a free state. Brown's first famous exploit was a senseless massacre at Os-

sawatamie, in which he led a raiding party in the cold-blooded murder of five men whose bodies were horribly mutilated. Of the five victims, two were not even southerners, and none owned slaves. "Old Ossawatamie's" second great moment was a raid on the federal arsenal at Harper's Ferry in October 1859, which turned out to be a mass of blunders and crazy dreams. The slaves rejected their "liberator," aware—as Abraham Lincoln noted at the time—that his plan could not possibly succeed. But Brown's final moment, his courageous stand in the courtroom and on the scaffold, seemed to redeem every past failure. Even though Thoreau had met Brown in the past, the real subject of his plea was the John Brown of the great courtroom drama.

Henry David Thoreau had little patience with institutions. As a transcendentalist, he believed that the solitary individual could seize reality as the artist does and dominate events by superior morality. In his famous protest against the Mexican War, the Essay on Civil Disobedience (1849), Thoreau argued rather abstractly that:

> Action from principle—the perception and the performance of right—changes things and relations; it is essentially revolutionary, and does not consist wholly with any thing which was. It not only divides states and churches, it divides families; aye, it divides the individual, separating the diabolical in him from the divine.

In Thoreau's case, the act of letting his "life be a counter-friction to stop the machine" was merely to go to jail for a night as a protest against paying taxes to support "a slaveholders' war." John Brown, however, offered Thoreau real proof of all he had always asserted. One man, acting from absolute principle, did change "things and relations," did divide state and churches, did help bring on a Civil War which achieved something of the goals of his extraordinary enterprise at Harper's Ferry.

Brown was the transcendental hero of Thoreau's dreams—dreams shared by thousands of romantic and idealistic Americans helpless before the dilemma of slavery. Now Brown had at last cut through all the ambiguities. Or had he? Did the single-minded pursuit of the destruction of evil improve the world or even the nation? Thoreau had said a loud yes. In the same era another major writer, Herman Melville, attacked the same problem in Moby Dick, and just as firmly said no.

I trust that you will pardon me for being here. I do not wish to force my thoughts upon you, but I feel forced myself. Little as I know of Captain Brown, I would fain do my part to correct the tone and the statements of the newspapers, and of my countrymen generally, respecting his character and actions. It costs us nothing to be just. We can at least express our sympathy with, and admiration of, him and his companions, and that is what I now propose to do.

First, as to his history. I will endeavor to omit, as much as possible, what you have already read. I need not describe his person to you, for probably most of you have seen and will not soon forget him. I am told that his grandfather, John Brown, was an officer in the Revolution; that he himself was born in Connecticut about the beginning of this century, but early went with his father to Ohio. I heard him say that his father was a contractor who furnished beef to the army there, in the war of 1812; that he accompanied him to the camp, and assisted him in that employment, seeing a good deal of military life, more, perhaps, than if he had been a soldier, for he was often present at the councils of the officers. Especially, he learned by experience how armies are supplied and maintained in the field—a work which, he observed, requires at least as much experience and skill as to lead them in battle. He said that few persons had any conception of the cost, even the pecuniary cost, of firing a single bullet in war. He saw enough, at any rate, to disgust him with a military life; indeed, to excite in him a great abhorrence of it; so much so, that though he was tempted by the offer of some petty office in the army, when he was about eighteen, he not only declined that, but he also refused to train when warned, and was fined for it. He then resolved that he would never have any thing to do with any war, unless it were a war for liberty.

When the troubles in Kansas began, he sent several of his sons thither to strengthen the party of the Free State men, fitting them out with such weapons as he had; telling them that if the troubles should increase, and there should be need of him, he would follow to assist them with his hand and counsel. This, as you all know, he soon after did; and it was through his agency, far more than any other's, that Kansas was made free.

For a part of his life he was a surveyor, and at one time he was engaged in wool-growing, and he went to Europe as an agent about that business. There, as every where, he had his eyes about him, and made many original observations. He said, for instance, that he saw why the soil of England was so rich, and that of Germany (I think it was) so poor, and he thought of writing to some of the crowned heads about it. It was because in England the peasantry live on the soil which they cultivate, but in Germany they are gathered into villages, at night. It is a pity that he did not make a book of his observations.

I should say that he was an old-fashioned man in his respect for the Constitution, & his faith in the permanence of this Union. Slavery he deemed to be wholly opposed to these, and he was its determined foe.

He was by descent and birth a New England farmer, a man of great common sense, deliberate and practical as that class is, and tenfold more so. He was like the best of those who stood at Concord Bridge once, on Lexington Common, and on Bunker Hill, only he was firmer and higher principled than any that I have chanced to hear of as there. It was no abolition lecturer that converted him. Ethan Allen and Stark, with whom he may in some respects be compared, were rangers in a lower and less important field. They could bravely face their country's foes, but he had the courage to face his country herself, when she was in the wrong. A Western writer says, to account for his escape from so many perils, that he was concealed under a "rural exterior;" as if, in that prairie land, a hero should, by good rights, wear a citizen's dress only.

He did not go to the college called Harvard, good old Alma Mater as she is. He was not fed on the pap that is there furnished. As he phrased it, "I know no more of grammar than one of your calves." But he went to the great university of the West, where he sedulously pursued the study of Liberty, for which he had early betrayed a fondness, and having taken many degrees, he finally commenced the public practice of Humanity in Kansas, as you all know. Such were *his humanities,* and not any study of grammar. He would have left a Greek accent slanting the wrong way, and righted up a falling man.

He was one of that class of whom we hear a great deal, but, for the most part, see nothing at all—the Puritans. It would be in vain to kill him. He died lately in the time of Cromwell, but he reappeared here. Why should he not? Some of the Puritan stock are said to have come over and settled in New England. They were a class that did something else than celebrate their forefathers' day, and eat parched corn in remembrance of that time. They were neither Democrats nor Republicans, but men of simple habits, straightforward, prayerful; not thinking much of rulers who did not fear God, not making many compromises, nor seeking after available candidates.

"In his camp," as one has recently written, and as I have myself heard him state, "he permitted no profanity; no man of loose morals was suffered to remain there, unless, indeed, as a prisoner of war. 'I would rather,' said he, 'have the small-pox, yellow fever, and cholera, all together in my camp, than a man without principle. It is a mistake, sir, that our people make, when they think that bullies are the best fighters, or that they are the fit men to oppose these Southerners. Give me men of good principles—God-fearing men—men who respect themselves, and with a dozen of them I will oppose any hundred such men as these Buford ruffians.'" He said that if one offered himself to be a soldier under him, who was forward to tell what he could or would do, if he could only get sight of the enemy, he had but little confidence in him.

He was never able to find more than a score or so of recruits whom he would accept, and only about a dozen, among them his sons, in whom he had perfect faith. When he was here, some years ago, he showed to a few a little manuscript book (his "orderly book" I think he called it) containing the names of his company in Kansas, and the rules by which they bound themselves; and he stated that several of them had already sealed the contract with their blood. When some one remarked that, with the addition of a chaplain, it would have been a perfect Cromwellian troop, he observed that he would have been glad to add a chaplain to the list, if he could have found one who could fill that office worthily. It is easy enough to find one for the United States army. I believe that he had prayers in his camp morning and evening, nevertheless.

He was a man of Spartan habits, and at sixty was scrupulous about his diet at your table, excusing himself by saying that he must eat sparingly and fare hard, as became a soldier or one who was fitting himself for difficult enterprises, a life of exposure.

A man of rare common sense and directness of speech, as of action; a transcendentalist above all, a man of ideas and principles—that was what distinguished him. Not yielding to a whim or transient impulse, but carrying out the purpose of a life. I noticed that he did not overstate any thing, but spoke within bounds. I remember, particularly, how, in his speech here, he referred to what his family had suffered in Kansas, without ever giving the least vent to his pent-up fire. It was a volcano with an ordinary chimney-flue. Also referring to the deeds of certain Border Ruffians, he said, rapidly paring away his speech, like an experienced soldier, keeping a reserve of force and meaning, "They had a perfect right to be hung." He was not in the least a rhetorician, was not talking to Buncombe or his constituents any where, had no need to invent any thing, but to tell the simple truth, and communicate his own resolution; therefore he appeared incomparably strong, and eloquence in Congress and elsewhere seemed to me at a discount. It was like the speeches of Cromwell compared with those of an ordinary king.

As for his tact and prudence, I will merely say, that at a time when scarcely a man from the Free States was able to reach Kansas by any direct route, at least without having his arms taken from him, he, carrying what imperfect guns and other weapons he could collect, openly and slowly drove an ox-cart through Missouri, apparently in the capacity of a surveyor, with his surveying compass exposed in it, and so passed unsuspected, and had ample opportunity to learn the designs of the enemy. For some time after his arrival he still followed the same profession. When, for instance, he saw a knot of the ruffians on the prairie, discussing, of course, the single topic which then occupied their minds, he would, perhaps, take his compass and one of his sons, and proceed to run an imaginary line right through the very spot on which that conclave had assembled, and when he came up to them, he would naturally pause and have some talk with them, learning their news, and, at last, all their plans perfectly; and having thus completed his real survey, he would resume his imaginary one, and run on his line till he was out of sight.

When I expressed surprise that he could live in Kansas at all, with a price set upon his head, and so large a number, including the authorities, exasperated against him, he accounted for it by saying, "It is perfectly well understood that I will not be taken." Much of the time for some years he has had to skulk in swamps, suffering from poverty and from sickness, which was the consequence of exposure, befriended only by Indians and a few whites. But though it might be known that he was lurking in a particular swamp, his foes commonly did not care to go in after him. He could even come out into a town where there were more Border Ruffians than Free State men, and transact some business, without delaying long, and yet not be molested; for said he, "No little handful of men were willing to undertake it, & a large body could not be got together in season."

As for his recent failure, we do not know the facts about it. It was evidently far from being a wild and desperate attempt. His enemy, Mr. Vallandingham, is compelled to say, that "it was among the best planned and executed conspiracies that ever failed."

Not to mention his other successes, was it a failure, or did it show a want of good management, to deliver from bondage a dozen human beings, and walk off with them by broad daylight, for weeks if not months, at a leisurely pace, through one State after another, for half the length of the North, conspicuous to all parties, with a price set upon his head, going into a court room on his way and telling what he had done, thus convincing Missouri that it was not profitable to try to hold slaves in his neighborhood?—and this, not because the government menials were lenient, but because they were afraid of him.

Yet he did not attribute his success, foolishly, to "his star," or to any magic. He said, truly, that the reason why such greatly superior numbers quailed before him, was, as one of his prisoners confessed, because they *lacked a cause*—a kind of armor which he and his party never lacked. When the time came, few men were found willing to lay down their lives in defence of what they knew to be wrong; they did not like that this should be their last act in this world.

But to make haste to *his* last act, and its effects.

The newspapers seem to ignore, or perhaps are really ignorant of the fact, that there are at least as many as two or three individuals to a town throughout the North, who think much as the present speaker does about him and his enterprise. I do not hesitate to say that they are an important and growing party. We aspire to be something more than stupid and timid chattels, pretending to read history and our Bibles, but desecrating every house and every day we breathe in. Perhaps anxious politicians may prove that only seventeen white men and five negroes were concerned in the late enterprise; but their very anxiety to prove this might suggest to themselves that all is not told. Why do they still dodge the truth? They are so anxious because of a dim consciousness of the fact, which they do not distinctly face, that at least a million of the free inhabitants of the United States would have rejoiced if it had succeeded. They at most only criticise the tactics. Though we wear no crape, the thought of that man's position and probable fate is spoiling many a man's day here at the North for other thinking. If any one who has seen him here can pursue successfully any other train of thought, I do not know what he is made of. If there is any such who gets his usual allowance of sleep, I will warrant him to fatten easily under any circumstances which do not touch his body or purse. I put a piece of paper and a pencil under my pillow, and when I could not sleep, I wrote in the dark.

On the whole, my respect for my fellow-men, except as one may outweigh a million, is not being increased these days. I have noticed the cold-blooded way in which newspaper writers and men generally speak of this event, as if an ordinary malefactor, though one of unusual "pluck" (as the Governor of Virginia is reported to have said, using the language of the cock-pit, "the gamest man he ever saw") had been caught, and were about to be hung. He was not dreaming of his foes when the governor thought he looked so brave. It turns what sweetness I have to gall, to hear, or hear of, the remarks of some of my neighbors. When we heard at first that he was dead, one of my townsmen observed that "he died as the fool dieth;" which, pardon me, for an instant suggested a likeness in him dying to my neighbor living. Others, craven-hearted, said disparagingly, that "he threw his life away," because he resisted the government. Which way have they thrown *their* lives, pray?—Such as would praise a man for attacking singly an ordinary band of thieves or murderers. I hear another ask, Yankee-like, "What will he gain by it?" as if he expected to fill his pockets by this enterprise. Such a one has no idea of gain but in this worldly sense. If it does not lead to a "surprise" party, if he does not get a new pair of boots, or a vote of thanks, it must be a failure. "But he won't gain any thing by it." Well, no, I don't suppose he could get four-and-sixpence a day for being hung, take the year round; but then he stands a chance to save a considerable part of his soul—and *such* a soul!—when *you* do not. No doubt you can get more in your market for a quart of milk than for a quart of blood, but that is not the market that heroes carry their blood to.

Such do not know that like the seed is the fruit, and that, in the moral world, when good seed is planted, good fruit is inevitable, and does not depend on our watering and cultivating; that when you plant, or bury, a hero in his field, a crop of heroes is sure to spring up. This is a seed of such force and vitality, that it does not ask our leave to germinate.

The momentary charge at Balaclava, in obedience to a blundering command, proving what a perfect machine the soldier is, has, properly enough, been celebrated by a poet laureate; but the steady, and for the most part successful charge of this man, for some years, against the legions of Slavery, in obedience to an infinitely higher command, is as much more memorable than that, as an intelligent and conscientious man is superior to a machine. Do you think that that will go unsung?

"Served him right"—"A dangerous man"—"He is undoubtedly insane." So they proceed to live their sane, and wise, and altogether admirable lives, reading their Plutarch a little, but chiefly pausing at that feat of Putnam, who was let down into a wolf's den; and in this wise they nourish themselves for brave and patriotic deeds some time or other. The Tract Society could afford to print that story of Putnam. You might open the district schools with the reading of it, for there is nothing about Slavery or the Church in it; unless it occurs to the reader that some pastors are *wolves* in sheep's clothing. "The American Board of Commissioners for Foreign Missions" even, might dare to protest against *that* wolf, I have heard of boards, and of American boards, but it chances that I never heard of this particular lumber till lately. And yet I hear of Northern men, women, and children, by families, buying a "life membership" in such societies as these—a life-membership in the grave! You can get buried cheaper than that.

Our foes are in our midst and all about us. There is hardly a house but is divided against itself, for our foe is the all but universal woodenness of both head and heart, the want of vitality in man, which is the effect of our vice; and hence are begotten fear, superstition, bigotry, persecution, and slavery of all kinds. We are mere figure-heads upon a hulk, with livers in the place of hearts. The curse is the worship of idols, which at length changes the worshipper into a stone image himself; and the New Englander is just as much an idolater as the Hindoo. This man was an exception, for he did not set up even a political graven image between him and his God.

A church that can never have done with excommunicating Christ while it exists! Away with your broad and flat churches, and your narrow and tall churches! Take a step forward, and invent a new style of out-houses. Invent a salt that will save you, and defend our nostrils.

The modern Christian is a man who has consented to say all the prayers in the liturgy, provided you will let him go straight to bed and sleep quietly afterward. All his prayers begin with "Now I lay me down to sleep," and he is forever looking forward to the time when he shall go to his "*long* rest." He has consented to perform certain old established charities, too, after a fashion, but he does not wish to hear of any new-fangled ones; he doesn't wish to have any supplementary articles added to the contract, to fit it to the present time. He shows the whites of his eyes on the Sabbath, and the blacks all the rest of the week. The evil is not merely a stagnation of blood, but a stagnation of spirit. Many, no doubt, are well disposed, but sluggish by constitution and by habit, and they cannot conceive of a man who is actuated by higher motives than they are. Accordingly they pronounce this man insane, for they know that *they* could never act as he does, as long as they were themselves.

We dream of foreign countries, of other times and races of men, placing them at a distance in history or space; but let some significant event like the present occur in our midst, and we discover, often, this distance and this strangeness between us and our nearest neighbors. *They* are our Austrias, and Chinas, and South Sea Islands. Our crowded society becomes well spaced all at once, clean and handsome to the eye, a city of magnificent distances. We discover why it was that we never got beyond compliments and surfaces with them before; we become aware of as many versts between us and them as there are between a wandering Tartar and a Chinese town. The thoughtful man becomes a hermit in the thoroughfares of the market-place. Impassable seas suddenly find their level between us, or dumb steppes stretch themselves out there. It is the difference of constitution, of intelligence, and faith, and not streams and mountains, that make the true and impassable boundaries between individuals and between states. None but the like-minded can come plenipotentiary to our court.

I read all the newspapers I could get within a week after this event, and I do not remember in them a single expression of sympathy for these men. I have since seen one noble statement, in a Boston paper, not editorial. Some voluminous sheets decided not to print the full report of Brown's words to the exclusion of other matter. It was as if a publisher should reject the manuscript of the New Testament, and print Wilson's last speech. The same journal which contained this pregnant news, was chiefly filled, in parallel columns, with the reports of the political conventions that were being held. But the descent to them was too steep. They should have been spared this contrast, been printed in an extra at least. To turn from the voices and deeds of earnest men to the *cackling* of political conventions! Office-seekers and speech-makers, who do not so much as lay an honest egg, but wear their breasts bare upon an egg of chalk! Their great game is the game of straws, or rather that universal aboriginal game of the platter, at which the Indians cried *hub, bub!* Exclude the reports of religious and political conventions, and publish the words of a living man.

But I object not so much to what they have omitted, as to what they have inserted. Even the *Liberator* called it "a misguided, wild, and apparently insane—effort." As for the herd of newspapers and magazines, I do not chance to know an editor in the country who will deliberately print any thing which he knows will ultimately and permanently reduce the number of his subscribers. They do not believe that it would be expedient. How then can they print truth? If we do not say pleasant things, they argue, nobody will attend to us. And so they do like some travelling auctioneers, who sing an obscene song in order to draw a crowd around them. Republican editors, obliged to get their sentences ready for the morning edition, and accustomed to look at every thing by the twilight of politics, express no admiration, nor true sorrow even, but call these men "deluded fanatics"—"mistaken men"—"insane," or "crazed." It suggests what a *sane* set of editors we are blessed with, *not* "mistaken men"; who know very well on which side their bread is buttered, at least.

A man does a brave and humane deed, and at once, on all sides, we hear people and parties declaring, "I didn't do it, nor countenance *him* to do it, in any conceivable way. It can't be fairly inferred from my past career." I, for one, am not interested to hear you define your position. I don't know that I ever was, or ever shall be. I think it is mere egotism, or impertinent at this time. Ye needn't take so much pains to wash your skirts of him. No intelligent man will ever be convinced that he was any creature of yours. He went and came, as he himself informs us, "under the auspices of John Brown and nobody else." The Republican party does not perceive how many his *failure* will make to vote more correctly than they would have them. They have counted the votes of Pennsylvania & Co., but they have not correctly counted Captain Brown's vote. He has taken the wind out of their sails, the little wind they had, and they may as well lie to and repair.

What though he did not belong to your clique! Though you may not approve of his method or his principles, recognize his magnanimity. Would you not like to claim kindredship with him in that, though in no other thing he is like, or likely, to you? Do you think that you would lose your reputation so? What you lost at the spile, you would gain at the bung.

If they do not mean all this, then they do not speak the truth, and say what they mean. They are simply at their old tricks still.

"It was always conceded to him," *says one who calls him crazy,* "that he was a conscientious man, very modest in his demeanor, apparently inoffensive, until the subject of Slavery was introduced, when he would exhibit a feeling of indignation unparalleled."

The slave-ship is on her way, crowded with its dying victims; new cargoes are being added in mid-ocean; a small crew of slaveholders, countenanced by a large body of passengers, is smothering four millions under the hatches, and yet the politician asserts that the only proper way by which deliverance is to be obtained, is by "the quiet diffusion of the sentiments of humanity," without any "outbreak." As if the sentiments of humanity were ever found unaccompanied by its deeds, and you could disperse them, all finished to order, the pure article, as easily as water with a watering-pot, and so lay the dust. What is that that I hear cast overboard? The bodies of the dead that have found deliverance. That is the way we are "diffusing" humanity, and its sentiments with it.

Prominent and influential editors, accustomed to deal with politicians, men of an infinitely lower grade, say, in their ignorance, that he acted "on the principle of revenge." They do not know the man. They must enlarge themselves to conceive of him. I have no doubt that the time will come when they will begin to see him as he was. They have got to conceive of a man of faith and of religious principle, and not a politician nor an Indian; of a man who did not wait till he was personally interfered with or thwarted in some harmless business before he gave his life to the cause of the oppressed.

If Walker may be considered the representative of the South, I wish I could say that Brown was the representative of the North. He was a superior man. He did not value his bodily life in comparison with ideal things. He did not recognize unjust human laws, but resisted them as he was bid. For once we are lifted out of the trivialness and dust of politics into the region of truth and manhood. No man in America has ever stood up so persistently and effectively for the dignity of human nature, knowing himself for a man, and the equal of any and all governments. In that sense he was the most American of us all. He needed no babbling lawyer, making false issues, to defend him. He was more than a match for all the judges that American voters, or office-holders of whatever grade, can create. He could not have been tried by a jury of his peers, because his peers did not exist. When a man stands up serenely against the condemnation and vengeance of mankind, rising above them literally *by a whole body*—even though he were of late the vilest murderer, who has settled that matter with himself—the spectacle is a sublime one (didn't ye know it, ye Liberators, ye Tribunes, ye Republicans?), and we become criminal in comparison. Do yourselves the honor to recognize him. He needs none of your respect.

As for the Democratic journals, they are not human enough to affect me at all. I do not feel indignation at any thing they may say.

I am aware that I anticipate a little, that he was still, at the last accounts, alive in the hands of his foes; but that being the case, I have all along found myself thinking & speaking of him as physically dead.

I do not believe in erecting statues to those who still live in our hearts, whose bones have not yet crumbled in the earth around us, but I would rather see the statue of Captain Brown in the Massachusetts State-House yard, than that of any other man whom I know. I rejoice that I live in this age—that I am his contemporary.

What a contrast, when we turn to that political party which is so anxiously shuffling him and his plot out of its way, and looking around for some available slaveholder, perhaps, to be its candidate, at least for one who will execute the Fugitive Slave Law, and all those other unjust laws which he took up arms to annul!

Insane! A father and six sons, and one son-in-law, and several more men besides—as many at least as twelve disciples—all struck with insanity at once; while the sane tyrant holds with a firmer grip than ever his four millions of slaves, and a thousand sane editors, his abettors, are saving their country and their bacon! Just as insane were his efforts in Kansas. Ask the tyrant who is his most dangerous foe, the sane man or the insane. Do the thousands who know him best, who have rejoiced at his deeds in Kansas, and have afforded him material aid there, think him insane? Such a use of this word is a mere trope with most who persist in using it, and I have no doubt that many of the rest have already in silence retracted their words.

Read his admirable answers to Mason and others. How they are dwarfed and defeated by the contrast! On the one side, half brutish, half timid questioning; on the other, truth, clear as lightning, crashing into their obscene temples. They are made to stand with Pilate, and Gesler, and the Inquisition. How ineffectual their speech and action! and what a void their silence! They are but helpless tools in this great work. It was no human power that gathered them about this preacher.

What have Massachusetts and the North sent a few *sane* representatives to Congress for, of late years?—to declare with effect what kind of sentiments? All their speeches put together and boiled down—and probably they themselves will confess it—do not match for manly directness and force, and for simple truth, the few casual remarks of crazy John Brown, on the floor of the Harper's Ferry engine house—that man whom you are about to hang, to send to the other world, though not to represent *you* there. No, he was not our representative in any sense. He was too fair a specimen of a man to represent the like of us. Who, then, *were* his constituents? If you read his words understandingly you will find out. In his case there is no idle eloquence, no made, nor maiden speech, no compliments to the oppressor. Truth is his inspirer, and earnestness the polisher of his sentences. He could afford to lose his Sharpe's rifles, while he retained his faculty of speech, a Sharpe's rifle of infinitely surer and longer range.

And the *New York Herald* reports the conversation *"verbatim"!* It does not know of what undying words it is made the vehicle.

I have no respect for the penetration of any man who can read the report of that conversation, and still call the principal in it insane. It has the ring of a saner sanity than an ordinary discipline and habits of life, than an ordinary organization, secure. Take any sentence of it—"Any questions that I can honorably answer, I will; not otherwise. So far as I am myself concerned, I have told every thing truthfully. I value my word, sir." The few who talk about his vindictive spirit, while they really admire his heroism, have no test by which to detect a noble man, no amalgam to combine with his pure gold. They mix their own dross with it.

It is a relief to turn from these slanders to the testimony of his more truthful, but frightened, jailers and hangmen. Governor Wise speaks far more justly & appreciatingly of him than any Northern editor, or politician, or public personage, that I chance to have heard from. I know that you can afford to hear him again on this subject. He says: "They are themselves mistaken who take him to be a madman. . . . He is cool, collected, and indomitable, and it is but just to him to say, that he was humane to his prisoners. . . . And he inspired me with great trust in his integrity as a man of truth. He is a fanatic, vain and garrulous," (I leave that part to Mr. Wise,) "but firm, truthful, and intelligent. His men, too, who survive, are like him. . . . Colonel Washington says that he was the coolest and firmest man he ever saw in defying danger and death. With one son dead by his side, and another shot through, he felt the pulse of his dying son with one hand, and held his rifle with the other, and commanded his men with the utmost composure, encouraging them to be firm, and to sell their lives as dear as they could. Of the three white prisoners, Brown, Stephens, and Coppic, it was hard to say which was most firm."

Almost the first Northern men whom the slaveholder has learned to respect!

The testimony of Mr. Vallandingham, though less valuable, is of the same purport, that "it is vain to underrate either the man or his conspiracy. . . . He is the farthest possible remove from the ordinary ruffian, fanatic, or madman."

"All is quiet at Harper's Ferry," say the journals. What is the character of that calm which follows when the law and the slaveholder prevail? I regard this event as a touchstone designed to bring out, with glaring distinctness, the character of this government. We needed to be thus assisted to see it by the light of history. It needed to see itself. When a government puts forth its strength on the side of injustice, as ours to maintain Slavery and kill the liberators of the slave, it reveals itself a merely brute force, or worse, a demoniacal force. It is the head of the Plug Uglies. It is more manifest than ever that tyranny rules. I see this government to be effectually allied with France and Austria in oppressing mankind. There sits a tyrant holding fettered four millions of slaves; here comes their heroic liberator. This most hypocritical and diabolical government looks up from its seat on the gasping four millions, and inquires with an assumption of innocence, "What do you assault me for? Am I not an honest man? Cease agitation on this subject, or I will make a slave of you, too, or else hang you."

We talk about a *representative* government; but what a monster of a government is that where the noblest faculties of the mind, and the *whole* heart, are not *represented.* A semi-human tiger or ox, stalking over the earth, with its heart taken out and the top of its brain shot away. Heroes have fought well on their stumps when their legs were shot off, but I never heard of any good done by such a government as that.

The only government that I recognize—and it matters not how few are at the head of it, or how small its army—is that power that establishes justice in the land, never that which establishes injustice. What shall we think of a government to which all the truly brave and just men in the land are enemies, standing between it and those whom it oppresses? A government that pretends to be Christian and crucifies a million Christs every day!

Treason! Where does such treason take its rise? I cannot help thinking of you as you deserve, ye governments. Can you dry up the fountains of thought? High treason, when it is resistance to tyranny here below, has its origin in, and is first committed by the power that makes and forever recreates man. When you have caught and hung all these human rebels, you have accomplished nothing but your own guilt, for you have not struck at the fountain head. You presume to contend with a foe against whom West Point cadets and rifled cannon *point* not. Can all the art of the cannon-founder tempt matter to turn against its maker? Is the form in which the founder thinks he casts it more essential than the constitution of it and of himself?

The United States have a coffle of four millions of slaves. They are determined to keep them in this condition; and Massachusetts is one of the confederated overseers to prevent their escape. Such are not all the inhabitants of Massachusetts, but such are they who rule and are obeyed here. It was Massachusetts, as well as Virginia, that put down this insurrection at Harper's Ferry. She sent the marines there, and she will have to pay the penalty of her sin.

Suppose that there is a society in this State that out of its own purse and magnanimity saves all the fugitive slaves that run to us, and protects our colored fellow-citizens, and leaves the other work to the Government, so-called. Is not that government fast losing its occupation, and becoming contemptible to mankind? If private men are obliged to perform the offices of government, to protect the weak and dispense justice, then the government becomes only a hired man, or clerk, to perform menial or indifferent services. Of course, that is but the shadow of a government whose existence necessitates a Vigilant Committee. What should we think of the oriental Cadi even, behind whom worked in secret a vigilant committee? But such is the character of our Northern States generally; each has its Vigilant Committee. And, to a certain extent, these crazy governments recognize and accept this relation. They say, virtually, "We'll be glad to work for you on these terms, only don't make a noise about it." And thus the government, its salary being insured, withdraws into the back shop, taking the constitution with it, and bestows most of its labor on repairing that. When I hear it at work sometimes, as I go by, it reminds me, at best, of those farmers who in winter contrive to turn a penny by following the coopering business. And what kind of spirit is their barrel made to hold? They speculate in stocks, and bore holes in mountains, but they are not competent to lay out even a decent highway. The only *free* road, the Underground Railroad, is owned and managed by the Vigilant Committee. *They* have tunnelled under the whole breadth of the land. Such a government is losing its power and respectability as surely as water runs out of a leaky vessel, and is held by one that can contain it.

I hear many condemn these men because they were so few. When were the good and the brave ever in a majority? Would you have had him wait till that time came?—till you and I came over to him? The very fact that he had no rabble or troop of hirelings about him, would alone distinguish him from ordinary heroes. His company was small indeed, because few could be found worthy to pass muster. Each one who there laid down his life for the poor and oppressed was a picked man, culled out of many thousands, if not millions; apparently a man of principle, of rare courage and devoted humanity; ready to sacrifice his life at any moment for the benefit of his fellow-man. It may be doubted if there were as many more their equals in these respects in all the country—I speak of his followers only—for their leader, no doubt, scoured the land far and wide, seeking to swell his troop. These alone were ready to step between the oppressor and the oppressed. Surely they were the very best men you could select to be hung. That was the greatest compliment which this country could pay them. They were ripe for her gallows. She has tried a long time, she has hung a good many, but never found the right one before.

When I think of him, and his six sons, and his son-in-law—not to enumerate the others—enlisted for this fight, proceeding coolly, reverently, humanely to work, for months, if not years, sleeping and waking upon it, summering and wintering the thought, without expecting any reward but a good conscience, while almost all America stood ranked on the other side, I say again, that it affects me as a sublime spectacle. If he had had any journal advocating *"his cause,"* any organ, as the phrase is, monotonously and wearisomely playing the same old tune, and then passing round the hat, it would have been fatal to his efficiency. If he had acted in any way so as to be let alone by the government, he might have been suspected. It was the fact that the tyrant must give place to him, or he to the tyrant, that distinguished him from all the reformers of the day that I know.

It was his peculiar doctrine that a man has a perfect right to interfere by force with the slaveholder, in order to rescue the slave. I agree with him. They who are continually shocked by slavery have some right to be shocked by the violent death of the slaveholder, but no others. Such will be more shocked by his life than by his death. I shall not be forward to think him mistaken in his method who quickest succeeds to liberate the slave. I speak for the slave when I say, that I prefer the philanthropy of Captain Brown to that philanthropy which neither shoots me nor liberates me. At any rate, I do not think it is quite sane for one to spend his whole life in talking or writing about this matter, unless he is continuously inspired, and I have not done so. A man may have other affairs to attend to. I do not wish to kill nor to be killed, but I can foresee circumstances in which both these things would be by me unavoidable. We preserve the so-called peace of our community by deeds of petty violence every day. Look at the policeman's billy and handcuffs! Look at the jail! Look at the gallows! Look at the chaplain of the regiment! We are hoping only to live safely on the outskirts of *this* provisional army. So we defend ourselves and our hen-roosts, and maintain slavery. I know that the mass of my countrymen think that the only righteous use that can be made of Sharpe's rifles and revolvers is to fight duels with them, when we are insulted by other nations, or to hunt Indians, or shoot fugitive slaves with them, or the like. I think that for once the Sharpe's rifles and the revolvers were employed in a righteous cause. The tools were in the hands of one who could use them.

The same indignation that is said to have cleared the temple once will clear it again. The question is not about the weapon, but the spirit in which you use it. No man has appeared in America, as yet, who loved his fellow-man so well, and treated him so tenderly. He lived for him. He took up his life and he laid it down for him. What sort of violence is that which is encouraged, not by soldiers but by peaceable citizens, not so much by laymen as by ministers of the gospel, not so much by the fighting sects as by the Quakers, and not so much by Quaker men as by Quaker women?

This event advertises me that there is such a fact as death—the possibility of a man's dying. It seems as if no man had ever died in America before, for in order to die you must first have lived. I don't believe in the hearses, and palls, and funerals that they have had. There was no death in the case, because there had been no life; they merely rotted or sloughed off, pretty much as they had rotted or sloughed along. No temple's vail was rent, only a hole dug somewhere. Let the dead bury their dead. The best of them fairly ran down like a clock. Franklin—Washington—they were let off without dying; they were merely missing one day. I hear a good many pretend that they are going to die; or that they have died, for aught that I know. Nonsense! I'll defy them to do it. They haven't got life enough in them. They'll deliquesce like fungi, and keep a hundred eulogists mopping the spot where they left off. Only half a dozen or so have died since the world began. Do you think that you are going to die, sir? No! there's no hope of you. You haven't got your lesson yet. You've got to stay after school. We make a needless ado about capital punishment—taking lives, when there is no life to take. *Memento mori!* We don't understand that sublime sentence which some worthy got sculptured on his gravestone once. We've interpreted it in a grovelling and snivelling sense; we've wholly forgotten how to die.

But be sure you do die, nevertheless. Do your work, and finish it. If you know how to begin, you will know when to end.

These men, in teaching us how to die, have at the same time taught us how to live. If this man's acts and words do not create a revival, it will be the severest possible satire on the acts and words that do. It is the best news that America has ever heard. It has already quickened the feeble pulse of the North, and infused more and more generous blood into her veins and heart, than any number of years of what is called commercial and political prosperity could. How many a man who was lately contemplating suicide has now something to live for!

One writer says that Brown's peculiar monomania made him to be "dreaded by the Missourians as a supernatural being." Sure enough, a hero in the midst of us cowards is always so dreaded. He is just that thing. He shows himself superior to nature. He has a spark of divinity in him.

Unless above himself he doth erect himself,
How poor a thing is man!

Newspaper editors argue also that it is a proof of his *insanity* that he thought he was appointed to do this work which he did—that he did not suspect himself for a moment! They talk as if it were impossible that a man could be "divinely appointed" in these days to do any work whatever; as if vows and religion were out of date as connected with any man's daily work—as if the agent to abolish Slavery could only be somebody appointed by the President, or by some political party. They talk as if a man's death were a failure, and his continued life, be it of whatever character, were a success.

When I reflect to what a cause this man devoted himself, and how religiously, & then reflect to what cause his judges & all who condemn him so angrily and fluently devote themselves, I see that they are as far apart as the heavens and earth are asunder.

The amount of it is, our *"leading men"* are a harmless kind of folk, and they know *well enough* that *they* were not divinely appointed, but elected by the votes of their party.

Who is it whose safety requires that Captain Brown be hung? Is it indispensable to any Northern man? Is there no resource but to cast these men also to the Minotaur? If you do not wish it, say so distinctly. While these things are being done, beauty stands veiled and music is a screeching lie. Think of him—of his rare qualities! such a man as it takes ages to make, and ages to understand; no mock hero, nor the representative of any party. A man such as the sun may not rise upon again in this benighted land. To whose making went the costliest material, the finest adamant; sent to be the redeemer of those in captivity; and the only use to which you can put him is to hang him at the end of a rope! You who pretend to care for Christ crucified, consider what you are about to do to him who offered himself to be the saviour of four millions of men.

Any man knows when he is justified, and all the wits in the world cannot enlighten him on that point. The murderer always knows that he is justly punished; but when a government takes the life of a man without the consent of his conscience, it is an audacious government, and is taking a step towards its own dissolution. Is it not possible that an individual may be right and a government wrong? Are laws to be enforced simply because they were made? or declared by any number of men to be good, if they are *not* good? Is there any necessity for a man's being a tool to perform a deed of which his better nature disapproves? Is it the intention of law-makers that *good* men shall be hung ever? Are judges to interpret the law according to the letter, and not the spirit? What right have *you* to enter into a compact with yourself that you *will* do thus or so, against the light within you? Is it for *you* to *make up* your mind—to form any resolution whatever—and not accept the convictions that are forced upon you, and which ever pass your understanding? I do not believe in lawyers, in that mode of attacking or defending a man, because you descend to meet the judge on his own ground, and, in cases of the highest importance, it is of no consequence whether a man breaks a human law or not. Let lawyers decide trivial cases. Business men may arrange that among themselves. If they were the interpreters of the everlasting laws which rightfully bind man, that would be another thing. A counterfeiting law-factory, standing half in a slave land and half in a free! What kind of laws for free men can you expect from that?

I am here to plead his cause with you. I plead not for his life, but for his character—his immortal life; and so it becomes your cause wholly, and is not his in the least. Some eighteen hundred years ago Christ was crucified; this morning, perchance, Captain Brown was hung. These are the two ends of a chain which is not without its links. He is not Old Brown any longer; he is an angel of light.

I see now that it was necessary that the bravest and humanest man in all the country should be hung. Perhaps he saw it himself. I *almost fear* that I may yet hear of his deliverance, doubting if a prolonged life, if *any* life, can do as much good as his death.

"Misguided"! "Garrulous"! "Insane"! "Vindictive"! So ye write in your easy chairs, and thus he wounded responds from the floor of the Armory, clear as a cloudless sky, true as the voice of nature is: "No man sent me here; it was my own prompting and that of my Maker. I acknowledge no master in human form."

And in what a sweet and noble strain he proceeds, addressing his captors, who stand over him: "I think, my friends, you are guilty of a great wrong against God and humanity, and it would be perfectly right for any one to interfere with you so far as to free those you wilfully and wickedly hold in bondage."

And referring to his movement: "It is, in my opinion, the greatest service a man can render to God."

"I pity the poor in bondage that have none to help them; that is why I am here; not to gratify any personal animosity, revenge, or vindictive spirit. It is my sympathy with the oppressed & the wronged, that are as good as you, & as precious in the sight of God."

You don't know your testament when you see it.

"I want you to understand that I respect the rights of the poorest and weakest of colored people, oppressed by the slave power, just as much as I do those of the most wealthy and powerful."

"I wish to say, furthermore, that you had better, all you people at the South, prepare yourselves for a settlement of that question, that must come up for settlement sooner than you are prepared for it. The sooner you are prepared the better. You may dispose of me very easily. I am nearly disposed of now; but this question is still to be settled—this negro question, I mean; the end of that is not yet."

I foresee the time when the painter will paint that scene, no longer going to Rome for a subject; the poet will sing it; the historian record
it; and, with the Landing of the Pilgrims & the Declaration of
Independence, it will be the ornament of some future
national gallery, when at least the present form of
Slavery shall be no more here. We shall then be
at liberty to weep for Captain Brown.
Then, & not till then, we will
take our revenge.

The unannounced arrival of President-elect Lincoln

MARGARET LEECH

Arrival of a Westerner

(1941)

Abraham Lincoln, with his mystic faith in the Union, his charity and humanity, his folk wisdom, and his identification with the former slaves, assumed a place in the American pantheon above all other heroes in our history. Northerners of the two generations after the Civil War especially made a cult of him, celebrating his birthday, naming their cities after him, and erecting statues to his honor. He became, as in the huge statue by Daniel Chester French that dominates the Lincoln Memorial in the nation's capital, larger than life, more exalted than the common man he somehow, mysteriously, represented. The martyred president became something separate from the homey philosopher and raconteur of frontier tales. What joined the two?

Lincoln the Westerner, arriving at the capital by a secret route, meeting—and being condescended to by—the mighty, seizes a part of the answer. Here (so few years before his martyrdom) was an upstart, his appearance rough, his pronunciation provincial, his worth largely untested. Faced with the threat of war, he lacked an equipped army; confronted with disunion, he had no sure following; pressed with the need to establish the power of his office, he had no reputation among the men he was supposed to command. Only the most optimistic democrat could expect him to rise to the occasion—as he rapidly did. Lincoln seemed great without preparation, one moment part of the folklife of the people, the next their transcendent leader, and last their martyr.

While preparations were being made for the inauguration of Jefferson Davis as president of the Confederate States, Abraham Lincoln was traveling eastward from Illinois. He was accompanied by his wife and three sons, and by a suite of State politicians, personal friends, relatives by marriage, secretaries and newspaper correspondents; and he also had a military escort of four Army officers appointed by the War Department. One was a friend, Major David Hunter, an honest, anti-slavery paymaster, with a dyed mustache and a dark-brown wig. Young Captain John Pope was the son of an Illinois judge, while Colonel Edwin V. Sumner was a good old white-haired cavalry officer from Massachusetts.

The militia system was represented by Colonel Elmer E. Ellsworth, the Zouave drillmaster, who was entrusted with the responsibility of passing the President-elect through the crowds at his stopping places on the route. The man on whom Mr. Lincoln placed most dependence, however, was Ward Hill Lamon, a younger lawyer who had been associated with him in practice on the circuit. Lamon, a native of Virginia, resembled the chivalry in his long hair, defiant eyes and drooping mustaches. He had brought his banjo in his baggage, and amused the party with Negro songs. Of these, *The Blue-Tailed Fly*, a buzzing ballad, was a favorite with Mr. Lincoln; and he loved to listen to many other simple tunes, both sad and comical, that Lamon sang. In addition to the banjo, Lamon carried an assortment of pistols and knives, a slingshot and brass knuckles. He was powerfully built and fearless, and he considered himself especially charged with Mr. Lincoln's safe-conduct to Washington.

It was a tour and a progress, rather than a journey. The special trains, preceded by pilot engines, ran on carefully arranged schedules between the big cities where the President-elect had appointments for speeches and receptions. Past cheering miles of people, in a confusion of bonfires, parades, salutes and handshakings, Mr. Lincoln moved to the ovation in Philadelphia. After a trip to Harrisburg on February 22, he was to proceed to Washington, where he was expected late on the following afternoon. Among the invitations with which he had been deluged, none had come from Maryland. The omission was the more conspicuous, since a slow transit through the city of Baltimore, where the cars were separately drawn by horses between the depots, was unavoidable in journeying by rail to the capital from the North.

This impending passage through a disaffected community had been a source of considerable anxiety to Mr. Lincoln's friends. The Baltimore gangs were notoriously lawless, and Maryland was boiling with secession agitation. There, as in Washington, military companies of suspect loyalty had been drilling; and threats had been heard that Mr. Lincoln would never go through Baltimore alive. The President of the Philadelphia, Wilmington and Baltimore Railroad,

Mr. Samuel M. Felton, not only felt the responsibility of conveying the President-elect across a hostile State, but he had been disturbed by reports of conspiracies to destroy railroad property. Some weeks earlier, he had sent for a trusted Chicago investigator, Allan Pinkerton, a Scottish barrelmaker who had founded one of the first private detective agencies in the United States. Pinkerton, who was also in the pay of Mr. Lincoln's Illinois advisers, placed spies in the military companies and secret societies in and about Baltimore. On receiving confirmation of the rumored plots to interrupt the railroad, Felton organized and armed some two hundred guards, whom he distributed in the guise of workmen along the line between the Susquehanna and Baltimore.

The dangers attendant on Mr. Lincoln's journey to Washington, as well as on his inauguration, had been recognized in Congress by the appointment of another committee of two, on which Congressman Washburne again represented the House, while Mr. Seward was the member for the Senate. As in the case of the committee on which Washburne served with Senator Grimes, there was close co-operation with General Scott. On February 21, Colonel Stone received a report from detectives he had placed in Baltimore that there was serious danger that Mr. Lincoln might be assassinated in passing through the city. Scott sent Stone posthaste to Seward, who agreed with the General's opinion that Mr. Lincoln should change his announced traveling schedule. To persuade him to do so, Seward dispatched his son, Frederick, to Philadelphia with a warning letter, enclosing Stone's report.

The Republicans of Washington were, in view of the ominous rumors, a stouthearted lot. They were erecting a large edifice in back of the City Hall for the inauguration ball. With eager anticipation, they were looking forward to receiving Mr. Lincoln at the depot on the afternoon of February 23, and they had prepared a quantity of banners with which to deck their wigwam. Meantime, the city was agog over the prospect of a military parade on Washington's Birthday. Early in the morning, the Avenue was cluttered with the wagons and drays of the country folk who had driven in to see the spectacle. By the market house, the City Hall and other vantage points, vendors set out tables of pigs' feet and gingerbread. Boys, with lettered placards on their breasts, offered patriotic songs for sale, and there were many flags with patriotic legends. Mr. Seward, since the New Year, had been agitating for a display of the national colors in the capital, and his efforts were rewarded on Washington's Birthday by an unusual show of red, white and blue. In the morning, the *National Intelligencer* carried the War Department's confirmation of the news for which everyone had been hoping, that the regulars would march, as well as the District militia.

At breakfast, however, General Scott had received an order countermanding the participation of the United States troops. The Virginian, John Tyler, was averse to this provocative exhibition of military force, and his protests had overwhelmed Mr. Buchanan. The militia proudly paced the Avenue, but there were no blue-clad regulars, no flying artillery nor plunging horses. Disappointment clouded the people's holiday spirits, as the rumor spread that the soldiers would not, after all, appear. The prevailing indignation was shared by Representative Daniel E. Sickles of New York, a close friend of the President. Two years earlier, Sickles had won great notoriety by shooting Mr. Philip Barton Key for trifling with his pretty wife. Key, the son of the author of "The Star-Spangled Banner," had been the District Attorney, and a popular figure in Washington society. His murder and the ensuing trial had made a tremendous sensation. Mr. Edwin M. Stanton, who conducted Dan Sickle's defense, had pleaded the unwritten law, and the verdict of acquittal had been cheered in the courtroom and received with delight by the President.

This impulsive congressman was enthusiastic for celebrating Washington's Birthday, and he rushed hotfoot to the War Office, where Secretary Holt was in conference with the President. Sickle's remonstrances induced Mr. Buchanan to change his mind, and Holt hurried off to General Scott's headquarters. The General felt a natural irritation. It was by this time midday. The officers had doffed their dress uniforms, and the soldiers had been dismissed. While a diminished force was hastily rounded up, Mr. Buchanan penned a note to ex-President Tyler, excusing himself for permitting Federal soldiers to be in evidence in the capital. In the afternoon, the people were appeased by a second parade. The artillery drill proved to be the high point of the exhibition. All were startled and amazed by the rapidity with which the guns were manned and prepared for action; and verisimilitude was lent to the martial scene by the dust of the Avenue, which floated about men and guns like the smoke of battle.

At six o'clock next morning, when the train from Philadelphia pulled into the Washington depot, the conductor might have been surprised at the sudden recovery of a sick gentleman, who on the preceding night had been quietly hustled into a berth at the end of the last car. The gentleman, in a soft, slouched hat, a muffler and a short, bobtailed overcoat, descended sprily to the platform. His tall and lanky figure would have made him an oddity in any gathering, and he had a plain, dark-skinned, melancholy face, with a stiff new crop of chin whiskers. He was closely attended by two companions, one of whom was big and heavily built, with bulges under his coat in every place where a man might carry arms; while the other was a short, bearded fellow, with a wary, peasant face. As they passed along the platform in the stream of sleepy-eyed travelers, they attracted attention from only one person in the depot, a man who had planted himself behind a pillar, and was peering out with a sharp, worried expression. As the lanky stranger passed, this man seized hold of his hand. "Abe," he cried in a loud voice, "you can't play that on me!"

"Don't strike him," the stranger hastily told his escorts. "It is Washburne." The President-elect had arrived in the capital of the United States.

The warning which Frederick Seward had carried to Philadelphia had already been sounded in a report from Detective Pinkerton of an assassination plot in Baltimore. Doubly disquieted by a second alarm, Lincoln's friends had prevailed on him to alter his published program. After his trip to Harrisburg, he had slipped secretly on the night train, accompanied only by Ward Hill Lamon and a Mr. E. J. Allen, otherwise known as Pinkerton. Frederick Seward had returned with the message that Mr. Lincoln might be early expected in Washington, and Congressman Washburne had hurried to the depot in the winter dawn. The three travelers climbed into Washburne's carriage, and drove off to Willard's.

The original plan, that Mr. Lincoln should occupy a rented house during the pre-inauguration period, had been changed on the advice of Thurlow Weed, the political manager of New York State. In a hotel, the incoming President would be accessible to the people, and Mr. Weed himself had written to Willard's to make the reservation. The best rooms in the house were, however, occupied when Mr. Lincoln made his unexpectedly early appearance, and a New York capitalist had to be hastily dislodged from the suite connected with Parlor Number 6, a large corner apartment on the second floor, overlooking the Avenue and the grounds of the Executive Mansion.

Mr. Seward was waiting at Willard's to receive the President-elect and congratulated him on his safe arrival. He was somewhat chagrined, Washburne thought, that he had not been up in time to go to the depot. At eight o'clock, however, the senator and the congressman sat down in high elation to breakfast, loading their plates with the first run of Potomac shad. Mr. Lincoln had retired to his rooms to rest. He did not share the exultation of his friends. He had yielded to the advice to change his plans, but he had not taken stock in the story that he risked assassination in Baltimore. Since his nomination, he had constantly received letters threatening his life. He believed that he was destined to suffer a violent death, had expressed the feeling that he would not return alive to Springfield; but Mr. Lincoln's apprehensions, though they may have been quickened by the menaces of his enemies or the nervous solicitude of his friends, were the shadowy alarms of premonition and anxiety, and the prospect of actual danger left him unmoved. For the rest of his life, he would regret the secret journey to Washington. It exposed him to bitter criticism from friends and enemies alike; and it seemed to many to cast reproach on a Government already sufficiently dishonored. Mr. Seward would laughingly agree with the detractors, and say that he had not believed in the Baltimore assassins, though General Scott had done so.

Mr. Lincoln breakfasted alone at nine in his parlor, and did not appear until eleven, when he left the hotel under the escort of Mr. Seward. Those solitary morning hours were the quietest he was ever to know in Washington. He would live thereafter at the mercy of the people, advancing eternally toward him in a jerking procession of faces.

The first duty of the President-elect was to pay his respects at the Executive Mansion. A special meeting of the Cabinet was in session, when the doorkeeper handed Mr. Buchanan a startling card. "Uncle Abe is downstairs!" the President cried, and hurriedly descended to the Red Room. He soon returned with the two Republicans. Mr. Lincoln was presented to the Cabinet, and paused for a few minutes' conversation before leaving to call on General Scott. One of the members, Attorney General Stanton, had a sneering contempt for Mr. Lincoln. Some years earlier, they had been associated as counsel for the defense in a famous case, a suit brought for infringement of patent rights by Cyrus McCormick, the inventor of the reaping machine. Stanton had snubbed and humiliated the backwoods lawyer, and Lincoln had not forgotten his mortification; but he had also retained a vivid impression of Edwin M. Stanton's abilities.

Mr. Lincoln was familiarly acquainted with Washington, where he had served a term as congressman from Illinois, but the capital could not return the compliment. In spite of his extraordinary figure, no one glanced a second time at the ungainly Westerner, as he walked with Mr. Seward through the streets. Rumors that he was in town caused unprecedented sales of the *Evening Star*, which was out in the early afternoon with a description of his arrival at Willard's. Many people still remained skeptical. Republicans declared that the story was a dodge to keep them from the cars; and, mounting on top of a big furniture wagon laden with their banners, they proceeded to decorate their wigwam to impress Mr. Lincoln on his way from the depot. Later, "squads of the incredulous" surged through the rain to meet the special train, and the Fourteenth Street entrance to Willard's was surrounded. The crowds were rewarded by the sight of the weary Presidential party, oppressed by the gloom of the Maryland threats and Lincoln's sudden departure. Mrs. Lincoln had become hysterical over the separation from her husband. Colonel Edwin Sumner was a very angry old soldier, thwarted in the performance of his duty; and Colonel Ellsworth had expected their train to be mobbed in Baltimore. To counteract the depression, Bob Lincoln had led the party in a rendition of "The Star-Spangled Banner," as the cars crossed the Maryland line.

Leaning on the arm of Mr. Seward, Mrs. Lincoln entered the hotel, and was received in the thronged hallway by the Messrs. Willard in person. Upstairs, the President-elect sprawled in an armchair with a beaming face, while his two spoiled boys, Willie and Tad, climbed over him. He had had a busy afternoon, for the tide of visitors had already set toward Parlor Number 6. General Scott, whom he had missed in the morning, had returned his call in full uniform, sweeping his instep with the yellow plumes of his hat as he bowed. Headed by Stephen A. Douglas, the Illinois senators and congressmen had paid their respects. Old Francis P. Blair had come in with his hatchet-faced son, Montgomery, who was hoping to be appointed Postmaster General. The Blair family, father and two sons, were a power in the Republican party. They were a fighting clan from the border slave States, Democrats who had swung into opposition to slavery. The elder Blair, formerly a famous newspaper editor and a member of Jackson's Kitchen Cabinet, was an acute politician who still wielded great influence behind the scenes. Frank, junior, former congressman, recently re-elected, was a Free-Soil leader in Missouri; while Montgomery, like his father, now lived and intrigued in Maryland. Mr. Lincoln reposed great confidence in the senior Blair, and submitted to him, as well as to his chief adviser, Mr. Seward, a copy of his inaugural address.

Soon after his family's arrival, Lincoln was informed that the delegates to the Peace Conference desired to wait on him. He appointed the hour of nine to receive them, and drove off to a seven o'clock dinner at Seward's, where the Vice-President-elect, Senator Hannibal Hamlin of Maine, was also present. The long parlor hall at Willard's was lined with people when he returned; and shaking hands on both sides, he was so interested, said the *New York Herald*, that he forgot to remove his shiny new silk hat.

Ex-President Tyler and the Honorable Salmon P. Chase of Ohio led the Peace delegates up the stairs to Parlor Number 6. Chase was as pompous as General Scott, and very nearly as antipathetic to slavery as Senator Sumner. Re-elected to the Senate after serving as governor of his State, he was the most prominent of the former Democrats in the Republican party. His rumored appointment to the Cabinet would satisfy the radicals, who were disgruntled with the conciliatory Seward. He was tall, imposing and handsome, with the noble brow of a statesman. As he stood beside Mr. Lincoln, presenting the delegates, it was Chase who looked the part of President of the United States, and Chase would have been the first to think so.

Curious and prejudiced, Easterners and men from the border slave States scrutinized the phenomenon from the prairies. The long, lean, sallow frontier lawyer was a shock to people who were unused to the Western type; and his homely phrases and mispronunciations grated on Eastern ears. It was impossible that Lincoln should have inspired confidence or admiration; but some saw shrewdness, honesty and even a natural dignity in his face. Its ugliness was partially redeemed by his eyes, though their dreamy, meditative expression did not bespeak either firmness or force. He had a pleasant, kindly smile, and was thought to be not so ill-favored and hard-looking as his pictures represented him. Chatting informally with the delegates, remembering like a good politician their claims to fame and their middle initials, Lincoln made on the whole a not unfavorable impression.

The next day was Sunday, and Mr. Lincoln attended St. John's Church with Mr. Seward. Under the same guidance he visited the Senate and the House on Monday, and also the Supreme Court; but almost his entire time during the pre-inauguration week was spent in the big, crowded parlor of the hotel suite. Willard's held an unprecedented collection of men notable in public affairs, civil, military and naval. Republican leaders were there to confer, and delegations to press their advice on the administration's policies and Cabinet appointments. The Peace Conference was winding up its session with resolutions that satisfied no one, and border slave State men came to beseech guarantees that there would be no Federal coercion. Past the new President, from early morning until late at night, streamed minor politicians, place seekers, editors, reporters and handshakers. He was still unknown to the passer-by in the street, but hundreds became familiar with his features in Parlor Number 6. Mr. Lincoln assured Mayor Berret and the Common Council of Washington, who called to tender a welcome, that he had kindly feelings toward them, and meant to treat them as neighbors. It was, he remarked, the first time since the present phase of politics that he had said anything publicly in a region where slavery existed. Again, in responding to a serenade by the Washington Republicans, Mr. Lincoln voiced his awareness of his peculiar situation in the capital city, whose population was almost entirely opposed to him in politics.

The new President had formed an inflexible determination to entertain no compromise on the extension of slavery, and to defend the Constitution, as his oath of office required. None of the multitude who, since his departure from Springfield, had casually met him or heard his speeches had been able to discern either his decision or his anxiety. In his public utterances, Mr. Lincoln had depreciated the seriousness of the crisis. His placid manner, the "jocular freedom" of his conversation, and his unceasing fund of anecdote gave the impression that he had but a shallow and provincial understanding of national affairs. Among the Republican leaders, none was more puzzled than Senator Charles Sumner. Mr. Lincoln had an amiable weakness for measuring heights with other tall men, and outraged Sumner's dignity by making the proposal to him. Sumner excused himself with the heavy pleasantry that it was a time for uniting their fronts and not their backs. The Washington Republican, Major French, who was chief marshal of the inauguration parade, declared that they all liked Old Abe, but wished "he would leave off making *little* speeches. He has not the gift of language," French went on, "though he may have of *western gab*."

With the appointment of Montgomery Blair as Postmaster General, the slate of Lincoln's Cabinet was complete. At the head of his advisers was Mr. Seward, balanced by the radical Mr. Chase, who was to be Secretary of the Treasury. Two selections had been virtually forced on Lincoln by bargains which his managers had made at the Republican convention which had nominated him. One was Caleb B. Smith of Indiana, the Secretary of the Interior, a prosaic-looking, lisping conservative. The other was Senator Simon Cameron of Pennsylvania, whom Mr. Lincoln had with much reluctance appointed Secretary of War. Cameron was the Republican leader in his own State, but his reputation for unscrupulous political practices shed no luster on the new Cabinet.

As a sop to New England, Mr. Lincoln had made Gideon Welles of Connecticut his Secretary of the Navy. He was tall and "venerably insignificant," with a flowing beard and a huge gray wig. Welles had been a newspaperman in Hartford, and did not know the stem from the stern of a ship, but he was an industrious and capable administrator. He was also very irritable, and those who undervalued him did not know that, with a pen dipped in gall, he kept a diary. In one respect, Welles was unique among the Cabinet members—he did not think himself a better man than the President.

The Attorney General, Mr. Edward Bates of Missouri, had been one of Mr. Lincoln's earliest selections. He was a former slaveholder, worthy, legalistic and reverential of the Constitution. The choice of the Marylander, Montgomery Blair, gave Lincoln two advisers from the border slave States. Blair was courageous, and had won abolitionist acclaim by acting as counsel for the slave, Dred Scott. However, while scarcely anyone could object to polite old Mr. Bates, the pinched and vindictive Montgomery had a host of enemies. He was detested by the radical wing of the Republicans, and disliked as an uncompromising and warmongering extremist by the moderates. He had plenty of secessionist relatives, and voiced his Union sympathies with challenge and defiance.

With the notable exception of sympathy with disunion, the President's advisers represented, like Mr. Chandlee's cockades, all shades of political sentiment. Four members of the Cabinet, Seward, Chase, Cameron and Bates, had been candidates for the Presidential nomination at the Republican convention, and for the first two the failure to secure it had been a rankling disappointment. It was not to be expected that these dissentient personalities should work together in harmony. Mr. Seward could foresee that it would be difficult to act as premier of the composite council. He sent in a last-minute resignation just before Mr. Lincoln's inauguration, but withdrew it in response to the President's firm request.

In spite of the pall of the national crisis, the President's party was not wanting in high spirits. Besides his oldest boy, Bob, a Harvard student of eighteen, it included three young men who had been law students in Mr. Lincoln's Springfield office, and he was on warmly affectionate terms with them all. John George Nicolay, capable, Teutonic, nearly thirty, was the private secretary. John Hay, the assistant secretary, was a clever, flippant, good-looking college graduate of twenty-two. The handsome little Zouave, Ellsworth, was not much older, and he had a magnetic boyish enthusiasm. He had worked out a plan for reforming the State militia system, and bringing it under Federal control; and he was hoping to be appointed to the chief clerkship of the War Department. Bob Lincoln had been educated at Phillips Exeter, and showed in speech and manner that he had enjoyed more advantages than his father. As a pendant to the campaign publicity for the rail splitter, Bob had been facetiously nicknamed "The Prince of Rails." Some people inevitably called him proud and affected, but he conducted himself sensibly during a prolonged ordeal of popular attention and flattery.

Nicolay thought that the bevy of ladies in the parlors made it seem like having a party every night. He was, however, occupied with the President's correspondence, while Ellsworth, though schoolgirls sighed over his black curls, was a moralist and a Spartan. John Hay and Bob Lincoln were the merry, carefree members of the party. Hay made a new friend in Henry Adams, another private secretary, who would soon be going off with his father to the Court of St. James's. In the evening, Bob sometimes tarried downstairs in the smoking room, listening to the music of the harpists and enjoying a cigar with the other men. Some disunionists, on one of these occasions, induced the musicians to play "Dixie," which Secessia had adopted as its national air; but the harpists quickly followed it with "Hail, Columbia." In Parlor Number 6, Mrs. Lincoln, attended by her sister, Mrs. Ninian Edwards, her two nieces and her cousin, Mrs. Grimsley, received a deferential throng in her stylish Springfield toilettes. The President's Kentucky wife was arrogantly pleased with her position, fancied herself of great importance in politics, and referred in company to Mr. Seward as a "dirty abolition sneak."

Every night, the new squads of militia were drilling in the open spaces of the city, but the fears of revolution had largely subsided. Many patriotic men thought that it would be ill-advised to make an ostentatious display of armed force at the inauguration. The threats to his own life, however, had convinced General Scott that the ceremony was a hazardous undertaking, and he prepared to guard the incoming President with every soldier in the city. He now had, exclusive of the marines at the Navy Yard, six hundred and fifty-three regulars at his command. He thought of Mr. Lincoln's drive from Willard's to the Capitol as a movement, and he planned to place a picked body of men, the sappers and miners from West Point, in the van. A squadron of District cavalry would ride on either side of the Presidential carriage, and infantry companies of militia would march in its rear. Squads of riflemen and a small number of United States cavalry were ordered to posts along the route. The main force of the regulars, headed by Scott in his coupé, was assigned to "flanking the movement" in F Street.

While one battery of artillery was situated near the Treasury building, two were stationed outside the north entrance to the Capitol grounds. At this latter important point, Scott himself proposed to remain during the ceremonies, and there, too, would be Major-General John E. Wool, the thin little old man who was the commander of the Department of the East.

On Saturday and Sunday, strangers, almost all men, were pouring into town in anticipation of the ceremonies on Monday. Baltimore plugs, tippling and shrieking their rallying cries, were but a noisy minority in the swelling influx of the Republicans. There were dignitaries among them—twenty-seven governors and ex-governors of States, and many former senators and congressmen—and there were also militia and civic organizations. Largest by far in number, however, were the plain men of the West—a type only recently familiar to Washington—who dodged forlornly about the city in travel-stained clothes, looking for a place to sleep. Hotel rooms were all preempted. The best accommodation to be had was a cot or a mattress in a parlor. The newcomers were not a spendthrift lot. Bonifaces noted that they were a cold-water army. Hack drivers and porters complained that they were given to walking and carrying their own carpetbags, reluctant to part with a quarter-dollar.

Sunday, with its roving crowds, did not seem like the Sabbath. In the morning, there was a rush to Fourteenth Street to see the President-elect depart for church. So many people congregated around the ladies' entrance to Willard's that police had difficulty in clearing a passage on the sidewalk. All tall men of only moderately good looks, said the tactful *Star*, were closely scanned, as they passed from the hotel. Uncle Abe, however, did not appear, and the sight-seers had to content themselves with the spectacle of the pugilist, John Morrissey, promenading in a stovepipe hat.

Willard's dined fifteen hundred on Sunday, and a thousand feasted at the National. In the evening, laborers were industriously scraping the entire width of the Avenue between the Capitol and the White House, a herculean assignment which they had been unable to finish on Saturday night. The wind whirled the thick dust into clouds, and, though there was now a water supply sufficient for the purpose, the city had no system for dampening the streets. At dusk, crowds of manifestly secular intention were walking toward the lighted Capitol, where the Senate flag was flying. Hundreds of homeless visitors slept on market stalls and lumber piles, or strolled about the streets all night. Orderlies and cavalry platoons rode through the dark. A rumor had reached Scott's headquarters that an attempt would be made to blow up the platform which had been erected at the east portico of the Capitol. A guard was placed under the floor of the stand, and at daybreak a battalion of District troops marched to form a semicircle around the foot of the steps.

The city was early astir with unaccommodated strangers, assembling to perform their toilets at the public fountains. People began to turn out for the parade. Boys screamed the morning newspapers, and there were lithographs of Uncle Abe's features, damp from the press. The sidewalks of the Avenue were filled from building line to curbstone. In the crush, Newton Leonard, aged four, with blue eyes and a full face, dressed in a plaid suit with tight knees, strayed from his parents, and was advertised for next day in the *National Intelligencer*.

In spite of bright sunshine, it was a raw, disagreeable day. Whipped by the gusty wind, the people stood waiting, while soldiers and District militia formed in line. It was not a festive gathering. The city seemed anxious and depressed. Few buildings had been decorated in honor of the inauguration. Some houses along the route had closed shutters, and many unfriendly faces frowned from balconies and windows. The story was being whispered that, if Mr. Lincoln were inducted into office in good order, a company of Virginia horsemen intended to dash across the Long Bridge and take the President captive at the Union Ball that evening.

Among the groups of spectators on the housetops, militiamen with loaded rifles moved to their posts overlooking the Avenue. It was a little after twelve when the word to present arms was passed along the line of cavalry on Fourteenth Street and infantry on the Avenue in front of Willard's. A band struck up "Hail to the Chief," and Mr. Buchanan and Mr. Lincoln emerged arm in arm from the side door of the hotel, and took their seats in an open barouche. In an hour, an Old Public Functionary would be free of a position which had covered him with ignominy and scorn. The Westerner at his side would be the man to trip over the obstacle of Fort Sumter, to guide, under the blows of hatred, an unruly country from which seven States had withdrawn. Mr. Buchanan sat in silence, as the barouche rolled toward the Capitol. His withered face was pale above his white cravat. Only four years before, he had taken this drive through cheering lanes of people, moving between two pretty floats, the Goddess of Liberty on her pedestal and a full-rigged ship, manned by sailors from the Navy Yard. Now, compact and short, the inaugural procession advanced like a military expedition, fearful of attack. There was little enthusiasm on the packed sidewalks. The spectators could scarcely see the new President through the escort of dancing cavalry. Colonel Stone, riding alongside, was digging his mount with his spurs, and he thought that he succeeded in making the militiamen's horses so uneasy that it would have been hard for even a good shot to take aim at the occupants of the carriage.

One hundred mounted marshals, with their trappings of orange, pink and blue, did their utmost to give the parade a garish air of holiday; but, after the disciplined ranks of the regulars and the sizable guard of militia, the civic procession looked straggling and insignificant. There were five hundred Washington Republicans in line, and a few delegations from the States. Thirty-four girls rode in a triumphal car, and were all later kissed by Mr. Lincoln. The *Star* made fun of the pegged boots of the New Englanders, cracking like air guns in the pauses of the Marine Band. No other startling sounds disturbed the progress on the Avenue. The rowdies had foregathered in the liquor shops. A few drunken men tried to obstruct the march of the soldiers, and one of them shouted insults at a delegation of Republicans from Virginia, and proposed three cheers for the Southern Confederacy. In the eastern park of the Capitol, a little man with red whiskers sat high in a tree and addressed the crowd with oratorical flourishes. These were, however, minor disturbances, soon silenced by the police. Chief Marshal French, after a long day on horseback, would be exultant over the perfect success of his arrangements.

The official party entered the Capitol by the north door, through a passage enclosed by a high, boarded fence, guarded by marines. While the ceremonies took place in the Senate Chamber, and Vice-President Hamlin and a few senators were sworn in, the multitude silently waited in the eastern park. They saw the spreading structure of the Capitol, with its unfinished dome surmounted by gaunt derricks braced with ropes of steel. The model of the statue of Armed Freedom, destined for its apex, stood in the grass among the littered and ruinous marbles. In every window of the stark new wings, two riflemen were posted; and Colonel Stone, looking from one of the windows, was satisfied that they perfectly flanked the steps. At last, the door opened, and the dignitaries took their places on the platform, over the heads of the fifty armed men concealed beneath it.

Silver-haired and eloquent, Mr. Lincoln's old friend, Senator Edward D. Baker of Oregon, stepped forward to introduce the new President. There was a faint ripple of cheers, as Lincoln made his way to the rickety little table provided for his address. Burdened with his gold-headed cane and glossy silk hat, he paused in embarrassment. As he laid his cane under the table, Senator Douglas smilingly reached out his hand for the hat. All the people could see Douglas, seated at the front of the platform, holding Lincoln's hat as a public profession of faith in a united country. In the background, Senator Wigfall of Texas leaned with folded arms against the Capitol doorway, watching the inaugural scene with contempt on his fierce, scarred face.

In a resonant, high-pitched voice, trained in the open-air meetings of the West, Mr. Lincoln began to speak. While his audience stood hushed in a painful silence, a tall man with a shrewd, impassive countenance detached himself from the crowd. Like one whom much familiarity backstage has robbed of interest in the play, Mr. Thurlow Weed of Albany turned his back on Mr. Lincoln, and wandered from the Capitol park. Perhaps he was too grieved to stay and see the sad-faced Westerner in the place where he had dreamed and schemed to put a subtle, smiling man. Mr. Weed was the most skillful political manager of his day, but he had failed in his fondest ambition, to manipulate the nomination of Seward by the Republican party.

As he walked north on Capitol Hill, Mr. Weed came upon two batteries of light artillery. Near one of them, General Scott drooped in splendid decay. Beside the other was General Wool, prim and perpendicular, in his high, choking collar. Like Scott, he bore in his stiffening body the scars of 1812. Mr. Weed started forward. In 1812, this cynical politician had been a drummer boy. Nearly half a century before, he had seen the two old generals, one so fat and the other so thin, as dashing, buoyant young officers. He hastened to present himself to them, and respectfully shake their hands.

Behind him, Mr. Lincoln's voice rang out, across the unenthusiastic multitude, across the sundered nation. "We are not enemies, but friends. . . . Though passion may have strained, it must not break our bonds of affection." The voice ceased. There was the noise of applause. Chief Justice Taney tottered forward, a cadaver in black silk. The old regime and the new faced each other, and a Bible lay between them, a pretty book, gilt-clasped and bound in cinnamon velvet. Mr. Lincoln solemnly swore to defend the Constitution of the United States.

There was a thundering salute from the batteries. Mr. Weed had been deeply moved by his chance encounter with the two commanders. He did not remember De Tocqueville's warning, that the army of a democracy tends to become weakened by a burden of old and unfit officers. Effulgent with that sentimentality to which the corrupt are prone, he gazed with veneration on the heroes of his boyhood; and failed to see in the antique tableau on Capitol Hill a presentation of the Union's unpreparedness for long and bloody war.